STATES IN A CHAN

STATES IN A CHANGING WORLD

A Contemporary Analysis

EDITED BY

ROBERT H. JACKSON

AND

ALAN JAMES

CLARENDON PRESS · OXFORD

Oxford University Press, Walton Street, Oxford OX2 6DP

Oxford New York

Athens Auckland Bangkok Bombay
Calcutta Cape Town Dar es Salaam Delhi
Florence Hong Kong Istanbul Karachi
Kuala Lumpur Madras Madrid Melbourne
Mexico City Nairobi Paris Singapore
Taipei Tokyo Toronto
and associated companies in
Berlin Ibadan

Oxford is a trade mark of Oxford University Press

Published in the United States by
Oxford University Press Inc., New York

First published in hardback (and paperback USA and Canada only) 1993
First published in paperback 1995

British Library Cataloguing in Publication Data
Data available

Library of Congress Cataloging in Publication Data
States in a changing world: a contemporary analysis / edited by
Robert H. Jackson and Alan James.
Includes bibliographical references.
1. International relations. 2. Regionalism (International
organization). 3. State, The. I. Jackson, Robert H. II. James,
Alan, 1933–
JX1391.S75 1993 327.1'01—dc20 93-3615
ISBN 0-19-827394-0
ISBN 0-19-827923-X (pbk.)

Printed in Great Britain on acid-free paper by
Biddles Ltd., Guildford and King's Lynn

ACKNOWLEDGEMENTS

This book had its genesis in a car journey made by the editors after an annual conference of the British International Studies Association. Subsequently, the various regional chapters of Part II were presented and discussed at the 1989 joint meeting in London of the US-based and the British International Studies Associations. The momentous historical changes which began in Eastern Europe in the summer of that year overtook the project. However, what initially seemed like bad luck now appears as a stroke of good fortune which gave every contributor a chance to update his chapter in the light of these remarkable developments and their consequences. The volume therefore presents an analysis of the world-wide experience with independent statehood from the end of the Second World War up to and including the recent upheavals which brought the era of the Cold War to a conclusion.

The sovereign State has long been and continues to be the focal point of world affairs, as we are reminded by (seemingly) contradictory developments: on the one hand the formation or reformation of independent States continues to occur when opportunities arise, which indicates the enduring appeal of the national independence idea; on the other hand transnational forces, such as communications, pollution, trade, and money markets, also continue to press upon sovereign States placing constraints upon public choice and (in some cases) provoking co-operation between independent governments. Thus in some places we see nationalities (often violently) asserting or reasserting demands for independence—as in parts of the former Yugoslavia and the former Soviet Union. In other places (not far away) we see States co-operating economically and in other ways pursuing common aims to an extent that is probably unprecedented historically, at least in peacetime—the EC States of Western Europe. We even see nationalities claiming independence while almost in the same breath also seeking membership in larger economic communities—Slovenia's and Croatia's separation from Yugoslavia and their immediate moves to associate themselves with the European Community. Yet whether new nations are being formed out of the ruins of multi-ethnic States or whether novel international communities are coming into existence by the co-operative actions of independent governments, the State remains the focus. These are only a few of the many important issues of contemporary statehood addressed by the contributors to this volume.

Our overall aim is to provide an account of the life of contemporary States which is alert both to specific features of particular regions and to general features of the States system as a whole, thus overcoming a common tendency of political science to study either one or the other but not usually both. The core chapters in Part II of the book analyse regional experiences with independent statehood from (and in some cases before) 1945. Additional chapters in Parts I and III take note of characteristics and concerns which are common to all contemporary States. Our goal has been to produce a volume which, by analysing every global region since the end of the Second World War and yet also by considering general problems of contemporary statehood, fills an important gap in the literature. We hope the result is a balanced and comprehensive study which may be of use to students of both comparative politics and international relations.

The book had an unusually lengthy gestation and the editors are grateful to the contributors for their efforts and patience in seeing it through to completion; to Tim Barton at Oxford University Press for his help and advice; to Andrew Lawrence, cartographer at Keele University, who, with considerable effort and care, prepared the maps for each of the regional chapters; to Annette Owen and, in particular, Maureen Groppe for the splendid editorial assistance they so willingly furnished during the earlier stages of the project; and to Terry Kersch and Jennifer Jackson who took on the responsibility of putting the chapters into one consistent format for publication. We also acknowledge very warmly the encouragement and support received from Margie and Lorna.

Robert H. Jackson
Alan James

Vancouver and Keele
January 1993

CONTENTS

FIGURES AND MAPS

THE CONTRIBUTORS

ALAN BRANTHWAITE is Director, Millward Brown International, and Honorary Research Fellow in the Department of Psychology, Keele University, UK

DAVID G. HAGLUND is Professor of Political Science and Director of the Centre for International Relations, Queen's University, Canada

ROBERT H. JACKSON is Professor of Political Science, University of British Columbia, Canada. During 1993–4 he is Visiting Senior Research Fellow at Jesus College, Oxford

ALAN JAMES is Research Professor of International Relations, Keele University, UK

DAVID B. KNIGHT became Dean of the College of Social Science at the University of Guelph, Ontario, Canada in January 1993; before that he was Professor of Geography at Carleton University, Ottawa

STEPHEN D. KRASNER is Graham H. Stuart Professor of International Relations, Stanford University, USA

RICHARD MATTHEW is Research Associate at the Institute of International Relations, University of British Columbia, Canada

J. D. B. MILLER is Emeritus Professor of International Relations, Australian National University, Canberra, and from 1989–91 was Executive Director of the Academy of Social Sciences in Australia

R. S. MILNE is Emeritus Professor of Political Science, University of British Columbia, Canada

W. H. MORRIS-JONES is Emeritus Professor and formerly Director of the Institute of Commonwealth Studies, University of London, UK

FRED PARKINSON is Honorary Research Fellow at the Institute of Latin American Studies of the University of London, and was formerly in the Faculty of Laws at University College London, UK

SIR ANTHONY PARSONS was formerly the UK's Permanent Representative at the United Nations, New York; he was also for a number of years a Research Fellow at the Centre for Gulf and Arab Studies, University of Exeter, UK

ANTHONY J. PAYNE is Reader in Politics and Chairman of the Department of Politics, University of Sheffield, UK

DONALD J. PUCHALA is Charles L. Jacobson Professor of Public Affairs and Director of the Institute of International Studies, University of South Carolina, USA

GERALD SEGAL is Senior Fellow (Asian Security) at the International Institute for Strategic Studies and Editor of the *Pacific Review*

WILLIAM V. (BILL) WALLACE was Director of the Institute of Soviet and East European Studies, University of Glasgow, UK, and is now Professor Emeritus and Honorary Senior Research Fellow

PART I
PHENOMENON

The Character of Independent Statehood

ROBERT H. JACKSON AND ALAN JAMES

GLOBALIZATION

One of the most remarkable features of the twentieth century is the globalization of independent—or sovereign—statehood. Most immediately, this development has been expressed through the rise of nationalism, the demand for self-determination, and the dismantling of all colonial empires. The Russian Revolution and the defeat of the Central Powers (Germany, Austria-Hungary, Turkey) in the First World War fed the nationalist movements which spawned many new States in the territories of the former Hohenzollern, Habsburg, Ottoman, and Romanov Empires in Eastern and Central Europe. (A comparable and indeed almost identical episode occurred in Eastern Europe at the end of the Cold War.) National self-determination became a ground for claiming independence which was acknowledged by the League of Nations even if it was not yet a principle of international law. This devolutionary process was blocked and turned back by the Bolsheviks in many parts of the former Russian Empire, renamed the Soviet Union. And outside Europe, League Mandates administered by victorious allied powers were set up to govern former Ottoman territories and German colonies. But this merely postponed the day when independent statehood would have to be granted.

That day was mightily advanced by the Second World War and also by the formation of the United Nations, many of whose members took up the cause of national self-determination not only for the Mandates (renamed Trust Territories) inherited from the League of Nations but also on behalf of colonial populations still under the control of European overseas empires, most particularly those of Britain and France. By 1960 the age of Western colonialism was fading fast and independence had become the political aspiration of peoples around the world. It was becoming impossible to justify—

either in morality or (increasingly) in law—the rule of a populated territory by the (foreign) government of another. This anti-imperial and pro-nationalist logic led to its inescapable conclusion in the 1989–91 disintegration of the last great European empire—the Soviet Union. Whether it will lead—as in Yugoslavia—to the breakup of informal empires within sovereign jurisdictions elsewhere—especially the Third World—remains to be seen. Whatever happens, it cannot alter the fact that, far from withering away in the twentieth century, the independent State has everywhere become the standard form of territorial political organization and all conflicting standards have been discredited and in most cases abandoned.

At the same time, and to some extent for connected reasons, the societal characteristics of the collectivity of States have become notably intensified. Sovereign States are more involved with one another in regard to more issues of common interest or concern than ever before. Diplomacy has expanded and the dialogue of States has intensified: nowadays almost everything (it seems) is a legitimate subject of international discussion. Diplomatic establishments, including the number of embassies and the staff and budgets of foreign ministries, are far larger than anything that existed previously. Diplomatic activity nowadays is a continuous dialogue marked by frequent meetings of State officials, including not only ambassadors and foreign secretaries but also finance and other ministers and even prime ministers and presidents—at summits. Diplomacy also involves participation in a far more elaborate scheme of international organization: a mark of diplomatic entry into the society of States is membership in various international organizations, notably of course the United Nations. But this is only the beginning of multilateral diplomacy for most States, as it extends not only to many organizations within the UN system itself—such as the WHO, the FAO, UNESCO among many others—but also to numerous international organizations outside the UN that are concerned with not only traditional diplomatic issues—such as war and peace—but also many modern functional issues—such as finance, transport, communication, energy, the environment, health, trade, agriculture, and much besides. The globe today is cross-hatched as never before by almost countless international organizations of one kind or another which service the society of sovereign States.

Furthermore, the common standards which States observe (however imperfectly) nowadays are more confining and touch on many more facets of their relationships than hitherto. International relations are more involved with legal norms than ever before: the Covenant of the League of Nations and the Charter of the United Nations are both far more elaborate than anything which existed previously. The rules of the UN Charter concerning the use of force are more restrictive and regulative than classical international law: the valid grounds for waging war have been reduced, almost to self-defence. At the same time the orbit of international law has expanded far beyond the traditional fundamental questions of force and non-intervention and now includes not only such issues as trade and commerce between States but also human rights, racism, terrorism, human migration, traffic in drugs, crime, the environment, even sport, and much else. This growth has been a consequence not only of international factors but also of the expansion and intensification of the domestic jurisdiction of States: the contemporary State is attempting to regulate a far larger sphere of human transactions in far greater detail than its predecessors ever attempted. This has led to the desirability and indeed necessity of expanded international communication and collaboration between States.

Finally, the economic connections of States are also far more extensive and elaborate than anything which existed before the twentieth century. Not only that, but nowadays important international institutions—the G-7, the OECD, the GATT, the IMF, the World Bank among others—exist for the express purpose of regulating the global economy by international means. In certain respects the OECD led by the G-7 major economic powers has become the principal co-ordinating body of international economic activity. Nothing like it has ever existed (at least during peacetime) since the emergence of the modern European State. The world's most important economies—Western Europe, North America, East Asia—have become subjects of international regulation through such bodies, and in the course of becoming so their sovereign governments have in recent decades increasingly acknowledged and followed a joint economic orthodoxy regarding exchange rates, inflation, interest rates, budget deficits, and other key elements of modern economic management. Economic blocs have been formed, such as the European Community, which have carried this effort at economic co-ordination considerably farther. Other regions of the globe, in particular North America, are moving in a similar direction.

In sum, the world has contracted dramatically during the twentieth century and has become (in a favourite cliché of popular commentators) a 'global village', and the process is continuing and in some respects even accelerating. Much of this reduction in the effective time and distance of human intercourse is due directly to mind-boggling technological innovations and developments which render the world of the 1990s a far more intimate and involved place than that of the 1890s. The automobile, the super-highway, the telephone, radio, television, radar, the jet airliner, the communications satellite, the transistor, and the microchip are only the most obvious examples of this technological revolution which already has gone far to conquer space and time in many parts of the world. Much of it is also due to the way in which sovereign governments have encouraged and sup-ported this technological process and attempted to take full advantage of it. As a consequence, governments and their populations nowadays are involved with each other to an extent that would be inconceivable in earlier times—and the interactions and transactions are continuing to increase with the march of technological innovation and the con-nected growing awareness of mutual advantage and mutual vulnerability which enters into both domestic and international political life.

SOVEREIGN STATEHOOD

And yet none of the above developments has reduced the significance of sovereign statehood as the fundamental way in which the world is politically organized. Indeed, in many respects a major effect has been to enhance that significance: the State has been a major supporter and beneficiary of economic, scientific, and technological advance. Many activities of the State, particularly but not exclusively war, have directly and profoundly provoked such advance. Nowadays no less than previously the population of the world is divided into separate, independent States each with their own identities, territories, and symbols which mark them off from one another. The vast majority of people still owe their allegiance to the independent countries to which they belong—which for most people is the primary loyalty. National identity and self-determination show no sign of receding; indeed, if anything, in recent years these sentiments have been voiced by more people around the world than ever before. The independent political entities referred to as 'States' have their own governments or-ganized according to their own political enlightenment and ideologies. And the governments decide their own policies, make their own decisions, and carry them out—for the most part—with their own agents, agencies, and resources. There is nothing to indicate that in the foreseeable future such entities will not continue to be the preferred and predominant form of political organization just as they are today and have been in previous centuries. Present indications are—if anything—that the desire and demand for independent statehood will remain strong, so that, as multi-ethnic States come under pressure from secessionists of one kind or another, independent States will perhaps continue to proliferate as they have done throughout most of the present century.

The fundamental characteristics of the international society formed by such sovereign political entities therefore give no indication of soon changing into something different or ceasing to exist. The world is still, in territorial terms, made up of separate political entities, each of which, by virtue of its independent status, enjoys certain basic rights (sometimes—often confusingly—called sovereign rights). Each State still has its own interests to advance and defend—whether by itself or in collaboration with others. The world is still an unequal society in power terms—indeed hugely so, and to a greater extent than previously now that membership is global and includes not only military superpowers and economic hegemons—at one extreme—but also—at the other—almost invisible micro-States. This unequal international distribution of power is not fixed but is ever changing, gradually or dramatically, as the case may be. The USA has lost the economic pre-eminence it enjoyed at the end of the Second World War, and the former Soviet Union has more suddenly and dramatically declined as a rival of the West. At the same time Western Europe and Japan have re-emerged as global centres of power and influence. This kind of change is only to be expected in a society of States which is, after all, based on the principle of freedom and consequently the possibility, if not indeed the inevitability, of change. We can expect other—and perhaps surprising—changes in the future. But we have few if any grounds for expecting the international society itself to change into something fundamentally different as long as most people retain their strong desire to live in independent States. As indicated, there is no evidence to conclude that this desire is declining; if anything, it is on the increase—as the close referendums in Denmark and France on the 1991 Maastricht Treaty indicate.

Furthermore, the society of States is still (strictly speaking) an ungoverned order. There is as yet nothing even remotely like a world authority with an attached government possessing express powers, budgets, staff, equipment, and material which are independent of the world's States and superior to them. The United Nations is no such entity; on the contrary, it is a characteristic institution of international society and the creature of its member States, reflecting, in the Security Council, the pre-eminence (or perhaps, the former pre-eminence) of some. Nor can one point to any other global political organization which transcends sovereign statehood. The only possible international government of substance is the European Community— but this is best conceived as the embryo of what *might* someday become a greater European State, enveloping the present independent States of that continent within some kind of federal arrangement. This is a realignment and an endorsement and not a superannuation of sovereign statehood. And it still seems far away when it comes to the greatest tests of sovereign statehood: foreign policy and war. In this regard the members of the European Community still seem strongly inclined to act not like a greater European State but like separate sovereign entities—as is evident in the 1992 financial and monetary difficulties Italy, Britain, Spain, and France experienced in attempting to operate within the EC Exchange Rate Mechanism. Moreover, obvious movements toward political unification on a greater geographical scale must be set alongside the equally obvious movements in the opposite direction, such as the breakup of Yugoslavia and the former Soviet Union.

Finally, the society of States continues to be noticeably and inescapably a militarized society, in which force or its threat can still play a crucial role. The Gulf War (1990–1) and the civil cum international wars in the Balkans (1991–3) are potent reminders of this reality. The possibility of war cannot be excluded as long as there are independent States—although the Gulf episode may give some grounds for hoping that future wars will be conducted more according to international law than those of the recent past have been. But the savage local wars in the Balkans offer far fewer grounds for such optimism. The end of the Soviet Union as an imperial State will not be marked by the end of great military power: its nuclear weapons will merely revert to the possession of successor States, including Russia, its principal descendant and inescapably a great power. If those weapons come into the possession of other successor States, then the end of the USSR will also be marked by nuclear proliferation, which may increase rather than reduce the risk of nuclear war.

Likewise, the military arms of the USA or even the major West European States cannot be expected to disappear in the future—although their size and firepower might be reduced significantly in balance with a similar reduction on the part of Russia. Militarized international association may in the future express itself in altered international alliances if NATO becomes less central to European defence, and other bodies—such as the Western European Union—acquire military significance. Perhaps a less likely but not inconceivable scenario is membership of the former Warsaw Pact in NATO. But none of this is a fundamental change; it is merely a redistribution, realignment, and reorganization of the military might of sovereign States. The independent State has always been and in the future will surely continue to be at least in significant part a machine of war.

Given the above-noted conditions and characteristics, certain international concerns follow which are shared by all States. First, they are all primarily concerned with protecting their territorial integrity—even if in many cases this concern does not need to be to the fore of their external relations, in so far as existing international boundaries are usually acknowledged and accepted in practice. Borders nevertheless continue to be a preoccupation of many States—as is indicated in the countries emerging (or re-emerging) in Eastern Europe and the former Soviet Union. Indeed, borders are so central to the society of States that they have acquired a new and heightened legitimacy in the present century. Thus, in the reunification of Germany the post-Second World War boundaries with Poland (which substantially reduced the extent of German territory from what it had been before the war) had to be accepted by the German government. Otherwise there would be a prospect of recurrent discord in its relations not only with Poland but also other States, particularly those of Eastern Europe. This principle of the legitimacy of the territorial status quo has been extended to internal borders in cases where States are breaking up. The borders which separated the constituent republics of the former Soviet Union were the only generally acceptable geographical definitions of the successor States. Thus, the historic Russian territory of the Crimea which has been part of Ukraine only in recent decades could not be returned to Russia without provoking serious discord—as Boris Yeltsin was advised by the Ukrainian government in late 1991. By the same normative logic Serbia stands condemned for using force to invade the territory of the neighbouring republics of Croatia and Bosnia-Herzegovina, thereby violating what were important internal borders of the former Yugoslavia. If negotiated settlements are eventually reached in these bitter disputes, they will have to make reference to pre-existing borders, either by accepting them or by justifying a mutually agreed departure from them.

Second, it follows that in the present society of States an equally basic concern is that of political independence. The principal value of a States system is, as indicated, the political freedom of its component parts. In other words, the main point in having a State of one's own is to enjoy the freedom (and bear the responsibility) that goes with it. States do not wish to be told, lectured, hectored, badgered, bullied, or otherwise pushed around by other States concerning what they should or should not do within their own jurisdictions. Rather, they desire to take their own counsel and decisions without external interference. The jealousy with which States regard their independence is well known and well nigh universal. Of course, this does not mean that States will not prudently take into account the interests or concerns of other States and, where necessary, consult them. Nor does it mean that States will not attempt to influence the decisions and policies of other States. Incentives, inducements, and even threats are a feature of international relations no less (and usually more) than other group and human relations. However, as with other groups, international society is also the scene of important courtesies, proprieties, and other civil practices—all of which acknowledge the independence of States. They are sometimes underestimated or even misunderstood by certain analysts who believe that power is everything in relations of States. But international society, like any other human society, could not exist if it were based exclusively on power. Consequently, it is also defined by norms and expectations concerning acceptable and unacceptable conduct which States would be wise to observe if they wish to be effective at least in the long term.

Lastly, States are concerned about their economic integrity. No State wishes to become overly dependent economically on another State; every State wishes to have some freedom of manœuvre in economic policy-making. This is why almost every country in the world has its own currency—which is a standard (but not a crucial) mark of sovereignty. This is also why virtually every State has its own central bank, ministry of finance, and other national economic bureaux—which it would be very reluctant to give up or combine with those of other States, as the 1992 experience of the EC States discloses. Such institutions are buffers between economies aimed at increasing national freedom and control. None of this is meant to deny the obvious fact of economic interdependence which—as indicated—is growing rapidly between States. Nor is it to dispute the general fact and desirability of international commerce. It is only meant to point out the obvious desire of all governments to retain some room for manœuvre in economic affairs, however large or small it can be in practice. Canada with an economy only one-tenth the size of its great neighbour obviously has far less room for manœuvre than the USA in their mutual economic transactions. Canadian economic policy is always profoundly affected by the performance of the US economy and by the economic policies of the US Treasury and the Federal Reserve. These constraints are inescapable realities for Canadian economic policy-makers. Yet Canada gives no sign of not desiring within this limit to control its own economic affairs and it would be surprising if it were otherwise. Even the USA, large and powerful as it is, has the same concern in its economic relations with Japan and the European Community. Independence is a form of freedom, and the desire for the maximum freedom possible in the circumstances extends not only to the political but also to the economic affairs of sovereign States.

In short, the independent State and the society formed by such States continue to be a marked feature of global political organization which gives no indication of disappearing or even declining in the foreseeable future. On the contrary, in recent years people in some parts of the world, particularly Eastern Europe and the former USSR, have been clamouring for control of their own national destinies free from outside authority. To all intents and purposes this means possessing an independent State of their own. Having one's own State remains a powerful definition of what it means to be free and to be in control of one's destiny—even if that control is in some or even many cases severely constrained by international or transnational factors which also are a distinctive feature of the contemporary world. Having such a State continues, in almost all cases, to be the most meaningful definition of a people, and the best sign that they are recognized and respected by others. This may be the most fundamental reason why sovereign States should not be expected to take their leave of the world for quite some time to come.

REGIONAL EXPERIENCES

Since States are geographically based political organizations, it follows that their regional location and relations with their neighbours is for many a central preoccupation. No State can disregard this factor, not great powers or even superpowers—as is evident from the historic American preoccupation with controlling or at least influencing international affairs within the Western hemisphere and particularly its 'backyard': Central America and the Caribbean. Thus for most States, including great powers whose interests also range far more widely, foreign policy is directed in significant measure at States within their own neighbourhood. International politics is played out in important respects within particular regional contexts, each of which is marked by a distinctive pattern of powers and agenda of concerns. It is impossible to ignore these various regional experiences if a balanced and rounded understanding of international politics is to be obtained. Indeed, they must be a central analytical focus. For this reason this book's core consists of eleven chapters in Part II, which examine the world's regional experiences of international politics. The regions are defined according to established conventions of contemporary international theory and practice. They consequently consist of Western Europe, Eastern Europe, the Middle East and North Africa, Sub-Saharan Africa, South Asia, South East Asia, North East Asia, Oceania, Latin America, the Caribbean, and North America.

The regionalism of the States system has increased in the twentieth century principally because of the decline and fall of the great European empires which together controlled the bulk of the territory and population in the Middle East and North Africa, Sub-Saharan Africa, South Asia, South East Asia, Oceania, and the Caribbean until the middle of the present century. Before that time international relations were far more centralized in the West and specifically in Western Europe. European imperial States not only had legal jurisdiction over vast territories and populations in what we now refer to as the 'Third World', they also directly governed most of them. What is today international relations was at that time the internal relations of imperial States. European decolonization created not only a large number of new sovereign States but also a far more regionalized States system. The contemporary States of the world in very considerable measure move in regional orbits all of which have distinctive features. For example, whereas prior to the Second World War South Asia was

almost entirely a British sphere of territorial jurisdiction and governance, today it is a region largely dominated by India—itself a vast internal empire—and its frequently acrimonious relations with Pakistan.
And whereas prior to 1960 most of Sub-Saharan Africa was partitioned
among five colonial powers (Britain, France, Belgium, Portugal, Spain),
today it is a decentralized global region of numerous weak States
which remain highly vulnerable to external interference, particularly
by the great powers. Other examples of the emergence of regions from
the ending of empires are contained in the chapters which follow.

Here we only wish to point out that this process of regionalization
which is such a marked feature of the contemporary State system is a
direct consequence of the globalization of the locally sovereign State.
If we grant the importance of this feature—which to us seems very
difficult to deny—it is perhaps ironic that many general studies of
international relations ignore it. This is perhaps owing to the difficulty
of bringing such political diversity within the compass of a single
volume. But if we really wish to understand the form and substance
international relations have acquired since 1945, regionalism is something we not only cannot ignore, we ought to make it a central subject
of analysis. This is why we have singled it out for special attention.

Each contributor has emphasized those experiences and relations
which have preoccupied the States of his region since 1945. Some of
these are distinctive to a region and contribute in large measure to its
international identity: for example, in North East Asia the rise of
Japan as an economic suzerain power and the massive presence
of China, in North America and the Caribbean the towering presence
of the USA, in Europe the emergence and development of the
European Economic Community. But some are indicative of more
general issues in international politics which are played out in a regional
context: for example, the protracted and poisonous Arab–Israeli conflict which for so long was a crucial point of confrontation between
the two rival superpowers, or the Vietnam conflict in South East Asia,
or the civil wars in Ethiopia and Angola which also served as regional
points of superpower rivalry for long periods during the Cold War.
In other words, regions are distinctive but they are not islands to
themselves anymore than are their component States. It is nevertheless
possible to discern differentiating regional patterns and preoccupations
in world politics, and it is these which receive the attention they
deserve in this volume. The regional chapters consequently indicate
not only which issues are distinctive of each region but also which

ones are variants of more general problems which have characterized international politics in the past half-century.

As relevant, each chapter pays attention to the birth (or rebirth), the death, and the life of States or in other words the ways in which international developments have occurred in each region of the world since 1945. The birth rate of States in this period—and frequently also the birth pain—has been high: there is nowadays about three times as many independent countries as existed at the founding of the United Nations. This proliferation of independent countries has of course been owing largely to the dismantling of Western overseas empires in Asia, Africa, Oceania, and the Caribbean, which has more than tripled the number of original UN members. More recently, however, it has been propelled by the sudden disintegration of what arguably was the last great European empire: the Soviet Union. Where one territorial leviathan previously existed there are now fifteen States, most of which by the start of 1992 were associating in a looser 'Commonwealth of Independent States' (which seemed to get even looser as the year progressed). Yugoslavia by then had also ceased for all practical purposes to exist, and at least five and possibly as many as seven successor States were emerging in the Balkan peninsula. And Czechoslovakia has divided (January 1993) into its two tributaries: the Czech Republic (Bohemia-Moravia) and Slovakia. The death of three States in Eastern Europe may consequently be matched by the birth of at least twenty-two and possibly as many as twenty-four new or restored sovereign jurisdictions. This would put the total number of independent States in the world near two hundred. If one recalls the new States born after the First World War which survived without being forcibly integrated into the Soviet Union, it is clear that the twentieth century has been a century of very high political as well as human birth-rates. The effects of such birth-rates on international relations have been nothing less than profound.

This process may not yet have run its course and we may see the emergence (or re-emergence) of additional States coincidental with the breakup of existing ones. All of the successor States of the former Soviet Union may not survive in their existing shapes: for example, Moldova could split into Romanian-speaking (majority) and Russian-speaking (minority) segments each of which could in turn be absorbed by Romania and Ukraine or Russia. This fracturing is perhaps most likely to happen in the Third World. In Africa alone the longing of numerous peoples to have their own State rather than remain part of a larger sovereignty is widespread and could intensify and spread even further in reaction to State secession elsewhere. In 1992 Eritrea was about to separate from Ethiopia. The birth of some new sovereignties could even occur in more developed parts of the world—for example, if Quebec secedes from Canada.

The main focus of each regional chapter, however, is on the way in which States in each region have coped with each other, with their ongoing international life both within the region and in relation to outside powers. As indicated, most of the regions dealt with in this book were colonial appendages of imperial powers in the past and were therefore not international regions as such. As a consequence, the international system is far more regionalized—in the sense of being defined and shaped by its locally independent States and not by distant colonial powers—than it was before the Second World War. For example, almost the entire continent of Africa became a new international region in a few years before and after 1960, consisting of about fifty independent countries. The newly formed and untried indigenous governments of the region had to learn not only how to govern their own countries internally but how to deal with their neighbours, and of course with former imperial masters and other major outside powers, such as the USA and the Soviet Union. Consequently, independence was marked by an enormous expansion of international borders and international interactions and transactions in that continent, with its usual features and problems— including diplomatic concords and discords, boundary disputes and settlements, economic relations and associations, population movements including problems of refugees, and in some cases warfare. It was also marked by the foundation and operation of regional international institutions which never existed before—such as the Organization of African Unity. As this example indicates, the regionalization of world politics is also reflected by the formation of numerous regional international organizations since 1945.

External relations of States are frequently affected, in varying and sometimes considerable degree, by factors which do not enter directly or immediately into the processes of international politics—internal factors, particularly those which influence the strength and stability of a country's political system. Consequently, a State's ability to act positively and effectively on the international stage can be enhanced or disadvantaged and in any event will always be influenced and even shaped by various domestic considerations. These will of course include most importantly the maturity, experience, and responsibility of national leaders who make the most important decisions which affect a country's prospects. When attention is given to the future success or failure, order or disorder, development or decay of Eastern Europe, the former Soviet Union and their component States, the focus is inevitably on the principal actors involved, such as (in 1992) Poland's Lech Walesa, Russia's Boris Yeltsin, or Ukraine's Leonid Kravchuk, and one wonders about the quality of their statesmanship. When attention is given to the prospects for *rapprochement* in the Middle East between Israel and its neighbours, one likewise wonders about the good faith and diplomatic skill of the statesmen involved, including the Prime Minister of Israel and the President of Syria, among others. And is there any solid reason to believe the leaders of the independent Balkan States of the former Yugoslavia will find the common ground that is necessary to resolve their conflicts by diplomacy rather than warfare?

However, leaders are never totally free agents. Any appraisal of decision-makers and their decisions (or indecisions) and actions (or inactions) must fundamentally take into account a country's consti-tutional, ideological, cultural, religious, economic, class, and ethnic make-up. Political decisions and actions are always taken within the context of circumstances such as these, and are to a varying degree affected by them. The significance and existence of particular cir-cumstances will of course vary from State to State and from region to region, often to a considerable degree. This makes it hard to generalize about them, except at a very high level of abstraction. These circum-stances will therefore be addressed, for the most part and as appro-priate, in the relevant regional chapters. They give to each region its distinctive characteristics and, indeed, personality. One becomes aware how far South Asia can be defined by the domination of India and its rivalry with Pakistan, or the Middle East and North Africa by the Arab–Israeli conflict, or Africa by a general preoccupation with boundaries and the problem of underdevelopment, or North America by the looming presence of the USA, or Western Europe by the pro-cesses and problems of moving toward greater European Community. There are certain fundamental incommensurabilities in these con-trasting regional identities about which one's ability to generalize is definitely limited. On the other hand, one gains a better impression of the diversity and personality of different regions in the contemporary world, and the necessity of regional studies for understanding them.

GENERAL PROCESSES AND PROBLEMS

There are nevertheless characteristics and concerns which are common to all independent States and which cannot be overlooked by any regional study of such States in a changing world. Indeed, the international relations of sovereign States are always in varying degrees a combination of the general and the particular. For example, as members of the same society all States share international boundaries with other States. Yet what they do within their own territorial jurisdictions will be affected by differences in national culture, tradition, ideology, wealth, and so forth. Likewise, all independent States possess their own national governments, but the constitutional shape and organization and policies and capabilities of those governments vary enormously from one to another. By the same token, while governments differ in these and other respects they all nevertheless have the same interest in independence, security, and survival which is a general characteristic of sovereign States.

In so far as we can speak of a global society of States there must be a set of features and issues common to all of them and exclusive to them alone which marks them off from other social systems. This book has singled out for separate analysis two general features which are at the very root of independent statehood and which affect every member of the contemporary States system: the geographical situation and configuration of States and the problem of the people's identification with the State and allegiance to its government. These issues receive a general examination in two separate chapters (Part I) before the regional studies (Part II) are embarked upon.

The reason these two elements (and not others) are singled out for general analysis is owing to the fact that they are part and parcel of what it means to be an independent State. There are certain elements (and connected problems) which are common to all States (*qua* States) and therefore can be discussed in a general way. These relate in the main to psychology and geography: no State can exist for long without a permanent population that identifies with it and gives allegiance to its national government; and no State can of course exist without a definite territory which belongs to it alone. The essential components of the generally accepted definition of a State in international law are population and territory along with an effective government. If a political system is to qualify as a State in law it obviously must be defined with sufficient precision. The legal definition makes no mention of culture or religion or ethnicity or economics or any other societal factors as defining characteristics of statehood. This is for the reason that these are not specific to States as such. This obviously is not the case with territory which ordinarily cannot be shared by two different sovereign jurisdictions: joint sovereignty or condominium is a very exceptional and very rare form of State jurisdiction. Nor is it the case with the national identity and allegiance of a population, which in the final analysis can be directed at one and only one focus of government authority. If among the population of a particular territory identity is divided between and allegiance is contested by two (or more) rival political claimants to national authority, there is good reason to doubt the internal coherence, and perhaps therefore the international effectiveness, of the State in question. For statehood to exist within a populated territory there can only be one national government.

The religions and cultures and even the languages of people who reside in particular States can and often do vary considerably. The modern State is a European and to a significant extent a Christian innovation—although it builds on the groundwork of the Romans who were Christians only belatedly and equivocally. Religion can frequently divide national populations (for example into Protestants and Catholics or Christians and Muslims) and bring them into at least spiritual kinship with people of similar religion in other States. This may explain why States have often attempted to control religion, even to the extent of proclaiming a State religion. But this is always a contingent endeavour which can only be more or less successful. The British State eventually had to tolerate and even legitimate Christians who were not members of the Church of England, and believers who were not Christian.

Circumstances such as religion or culture or language or—for that matter—economics or class are often crucially important for understanding the domestic politics and external relations of States. Our regional contributors consequently pay a good deal of attention to them. But such factors are not a part of the defining characteristics of independent statehood. An independent State is no less (and no more) a sovereign State for having a form of government which is democratic rather than dictatorial or a population that is Christian (rather than Muslim) or a dominant language that is European rather than Asian or an economy that is capitalist (rather than socialist). These are all important facts about countries but they are contingent and not essential facts about statehood. Their contingency is usually disclosed by the use of adjectives: we commonly refer to democratic or authoritarian States, Christian or Islamic countries, socialist or capitalist economies, and so forth. These factors are essential not in defining that which is general to States but in differentiating between States.

It might be objected that all States have cultures, economies, and so forth, which must therefore figure in any definition of statehood. And therefore to leave them out of a political analysis is to overlook something fundamental about statehood. But this is a category mistake in the sense that all peoples have these characteristics—and many other besides—but not all peoples have their own independent States. Neither a culture nor a language nor an economy nor any similar social characteristic is sufficient for a population to possess statehood. For that to happen they must occupy an exclusive territory under a national government of their own which is constitutionally independent of all other sovereign governments. This may serve as a definition of what we mean by sovereign statehood in this book.

Even though every State must possess a basis in geography and psychology these defining characteristics of statehood are, as the two chapters in Part I indicate, subjects in their own right. There are very significant geographical differences within and between States, which merit attention by any study that seeks to investigate the contemporary global States system. Although every State has territory, and certain opportunities and responsibilities which flow from the occupation of a definite piece of real estate, what a State does with its territory can vary considerably. Territory is what humans choose to make of it. Territory is not value-free. People ordinarily become attached to the place in which they live. But territories differ in the opportunities (resources, climate, landscape, etc.) they afford to the people who live in them. Some State territories can barely sustain a population—such as those in the drought-stricken African Sahel. Some State territories can easily sustain a population even though their size is extremely limited—Singapore is a case in point. Consequently, though every State requires territory it can vary enormously in size and endowment. One noteworthy feature of the recent expansion of the States system is the number of new States whose territorial size and endowment is extremely limited: for example, the numerous micro-States of the Caribbean and Oceania. Why and how such States can exist and survive is discussed in several chapters.

The psychological basis of statehood also discloses a distinctive dynamic. Although the need of people to identify with a group of some kind is probably universal, the objects of group identification are enormously diverse in form and substance. The State is one of these, but there are many others: family, clan, tribe, caste, race, class, locale, occupation, profession—the list is long. Moreover, such group identifications can be harmonious but they can also be discordant. One ordinarily thinks of national identities embodied in sovereign States—Germany, France, Britain—as a fundamental element of international conflict—which it has been on two occasions in the present century. But identities within States may also conflict: as the chapters on Eastern Europe and Sub-Saharan Africa indicate. There is a sense in which identification with a State as citizen or subject must take precedence over all other identifications an individual may have for that State to survive and flourish. This is not usually a problem since most identities an individual possesses—family, occupation, city, and so forth—can be accommodated within the framework of statehood. But certain identities at certain times cannot: ethnonationality, for example. When such identities displace attachments to an existing State the psychological foundation upon which it rests is undermined and the State, deprived of a fundamental support, may collapse—as evidently happened in the case of Yugoslavia. Generating and sustaining identification with the State is a recurrent 'nation-building' project. Thus many governments try to instil in their populations positive identifications with the country, for which a repertoire of flags, emblems, anthems, and the like, is available. Although some States are extremely successful in this regard, developing a loyal citizenry is not something that can be taken for granted even by the most successful States. This is often most evident during wars when identification and attachment to the State is put to the severest of tests. Both the geographical and the psychological bases of statehood for these reasons merit special study in a volume such as this.

In Part III, following the regional chapters, the focus is on another set of general issues which, although they are not strictly speaking components of the definition of statehood, are crucially important contingent issues that most States if not all must be concerned with to some degree: the economic interdependence of States, and the problems to which their ethnic composition might well give rise. For States find that these processes increasingly impinge upon them. Any discussion of States in contemporary world politics cannot get away from these two issues, as they raise fundamental questions about the future of the society of States. One has been on the agenda for some time: the question of whether many States are being undermined over the longer term by the process of economic interdependence. The other, perhaps more contemporary and urgent, is whether certain States are threatened with fragmentation and the international society with disorder because of internal nationalist or ethnic tensions.

Even a cursory glance around the world at the present time will make it apparent why these two issues are singled out—among the many which could be—for separate analysis. The existing and growing interdependence between States both more generally and within particular regions is a very noteworthy feature of contemporary international relations. States today are more involved with one another than they have ever been: commercial exchanges and financial entanglements as well as human intercourse and technological transactions between independent countries—particularly the developed capitalist States of Western Europe, North America, and East Asia—are already extensive and intensive and they continue to increase—in most cases rapidly—as the world continues to shrink. The States of the world are interconnected and interwired as never before. Consider only two international and transnational dynamics which are such a marked characteristic of the present and future age which differentiates it sharply from the past: the rapid mobility of large numbers of people around the world by means of jet aircraft and the even faster mobility of huge sums of money around the world by means of computers and electronic communications. These two features alone are changing the global landscape. Furthermore, the economic (and political) integration of Western Europe in the past four decades—both in the growing number of socio-economic activities brought within the compass of the process and in the number of States involved—is perhaps sufficient evidence of economic interdependence and co-operation at the regional level of international relations. Similar and somewhat imitative processes are also in evidence, even if they are not so far advanced, in other parts of the world.

Does economic interdependence undermine political independence and contribute significantly to a long-term prospect of the withering away of the sovereign State as we have known it? In this respect is the future of the State to become a residual category or empty shell—as Stephen Krasner puts it. Or does it reinforce sovereign statehood—

perhaps by increasing the prospects of economic growth and development and therefore the welfare and security of national populations beyond what can be provided by the largest national economy or by the most successful free-trading States? These questions are addressed in the chapter on economic interdependence and independent statehood.

The widespread fact of awakened and mobilized ethnicity or nationalism is perhaps even more obvious to any observer of contemporary States, and for that reason also warrants a separate chapter in the final part of the book. The contemporary era has perhaps been witness to a resurgence of politicized and mobilized ethnicity with immediate consequences for the autonomy and unity of sovereign States. This general phenomenon is of course strikingly evident from the dramatic events which have unfolded in Eastern Europe and the former Soviet Union since 1989. The grounds for independence which are being asserted successfully in that part of the world are those of ethnonationality. People who share a language or a religion (or some other socially relevant characteristic which binds them together and separates them from other people) want to enjoy the right of living together within their own State under their own government. They patently do not wish to live under a government which is dominated by a different nationality or ethnic group—as the case of Croatia and Slovenia in the former Serbian-dominated Yugoslavia makes clear. To all intents and purposes this means forming an ethno-national State or in practice a State which is under the majority control of one linguistic or cultural or religious group. This is a form of State in which minorities can at best only be tolerated and protected but cannot be equal partners, for that would deny the ethno-national justification of separate statehood.

This logic denies the legitimacy of multinational and multi-ethnic statehood. Thus, the Soviet Union, Yugoslavia, and even Czechoslovakia could not fully accommodate ethnonationalism and remain single sovereign entities in the same shape as before. Likewise, perhaps Canada must also cease to exist as a unified State in its present geographical configuration. If this ethnonationalist logic were widely adopted in the contemporary world, in which multinational and multi-ethnic States constitute the vast majority of independent countries in most regions, it could present a threat of national disintegration and therefore international instability. Minority populations who could not accept (or be accepted by) such an arrangement would be sorely tempted to move to another State, perhaps where they might be in a majority or at least could be accepted as joint and equal partners in sovereign statehood. They might even be tempted—as in the case of the Serbian minority living in Eastern Croatia—to move the border instead of themselves so as to live within what had been the neighbouring territory of Serbia. Either eventuality could be another profound source of instability, both domestic and international. And, when the focus is turned from Europe and North America to Africa and Asia one can only be staggered by the number of multi-ethnic States which would be seriously threatened by ethnic discord should this logic prevail.

At some point the existing society of States could be at risk from such developments. For this reason—if for no other—concerted international efforts might well take place to try to forestall them. Furthermore, there is a noteworthy paradox in the assertion (or reassertion) of ethnonationality as a definition of independent statehood at a time when human population movements and communications are high, and many States (particularly in North America and Western Europe) are receiving as temporary residents or permanent immigrants many people of different nationality or ethnicity or religion or race from other parts of the world. Many if not indeed most Western countries are nowadays becoming increasingly multicultural and multiracial in the composition of their populations. The USA, Canada, and Australia are perhaps the best examples, but the process is also well advanced in Germany, France, Britain, and other West European countries. At a time when multiculturalism and multiracialism are becoming not only a demographical fact but even a social orthodoxy in some of the leading countries of the world—Canada has a multicultural provision in its constitution—it may seem ironical that there is also a reassertion of ethnonationalism as a definition of statehood. However, the two processes are linked—as is evident in strong political demands and even political movements in some countries for the repatriation of racially different immigrants. Ethnonationalism and multiculturalism are conflicting standards. But if some of the most important States are multicultural or multiracial, or are rapidly moving in that direction, one could speculate that this may be another reason to doubt that there will be any widespread redrawing of borders to accommodate demands for ethnically homogeneous States.

Finally, in the last chapter an assessment is made of the overall picture that emerges from this book, asking whether that picture is in need of revision and if so to what extent. Some international relations scholars believe that the forces of change outlined above, particularly economic changes but also demographic, technological, ideological, and similar changes, undermine the foundations of sovereign statehood and make a reorganization of world society on some other basis likely. Other scholars believe, however, that the current States system—which has existed in the same fundamental organizational shape based on the principle of sovereignty for more than four centuries—is a highly flexible political arrangement that is likely to adapt to all such changes without undue difficulty. What this global survey strongly suggests is that the vast majority of contemporary States have a very good prospect of existing indefinitely in their current territorial shapes and identities. This means, among other things, that States will continue to enjoy a measure of international freedom to be themselves—within, of course, international social, economic, and technological constraints. It therefore means, which cannot come as any surprise, that States will continue to possess individual personalities which sets them apart from other States. And the same distinctiveness is likely to characterize the various regions of the States system in the years to come. In short, the volume gives us many good reasons for believing that sovereign statehood is alive and well in the contemporary world and is likely to be in this robust condition for the foreseeable future.

However, this should not be taken to mean that the States system is a conservative world devoid of change. It is a conservative world, but it is not a changeless world. International change, however, is not of the fundamental or revolutionary variety—such as would be involved if the system of sovereign States were replaced by some alternative political arrangement. Rather, it is change in the character and capabilities of sovereign States and consequently in the shape and substance of their relations. For example, national and international economies continue to provide increased levels of welfare and well-being to the populations of most developed and many developing countries. Change in the opposite direction is also occurring—the case in many Sub-Saharan countries during the 1980s. Technological capabilities of States and the life-styles of their citizens also continue to change. Changes such as these are anything but new and have, in fact, been going on ever since the modern sovereign State first emerged about 500 years ago. This sort of change in which sovereign States, both individually and collectively, adapt to human innovations (or fail to adapt to them) is what we should probably expect in the years to come and what has in fact been continuously occurring since the foundation of the modern State. What is perhaps most important is the way the sovereign State *as an institution* has been able to accommodate such changes. Whereas some individual States have been more successful and some have been less successful in responding to change, the institution of sovereign statehood has been, in this regard, an amazingly flexible political arrangement which has successfully responded to every challenge presented to it during the last half millennium.

FURTHER READING

Boyd, A., *An Atlas of World Affairs* (London, 1991).

Bull, H., and Watson, A. (eds.), *The Expansion of International Society* (Oxford, 1984).

Clark, Sir George, *The Seventeenth Century* (Oxford, 1947).

Holland, R. F., *European Decolonization: 1918–1981* (London, 1985).

Jackson, R. H., *Quasi-States: Sovereignty, International Relations and the Third World* (Cambridge, 1990).

James, A., *Sovereign Statehood: The Basis of International Society* (London, 1986).

Manning, C. A. W., *The Nature of International Society* (London, 1962).

Wight, M., *Power Politics*, eds. H. Bull and C. Holbraad (Leicester, 1978).

2

Geographical Considerations in a World of States

DAVID B. KNIGHT[1]

Whereas all States are legally equal within the international system, in geographical terms there are great differences within and between States, including differences which find reflection in the way individual States may be perceived and accepted as participants in the system. This chapter identifies a series of geographical considerations that deserve examination when focusing on States, both internally and from an international perspective, and concludes with some comments on the geographic basis for State viability. States should be examined within their national and international geographical contexts, and the latter must be considered in interrelated terms, with concern for both human and physical patterns and processes. Particular emphasis is given to the concept of territory—a physical and behavioural concept—for it has significance for both intra- and inter-national State structures and processes.

What is the geographical perspective? Geographers focus on spatial patterns, processes, and relationships between human societies and their physical environments and the resulting regional structures at various local, national, and international scales. Such a focus means that there is need to take into account physical environmental considerations and also human elements. Human elements here refers to those facts and beliefs, patterns and events that relate to, reflect perceptions of, and result in various forms of territorial-organizational and landscape impacts on the surface of the earth. What is of concern here is the identification of some of the key geographical factors and processes that one must consider when critically examining the State and the international system of States.

TERRITORY AND STATE

The concept of territory is involved in every type of political organization.[2] The State, a physical, legal, and governmental entity, is a bounded container for the contents of a particular area on the earth's surface, which includes the people, resources, and means for communication and movement. The State, in theory if not always in fact, is also 'the chief custodian of overall social order; it is monitor, comptroller, arbitrator' of all people, things, and processes operating within the delimited bounds.[3] Further, as Johnston has observed, the State undertakes three basic roles: it acts as the promoter of accumulation, as the legitimator of capitalism, and as the creator of social consensus and order.[4] Of course, the State is necessary not only within capitalism, for the State acts as promoter, legitimator, and creator for other socio-economic systems too. In order to undertake these three roles, each State develops its own instruments and mechanisms by which the structural links between social formation and the State can function hierarchically and so enable the reproduction of the system.[5]

The State is thus itself a geographical factor, for things happen which have spatial consequences as a result of decisions and actions by State agents and institutions.[6] All States have territory that is bounded, formally or informally, by human decisions and actions. Its contents include terrain, flora and fauna, resources, and human inhabitants and their way of life. Since territory itself is passive and it is human beliefs, decisions, and actions that give territory meaning, it has been concluded that territory is not, rather, it becomes.[7] Two considerations which developed from this conclusion can be noted here.

First, not everyone would accept the statement that 'territory is not, it becomes', for many people obtain meaning from territory and the landscape within it by believing that the territory and its landscape are living entities which are already filled with meaning.[8] Such meanings may be reflected in a people's cultural ecology, the spatial patterning of their settlement and land use systems, their naming of places, in their patterns of movement, and perhaps in reverential beliefs they hold about specific parts of the landscape around them. To suggest that these meanings are simply figments of the collective imagination—parts of the 'geographies of the mind'—is to be heretical, at least for those people who accept the apparent truth of such meanings. Meanings gained from territory—but which really are attributions to the territory—reflect a cultural relationship with the territory. Further, however, and of particular importance, these geographies of the mind can form significant parts of the territorial component of national and ethnic identities.[9]

Second, since territory 'becomes', States have no basic geographical 'givens'. The dimensions of States, their shapes, bounds, contents, and longevity clearly are not givens: they generally result from long-term processes. Some aspects, such as territorial boundaries, may have resulted from relatively short-term processes. The imposition of boundaries by colonial powers are examples of some short-term processes. No State exists as a result of firm geographical factors! States exist because human actions and various local and world societal processes have led to their creation. These actions and processes occur in specific time-space settings, however, and so involve (sometimes critically important) geographical considerations, with resulting actions and processes having sometimes profound and sometimes subtle geographical impact.

A State's territory is not value-free, for it holds different kinds of meanings, depending upon the context of the part involved. For instance, colonial authorities may perceive a territory in strategic and economic terms, missionary organizations may understand it in terms of a place where souls can be saved, multinational corporations may see it as a resource supplier and as a place with a cheap labour force, all of which would be in marked contrast to the varying types of perceptions that people who are of the territory would have, whether or not their perceptions are part of a nationalism or something less than that. For the latter, the people of the territory, there would undoubtedly be powerful symbolic links to their State's sacred territory, no matter how little the territory was actually known or how weakly it was perceived; it would be enough that it was and is theirs.

As suggested above, the attachments people of a State have to their territory can have psychological and spiritual bases and thus go far deeper than anything generated simply by economic factors. These attachments and linkages may have national and/or various levels of subnational bounds, but to whatever scale the attachments are linked, the meanings and linkages really exist only in the mind (although, to repeat, there may be spatial and landscape consequences). To appreciate this, consider how groups in neighbouring States will hold contrasting perceptions: one group of people will not like, admire, revere, or gain strength from the other group's State territory in the way they will admire their own. The contrasting perceptions are influenced by what territory does and does not belong to the people in question, and also reflects historical interactions between peoples. Even if relations between the two groups always have been superb, there will nevertheless always be contrasting attachments to the territories in question. To take this latter thought further, it must be asked, what does territory provide?

Territory, when delimited with a system of government that has effective control over it, generally provides both security and opportunity for those who live within its bounds. On the one hand there is security to be gained from being an isolated community whereas, on the other hand, there is opportunity to be derived from being a part of a larger whole. Stress is caused by these two contradictory dimensions of territory, for elements of both undoubtedly always are present in any situation. In terms of foreign policy and international trade and other linkages, States may be further along the continuum toward one extreme or the other at different times. That there is interplay between the two contrasting, fundamental dimensions of territory is vital to any understanding of the political geography of both specific States and the international system of States.

The concept of territory is related to two additional powerful concepts, namely 'place' and 'territoriality'. Place refers to the locale in which people live (at personal and local scales), with attachments to place being strongly related to meanings that are both inscribed to and gained from place. Territoriality refers to the attempt by individuals or groups to affect, influence, and control people, phenomena, and relationships, by delimiting and asserting control over a geographic area.[10] Each of these concepts—territory, place, and territoriality—cannot be understood without reference to other territorial units, for implicit in each of them are this–that and we–they dichotomies, and, of course, each concept implies power, at local, regional, or national scales.

INTRASTATE STRUCTURES AND PROCESSES

What intrastate geographical elements are pertinent? Some points relating to spatial structures, including size and shape, resources, core and peripheral areas, capital cities and the overall settlement pattern, and frontiers and boundaries can be mentioned. From these other considerations are raised, including some further comments on attachments to territory within the State that are directly linked to sometimes competing conceptualizations of group 'self'.

There is probably no ideal size, shape, or real extent for any State. Obviously leaders of every State would like their State to be ideal, containing a just-right distribution and mix of renewable and non-renewable resources, an infrastructure that meets the needs of the State, an economy that is adequate to maintain an acceptable, perhaps even fine standard of living (but how measured?) for all of the State's population, and international linkages that serve to further the interests of the State. But some States are huge, others are tiny, and still more are in between; some are essentially round, but may be small or large, while others are long, thin, and tiny, or perhaps long, thin, and large, and so on. There is no meaningful statement that can validly be made concerning the ideal size. Does it matter what shape and size a State is, if the resources contained within it are inadequate (that is, difficult to get to, economically unviable to retrieve, poor in quality, small in amount), the terrain is an impediment to movement, the coastline is inhospitable, or the State is landlocked and has poor means for movement to the sea? Such geographical factors can be of significance when considering a State's viability.

An underlying element in these thoughts relates to the natural endowment of a territory, for the resources of a territory may seem inadequate at one time yet at another time (due, for example, to technological developments or pricing changes) may become extremely important. And some States are large with few resources whereas others are small with a rich endowment. The combinations are almost endless. When considering natural endowment, thoughts should not be confined to non-renewable resources—although such can be exceedingly valuable in many cases—for renewable resources should also be considered. Soils and agricultural output (linked to terrain and climatic factors) also need to be considered in association with population size and growth dynamics as well as levels and types of technological input. The nature of the State's external linkages may have to be highlighted too if, for example, the best soils and extensive plots of land are used for export cash crops rather than for indigenous food needs.

Contrary to the way too many social scientists seem to think as they write about various States, the earth is not an isometric plane. Thus, obviously within States' territories there is never an even spread of resources or settlement—there is always an uneven spread. The basic dichotomy in all settlement systems is urban versus rural, although numerous variations in patterns within rural and urban sectors abound, as do differing types of hierarchies in all settlement systems, all of which, with communication systems, relate in varying ways to technological levels of development present within any State. Industrial and agricultural outputs, levels of employment, of wealth and poverty, and so on, also have different spatial patterns within States, patterns which may inhibit or enhance the State's relative standing *vis-à-vis* other States.[11]

Distance can be an obstacle, although one that can be overcome with varying degrees of success, by the development of transportation and communication links. For example, Canada's huge territory once served as a major barrier to national development; the creation of linear links by rail, road and, later, air served to bring the country together. Of course, there still remain sections of that State which are remote, although many isolated communities are linked with populous regions by satellite. Distance as a factor to be overcome also applies internationally. New Zealand's long-standing linkages with Britain illustrates this well. Interestingly, New Zealand also can be used to illustrate that relative closeness in locational terms need not lead to other forms of closeness, for colonial New Zealand communicated officially with neighbouring Australia via London for many decades before links across the Tasman Sea were formed. Similar periphery–metropole/centre–periphery routings for communications also existed between some neighbouring former British colonies in Africa, as well as between some former French colonies in Africa, whereas communication routings between British and French African colonies sometimes had an unusual periphery–metropole–metropole–periphery arrangement.[12] Of course, in contrast, adjacency can lead to close communications, as demonstrated by Western Europe where the many neighbouring States have intricate webs of transportation and communications linkages, both within each State and between them, so it is correct to talk of networks.

Linkages, whether or not they form complex networks, can be examined from a time-space convergence perspective, for unless space is collapsed by at least reasonably efficient communication and transportation systems a State's infrastructure may be inadequate. Of concern, an old infrastructure and relict features on the landscape, when linked to societal inertia and a reluctance to change, may cause functional friction whereby bottlenecks may develop in a system now inadequate to meet contemporary or future needs. Instances of this exist in all States, even in the most advanced States. For example, Britain's road and rail systems are inadequate in many places (especially at bridging and tunnelling points) and so expensive upgrading is needed in order for Britain to fit into the European network once the Channel Tunnel link with France is opened. And in many Third World States limited development of road and rail systems often hinders the movement of goods for export or may lead to backups in the supply and distribution of, for example, imported goods or possibly needed food aid.

Whether a State's infrastructure is developed as a series of linear links or a complex network, it normally will find focus in the State's major core area wherein there is a major clustering of population, economic activity, and political decision-making. In many States, especially in the Third World, such a core is focused on a primate city, that is, a State's largest city which so dominates the urban hierarchy that no other city within the territory can match its size and importance.[13] The dominant clustering of people and urban-based activities in one centre reflects a severe spatial imbalance in the State, for it means that everywhere in the State that lies outside the capital city is the periphery and this may have detrimental consequences for many developmental processes. Not all States have primate cities. Indeed, most (especially developed) States have a stepwise hierarchy of settlements that range from villages, to small towns, to regional centres, to the largest cities. The nature of and linkages within the urban hierarchy can be a significant geographical factor, for various demographic, economic, and political elements find focus in contrasting ways within all settlement, transportation and communication systems. Also, whether or not a State has a primate city, most States today have experienced or are experiencing shifts in population location, with urbanization processes increasing rural–urban and within-urban inequalities. Such today generally is the case in Third World States which are experiencing rapid population growth and rapid urbanization, although sections of all States and their populations suffer from a maldistribution of wealth and of services, including health care. Measures of income distribution and quality of life indicate great variability both within and between States. Where there are great disparities there likely will also be the considerable potential for violence. Some violence can occur because of the State itself, for the structure and policies of the State may cause subjugation, alienation, and suffering.[14]

It is worth noting too that contemporary cores may not be the original cores of States, for other centres of concentration may have been historically important.[15] Capital cities—which always more than any other cities within their respective States reflect the focus of political decision-making powers and their often quite distinctive landscapes—generally are located in States' cores but may be beyond them, sometimes purposely being located in other regions of States so as to be freed from core pressures and competing cities located within the core (as in Australia, Canada, and Brazil) or away from areas with traditions of tribal rivalries (as in Botswana and Malawi).[16] State structures and processes have many geographical dimensions, including the ways the State is administered (as with various forms of unitary or federal systems), development policies (which may involve development from above or below,[17] and, for some States, means responding to directives from external sources such as the World Bank), migration patterns, production and movement of agricultural, mining, and industrial products, educational patterns, health patterns, the spread and impact of the media.

Of significance may be the way people within States respond to their leaders' directives. In some States, of course, elections may be permitted and the geographical patterns may provide vitally useful means for determining an understanding of power relations within the State, the reaction to party policies and practices, and measures of concern for regional versus statewide attachments to the State itself.[18] Elections as well as other forms of demonstrations (State approved or not) can reveal some insights into whether or not a State's population regards the government in power to be legitimate, as illustrated by recent events in China, the former Soviet Union, and Eastern Europe. If a government is challenged and has difficulty in responding without violent means, or in fact if it can only respond by using violence, then some people would charge that the viability of the State is in question. It may be, however, that it is simply the particular regime in power that is not viable.

In modern Western terms, State bounds are seen generally to be firm, to be lines, hence we talk of boundaries. In contrast, before the age of European imperialism, the traditional non-Western situation was comprised of suzerain-State systems (rather than sovereign State systems) which were defined not only by zones of transition between the component parts but also by formal hierarchical relations between a suzerain and the non-suzerain members of the system, thus not only the bounds but also the systems were different. Indeed, since zones of transition were a significant feature of suzerain-State systems, the imposition of the Western territorial principle (including delimited and demarcated boundaries) by colonialism was a radical system change.[19]

A State's boundaries may be permeable, permitting free or at least measured flows of people, goods, and ideas, or they may be impermeable to goods and people but perhaps not to ideas. The location on an interaction continuum from totally open to totally closed boundaries and frontiers reflects something of the nature of relationships between neighbouring States. Bounds of States of course may include peaceful or contentious ocean delimitations as well as land-bound issues, and questions of access to the waters and their resources may represent particular challenges. The longevity of boundaries may reflect the nature and intensity of relationships between States, hence may be useful barometers for measuring issues of peace versus war. Sometimes boundaries will remain fixed even as war rages across the territories and their bounds, although after most conflicts boundary changes occur. To avoid war between two major powers other generally weaker States may be used as an intermediary zone, whereby a buffer is created between the competing powers.[20] To all intents and purposes the boundaries of the small State or States may seem normal but there will always be the threat of invasion from one or other of the competing States if the balance of power changes. Relative location and relatively weak power thus may combine to place a State at some risk although, if all works well, advantages may be gained during times of stability and peace. If a State is located within a shatterbelt—that is, a region 'over whose control great powers seriously compete'[21]—then the chances of interstate conflict are high.

Putting the above thoughts together it will be realized that location must be considered from two perspectives: absolute location (which cannot change although the internal arrangements of the territory's contents can be altered by new discoveries, developmental processes, and economic and political policies and decision-making) and relative location (which can change as a result of a variety of linkage factors). The internal characteristics of States, in their fullest sense, clearly relate to the question of viability, for the human and physical environmental patterns and interactions find reflection in and gain meaning and guidance from the realities of absolute location, if taken at the statewide scale. Equally, the relative location of States may be significant, for States do not exist in isolation, no matter how much some governments may seek to be isolated from the broader international States' system. These matters suggest a need to consider the issue of power, for power (to control or manipulate other States, and the ability to provide alternatives) can be gained from a variety of internal-to-a-State factors (such as numerous or scarce resources and major industrial output) when related to such things as import–export ratios, international loans, and balance of payments.

STATE INTERACTIONS AND POWER CONSTRUCTIONS

Within political geography, as in other political studies disciplines, concern for geopolitical and geostrategic issues has a long history. Many constructions have been developed which suggest ways for approaching international interactions, although most have been biased by their respective authors' time-frame, national attachments, and ideological orientations.

Political geographer Saul Cohen recently has sought to provide a counter to US foreign policy by encouraging foreign policy-makers in Washington, DC—and elsewhere—to think of the complex world geopolitical system as a flexibly hierarchical, specialized, and integrated spatial structure.[22] Rather than seeing a strategic unity of space Cohen has recognized geostrategic realms, and, within them, geopolitical regions. There are two realms: the trade-dependent Maritime realm (essentially an open system based upon specialized exchange with global reach) and the Eurasian Continental realm (which is a much more closed, land-orientated system). The realms are divided into second-level geopolitical regions, thus the Maritime realm includes Anglo-America and Caribbean, Maritime Europe, Maghreb, Offshore Asia, South America, and Sub-Saharan Africa, whereas the Eurasian Continental realm consists of the Soviet heartland and East Asia. Three second-level regions lie outside the realms: the Middle East Shatterbelt, a zone of contention, is caught between the two realms; the East European Gateway is beginning to

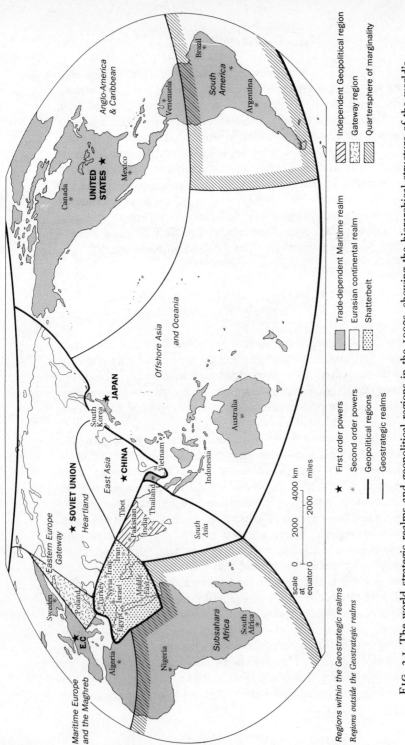

Fig. 2.1 The world strategic realms and geopolitical regions in the 1990s, showing the hierarchical structure of the world's geopolitical framework. *Source:* Reproduced with permission from Saul Cohen, 'Global Geopolitical Change in the Post-Colonial War Era', *Annals of the Association of American Geographers*, 81/4 (1991), 553

link them; and South Asia is geopolitically independent. National States form the third level of the hierarchy. Within the latter, that is, at the sub-state level, there exists a fourth level of embryonic States which may someday (violently or peacefully) spin off from existing States to become, in Cohen's words, Gateway States. Cohen suggests that global imbalance is a function of changes among and between geostrategic realms and their geopolitical regions, and that the imbalance reflects differences in entropic levels of major national States, particularly first- and second-order powers.

Cohen's model is suggestive of the interconnectedness of regions and of States within their regions, and acknowledges that the geographic patterns of States interacting one with the other have differential characteristics and impacts. Other recent models lay special focus on interconnectedness and on the impact of world economy perspectives.[23] The point here is not to stress any one model but to suggest that to appreciate the geographical basis of statehood and viability one must be concerned not only with the internal political geography of a State but also with its external linkages, and its relative standing as a State within the international system of States from both regional and systems-wide perspectives.

STRESSES, RIGIDITY, AND CHALLENGES

The discussion of models may suggest that external-to-the-State considerations are to the fore when focusing on geopolitical issues; however, internal-to-the-State considerations are also always involved. Clearly a variety of factors other than just political and economic power must be considered. These include peoples' sense of group-self (as with, especially, nationalism, an ingredient of which is a particular territory that is held or coveted), and questions of control. Some groups form distinctive regionalisms within their State's territory. Some regionalisms may be politicized and so may represent a threat to the central government. The threat may remain sub-state, with the result simply being a minor restructuring of territory and, possibly, the creation of a new sub-unit—as with Jura in Switzerland—or the State may have to be redivided with a significantly different structure (or structures) due, for example, to the need to better accommodate marked cultural-linguistic differentiation—as in the cases of Belgium and Nigeria. Some solutions to regionally focused sub-state conflict may be territorially based yet may not involve territorial change, for a redistribution of (constitutional and other) powers may be enough to meet minority demands—within existing territorial delimitations. Clearly, there are numerous means for dealing with sub-state conflict, only some of which are territorially focused.

Intrastate reconstructions are not new, for regional divisioning of States has been occurring for centuries. Without doubt, the intra-administrative territorial structuring of States will continue to alter as governments face sub-state peoples who desire to be either totally or at least partially in control of themselves. Of course, States can use the State apparatus for manipulating sub-state regional groupings even as the apparatus is used to help develop the State and all of its people within a national framework.

There is rarely a complete areal fit between one clearly defined nation and a State, thus it is generally quite misleading to use the phrase 'nation State'.[24] Some States have lost or never had a full sense of nationhood due to, for example, competing senses of group-self. In a few instances, where societal divisions and competing senses of group identity run especially deep, there may be severe sectarian-based violence, as in Northern Ireland and Lebanon, with little sense of common national identity. Perhaps still further territorial divisions may be needed in these territories if peace between the competing communities is to be given a chance. Elsewhere, where a State is unable to control or manage dissident groups within the total population, especially if the dissident groups are located in peripheral parts of the States' territory, secessionist consequences may threaten. That such threats exist in many States is no surprise for there are numerous instances where significant mismatches between the distribution of groups with separate identities and the contemporary delineation of international boundaries.[25]

How real is the possibility of secessionist threats succeeding? Many international instruments declare that all peoples have the right to self-determination, but UN pronouncements also give stress to national unity and territorial integrity rather than permitting a genuine concern for a people freed from a geographical (that is, statewide) context. Indeed, an overriding primacy is currently retained for the centuries-old foundations of international law and the system of States: recognition, State sovereignty, and territorial integrity. Thus, for example, the Congo (Zaïre) and Nigeria were supported internationally as they forcibly denied secessionist threats. Perhaps surprisingly, in contrast,

Pakistan was not so supported as it sought to keep East Pakistan from becoming Bangladesh, but this was largely due to the unusual physical and cultural geography of Pakistan and also to India's interventionist support of Bangladesh. Indeed, the international community chose not to endorse a Bangladeshi claim to self-determination but instead took the easier—and safer—course by declaring their support for the new State because of their humanitarian concerns over the huge losses of life.[26] Sadly, similar international concern has not been shown for East Timorese whose claim for self-determination (once the Portuguese colonialists had departed) was denied by invading Indonesians who first claimed they had a pre-colonial claim to the territory and then proceeded to slaughter the East Timorese.[27] And while the world did not condemn Indonesia, there was near-universal and violent reaction to Iraq's invasion of Kuwait. These examples illustrate that the application of international law is far from being free of inconsistencies and double standards. Above all, in issues involving the possibility of self-determination, the international community is hesitant to set an example, largely because numerous States could suffer from secessionist threats from their sub-state minorities.[28]

Politico-territorial or constitutional restructuring—or the use of force—may solve most intrastate pressures, but new forms of international linkages also may help to release some pent-up tension. Three Canadian examples may illustrate this point: the Canadian Government has permitted the provinces of Quebec and New Brunswick to have associate membership status in la Francophonie and so sit with the State of Canada, which is a full member; Canadian provinces may and do have trade and cultural offices in other countries, in the USA, UK, and France; and (but not with the full blessing of the Canadian Government) some groups of Canada's indigenous peoples have non-governmental recognition within the UN, via its Working Group on Indigenous Populations.[29]

Do these recently created forms of international linkages and recognition for sub-state units and peoples indicate that a freeing of the notion of sovereignty is possible? At once it must be noted that the Canadian State still holds primacy and is not about to release total responsibility to any sub-state unit. And too, it must be admitted that similar linkages will always be inadequate for peoples—such as Quebecois nationalists—who will accept nothing less than their own State; thus there will always be pressures from sub-state peoples who want nothing less than to have self-determination mean total self-government, i.e. independence. In some instances, force may be used by peoples desirous of liberation as they seek to highlight their demands and as a means for bringing pressure to bear upon the dominating States. Indeed, sadly, violence and the threat of violence will undoubtedly continue to be expressed around the world, as competing claims are made to territory by different States and by particular States against some of their sub-state minorities. Underlying such threats are questions that will continue to be raised concerning how power is to be used, what methods of control and what degrees of control are acceptable, and, perhaps ultimately, about self-determination. Each of the questions, and the answers arrived at through practice, will have territorial consequences.

TENSIONS, SOME CONSEQUENCES, AND THE ISSUE OF VIABILITY

Tension exists in our world between parochial State-centred views and world-wide needs, as witnessed, for example, by the increased realization that we live on a globe that is sensitive to harmful human-generated processes which, at the same time, may be perceived as essential to individual States' socio-economic and political well-being. Increasingly rapid changes are altering power relationships within and between States due to major changes in world economic and social conditions, challenging ideological developments, military technology and hardware advances, Great Power disarmament efforts, new trade patterns, and numerous regional conflicts. Of major significance, both capitalism and State socialism (communism) are being challenged as peoples within numerous States create and recreate their myths and symbols of identity and seek to better construct their worlds along new lines. Thus, even as international linkages are being forged and reformulated, some intrastate identities also are being reformed and even hardened. The tension between these contrasting forces reflects the two opposites that territory itself embodies: outward orientated opportunity versus inward-looking security. Some peoples desire to reform their States' governments (witness recent changes in Poland, Hungary, and what was East Germany and the Soviet Union) while others wish to use their former sub-state territory as a means for obtaining new opportunities apart from existing State structures (witness, for instance, the situations in Lithuania, Ukraine, Slovenia, and Croatia).

As new States are created, their new governments initially have to stress the security dimension of territory, a need that stands in contrast to the opportunity dimension of territory. There is tension if not also friction, since any stress on security clashes with pressures from the increasingly integrated international system of States which, at least in theory, provides opportunities that otherwise might not be experienced. Of course, it is fair to add that all existing States—and not just potential States—will continue to have to deal with the contradictions between security and opportunity. Inherent tensions and possible conflicts arising from these contradictions will lead to contrasting outcomes which thus will have differing State and inter-national consequences.

When considering, therefore, how one can measure the geographical basis for State viability, the best answer is that there is no simple answer since numerous factors, at local, broader regional, statewide, world regional, and world-systems-wide scales have to be considered. Numerous States exist which from any rational standpoint should not exist since they are economically non-viable, and cannot exist without (sometimes massive) external support. Yet they do exist as independent States for they have been granted recognition within the international system of States. Indeed, once recognized internationally it is difficult to be denied that recognition, as evidenced by the fact that wartorn, internally shattered Lebanon has remained as an internationally re-cognized State with a seat in the UN during its times of dreadful trial. The Lebanese case would suggest that internationally stress is given to the formal legal norm of equal sovereignty rather than to empirical reality.

To take this thought further, the politically independent (and genuinely democratic) country of Botswana is a viable State for it has international recognition, despite being dependent on considerable external aid (most notably during drought years) and being vulnerable to numerous economically crippling pressures that neighbouring South Africa holds as a threat over it. In contrast, the nearby territorially fragmented BaTswana Bantustan within the Republic of South Africa called Bophuthatswana is not recognized internationally, despite South Africa's declaration that the territory was independent. Ironi-cally, some of the South African Bantustans—misleadingly called 'homelands' by the white regime—as sub-state territories are more

economically and politically substantial—even while still being intimately tied to the South African political economy—than some
independent Black States to the north which have been granted UN
status. The South African Bantustan example clearly indicates that it
is not enough simply to have a self-made claim by the people of a
territory (or the people who claim to speak for them), or even that
they have an internally accepted form of government, for the State
itself has to be granted international recognition.

Recognition generally comes from an acceptance that the State
has the attributes of statehood, the ruling regime is the effective
government, and the State fits into the international system of States.[30]
Recognition is rarely retracted once given. However, it may be that
an existing State's governmental regime may not be accorded recognition if the regime in question comes to power by unconstitutional
means, such as by a *coup d'état*, so non-recognition of the regime may
occur even though the State itself is recognized. In a sense, then,
recognition implies a form of viability, although functional viability
may be another question.

Consider the following questions. What if a State's economy is not
strong? If exports are principally unrefined non-renewable resources,
or are largely limited to a crop that is regarded as a luxury food in the
Western world? Or if changing trade patterns threaten a State's
access to traditional markets? Or if a country's exports and imports
are potentially or actually controlled by a neighbouring State through
whose territory access to the sea must be gained? Or if a State is
dependent upon external assistance? Or if there is a perennial trade
deficit? Or if a State is dominated politically, ideologically, and militarily
by another State? Do these various considerations mean a State faced
with such functional problems is not viable? There is no easy answer
to the question. As suggested in this chapter, to gain an understanding
of the geographical basis of any State's viability there is a need for an
integrated examination of the many human, physical-environmental,
and locational factors that together have led to the changed (and still-
changing) patterns and processes operating within and on the State.
The territory's absolute and relative location, contents, spatial and
functional organization, and ideological, political, legal, psychological,
trade, and possibly military linkages are all factors to be considered.

Clearly, there is an enormous variation in the substance and capability of independent States. In most cases equal sovereignty—a
legal norm—seems able to withstand enormous inequality between

States—an empirical reality. Hence sovereign States may remain in existence in spite of their palpable lack of functional viability. In short, only if many factors and several scales identified earlier are considered in an integrated fashion can we begin to truly appreciate what the geographical factors are that underlie any State's viability.

NOTES

1. The author gratefully acknowledges the research support of the Social Sciences and Humanities Research Council of Canada, the Visiting Fellowship from Corpus Christi College, Cambridge, and the International Geographical Union Commission on the World Political Map.
2. See the thoughtful writings of E. W. Soja, *The Political Organization of Space* (Washington, 1971); I. D. Duchacek, *The Territorial Dimensions of Politics Within, Among, and Across Nations* (Boulder, Col., 1986).
3. S. Greer and P. Orleans, 'Political Sociology', in R. E. L. Faris (ed.), *Handbook of Modern Sociology* (Chicago, 1964), 810.
4. R. J. Johnston, *Geography and the State* (London, 1982).
5. G. L. Clark and M. Dear, *State Apparatus: Structures and Language of Legitimacy* (Boston, 1984).
6. R. J. Johnston and P. Taylor (eds.), *A World in Crisis: Geographical Perspectives* (Oxford, 1989).
7. D. B. Knight, 'Identity and Territory: Geographical Perspectives on Nationalism and Regionalism', *Annals of the Association of American Geographers*, 72 (1982), 517.
8. Y.-F. Tuan, *Topophilia* (Englewood Cliffs, NJ, 1974).
9. R. J. Johnston, D. B. Knight, and E. Kofman (eds.), *Nationalism, Self-Determination and Political Geography* (London, 1988).
10. R. D. Sack, 'Territorial Bases of Power', in A. D. Burnett and P. J. Taylor (eds.), *Political Studies from Spatial Perspectives* (Chichester, 1981), 53–71; R. D. Sack, *Human Territoriality: Its Theory and History* (Cambridge, 1986).
11. For interstate comparisons see N. Ginsburg, *Geographic Perspectives on the Wealth of Nations* (Chicago, 1986) and M. Kidron and R. Segal, *The New State of the World Atlas* (London, 1987).
12. 'Periphery' is used advisedly here for it is accepted that people of States which 'theory' place in the periphery do not necessarily see themselves as being anywhere other than the 'centre' at least in their own view of the world.
13. N. Keyfitz, 'Political-Economic Aspects of Urbanization in South and Southeast Asia', in P. M. Hauser and L. F. Schnore (eds.), *The Study of Urbanization* (New York, 1966), 265–309; T. G. McGee, *The Southeast*

Asian City (London, 1967). Mark Jefferson's 1939 paper remains provocative: repr. 'The Law of the Primate City', *Geographical Review*, 79 (1989), 226–32.

14. R. J. Johnston, J. O'Loughlin, and P. J. Taylor, 'The Geography of Violence and Premature Death', in C. Schmidt, D. Senghaas, and R. Vayryenn (eds.), *The Quest for Peace* (London, 1987).

15. N. J. G. Pounds and S. S. Ball, 'Core Areas and the Development of the European State System', *Annals of the Association of American Geographers*, 54 (1964), 24–40; and M. I. Glassner and H. de Blij, *Systematic Political Geography* (New York, 1989), 94–100.

16. For instance, O. H. K. Spate, 'Two Federal Capitals: New Delhi and Canberra', *Geography Outlook*, 1 (1956), 1–8; D. B. Knight, *Choosing Canada's Capital: Conflict Resolution in a Parliamentary System* (Ottawa, 1991); J. Augelli, 'Brasilia: The Emergence of a National Capital', *Journal of Geography*, 62 (1963), 241–52; D. B. Knight, 'Gaberones: A Viable Proposition', *Professional Geographer*, 17 (1965), 38–9; D. Potts, 'Capital Relocation in Africa: The Case of Lilongwe in Malawi', *Geographical Journal*, 151 (1985), 182–96.

17. e.g. W. B. Stohr and D. R. F. Taylor (eds.), *Development from Above or Below?* (Chichester and New York, 1991).

18. See R. J. Johnston, F. M. Shelley, and P. J. Taylor (eds.), *Developments in Electoral Geography* (London, 1990), and R. J. Johnston, C. J. Pattie, and J. G. Allsopp, *A Nation Dividing? The Electoral Map of Great Britain: 1979–1987* (London, 1988).

19. For a discussion of some geopolitical concerns that relate, in part, to traditional non-Western boundaries, see Lim Joo-Jock, *Territorial Power Domains, Southeast Asia and China* (Singapore, 1984). Generally on boundaries and frontiers, see J. R. V. Prescott, *Political Frontiers and Boundaries* (London, 1987).

20. J. Chay and T. E. Ross (eds.), *Buffer States in World Politics* (Boulder, Col., 1986).

21. P. L. Kelly, 'Escalation of Regional Conflict: Testing the Shatterbelt Concept', *Political Geography Quarterly*, 5 (1986), 161.

22. S. Cohen, 'Global Geopolitical Change in the Post-Colonial War Era', *Annals of the Association of American Geographers*, 81 (1991), 551–80.

23. e.g. I. Wallerstein, *The Capitalist World Economy* (Cambridge, 1979), and P. J. Taylor, *Political Geography* (London, 1989).

24. M. W. Mikesell, 'The Myth of the Nation State,' *Journal of Geography*, 82 (1983), 257–60.

25. D. B. Knight, 'The Dilemma of Nations in a Rigid State Structured World', in N. Kliot and S. Waterman (eds.), *Pluralism and Political Geography: People, Territory, and State* (London, 1983), 114–37; M. W. Mikesell and A. B. Murphy, 'A Framework for Comparative Study of

Minority-Group Aspirations', *Annals of the Association of American Geographers*, 81 (1991), 581–604.

26. V. P. Nanda, 'Self-Determination Outside the Colonial Context: The Birth of Bangladesh in Retrospect', in Y. Alexander and R. A. Friedlander (eds.), *Self-Determination* (Boulder, Col., 1980), 193–220.

27. R. S. Clark, 'The Decolonization of East Timor and the United Nations Norms on Self-Determination and Aggression', *Yale Journal of Public Order*, 7 (1980), 2–44.

28. For a guide to numerous theoretical discussions and case-studies see D. B. Knight and M. Davies, *Self-Determination: An Interdisciplinary Annotated Bibliography* (New York, 1987).

29. See C. Old, *Quebec's Relations with Francophonie* (Ottawa, 1984); On international action by indigenous peoples see Knight, 'Self-Determination and Indigenous Peoples', in R. J. Johnston, D. B. Knight, and E. Kofman (eds.), *Nationalism*, 117–34.

30. D. B. Knight, 'Statehood: A Politico-Geographic and Legal Perspective', *GeoJournal*, 28 (1992), 311–18.

FURTHER READING

Blake, G. (ed.), *Maritime Boundaries and Ocean Resources* (London, 1987).

Burnett, A. D., and Taylor, P. J. (eds.), *Political Studies from Spatial Perspectives* (Chichester, 1981).

Glassner, M. I., *Political Geography* (New York, 1993).

Johnston, R. J., Knight, D. B., and Kofman, E. (eds.), *Nationalism, Self-Determination and Political Geography* (London, 1988).

—— and Taylor, P. J. (eds.), *A World in Crisis?: Geographical Perspectives* (Oxford, 1989).

Kliot, N., and Waterman, S. (eds.), *Pluralism and Political Geography: People, Territory, and State* (London, 1983).

—— and Waterman, S. (eds.), *The Political Geography of Conflict and Peace* (London, 1991).

Prescott, J. R. V., *Political Frontiers and Boundaries* (London, 1987).

Rumley, D., and Minghi, J. (eds.), *The Geography of Border Landscapes* (London, 1991).

Taylor, P. J., *Political Geography: World-Economy, Nation-State and Locality* (London, 1989).

Wallace, I., *The Global Economic System* (London, 1990).

3

The Psychological Basis of
Independent Statehood

ALAN BRANTHWAITE

INTRODUCTION

The psychological basis of independent statehood lies in the attachment ordinary people form with their nation or country. This relationship arises because a group of people perceive themselves as having something in common, and believe they share an identity, which provides security. Out of this attachment grows an ideology that there is something special about a land mass and a way of life.

As a method of social-political organization, this is almost universal; families and tribes group themselves into larger political units. Psychologically, self-perception, identification, and labelling are fundamental in committing a group of people to larger political categories. The power of categorization and labelling to affect attitudes and behaviour is widespread (and has been noted in fields as diverse as mental illness, delinquency, and marketing).

By and large, citizens' self-categorizations correspond with the political units of nation States, although in certain circumstances they may prefer to emphasize their nationality or ethnic group. The reasons why one level of affiliation should be more satisfying than another are instructive about the psychological basis of statehood and are examined later in the chapter.

Attachments to a State can be based on different mechanisms, which may be overlapping.[1] The values and beliefs involved provide the psychological justification for statehood in human social organization.

Cultural identity

People identify certain common characteristics in themselves such as tradition, ownership of land, language, and way of life. These values are derived through kinship and heritage which the people share. These beliefs and values can exist without the possession of a nationally based sovereign State, as with Zionism in Israel, or Armenians and Georgians in the former USSR. The underlying values here are similarity and cohesion: people want to live their lives with others who they feel are similar and they can trust.

Statism

Statism exists where the national ideology centres around the State itself as a political entity with sovereignty, power, and authority over the people, who owe respect and allegiance to it. The State is believed to function to provide security and to advance the national interests of its people. Central to this ideology are leaders (monarch, president, etc.) and the symbols and trappings of their office. The example of strife in former Yugoslavia is illustrative: Tito as a leader-figure played a crucial role in holding together the constituent republics and ethnic groups; after his death alternative leadership based on cultural (religious and ethnic) identity helped pull the country apart. The underpinning values are related to power and control: people want to live in a place under their own control, to exercise their rights, and further their goals.

Institutional ideology

Institutional ideology focuses on the institutions, 'philosophies' and policies of the group, which are considered right and proper, such as free enterprise, freedom of speech, human rights, etc. 'Our' way of doing things is believed to be the best, whether it be a democratic system or socialist. Nationalism centred on this type of belief provided an important rationalization to the expansion of the British Empire and conquest by Germany in the Hitler era. The essential values of this type of nationalism are moral: people seek to live according to principles which they cherish and which justify their way of life.

Although these value and belief systems provide the basis for different collective experiences of statehood, individual citizens' appreciation of them varies. Ideas of the State may be relatively primitive or sophisticated, for example, in regarding the leader as inherently superior, or a mutually agreed device to bring organization and coherence to the group. In practice, these values of the State are manifest through symbols: the flag and emblems of a country, its great statesmen and heroes, a passport, the style of a car number plate, buildings that house national institutions belonging to the people. These serve as overt points of attachment to the values and beliefs of the group. Integration of the group is through shared awareness of these symbols, and emotional investment in them which gives them an agreed sense of importance.

Of the three bases for attachment, cultural identity and statism are most important as emotional mechanisms linking the individual and State. Institutional ideology evolves out of this as a cognitive and philosophical rationale for a specific way of life. As a consciously adopted belief, it can be a potent commitment to the State, depending on the extent of personal consideration given to it, overtness of publicly expressed opinions, and links with other cherished ideas and attitudes.

At this point, it should be acknowledged that psychologists in their work have focused on the nation (as a human group) and nationality (as a part of social perception) rather than the State (as a political organization), nevertheless, there are three questions to address in this chapter relating to statehood as seen from a psychological point of view: (1) How and why do individuals become identified with their nation? (2) Why do people emphasize differences between their nation and others? (3) Why is so much emotion invested in nationality that people are prepared to die for what might otherwise be almost an arbitrary clustering of people?

IDENTIFICATION WITH NATION-STATES

The importance of national identity can be illustrated from the case of a student who was stateless, a refugee from Eastern Europe. Without a passport and having only limited travel documents, movement between his country and that where his family resided was fraught with difficulty. He had no right to stay in Britain except while studying. Without a nationality he had only a tentative hold on a place in the world to live, work, have friends, a family, and conduct his life.

A sense of who we are, and our place in society is important in human consciousness. Individuals' self-concepts are made up from personal qualities and self-attributions, together with features ascribed to them from membership in groups and social categories that they belong to, or fancy they belong to.[2] Individuals seek to achieve a positive and distinctive identity by differentiating themselves from others in order to demonstrate their nature and worth in society. Social groups behave similarly, seeking to gain a more positive identity through social comparisons with other groups to achieve a more superior and respected position.[3] Such comparisons are often based on social and geographical proximity, consequently territorial neighbours and surrounding social groups are very important in the acquisition of identity.

Where comparison does not produce a secure positive identity for the group, it leads to tension and conflict. Social psychologists have shown that this is an important mechanism underlying conflict and aggression operating independently of competition for finite resources and wealth. Individuals, acting as part of a social group, will forgo rewards for their group if the achievement of them entails giving more benefit to other groups, thus enhancing the other group's status relative to their own. They act in this fashion even when it is against the rational interest of their group to maximize absolute gains. What matters in establishing identity is not the absolute but the relative standing of the groups in comparison with each other. The power of labelling and categorization to affect identity and behaviour has been demonstrated in experiments where temporary and arbitrary categories (which were socially meaningless outside of the research) were imposed by the researcher. These categorizations were sufficient to evoke discriminatory behaviour between groups. The conclusions from research in this field are that groups strive for positive identity in comparison with other groups.

We can see the importance of nationality as part of individuals' social identities in a similar experiment.[4] (The importance of an experiment here is that its very artificiality allows us to isolate the variables we are interested in and measure their influence while other factors are controlled.) Students at the same university were assigned to Welsh or English groups according to their nationality, so that this was the only salient aspect of their social identities. In allocating resources to each other they exhibited conflict which was against their rational interests. This resulted in less absolute rewards for their group than could have been achieved, but relatively more than for the other group. The conflict and discrimination was greatest on the part of the Welsh students whose identity, as the underdog in the comparison, was most threatened.

The search for distinctive social identity presents a paradox in human psychology. On the one hand, our identity in groups gives us a sense of belonging, while on the other hand we constantly seek to differentiate ourselves from those around us and attempt to stand out from the crowd (individualism). By belonging we achieve a sense of security, but we fear being absorbed, undifferentiated, and anonymous. By being different, we achieve distinctiveness but we fear becoming detached and isolated. Fig. 3.1 illustrates these tensions in social relationships. These tensions are also true for groups and nations, since we seek to work out our identity through the groups we are members of. States, as directed by leaders and with the support of the people, are similarly ambivalent in relation to their neighbours— attracted for security, recognition, and influence, but also anxious about losing out in the comparison or even being absorbed by them.

This tension is especially acute for smaller nations in relation to their dominant neighbours. Anxiety about being shut out and insecurity about being taken over increase the chances of conflict hardening, so that impenetrable, non-co-operative 'walls' are set up. It is in conditions which provide a sense of security and recognition of independent identities, that nations are most likely to replace these walls by permeable 'boundaries' and co-operate with each other. Kaplan and Markus-Kaplan[5] argued that as Turkey and Tunisia developed stronger national identities (between 1948 and 1982) so they became more secure and less anxious about being absorbed by other cultures, particularly Western culture which they were attracted to because of its success and prosperity. This culture conflict was especially

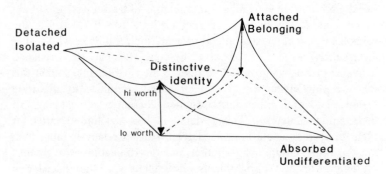

FIG. 3.1 Tensions in social relationships

manifested in the Arab world by Israeli economic achievements. Turkey and Tunisia's increased sense of security enabled them to drop their 'defensive walls', set up to protect their distinctive identity as Arab and Islamic States, and engage in greater dialogue and more harmonious relationships with Israel. Egypt achieved a sense of national identity later, after the removal of Western interests and rejection of pan-Arab aspirations. This was followed by *rapprochement* with Israel. The Palestinians, who had not achieved independent statehood, nor a national or geographical identity, have not recognized the legitimacy of Israel. Interestingly, since Kaplan and Markus-Kaplan's paper was written, Palestinian claims to statehood have been acknowledged in the international community while they have moved towards re-cognition of Israel, admittedly under pressure. However, in the past, Western pressure had not been successful and might be said to have been translated into terrorist actions. While this analysis may not prove the effects of identity on 'walls' and 'boundaries', as the authors acknowledge, it is illustrative of the psychological processes involved in the development of independent statehood.

The value of statehood for the citizen

Statehood, as part of the citizen's identity, has certain values and functions for the individual.

Security. It gives a feeling of belonging to a group and provides a sense of security. A Palestinian Arab leader is quoted as saying:[6] 'A flag, a sense of nationality, a passport are essential. In the modern world, State membership is a fundamental part of identity . . . With a passport we would not be pariahs. We could be the beneficiaries of reciprocity . . . We would have a place to go back to if in a plight.' An Israeli general is quoted as making a similar point. Recalling his experience as a 14-year-old boy arriving in Israel, he spoke of how important it was for him to feel 'like a normal person, with land, a State and an army'.[7] This sense of security in a State arises out of individuals' experiences within families, which gradually widens and is generalized to other social groups that enclose us. The spatial hierarchy—'member of a family, living in a house, situated in a street of a town in a country'—gives a sequence of enveloping physical categories which form a distinct progression. This special sequence, radiating outwards from the home, helps in generalizing the ties of affection and loyalty that begin in the family.

Sociobiologists have argued that there is a genetic basis to loyalty and altruism within in-groups. Since we share genes with our kin, it is in our interest to assist in the survival and procreation of kin. In-group loyalties are a generalization from kinship ties, and have survival value. The cultural and psychological importance of groups is an extension of these kinship ties, which enables us to determine whom we can trust.

Structure. Groups give society its structure and our membership in groups gives us a position in society. Thus nationality provides a sense of order in the international world, through knowing which groups are allies, that can be trusted, and which are enemies. Media news increasingly penetrates into the lives of ordinary citizens and focuses awareness on 'national' and 'international' events, which heightens the sense of being a nation, and the need to appreciate where one stands in the international scene.

Worth. In general, being associated with 'our country', its heritage, and achievements[8] gives pride and a sense of worth. Many people living abroad do not change their citizenship and cannot understand how anyone could do it. For them this would be tantamount to rejecting their self-image. Nationality, as part of identity, sets up simple ways of understanding the world in terms of in-groups and out-groups. These divisions help in evaluating the world, deciding where loyalties lie on issues, and what is right and wrong. Nationality acts as a guide to the interpretation of events and attributing blame and responsibility so that we have a coherent and self-justifying perception of the world around us.[9] This can have unfortunate repercussions: a rapid flow of refugees or immigrants into a country is met with hostility and disgust because it is felt to devalue the currency of national membership, by diluting the specialness and dignity of the people who make up the country.

Heritage. National identity has a strong time-dimension, which links generations. It is one of the few group identities which provides an individual with this sense of place in time as well as space.

Social control. The State is important because of its control over our daily lives in telling us what we can do, what we cannot do, and what we must do. There is a tendency to identify with dominant sources of authority as a way of managing the emotions that such control produces. By allying ourselves with the controller we feel we are directing and restraining ourselves (self-determination) rather than being restricted by others.

DEVELOPMENT OF IDENTIFICATION
DURING CHILDHOOD

Children prefer their own country to others well before they understand what it is.[10] Preference precedes knowledge. At first a country is simply a word[11] which is often personalized through its leaders. Allegiance develops quickly to this label and its associated symbols (flags, emblems, anthems) before children properly understand the spatial meaning of the concept.[12] Before 6 years of age, children are conscious of their nationality as part of their self-concept[13] though it is less significant than their age or sex. Thus emotional attachments are basic to the developing concepts of country and nationality, which helps to explain the strength of feelings they generate.

The term country becomes attached to a spatial entity as children's familiarity with places widens outwards from their immediate vicinity and they are able to co-ordinate their grasp of place and space. Young children have poor understanding of the inclusive spatial categories of town, country, and continents. Five- and six-year-olds are just as likely to mention a city or continent when asked which country they live in. Paradoxically, this logic of inclusive spatial categories, which makes it difficult to understand the concept of country in the first place, may in the end serve to strengthen the ties of country by forming a special sequence of enveloping geographical categories expanding from the family and home to the State. Few other group memberships (if any) have the same hierarchy.

Later on (8–10 years) national preferences are justified using knowledge that has been acquired of distinctive national features,[14] such as lifestyles (including games, possessions) and language (the way people talk). Awareness and knowledge of children's own country precedes that of others, which are poorly differentiated. It is the focal point in comparisons with other countries, so that its salience becomes magnified. Thus children develop an egocentric view of their nationality in relationship with other individual countries, which are not seen as having independent existences. Eight- and nine-year-olds go through a stage of being repelled by the strangeness of other nationalities and judge countries favourably in proportion to their perceived similarity with their home country and people.[15]

By the age of 10–12, much more sophisticated concepts of countries exist. There is greater accuracy in using the spatial concepts involved, greater differentiation in attitudes to individual foreign countries, based on less concrete thinking, and more awareness of contemporary events, such as technological achievements and success in international sport. Abstract values (freedom, democracy, etc.) are more prominent in explanations of what is good about a country[16] and evaluations focus more on the people than aspects of scenery, flags, or stamps, etc. There is also greater stability in attitudes and wider consensus about preferences.[17]

The increasing prominence of sport and international affairs on television over the years since much of the research was conducted may well have accelerated awareness of nationality and development of international attitudes. The development of ideas about countries shows little influence from formal education.

Exceptions in developmental patterns

While children in most countries are satisfied with their attachment to their own nationality, there are exceptions where children's growing understanding about their own and other nationalities, leads them to devalue their own group. This occurs in two circumstances.

The first is children of a country whose international standing is in some way tarnished. Children studied in Japan and Germany during the 1960s[18] saw their own people less positively than those from countries they admired.

The second is children who belong to a minority group in multi-cultural countries where there are internal divisions. Belgium, for example, has people of French and Flemish descent and both languages are in use. Because of this ambiguity in the ethnic structure of Belgium, Flemish children do not acquire a sense of national pride (as either Belgian or Flemish) until later in their development. Where children belong to less privileged groups in the social hierarchy, they may never develop pride to the same extent as in more integrated nationalities. In Scotland, older children devalued being Scottish as against being English. In Israel, children displayed a strong liking for being Israeli. But children from both 'European' and 'Oriental' origins, preferred 'European' compatriots and were more likely to classify pictures of European extract as 'Israeli'.[19] Similarly, Bantu and Lebanese children when describing their own people, use phrases such as 'they are like us', or 'they dress as we do'. These 'similarity' statements indicate that children in some countries do not feel integrated, full-fledged members of their nation, even though they recognize they are included by the national label. Such ethnic, religious, and linguistic divisions in a country 'divide children's allegiances, making it difficult to identify with or form a clear concept of the superordinate national group'.[20]

VARIATIONS IN THE SALIENCE OF STATEHOOD

The individual's role as a member of the State is often latent: he or she is not called on for much of peacetime to perform 'national duties'. The life of an ordinary citizen is devoted to other roles as a member of an occupation, of his family, and the local community. The same is not true for a leader. Prime ministers or presidents will be more conscious of their national identity and it will have greater influence on their actions and decisions.

There are however variations in the importance that individuals attach to nationality, which depend on situations of confrontation and personality factors.

Confrontation

For the ordinary citizen, situations of cross-national confrontation temporarily heighten feelings of national awareness and pride. Comparisons between countries that are more sharply separated (Russia and America) have a greater effect in heightening feelings of nationality, than comparisons of more closely aligned nations (America and Canada).[21] These effects can result from direct contacts with other nationals or communications from leaders through the media which draw attention to national interests and national security (statism) that may threaten rewards (wealth, prosperity) or security for the citizen. One does not have to look far for examples of leaders exhorting their compatriots to work harder, or for less money, in order to outstrip foreign competition for trade. National symbols and the virtues of nationally made products have a long history in marketing and advertising.[22]

For a variety of historical reasons, the geographical boundaries of a State may not coincide with the boundaries of ethnic and cultural identities ('multinational States'). The physical boundaries of a State's authority (statism) may exceed the cultural and ideological boundaries perceived by the people. Ethnic diversity is a common feature of many modern States which has implications for the identity and commitment of its citizens. In both the former Soviet Union and Yugoslavia it was a major problem in cementing State identities with psychological value and relevance for their 'citizens'. It continues to be a problem for some of their successor States and for many other multinational States of which there are many in the world today.

Belonging to a State does not guarantee a sense of statehood in the people. This is illustrated in the relationship between identity and conflict in multicultural States, such as Cyprus or former Czechoslovakia. Turkish and Greek Cypriots have had separate identities and loyalties for some time. Cypriot nationalism before the Turkish invasion was dominated by Greek culture which failed to integrate the Turkish minority, and failed to inculcate values for nationalism based on cultural identity, State control and security, or a national ideology. Apart from physically living on the same island, the two groups had little in common to generate a distinct Cypriot identity. Few specifically Cypriot symbols developed which would have emphasized their unity and given them a shared culture.[23] In former Czechoslovakia the boundaries of the State did not correspond with the feelings and identities of its population. With relaxation in the dominance of the neighbouring former USSR, attention turned to a comparison of identities on a more local basis and the Slovaks in particular felt the need to create a more positive identity for themselves free from the domination of the Czechs.

In sum, effective statehood cannot be an arbitrary categorization imposed by government and law. There must be a meaningful, collective, and satisfying sense of identity. Geographic location is not sufficient; it requires authentication by things which are shared, enduring, and which positively differentiate the group from others (such as culture, history, or language).

A similar situation of confused loyalties and identities exists between Catholics and Protestants in Northern Ireland. However, there is evidence that identities there (Northern Irish, Irish, British, and Ulsterman) can converge, to some extent, in particular situations, where there is some common cultural heritage. Protestants do feel 'Irish' on occasion, particularly when watching Ireland play rugby. While Protestants have a complicated social identity in Northern Ireland with overlapping or fuzzy boundaries, Catholics (the minority group) adhere more strongly to their Irish identity and were never found to feel 'British'—only more or less Irish.[24] None of the situations tested engendered an integrated, common 'Northern Irish' identity.

Equally there are examples of cultural or ethnic identity without statehood (such as the Palestinians or Estonians before the breakup of the USSR) and also where ethnic identities cross State lines which dissect the people in arbitrary ways, as in the creation of African States by colonial powers. Ethnic groups without statehood have some of the values of nationality (common identity) but not others (statism, self-determination). This is an unstable position and a potential source of terrorism and revolution.[25]

National identity is strongest when there are external threats to the State. Conversely, separate ethnic or cultural identities are more salient in times when international tension is low. Divergence between State and ethnic identification occurs in political minorities who perceive unequal treatment and relative deprivation in the distribution of benefits within the State. The existence of separate identities fosters sensitivity to detecting such unequal treatment. In recent decades, separate nationality has been a strong issue among ethnic minorities in enclaves of larger dominant nations. Separatist movements have arisen among the Bretons in France, Catalonians in Spain, Welsh and Scots in Britain, and the French Canadians (Quebecois) in Canada. Tensions between majority and minority cultures, which have strengthened ethnic awareness and identity, have been a feature of politics for longer in India, Yugoslavia, and Belgium for example. Language is frequently central to these conflicts of identity and nationality so it often seems that a State without a common language is only half a nation.[26]

The rise of separatist ethnic movements illustrates some of the conditions where national identity becomes more or less salient. Subgroups in the population become increasingly concerned about their separate and distinctive identity when collectively they perceive a danger of their culture and language being submerged, leading to some kind of cultural anomie. This realization may reflect economic and political pressures on the group. Bourhis *et al.*[27] describe tensions in Belgium. Groups perceive discrimination and unequal treatment for their people (or region), so that there is a collective feeling of relative deprivation.[28] Threats to culture and language also arise out of the widespread trend towards the creation of larger administrative units in a country, increasing dependence on larger social and economic units and greater interaction with other groups. This is manifest in more centralized control of government, media (with growing importance of nationally based, rather than regional, newspapers and radio or television programmes) and even centralized shopping chains. In a world which seems increasingly to be a global village, one's own ethnic corner feels less and less significant. This turns to political action when there is a collective realization by minority group members of injustice and erosion in their status. Even if dominant majority groups recognize inequalities of opportunity, and attempt to equalize treatment for minority citizens, they can backfire. When minority groups have perceived that this cultural assimilation was destroying their ethnic distinctiveness, they have rejected such 'patronizing' moves, preferring to find an integrity and identity of their own.[29]

There are several aspects of language which make it a highly central and emotive dimension of ethnic experience in asserting separate identities.[30] A certain speech style is often a defining characteristic of nationality or ethnic group membership, and it is a feature frequently used by others for recognizing and distinguishing identities (an American from a Canadian or a Catholic from a Protestant in Northern Ireland). Because of its fundamental role in communication and social interaction, language is treated as a basic indicator of a person's eligibility and desire to be treated as a group member. French Canadians feel closer to an English Canadian who speaks French than to a resident of Quebec who does not. In this it is not essential to have a distinct language but simply to have distinctive accents in the use of the host language. Language is a dynamic symbol of ethnic identity, in that it both reflects the cultural and historical ancestry of a group (their 'mother tongue') and can be actively used to create distinctiveness. As such, language is a better clue to an individual's loyalties and self-concept than inherited tokens of ethnic identity such as colour or physiognomy. Devices used to make language a cause and expression of distinct identity have been reviewed by Giles who concludes 'The use of an ethnic speech style is hence a reminder of a shared past, of a shared solidarity in the presence of shared destiny in the future . . . as well as a means of excluding outgroup members from within-group transactions.'[31]

Personality factors

Strong attachments to nation or State can result from personality needs. Nationalism can become an exaggerated component of identity as a means of compensating for personal insecurities or resolving personal conflicts. The authoritarian personality found in some individuals develops a style of handling self-doubt, frustration, and personal inadequacies by making rigid distinctions between in-group and out-group members, and projecting their frustration and hostility on to the out-group. They are highly critical of out-groups such as Jews and immigrants who are blamed for personal and national failings. Authoritarians are noted for their prejudice and ethnocentrism, favouring members of their own nationality and rejecting foreigners. Authoritarians are loyal and patriotic and emphasize values associated with the power and authority of the State (statism). They are attracted to extremist political parties and nationalist movements. They are also attracted by the order and discipline of military careers which offer security and an outlet for feelings of anger and frustration. They may be very successful and achieve promotion, although ultimately they are not effective leaders and decision-makers.[32]

Case-histories give examples of compensatory national identification whereby individuals compensate for personal insecurities or work out their inner conflicts and anger through espousing nationalist causes. Mack[33] describes an unpublished study by Knutson of a Croatian revolutionary: 'Identification with the idea of the Croatian "nation" and its humiliations proved a vehicle and a justification through which passivity could be converted to self-assertion and aggression, childhood death anxieties transcended, personal historical wounds healed and injustices redressed.'[34]

The case of Sirhan Sirhan who assassinated Robert Kennedy, has been documented.[35] After experiencing tragedy and suffering as a child of a Palestinian family in Jerusalem, and failure in starting work in California, his thoughts began to focus on the Middle East conflict and his personal hostility to Israel. Sirhan's hopes of returning to his homeland were dashed by the 1967 Arab–Israeli war. Although at first he had admired Robert Kennedy for trying to understand the Arab cause, his anger became directed at Kennedy when he proposed the sale of Phantom jets to Israel. Eighteen days before the assassination, Sirhan wrote that his determination to eliminate Kennedy was becoming an unshakeable obsession. The case illustrates how insecurity experienced in childhood out of political conflict, together with personal failure later in life, can become channelled into nationalistically motivated violence.[36]

While ethnic nationalist movements result from an emphasis on

cultural identity, personality factors leading to exaggerated attachments to a State are more likely to be based on statism (as in the
authoritarian personality) or institutional ideology. The intellectual
aspect of institutional ideology appears to be important in heroic
patriotism where individuals die for their country in a personal
gesture. (This should be distinguished from the thousands of soldiers
who obey orders which lead to their death.) Contrary to popular
expectation, it is not an emotional investment in statehood, but a
thought out decision which results in such heroics. Youthful intellectual commitment to an ideology, coupled with cultural identity,
were instrumental in the suicides of Jan Palach and Japanese kamikaze
(or shimpu) pilots.[37]

CHANGING NATIONAL IDENTITIES

Attempts to change national identities also testify to their latent force
and vigour. Aims to create a European identity among citizens of the
European Community have not been notably successful so far. The
most important line of cleavage in public opinion for or against
European integration is based on nationality.[38] This is a more important predictor of attitudes than national political affiliations, social
class, age, occupations, or religion. A European identity is perceived
as a potential threat to existing national identities and loyalty to the
traditions and heritage of a country. So, at least among students,
positive attitudes to Europe are related to positive, secure feelings
about one's nationality. Europe may be perceived positively if it is
conceived of as compensating for weakness in one's own country; but
still national attitudes predicate views of this wider union.[39] There is
little evidence of European unity being able to offer a compensatory
identity to replace national identities, though it might be complementary. In general, a United Europe is perceived as an artificial
entity for which there are no natural feelings or sympathy. The
failure so far to make the European Community a psychologically
attractive and satisfying identity may illustrate arguments made by the
editors in the introductory chapter concerning the continued attraction of sovereign statehood as the preferred model for organizing and
expressing the political identities of the world's diverse population.

   It has been argued that for a European identity to become meaningful
and relevant, it will have to be seen as offering greater standing in

the world than membership of people's own country, and a more expansionist attitude through which citizens see their own power and influence extended.[40]

These findings are instructive in showing some of the general requirements to achieve an effective psychological basis for an independent statehood. These are: (1) a conceptual unity for the State. This may be achieved through emphasizing external geographical boundaries (and weakening internal demarcations), but more importantly through symbols which give coherence and reality to the concept, preferably by drawing on tradition and shared cultural features (language, architecture, traditions); (2) feelings of security and warmth from membership in the State coupled with beliefs in solidarity and caring for the citizen. Here the State is a 'haven' or a 'home' meeting the needs traditionally associated with the mother figure in a family; (3) feelings of status and pride, arising from achievements and successful activities. Physical innovation, explorations and engineering construction can be the symbols for national pride (such as, the Acropolis, the conquest of Everest, the Panama canal, for example). These are satisfactions normally associated with the role of father in a family; (4) a framework of other groups (States) in which the State is positioned, and in which it stands in contradistinction to other groups (e.g. the European Community in relation to the USA and the CIS); and (5) perceived respect and approval from other States.

CONCLUSION

The psychological basis for statehood lies in group identity and the way national and ethnic identities form part of an individual's self-concept. The groups and categories that society assigns us to, or we fancy we belong to, contribute to an identity which gives individuals character and reputation, a sense of belonging and security, and distinctiveness from others.

The basis for effective (psychological) statehood lies in three features which are recognized, valued, and emphasized by the people: (1) characteristics which the people share in *common* (culture, language, history, and the symbols of the country which arise from its tradition); (2) *stable* and enduring characteristics that are authenticated by tradition and the passage of time; and (3) characteristics which provide *positive distinction* from other groups.

Identification with a State leads potentially to cohesion and conformity, so that national identity plays an integral part in welding a country together. Different forms of attachment to the State may be differentially successful in the integration they achieve. Psychologists have recognized three levels of conformity.[41] The shallowest level is *compliance* in which conformity is produced by social pressure, and maintained by rewards and punishments. This kind of conformity depends on hierarchies of authority and the power of leaders to exercise control. When authority sleeps, conformity will disappear. The second level is *identification* where people conform out of a desire to be like other people whom they admire (heroes). Conformity here depends on the attractiveness of the leader or group and the psychological needs which membership in the group can satisfy. Conformity is more inwardly (personally) motivated and also maintained by social incentives. The third level of conformity is *internalization* which involves the strongest personal commitment to group norms and standards. Here there is conformity to norms because they make sense, and are believed by the individual to be right and worthy.

Statehood which functions through statism (to use Katz's term, as described in the Introduction) can be compared with compliance, and is unlikely to be a satisfactory source of nationalism, involving only weak commitment by the citizens and little group cohesion. It depends on the power of the State to control the population. The exception depends on personality needs (as in the authoritarian personality).

Statehood based on cultural identification is more likely to lead to cohesion and integration in a country, being based on stronger individual commitments to the group as a whole, arising out of the capacity of the country to satisfy individual needs. This form of nationality rests on the atttractiveness of the country in satisfying collective needs for security, pride, and distinctive identity. Institutional ideology is potentially the deepest individual attachment to the State, in which the citizen internalizes the ideology of the country and adopts these principles as just and worthy. This depends on the ideology being assimilated into an individual's belief structure and not just parroted. The values and beliefs then become fundamental justifications for a way of life. These different forms of nationality produce different levels of cohesion, integration, and commitment to the State, but they are also likely to produce potentials for conflict with other nations in order to establish a distinctive identity.

NOTES

1. D. Katz, 'Nationalism and Strategies of International Conflict Resolution', in H. C. Kelman (ed.), *International Behavior* (New York, 1965).
2. A. Branthwaite, 'The Development of Social Identity and Self-concept', in A. Branthwaite and D. Rogers (eds.), *Children Growing Up* (Milton Keynes, 1985).
3. H. Tajfel (ed.), *Differentiation between Social Groups* (London, 1978); J. C. Turner, *Rediscovering the Social Group* (Oxford, 1987).
4. A. Branthwaite and J. E. Jones, 'Fairness and Discrimination: English versus Welsh', *European Journal of Social Psychology*, 5 (1975), 323–38.
5. K. J. Kaplan and M. Markus-Kaplan, 'Walls and Boundaries in Arab Relations with Israel', *Journal of Conflict Resolution*, 27 (1983), 457–72.
6. J. Mack, 'Nationalism and the Self', *Psychohistory Review*, 11 (1983), 47–69.
7. Ibid. 55.
8. Mack, 'Nationalism and the Self'.
9. H. Tajfel, *Human Groups and Social Categories* (Cambridge, 1981).
10. H. Tajfel, 'The Development of Children's Preferences for Their Own Country: A Cross-National Study', *International Journal of Psychology*, 5 (1970), 245–53.
11. J. Piaget, *Judgement and Reasoning in the Child* (New York, 1928).
12. E. D. Lawson, 'Development of Patriotism in Children: A Second Look', *Journal of Psychology*, 55 (1963), 279–86; E. L. Horowitz, 'Some Aspects of the Development of Patriotism in Children', *Sociometry*, 3 (1941), 329–41; E. D. Lawson, 'Flag Preference as an Indicator of Patriotism in Israeli Children', *Journal of Cross-Cultural Psychology*, 6 (1975), 490–6.
13. W. E. Lambert and O. Klineberg, *Children's Views of Foreign Peoples* (New York, 1967); G. Jahoda, 'Children's Ideas about Country and Nationality', *British Journal of Educational Psychology*, 33 (1963), 47–60.
14. R. D. Hess and J. V. Torney, *The Development of Political Attitudes in Children* (Chicago, 1976).
15. G. Jahoda, 'Development of Scottish Children's Ideas and Attitudes about Other Countries', *Journal of Social Psychology*, 58 (1962), 91–108.
16. O. Egan and J. K. Nugent, 'Adolescent Conceptions of the Homeland', *Journal of Youth and Adolescence*, 12 (1983), 185–201.
17. J. M. F. Jaspars, 'On the Development of National Attitudes in Children', *European Journal of Social Psychology*, 3 (1973), 347–69.
18. Tajfel, *Human Groups and Social Categories*.
19. H. Tajfel, 'The Devaluation by Children of Their Own National and Ethnic Group: Two Case Studies', *British Journal of Social and Clinical Psychology*, 11 (1972), 235–43.

20. Tajfel, *Human Groups and Social Categories*.
21. A. H. Buss and N. W. Portnoy, 'Pain Tolerance and Group Identification', *Journal of Personality and Social Psychology*, 6 (1967), 106–8; Turner, *Rediscovering the Social Group*.
22. R. Opie, *Rule Britannia: Trading on the British Image* (Harmondsworth, 1985).
23. L. W. Doob, 'Cypriot Patriotism and Nationalism', *Journal of Conflict Resolution*, 30 (1986), 383–96.
24. N. Waddell and E. Cairns, 'Situational Perspectives on Social Identity in Northern Ireland', *British Journal of Social Psychology*, 25 (1986), 25–31.
25. L. E. Dutter, 'Ethno-Political Activity and the Psychology of Terrorism', *Terrorism*, 10 (1987), 145–63.
26. H. Giles and P. Johnson, 'The Role of Language in Ethnic Group Relations', in J. C. Turner and H. Giles (eds.), *Intergroup Behavior* (Oxford, 1981).
27. R. Y. Bourhis, H. Giles, J. P. Leyens, and H. Tajfel, 'Psycholinguistic Distinctiveness', in H. Giles and R. N. St Clair (eds.), *Language and Social Psychology* (Oxford, 1979).
28. S. Guimond and L. Dubé-Simard, 'Relative Deprivation Theory and the Quebec Nationalist Movement', *Journal of Personality and Social Psychology*, 44 (1983), 526–35.
29. H. Giles, 'Linguistic Differentiation in Ethnic Groups', in H. Tajfel (ed.), *Differentiation between Social Groups* (London, 1978).
30. H. Giles and P. Johnson, 'Perceived Threat, Ethnic Commitment and Inter-Ethnic Language Behavior', in Y. Kim (ed.), *Inter-Ethnic Communication: Recent Research* (Beverly Hills, Calif., 1986).
31. Giles and Johnson, 'Perceived Threat', 205.
32. N. F. Dixon, *On the Psychology of Military Incompetence* (London, 1979).
33. Mack, 'Nationalism and the Self.'
34. Ibid. 58.
35. J. W. Clark, *American Assassins: The Darker Side of Politics* (Princeton, NJ, 1982).
36. K. Heskin, 'The Psychology of Terrorism in Ireland', in Y. Alexander and A. O'Day (eds.), *Terrorism in Ireland* (New York, 1984).
37. I. Morris, *The Nobility of Failure* (London, 1975).
38. R. Inglehart, *Continuity and Change in attitudes of the European Community Publics 1979–1984*. Research report for the Commission of the European Communities, 1984.
39. M. Hewstone, *Understanding Attitudes to the European Community* (Cambridge, 1986).
40. IMADI (Instituut voor Marketing-Diagnostiek), *An Exploratory Study into the Motivational Dynamics that could play a Role in the Europeanization of E.C. Citizens*. Report for the EC Directorate-General Information, 1984;

CRAM (Cooper Research and Marketing Ltd.), *Exploratory Study into the Motivational Dynamics of the British Relating to Europeanization*. Report for the EC Directorate-General Information, 1985.

41. E. Aronson, *The Social Animal* (San Francisco, 1988).

FURTHER READING

Tajfel, H., *Human Groups and Social Categories* (Cambridge, 1981).
Turner, J. C., and Giles, H., *Intergroup Behavior* (Oxford, 1981).

PART II
EXPERIENCE

4

Western Europe

DONALD J. PUCHALA

The Westphalian State system in Europe lasted for three hundred years, roughly from 1648 to 1948. Its signal characteristics were the absence of transcendent political authority, power politics among States, and insecurity for people, particularly those who made their homes in the Franco-German, Franco-Italian, and Austro-Prussian marches. During the Westphalian centuries Europe was the theatre for 106 interstate wars that killed by conservative estimate some 150 million people.[1] The incessant warfare also ravaged inestimable amounts of property and wasted immense quantities of resources. Altogether, Westphalian warfare and diplomacy created ten new States in Western Europe, and extinguished forty-two. The last of these was Nazi Germany in 1945. The Second World War was the last general war of the Westphalian State system. It may well have been the last intra-Western European war ever, because the Westphalian system of international relations in Western Europe has ended.

Intra-Western European international relations in the post-Second World War era are taking place in the political psychological setting of what Karl W. Deutsch identified as a 'pluralistic security community'. The signal characteristics of this new setting are (1) that the separate States maintain their sovereignty and ultimately decide their own destinies, and (2) that the different peoples do not arm against one another or contemplate fighting one another. On the contrary, they expect that their conflicts will be peacefully resolved.[2] It is true that the States and peoples of Western Europe today do not yet constitute a completed security community. The governments and peoples of Greece and Turkey, for example, deviate from security community norms in their mutual relations, factions in Northern Ireland perceive themselves to be at war with England, extremist Basques are at war with Spain and France, and separatist Corsicans also engage in intermittent violence against France. Shots were fired in the Anglo-Icelandic Cod War of 1973. Yet overall, and in remarkable contrast to the last three hundred years' international relations, Western Europe is today a region of unfortified internal frontiers and amity among peoples, social-psychologically underpinned by Franco-German-British conciliation, finally emergent after centuries of hostility.

Early European jurists invented the notion of State sovereignty,

FIG. 4.1 Western Europe

and European statesmen endorsed it at Westphalia. Yet European diplomatic history after Westphalia, exactly as before, was much more conditioned by the inequality of power than by the equality of sovereignty. Many States in the Westphalian State system were legally sovereign, but only the powerful benefited from being so, since only they could fully exercise the privileges and enjoy the immunities that sovereignty bestowed. Power meant independence. But the practical meaning of sovereignty, particularly as it applied to the smaller States, was unclear.

Relationships surrounding both power and sovereignty are different today. For one thing, the relative autonomy of States, their diplomatic effectiveness, the stability of the State system, and the distribution of rewards in it are all today far less contingent upon relative power than certainly was the case during the Westphalian system. Naturally, one must not exaggerate this point: Dutch, Belgian, Irish, and Luxembourgeois statesmen among others are quick to point out that relative power is anything but irrelevant in intra-European affairs. But its role has none the less changed, especially since the unleashing of military force against regional neighbours is virtually out of the question. So too has the significance of equal sovereignty changed. Mutual respect for State sovereignty is a foundation of the pluralistic security community itself. Sovereignty maintained and sovereignty exercised are what make the security community pluralistic. In a more practical way the relationship between sovereignty and diplomatic influence has been enhanced in postwar Western Europe by the fact that a great deal of intergovernmental business today is transacted within multilateral international organizations where the legal equality of member States is assumed and respected.

THE EMERGENCE OF POST-WAR WESTERN EUROPE

Western Europe is a politically defined region, not a geographic theatre. The Soviet–American Cold War created Western Europe, just as it created Eastern Europe, of which neither had a pre-Second World War identity or any particular historical significance as a distinct region. Even as this chapter is being written the zones of Western and Eastern Europe created by the Cold War are fading in geostrategic significance, though because of the Cold War the 'two Europes' remain distinct economic subregions.

If one counts mini-States and sovereign principalities as well as the more familiar countries, there are today twenty-six States in Western Europe. The only Western European State to perish in the Second World War was the German Third Reich—Adolf Hitler's Nazi Germany. A number of Western European States lost their sovereignty during the Second World War when they were absorbed into Germany's expanding empire or otherwise militarily occupied. Most of them—France, Norway, Denmark, The Netherlands, Belgium, Luxembourg, and Greece—rejoined the European States system at war's end. Italy capitulated to the Allies in 1943, endured occupation by both the Nazis and the Allies and rejoined the society of sovereign States as a new republic in 1946. Austria rejoined the system in 1955, the beneficiary of a temporary thaw in the Cold War. The United Kingdom preserved its sovereignty during the Second World War by successfully resisting Nazi Germany. Sweden, Switzerland, Ireland, Spain, Portugal, Turkey, Liechtenstein, Vatican City, Andorra, Monaco, and San Marino all protected their sovereignty by declaring their neutrality, though the Allies bombed San Marino by mistake. Iceland dissolved its union with the Danish Crown in 1944 to become an independent State. Finland fought Russia and Germany in succession between 1939 and 1945, and while it preserved its sovereignty it was none the less compelled to cede territory to the Soviet Union.

By far the most important new entrant into the Western European States system after the Second World War was the Federal Republic of Germany. Cold War politics transformed West Germany from an occupied territory into a sovereign State, the *wirtschaftswunder* re-established West Germany as a European power, and the end of the Cold War allowed West and East Germany to unify in 1991 into Western Europe's largest and most powerful State.

The Republic of Cyprus joined the Western European States system in August 1960 upon obtaining independence from its most recent colonial master, Great Britain. Communal conflict between Greek and Turkish Cypriots resulted in an invasion from Turkey in 1974 and the establishment on Cyprus of a semi-independent Turkish Republic of Northern Cyprus whose government controls the northern third of the island. The Republic of Malta became an independent constitutional monarchy in the British Commonwealth in 1964 and a republic in 1974. For geographic and cultural reasons we might like to include Slovenia and Croatia among the States of Western Europe, though even in 1992 their international status, like that of other Yugoslav successor entities, remained unclear. The likelihood that other new States will emerge in Western Europe in the foreseeable future is remote.

It is similarly unlikely that State borders in Western Europe will be disturbed from without. There are no outstanding border disputes among Western European States, and, save perhaps for the situation in Cyprus and Northern Ireland there are no irredentist movements. None of the major States in Western Europe entertains expansionistic or imperialistic designs. Nowadays, the threat of an aggressive 'onslaught from the East' is rather fanciful. It may never have been more than this! The Western European States system then is remarkably stable; it has been for most of the post-Second World War era; it looks to remain so.

WESTERN EUROPEAN POWER IN THE POST-WAR ERA

There is no question but that the States of Western Europe between 1945 and the present day have been prime beneficiaries of what John Lewis Gaddis has termed 'the long peace'.[3] For the better part of the last half-century Western Europeans have been generating and investing wealth and building new power. They have been stocking and using rather than bombing, burning, and sinking their machines and they have been educating and employing instead of killing their young people. One result of such productive allocations of resources has been some rather remarkable economic growth. Another result has been an equally remarkable accretion of power at the disposal of Western European States.

Practically speaking, power is *the capacity to act*. It is the ability to initiate and sustain a course of action. With regard to a State, the pursued course of action might be a military adventure, or it might be any of a myriad of other public undertakings. In all cases, having power means having the wherewithal to engage in the given pursuit, or, in other words, having the resources to allocate to the chosen task. In our day, real money is the most fungible of resources, and the amounts of it at the discretionary disposal of governments are today's best measures of States' power. Unless a government chooses to engage in international plunder, the amount of money at its disposal depends upon (1) the wealth of the society it governs and (2) its ability to accumulate that wealth via fiscal or other more crudely extractive means. Ultimately, the government's capacity to act towards any particular goal will depend upon funds available and allocative discretion allowed by political processes. But the point that needs to be underlined is that *Western European States have become increasingly powerful in the postwar era, (1) because Western European societies have become increasingly wealthy, and (2) because governments have been able to accumulate increasing proportions of the increasing societal wealth.*

Table 4.1 illustrates the relationship between wealth and power in post-war Europe.

The figures in Table 4.1 need very little interpretation. The societies of Western Europe experienced impressive economic growth in the post-war era. Most had recovered economically from the war by the early 1950s and were by that time already producing and consuming well above pre-war levels. As indicated in Column 1 most of the OECD countries nearly doubled the size of their economies in real terms between 1960 and 1985 and some more than doubled. Only the United Kingdom lagged somewhat in economic growth, but this situation turned around by the 1990s to the point where the UK was for a time the fastest growing of the Common Market group and among the fastest growing in Western Europe at large. Already among the wealthiest peoples in the world for quite some time, Western Europeans have become even wealthier in the post-war era. Because of this, governments in Western Europe have also become more powerful in the post-war era in the sense that they have had increasing amounts of resources at their disposal and their capacities to act have been accordingly enhanced.

As Table 4.1 rather strikingly indicates in Columns 2–3, Western European governments annually accumulate for their needs and spend for their purposes large proportions of their respective countries' national incomes, ranging on the revenue side from just over one-third of GDP in Portugal to well over one-half in Sweden. On the spending side, the range in 1985 was from just over one-third of GDP for Iceland to almost two-thirds for Sweden. Columns 4–5 of the table show that Western European governments have not only been accumulating and spending large proportions of national income, but that the proportions themselves have been increasing over time. The average growth of the proportion of GDP received as revenues by national governments for the period 1960–85 across the eighteen

TABLE 4.1 National wealth and State power in post-war Western Europe

Country	% Grth. GDP 1960–85 (1)	Govt. receipt as % of GDP 1985 (2)	Govt. outlay as % of GDP 1985 (3)	% Grth. of govt. receipt GDP 1960–85 (4)	% Grth. of govt. outlay GDP 1960–85 (5)	% Grth. civil srvc. 1960–85 (6)	% Grth. labour force 1960–85 (7)
GER	77.50	45.40	47.20	29.71	45.68	70.00	5.00
FRN	97.50	48.50	52.40	38.97	51.45	37.50	17.50
UK	57.50	42.70	46.50	42.33	44.58	42.50	12.50
ITY	92.50	44.10	58.40	53.13	94.02	65.00	5.00
AUS	92.50	47.70	50.70	38.66	42.02	70.00	2.50
BEL	85.00	46.50	54.50	69.09	79.87	57.50	15.00
DEN	80.00	57.00	59.50	108.79	139.92	127.50	23.75
FIN	97.50	40.50	41.50	36.36	56.02	110.00	17.50
GRC	127.50	34.60	43.20	63.98	148.28	n/a	7.50
ICE	110.00	33.40	35.60	–8.24	26.24	n/a	55.00
IRE	97.50	44.30	54.60	55.98	92.85	n/a	15.00
LUX	75.00	53.30	51.20	64.00	67.86	n/a	n/a
NTH	82.50	54.40	60.20	60.47	78.64	42.50	32.50
NOR	105.00	56.10	48.10	69.49	60.87	92.50	n/a
POR	117.50	33.30	43.90	89.20	158.24	n/a	n/a
SPN	117.50	34.50	42.10	90.61	97.65	n/a	15.00
SWD	75.00	59.40	64.50	85.05	108.06	117.50	20.00
SWT	65.00	34.40	30.90	47.64	79.65	75.00	17.50
TUR	137.50	n/a	n/a	n/a	n/a	n/a	32.50

Notes: n/a = data not available
For Ireland and Luxembourg computations concerning government receipts and outlays are based on 1984 figures; for Portugal these computations are based on 1981 figures; for Spain the base year for these computations was 1968.

Sources: OECD Economic Outlook, *Historical Statistics, 1960–1985* (OECD, Paris 1987): 10–18, 26, 30, 38, 44, 64. Organization for Economic Cooperation and Development, *OECD Economic Outlook 44* (OECD, Paris, Dec. 1988): 179–80.

countries for which data are available was 52 per cent. Columns 6–7 of Table 4.1 offer an additional index of the growth of the power of Western European States in the post-war era. The numbers of people in the employ of national governments reflect these governments' capacities to act, and, as the table shows, these numbers have expanded rapidly in the post-Second World War era, and well out of proportion to the general expansion of respective national labour forces.

THE REDIRECTION OF WESTERN EUROPEAN POWER

In historical perspective, what is most intriguing about Western European States, given the power at their governments' command, along with disparities among them, is that these States no longer prey upon one another militarily or otherwise. Traditional 'power politics' no longer characterizes intra-Western European international relations. Typically, historical periods of 'peace' in Europe were actually periods of recuperation from the exhaustion of wars. They were also periods of preparation for future wars. Power, founded and enhanced by tapping into societal wealth, was nurtured and harboured by governments. Then it was largely allocated to preparing for and finally fighting wars with neighbours. Wars would drain power and exhaustion would ultimately require peace. Treaties were signed, and the accumulation of power would begin anew so that ultimately the wars could begin again. What is historically rather remarkable is that this war–exhaustion–peace–war cycle is no longer being played out in Western Europe. The power of States is no longer being spent on preparing for intra-regional warfare; it is no longer being applied to altering the territorial *status quo*, to aggrandizing the stature or stroking the pride of political leaders, to dispersing the boredom of knightly classes and their successors, or to supporting messianic political philosophies. The States of Western Europe do today continue to engage in military preparations, but not with the vigour they displayed historically, and clearly not with the aim of fighting among themselves.

There are at least four reasons for Western Europe's break from its traditional politics of power and predation. First, in the political-strategic and economic-strategic contexts of the post-Second World War era, preying upon regional neighbours in Western Europe has become irrational. Second, the balance of power between State and society has been altered in every Western European country in such a way that societies are now able to constrain States. Third, there has been a notable depoliticization of Western European nationalisms, and the emergence of at least the beginnings of a trans- or supranational community of Europeans. Fourth, to a much greater extent than ever before the prime source of every Western European society's wealth is markets beyond its State borders in a regional nexus of commercial interdependence. To disrupt the economic interdependence of the demi-continent by retrogressing toward traditional predatory politics is unacceptable to Western Europeans.[4]

Strategic and economic rethinking after 1945

Exactly when the political-military imperatives of co-operation came to be understood in Western Europe, and conversely when the traditional patterns of intra-regional suspicion, hostility, and combativeness began to break down are unclear. Traditional thinking about old intra-regional animosities was still very much in evidence in the immediate post-war years. At that time Germany and a possible new German threat were the main focuses of attention, particularly in France, the United Kingdom, and the Low Countries, where many people continued to believe that the end of the Second World War merely signalled the temporary exhaustion of the contenders' power. A Frenchman, for example, told a poll-taker in 1955 that he fully expected another war with Germany because 'the Germans came in 1870; they came again in 1914 and again in 1940; why should I not expect them to come yet again?'[5] This respondent, like countless others at the time, believed that the new post-war era would be like the last one, and the countless post-war eras before. Such times were pauses to accommodate the regeneration of wealth and power and allow for the generation of new young people to refill depleted military ranks. One immediate response of non-Germans at the Great War's end, then, was to begin to prepare for the next intra-European war—against Germany. The Anglo-French Dunkirk Treaty of 1947 was essentially a pact against an expectedly re-emergent and *revanchist* Germany. This was also the purpose behind the Brussels Treaty of 1948 which joined France, Britain, and the Low Countries in a defensive alliance essentially against Germany. French efforts to separate the Saar from Germany were directed toward denying the

Germans an important part of their industrial heartland, and even
the European Coal and Steel Community was admittedly a French
design to constrain German war potential.[6] Traditional thinking died
very hard.

The ascendance of the superpowers on Europe's eastern and
western flanks after 1945 dramatically changed the global environment surrounding intra-European international relations, and eventually compelled Europeans to think about one another in altered
fashion.[7] Perhaps in the course of the Berlin Airlift, or after the Suez
and Hungarian crises, it began to be accepted in Western Europe
that the global balance of power was dramatically altered and that the
most likely threat to sovereignty and security came from the superpowers, who could, if they chose, impose their will by overwhelming
force. In this new geostrategic setting, intra-European political-military competition could only redound to the advantage of either the
Soviet Union or the USA and to the disadvantage of Europe as a
region. Intra-European co-operation, by contrast, could fortify Europe
against superpower incursions. Practically speaking, only the Soviet
Union threatened Western Europe militarily after 1945; perceived
threats from the USA came later, and these were primarily economic.
But the illogic of intra-European disunity was the same: a falling-
out among Europeans could only weaken their capability and resolve
to stand fast against the Russians. The INF/MLF controversies of
the mid-1960s illustrated this early, and each ensuing NATO 'crisis'
in its intra-European as well as its transatlantic aspects retaught the
same lessons about the costs of disunity. So too have there been more
positive lessons learned about the relationships between Western
European unity and Western European security in the age of the
superpowers. Fundamentally speaking, Western Europeans recognized that nothing could possibly be gained, and everything might be
lost, from preying militarily upon each other.[8]

Later, some of the same kinds of thinking about the costs of intra-
European combativeness and the rewards from regional co-operation
came to underpin the different peoples' economic outlook. For the
better part of the century prior to 1945 the international economic
strategies of a number of the major Western European countries—
France, Austria-Hungary, and Prussia/Germany, for example—called
for defending home markets against continental rivals while establishing safe markets in lesser developed areas within and beyond
Europe.[9] Industrial autarky also had considerable traditional appeal
in Western Europe, especially autarky in the industries associated

with war-making potential and food production, and this offered all
the more reason for insulating against continental neighbours who
more than occasionally became wartime enemies. Great Britain kept
her home markets open longer than most of her European neighbours, but at the same time she looked outward economically toward
the Empire and North America and limited her dealings with the
Continent.

In the new post-Second World War context European economic
nationalism as traditionally practised no longer made sense, because
the new economic challenges coming from economic giants outside
Europe were much more worrisome than the old ones coming from
regional neighbours. Western Europeans by and large welcomed
American military power in their region in the post-war era, but as
time went on they became increasingly nervous about their superpower ally's economic might. Meeting the perceived 'American challenge' however required altered Western European thinking about
their international economic behaviour, just as much as responding
to the Soviet challenge required new thinking concerning political-
strategic behaviour. Starting again to defend economically against one
another might have been feasible for some of the Western European
countries after the post-war recovery was completed, and there were
indeed pressures in this direction. But keeping their markets separate
and mutually insulated denied all of the Western European countries
the capability to compete with the continent-sized US economy, or
even to bargain effectively with the US government on commercial matters. The new global economic setting implied either that
Western European countries must amalgamate their economic might
to compete abroad or separately slip toward deepening dependency
on the USA in all leading economic sectors. The new thinking about
the efficacy of Western Europe as a 'common market' and the economic illogic of traditional alternatives probably took final hold of the
business and public policy élites only around 1985. Such thinking
was symbolized in the psychology of '1992', the drive to 'complete
the common market', and the impetus to move through economic and
monetary union to a full economic union of genuinely continental
dimensions.

Societal constraints on State power in the post-war era

If all of the Western European States have become more powerful in
recent decades as a result of having increasing resources at their

disposal, and if this enhanced power is not being used for international predatory purposes, for what then is the power being used? As noted, some of the resources available to Western European States are in fact being allocated to national defence in preparation for extra-regional military contingencies, including United Nations peacekeeping, or to participation in collective regional defence under NATO or the Western European Union. Overall, however, when measured either as a proportion of national income or a proportion of public outlays, post-Second World War military spending in Western Europe has not nearly approached historical levels and has proportionally either remained about constant or decreased over time. More revealingly, amounts of State resources allocated to defence in Western Europe are not nearly as large as the amounts allocated to other purposes. What has risen in almost every Western European country

TABLE 4.2 Social security transfers as % of GNP and total government spending in Western European OECD countries, 1960 and 1985

	Social security transfers/GDP 1960	Social security transfers/GDP 1985	Change (%)
GER	12.00	16.10	34.17
FRN	13.50	26.40	95.56
UK	6.80	14.00	105.88
ITY	9.80	19.50	98.98
AUS	12.90	20.10	55.81
BEL	11.30	22.00	94.69
DEN	7.40	16.40	121.62
FIN	5.10	10.80	111.76
GRC	5.30	14.90	181.13
ICE	7.10	5.10	−28.17
IRE	5.50	16.20	194.55
LUX	11.60	23.20	100.00
NTH	16.20	27.00	66.67
NOR	7.60	14.80	94.74
POR	2.90	11.60	300.00
SPN	2.30	16.00	595.65
SWD	8.00	18.20	127.50
SWT	5.70	13.70	140.35
TUR	1.30	n/a	n/a

TABLE 4.2 (*cont.*)

	Social security transfers/govt. budget 1960	Social security transfers/govt. budget 1985	Change (%)
GER	·34	·35	3.43
FRN	.38	·54	40.71
UK	.22	·32	44.64
ITY	·34	·44	29.94
AUS	·37	.42	12.36
BEL	.41	·47	15.13
DEN	.27	.28	6.14
FIN	.17	.26	55.29
GRC	.25	·43	71.44
ICE	.19	.15	−21.71
IRE	.22	.36	64.89
LUX	·35	·43	21.95
NTH	·47	·49	3.86
NOR	.22	.26	14.89
POR	.16	·34	111.41
SPN	.12	.46	264.96
SWD	.24	·30	22.94
SWT	.24	·54	122.21
TUR	n/a	n/a	n/a

Notes: n/a = data not available
Terminal year for UK, 1984; Iceland, 1984; Ireland, 1982; Portugal, 1981; Spain, 1984. Base year for Netherlands, 1968.
Source: OECD Economic Outlook, *Historical Statistics, 1960–1985* (OECD, Paris 1987), Table 6.3, Social Security Transfers as a Percentage of GDP, p. 63.

over the course of the last two decades is public spending on a variety of undertakings aimed at improving the well-being of people and the comfort of their lives. Table 4.2 indexes some of these trends in governmental spending by comparing social welfare allocations in 1960 and 1985.

As Table 4.2 indicates, programmes of the Welfare State all over Western Europe were allocated increasing amounts of State resources over time, so that by the mid-1980s such allocations accounted for very sizeable proportions of total public outlays. Add to these governments' annual expenditures on education and public works and it becomes apparent that State power in Western Europe after the war was increasingly directed to elevating internal, societal well-being.

One more important reason why Western Europe has abandoned intra-regional warfare, a traditional 'sport of kings', is that Western Europeans have abandoned kings. More precisely, Western European polities have progressively shed autocratic politics and nearly universally introduced publicly responsible democratic regimes. What democracy has done is to permit civil society to intrude upon and constrain the State. Few democratic States can for very long accumulate the resources of society, transform them into power, and use that power in ways that are oblivious or detrimental to the well-being of the society. Autocratic States can do this; traditional European autocracies did it; existing autocratic States do it today. Democratic States, on the other hand, are constrained to allocate public resources to popular undertakings, and the Western European Welfare States are thus constrained at present. Naturally, democratic States arm, and they also fight, but most often only when electorates feel threatened. Both because of American security guarantees and as a result of periodic reconsiderations of Soviet motives, Cold War-era Western Europeans did not feel sufficiently threatened to demand better-armed States. Instead they demanded more materially secure lives, and their governments complied.

The Depoliticization of Western European nationalism

There has been a good deal of research in the field of Integration Studies directed toward determining whether a 'European' nationality is emerging to bind together and supersede Europe's traditional communal identities.[10] While there is not much to suggest that cross-cultural assimilation is occurring or that national identification is diminishing among Western Europeans in the Common Market countries or otherwise, considerable evidence shows that international *alienation* is lessening significantly. Communal passions and hostilities fired during the rather terrible last century of integral European nationalism are subsiding everywhere, except perhaps in the very few subnational regions where ethnic minorities are still violently pursuing self-determination. Generally speaking, mutual trust and confidence among many of Western Europe's peoples have risen notably over time. This has particularly (and rather remarkably) been the case with regard to Frenchmen and West Germans.[11] Amity among peoples, measured in quantities and qualities of 'good feeling' expressed in public opinion polls, has also risen significantly over time.[12] Many negative stereotypes have been displaced by more positive images of neighbours, and, most significantly, there is evidence that sentiments associated with 'security community' are prevalent in Western Europe today. The great majority of Western Europeans no longer expect that they will ever again war among themselves: the notion has become alien to their thinking. As long ago as 1968, for example, 74 per cent of Frenchmen polled by the French survey organization SOFRES agreed that 'Wars between Germans and Frenchmen are now finished: it is time to forget the past.' Fifty-three per cent of Frenchmen polled at that time also agreed that 'the Germans are now sincere Europeans in whom one can have confidence.'[13] Polls taken in West Germany about the same time suggest in less specific ways that these French sentiments were reciprocated.[14]

In recent years, and more particularly perhaps with the peoples of the European Communities than with all of Western Europe, there has emerged the beginning of a *European world view* that takes the form of a commonality of perceptions and expectations about Western Europe and the outside world. It includes a set of assumptions about the inefficacy of isolated national action and the consequent imperative for collective action over a range of issues like combating terrorism, aiding the Third World, securing energy supplies, and conducting research and development. This emergent common world view also prefers that Europe be geopolitically separated from the USA, that Europe expand its development assistance activities in the Third World and among the peoples of the former Soviet Union, and that Europe play a civilian rather than a military role in world affairs. Naturally, not all Western Europeans think alike about world affairs, but there is nevertheless a surprising degree of transnational similarity in outlook.[15] Differences of nationality, then, neither embitter peoples against their neighbours in Western Europe today, nor set them as perceptually far apart as it surely did only a few decades ago.

The reasons why the political edge has been taken off European nationalism are several. The Second World War (indeed a *second* great intra-European war in less than a full generation) catalysed the emergence of the European security community by provoking almost universal abhorrence against the uselessness of mass slaughter and the senselessness of chauvinism. Meanwhile, open borders, expanded trade and all manner of enhanced international communication bred cross-cultural familiarity and reduced cultural alienation. The Western European national media also became more attentive to regional neighbours and regional affairs as the post-war era progressed and the symbolic content of the reporting became in general increasingly positive toward other Western European countries and peoples and toward the institutions and activities associated with European unity.[16]

Regional economic interdependence

As noted earlier, the basis of the power of Western European States, and thus the source of their welfare-enhancing programmes, is societal wealth. Progressively over the last three decades, increasing proportions of the annual growth of the societal wealth of Western European countries have been generated through foreign trade, and also progressively over the last three decades increasing proportions of almost every Western European country's foreign trade have been accounted for by intra-regional trade. In this way, the different States of Western Europe have been contributing directly and increasingly to one another's power, and because State power has been increasingly applied to enhancing societal well-being, the different peoples have therefore been contributing directly and increasingly to one another's well-being. This is sensed and appreciated.

Table 4.3 suggests something of the current level of intra-Western European economic interdependence.

The averages inserted at the bottoms of Columns 4–5 of Table 4.3 reveal that, overall, foreign trade plays an especially important part in generating wealth in Western Europe, or, in other words, that Western European economies are externally orientated and externally dependent for annual growth. These averages also indicate that prime markets of Western European traders are regional markets. Western Europeans are one anothers' best customers.

Like the other factors already enumerated in this discussion, economic interdependence constrains international predatory behaviour and a politics of power because such behaviour would risk destroying the enhanced material well-being that results from the economic interconnectedness. The Western European market operates in the environment of, and according to rules developed within, an elaborate set of international economic institutions. *Interdependence is managed*

TABLE 4.3 Trade, GDP, and trade/GDP indices for Western European countries, 1985

	GDP 1985 $bn. (1)	Total trade 1985 $bn. (2)	WE trade 1985 $bn. (3)	Total trade/ WE trade (4)	Total trade/ GDP (5)	WE trade/ GDP (6)
AUS	66.05	38.20	26.09	0.68	0.57	0.39
BLX	82.65	109.85	84.14	0.76	1.32	1.01
DEN	57.87	35.29	25.13	0.71	0.60	0.43
FIN	54.11	26.87	15.22	0.56	0.49	0.28
FRN	510.32	208.00	127.91	0.61	0.40	0.25
GER	624.98	341.00	222.00	0.65	0.54	0.35
ICE	2.66	1.72	1.12	0.65	0.64	0.42
IRE	18.25	20.38	14.76	0.72	1.11	0.80
ITY	358.66	170.06	96.21	0.56	0.47	0.26
NTH	124.97	133.28	96.86	0.72	1.06	0.77
NOR	57.91	35.41	27.53	0.77	0.61	0.47
SPN	164.25	54.20	26.47	0.48	0.33	0.16
SWD	100.25	58.48	41.06	0.70	0.58	0.40
SWT	92.69	58.14	40.54	0.69	0.62	0.43
UK	449.73	209.00	127.74	0.61	0.46	0.28
CYP	n/a	1.72	0.95	0.55	n/a	n/a
GRC	32.78	14.69	8.15	0.55	0.44	0.24
MAL	—	1.15	0.89	0.77	n/a	n/a
POR	20.69	13.35	8.00	0.59	0.64	0.38
TUR	52.70	18.82	7.98	0.42	0.35	0.15
Average				0.64	0.62	0.42

Notes: n/a = data not available

Sources: OECD Economic Outlook, *Historical Statistics, 1960–1985* (OECD, Paris 1987), Table B, Main Aggregates of the National Accounts in US Dollars: 1985, 14–17; International Monetary Fund, *Direction of Trade Statistics Yearbook, 1986*, country tables.

in Western Europe, as it must be if the frictions it invariably generates are not to cumulate and overwhelm the benefits that it also generates. The effective management of interdependence—the monitoring, the anticipating, the trouble-shooting, the crisis-resolving, and the consensus-building and compromise-making in the interest of keeping markets productively functioning—requires high levels of inter-governmental co-operation on a continuing basis. Such co-operation precludes predatory behaviour and proscribes power politics.

STATE SOVEREIGNTY AND THE INSTITUTIONALIZATION OF WESTERN EUROPEAN INTERDEPENDENCE

The twenty-six States of Western Europe remain legally sovereign and are therefore diplomatic equals in international councils established by interstate treaties. What is most important to understand regarding sovereignty today is that *the overwhelming proportion of intra-Western European diplomatic business is conducted within international organizations established by such interstate treaties and founded on the principle of the equal sovereignty of member States*. The management of intra-European economic interdependence requires the continuous operations of more than a dozen international organizations, including the several organizations that comprise the European Communities (EC), the European Free Trade Association, the Organization for Economic Co-operation and Development, the several organizations concerned with collective defence, and the many newer organizations attending to matters like environmental deterioration and technological development.

Table 4.4 illustrates the expansion of the intra-Western European international organization network in the post-war era.

While impressive, especially among Nordic and EC countries, the expansion of international organizational activities indicated in Table 4.4 actually understates the institutionalization of Western European diplomacy in the post-war era. In addition to their intense and continuous interactions within regional organizations, Western European governments also continuously deal with one another in the context of larger multilateral organizations like the United Nations and its many agencies, the Economic Commission for Europe, the GATT, the World Bank, and the International Monetary Fund.

The combination of legal sovereignty and organizational context has fundamentally altered the tenor of intra-European international relations. It would be politically naïve to assume that equal influence accrues to different States within the regional organizations as a result of all of them being legally sovereign. The prerogatives of

TABLE 4.4 Memberships in Western European regional inter-governmental organizations, selected countries, 1950 and 1988

State	1950	1988
France	8	26
W. Germany	7	29
Belgium	11	22
Luxembourg	10	16
Netherlands	11	26
Italy	7	18
United Kingdom	9	18
Denmark	8	45
Sweden	7	49
Norway	8	45
Iceland	4	33
Finland	4[a]	44
Switzerland	7	20

[a] 1964

Sources: A. H. Robertson, *European Institutions: Co-operation, Integration, Unification* (New York, Frederick A. Praeger 1958); Union of International Association, *Yearbook of International Organizations, 1965* (Brussels, IIA 1966); Union of International Association, *Yearbook of International Organizations, 1988/89* (Munich, K. G. Saur 1989), ii, Table 4.

power naturally infringe upon the privileges of sovereignty when it comes to bargaining about organizational policies. What is significant about intra-Western European international organizational politics, however, is that 'power plays' by the large States at the expense of the small have been few and far between, partly because organizational politics are coalitional and seldom align the large States against the small, and partly because even the small States ultimately have the sovereign prerogative to say 'no'. When the people of Denmark in a 1992 referendum said 'no' by a slim majority to the Maastricht Treaty on further European integration it was noticed. Organizational politics in Western Europe take the form of quests for the common positions that underpin and activate collective behaviour. For all of the reasons elaborated earlier in this chapter, Western European governments agree that they need to co-operate. That all States operating within Western European regional organizations ultimately have the sovereign prerogative to say 'no', means that every member State in every organization can disrupt the quest for common positions and therefore sidetrack processes of international co-operation. In this sense, in internationally institutionalized diplomacy, sovereignty translates into influence in a much more meaningful way than was ever the case in traditional European power politics, and vestiges of Europe's power-political past further fade.

Notably, the sovereign equality of member States, and its implications, also hold true within the European Communities, where members have agreed to constrain their autonomy in order to facilitate collective action. But, myths, wishes, and Commission propaganda notwithstanding, the EC member States have relinquished no sovereignty. After what appeared to some analysts as an early dash 'beyond the nation-state' in the early 1960s, the European Communities have settled into an intergovernmental mode of decision-making centred in the Council of Ministers. Though the Single European Act calls for the expanded use of majority voting and the Maastricht agreements of December 1991 and January 1992 further this tendency, these developments hardly represent a leap into supranationalism. More frequent majority voting in the EC Council will alter the balance of political prerogative by possibly shifting policy initiative to the most dynamic community-builders among member governments. Majority voting will also reinforce political pressures for agreement on collective policies. But it will not necessarily hasten or broaden compliance. Many other international organizations, including the General Assembly of the United Nations, also operate on the basis of majority voting, but compliance in the end with organizational dictates remains in the realm of national choice. Neither the Single European Act nor 'Maastricht' has altered any member State's prerogative to ultimately say 'no', not even after 1992.

EUROPE DES ÉTATS

More than three decades ago, in May 1960, President Charles de Gaulle said that with regard to Western European unity, 'the path to be followed must be that of organized co-operation between States.'[17] 'States are the only entities that have the right to make decrees and the authority to act,' de Gaulle said. 'To imagine that we can create effective means of action, supported by the peoples above and beyond the States, is nothing but an illusion.'[18]

In October 1961, the French president's thinking about European unity was written into a draft treaty to establish a 'Union of States'. The first article of the French document called for a regional union based on 'respect for the personality of the peoples and member States, and . . . the equality of their rights and obligations'. Succeeding articles called for the 'adoption of a common foreign policy' where 'member States have common interests', the protection of 'the security of member States against any aggression by means of a common defence policy', and co-operation in science, culture, human rights, and the furtherance of democracy. In economic affairs, the French plan preserved the Common Market and sought to fill 'gaps of the Rome Treaty', particularly in areas concerning credit policy, taxation, long-term planning, and monetary policy.[19] Policy-making pre-eminence in the union was assigned to a Council of Heads of States, which might, according to a West German amendment, have eventually moved to a system of majority voting.

President de Gaulle's plan for Europe was poorly received by the European federalists. It died with the collapse of the Fouchet Plan negotiations in the spring of 1963. In retrospect, however, and with all of the federalist rhetoric swept aside, it appears that what Western European governments and peoples have actually been constructing for the last thirty years is a 'Europe of the States'. Even now, they are at the point of 'filling gaps of the Rome Treaty'. Closer economic integration will be realized. Common foreign policy in areas where there are genuine European interests is emerging, along with the mechanisms for making it. The recent revival of the Western European Union, and talk about a 'security identity' and nuclear collaboration, all point toward at least a common conception of defence, if not yet a common policy for defence.

But, as de Gaulle preferred, Western European unity has been achieved, and is being strengthened, in a framework of co-operation among States which does not require supranational amalgamation. In this sense, Margaret Thatcher's 1988 speech at the College of Europe at Bruges captured an enduring Western European reality. 'Willing and active co-operation between independent sovereign States is the best way to build a successful European Community,' Thatcher said. 'To try to suppress nationhood and concentrate power at the centre of a European conglomerate would be highly damaging and would jeopardize the objectives we seek to achieve.'[20]

What Western Europeans originally wanted from European co-operation were peace and prosperity. They have got both, and they have achieved this without homogenizing their cultural diversity or abandoning their separate sovereignties. Given its practical success to date, it is likely that *L'Europe des États* will continue to model the Western European regional system for some time to come.

NOTES

1. P. A. Sorokin, *Social and Cultural Dynamics*, iii (New York, 1962): 547–75. The casualty estimates are mine. Sorokin estimates about 34 million military casualties in European wars between 1650 and 1918. The standard estimate for military and civilian casualties in Europe in the Second World War is about 40 million. To include civilian casualties in historic European wars, including the Thirty Years War, I estimated about 75 million. Reading the history of many of the wars in question leads me to believe that this is a rather low estimate.

2. K. W. Deutsch, *Political Community and the North Atlantic Area: International Organisation in the Light of Historical Experience* (Princeton, NJ, 1957): 5; see also R. W. Van Wagenen, *Research in the International Organisation Field: Some Notes on a Possible Focus* (Princeton, NJ, 1952).

3. J. L. Gaddis, *The Long Peace: Inquiries into the History of the Cold War* (New York, 1987), 215–46.

4. For a fundamental discussion of the issues involving economic openness and international harmony, see K. Polanyi, *The Great Transformation: The Political and Economic Origins of Our Time* (Boston, 1957), Pt. 2.

5. United States Information Agency, *International Survey XX-3* (Washington, 1955). The open-ended responses to questions asked on the USIA 'XX-Series' of international surveys (conducted in Western Europe between 1952 and 1963) have never been thoroughly analysed, and the data may now be lost forever. I came upon the particular response cited here when I was a graduate student at university in 1963 charged with organizing the international survey data that had been deposited at the Yale Political Science Research Library by the USIA. At that time, this quotation about the 'Germans coming' seemed a particularly poignant indicator of the absence of a security community in Western Europe.

6. D. Lerner and R. Aron (eds.), *France Defeats EDC* (New York, 1957), 3.

7. H. Holborn, *The Political Collapse of Europe* (New York, 1957), 182–94; J. Freymond, *Western Europe Since the War*, 3–28.

8. A. W. DePorte, *Europe Between the Superpowers: The Enduring Balance* (New Haven, Conn., 1986), 188–243.

9. S. B. Clough and C. W. Cole, *Economic History of Europe* (Boston, 1952), 610–21.

10. K. W. Deutsch, *France, Germany and the Western Alliance: A Study of Élite Attitudes on European Integration and World Politics* (New York, 1967), 213–83; R. W. Cobb and C. Elder, *International Community: A Regional and Global Study* (New York, 1970), 28–40; R. Inglehart, 'Trends and Non-Trends in the Western Alliance: A Review', *Journal of Conflict Resolution*, 12 (1968), 120–8; P. Cornelis, *Europeans About Europe* (Amsterdam, 1970); J. J. Rabier, *Les Européens et L'Unification de L'Europe* (Brussels, 1972). Continuing documentation concerning the assimilation of European attitudes is to be found in the results of the European Commission's periodic *Euro-Barometer* surveys.

11. Deutsch, *France, Germany and the Western Alliance*, 245–51; R. L. Merritt and D. J. Puchala, *Western European Attitudes on Arms Control, Defense and European Unity, 1952–1963* (New Haven, Conn., 1966), 39–44; R. Inglehart and J. Rabier, 'Trust between Nations: Primordial Ties, Societal Élites and Economic Development' (MS, 1983).

12. Deutsch, *France, Germany and the Western Alliance*, 245–51.

13. SOFRES (Société d'enquêtes par Sondage), 'L'Europe et le nationalisme' (Paris, 1968).

14. At the conclusion of a study of European nationalism in 1970 I wrote that: 'The extent of community formation in Western Europe during the two decades since the end of World War II is perhaps nowhere reflected more dramatically than in the Franco-West German relationship. . . . [In the fall of 1954] probings of . . . French responses uncovered strong latent fears of renewed German militarism, visions of another Franco-German war, and general and bitter anti-Germanism. . . . While West German attitudes toward France and Frenchmen during the 1950s were not as specifically documented as French attitudes, available poll data strongly suggest that ill feelings harboured in France were reciprocated in West Germany. Therefore, up to 1954 at least, Frenchmen and West Germans remained deeply and mutually estranged. . . . Yet by 1968 (actually probably somewhat earlier) the same kinds of indices that marked Franco-German estrangement in the 1950s were registering amity and confidence between the two peoples.' For relevant documentation see D. J. Puchala, 'International Transactions and Regional Integration', *International Organization*, 24 (1970), 744.

15. D. J. Puchala, 'Europeanism in the Nineteen Eighties', *Il Politico*, 51 (1986), 181–97.

16. F. Spalla, *La Stampa Quotidiana e L'Integrazione Europea* (Genoa, 1985), 127–35; J. Zvi Namenwirth, *Changing Editorial Concerns with Atlantic and European Politics* (New Haven, Conn., 1966), 12 ff.

17. C. Johnson, 'De Gaulle's Europe', *Journal of Common Market Studies*, i (1962), 154.
18. Ibid. 160.
19. Ibid. 162.
20. Bruges, 20 Sept. 1988, *Official Text*; also see commentary in *The Economist*, 24–30 Sept. 1988, 61.

FURTHER READING

DePorte, A. W., *Europe Between the Superpowers* (New Haven, Conn., 1986).
Deutsch, K. W., *France, Germany and the Western Alliance* (New York, 1967).
Holborn, H., *The Political Collapse of Europe* (New York, 1957).
Katzenstein, P. J. (ed.), *Between Power and Plenty* (Madison, Wis., 1978).
Taylor, A. J. P., *The Struggle for Mastery in Europe: 1848–1918* (Oxford, 1957).
Wallace, W., *The Transformation of Western Europe* (London, 1990).

5

Eastern Europe

WILLIAM V. WALLACE

In appearance, the political geography of Eastern Europe and what used to be the Soviet Union was little different after the Second World War from what it had been before. Certainly the formerly independent States of Estonia, Latvia, and Lithuania had been seized by the Soviet Union in 1940, and a new German Democratic Republic was gradually crafted out of the ruins of the Third Reich after 1945. Otherwise there was a great similarity. The Soviet border was moved westwards; but that merely served to re-emphasize its permanence. The frontiers of Poland, Czechoslovakia, and Romania in particular were adjusted; but along with Hungary, Yugoslavia, Bulgaria, and Albania they were all recognized as continuing the political entities that had first won their independence in the half-century or so culminating in the First World War.

However, the reality was somewhat different. There was an enormous disparity between the largest and the smallest States in the region, the Soviet Union and Albania. There was also a vast asymmetry between the Soviet Union and all the others put together. So while in the formal sense they enjoyed equal status, the freedom of action of the smaller States was almost bound to be restricted by the overweening power of the largest. This likely outcome was made inevitable by the expansionist nature of Soviet communism that saw in the condition of Eastern Europe a suitable opportunity for spreading its revolutionary doctrine and by the onset of what came to be termed the Cold War, a struggle with the USA that impelled the Soviet Union to think in terms of a military frontier extending into the heart of the old Germany.

So in part deliberately, in part unwillingly, the Soviet Union proceeded to exercise a hegemony over its East European neighbours. In 1948 it threw Yugoslavia out of its sphere of dominance in the perverse and mistaken belief that this was the way to reduce it to complete subservience. Albania, on the far side of Yugoslavia, managed to slip away under fire early in the dispute with China. And Romania was latterly half-insubordinate. But East German resentment was crushed in 1953; Polish dissatisfaction was contained and the Hungarian uprising obliterated in 1956; and Czechoslovak liberalism in 1968 was met with a full-scale invasion and the declaration of the so-called Brezhnev Doctrine that was nothing if not an external limitation upon the political freedom of all the East European States. There had indeed been severe restraints upon them before the Second World War, but afterwards their independence was a sham.

Yet, quite apart from resentment at Soviet hegemony, discontent at the economic and social failure of a Moscow-style communism gradually fuelled a popular wish to reassert national independence, particularly in Poland. But even the Solidarity movement in 1980–1 could not break the Soviet hold. It took change within the Soviet Union itself to give the East Europeans their chance to escape from what had become the (outer) Soviet Empire. On rising to power in 1985, Mikhail Gorbachev's concern was not, of course, to free the colonies but to save the motherland's economy and ideology from bankruptcy. But that took him along the road of reducing military expenditure, seeking an end to the Cold War, and withdrawing from a financially unrewarding and politically embarrassing involvement in Eastern Europe. Not entirely a convert to the doctrine of national self-determination and still hankering after some kind of 'common European home' to unite East and West, he nevertheless turned the Brezhnev Doctrine on its head by encouraging self-management in East European politics. By mid-1988 he had made it possible for each and every member of the Council for Mutual Economic Assistance to conclude its own agreement with the European Community, and by mid-1989 he was prophesying the demise of the Warsaw Treaty Organization. In the autumn and early winter of 1989–90 all the East European peoples overthrew their Moscow-inspired communist governments and, in so far as it lay in the power of still small peoples, reasserted their independence. The Soviet sham was at an end.

The movement Gorbachev started in Eastern Europe, or certainly encouraged, in due course outran him and proved not merely his own undoing but that of the entire Soviet Union as well. This might not have been so if he had been able to reinvigorate the economy and improve the standard of living. The reverse happened. Flawed or

FIG. 5.1 Eastern Europe

impeded reforms reduced production and disrupted distribution, and the peoples of the Soviet Union began to seek fresh means to achieve the prosperity Gorbachev had promised. And what better than the nationalist medium allowed to the East Europeans? This was certainly natural to the ethnic Estonians, Latvians, and Lithuanians whose elders could remember independence and its destruction. But although the rest of the Soviet Union had operated for most of its existence as if it were a single national State, it was soon revealed as an unwilling amalgam of more than a dozen historically or potentially independent units.

The moment of truth came in August 1991 when Gorbachev was first kidnapped by a blundering group of anti-reformers and then

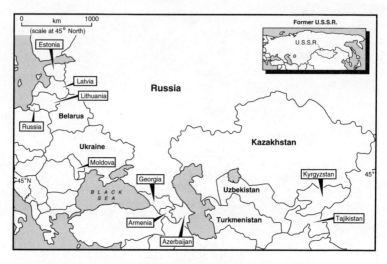

FIG. 5.2 Former USSR

rescued by a decisive and very Russian Boris Yeltsin. The Baltic
Republics almost immediately declared their independence. Ukraine,
whose long bid for nationhood had been foiled within a few years of
the Bolshevik Revolution, quickly prepared to follow suit as did the
ancient lands of the Armenians, the Azerbaijanis, and the Georgians
that had fallen prey to the nineteenth-century Russian tsars. In
December the Soviet Union was dissolved. The eleven of its formerly
fifteen constituent republics that proclaimed themselves still to be
linked in a new Commonwealth of Independent States were in fact as
separate as the four that did not. All fifteen started the new year in
1992 on a par with the host of other States they were soon to join in
membership of the United Nations.

This does not mean to say that the Commonwealth of Independent
States is without content—nor that emerging bilateral and multinational agreements have no validity. New links are also developing
between the States of the Commonwealth and those of Eastern
Europe, particularly through the Conference on Security and Co-
operation in Europe. But the prevailing trend is still towards an even
greater fragmentation into, if not nation-states, then ethnically based
States. The Russian Federation's parliament building in Moscow
somewhat awkwardly flies nineteen republican flags. And further to

the west the Czechs and Slovaks have discussed and implemented a divorce, while the Yugoslavs have disintegrated—so far—into five separate States. A great dependency region has shattered into its apparently constituent parts—and yet there are already interesting new links keeping them in touch.

THE EMERGENCE AND DISAPPEARANCE OF THE GERMAN DEMOCRATIC REPUBLIC

It was a typical historical irony that Hitler's attempt to create a single united German nation in fact led to the reestablishment of a separate Austria and the division of the contracted remainder into two distinct States. His victorious enemies were determined to ensure that such an attempt, with all its attendant horrors, should never be made again. But disagreeing on how best to achieve this purpose, as well as on many other broader issues, they ended up supporting and enabling the emergence of two Germanies.

The process was complicated, proceeding from wartime decisions based on a combination of military probabilities and diplomatic sensitivities to post-war assertions of territorial authority arising from political misunderstandings and ideological differences. In other circumstances a single, if physically reduced and psychologically reformed State might gradually have taken its place among the established nations of Europe—as was the case with Italy, which was not divided—and a substantial majority of Germans would have been pleased. The emergence of two Germanies was the work of outsiders; during and immediately after the war there was no suggestion that separate internal movements wished to replace one State with two.

It is necessary to describe the peculiar circumstances that gave birth to the German Democratic Republic (GDR) in 1949, not for reasons of morbid curiosity, but because they greatly influenced its subsequent development and had some bearing on how little of a history it ultimately had. That it increasingly assumed the characteristics of a separate State was due to the deteriorating relationship between East and West in the years of the Cold War; the building of the Berlin Wall in 1961 was a symbol as much of international as of German division. Paradoxically, the period of *détente* in the 1970s further enhanced the separateness of East Germany; the Helsinki Final Act recognized its frontiers, as well as those of the rest of Europe, as sacrosanct. It seemed as if it had outgrown the disadvantages of its birth.

Equally it has to be admitted that there were internal differences in Germany at the end of the war and that some of these attached themselves to the separating States. The fact that the GDR emerged as a 'socialist' State was not entirely due to the enforced patronage of the Soviet Union. And although outspoken protests by many of its workers in 1953 provoked the intervention of Soviet tanks, it was latterly more 'socialist' than the Soviet Union itself and entitled to feel totally distinct from the Federal Republic. Countries can speak the same language—and even be contiguous—and yet enjoy independent status. The fact remains, however, that the two Germanies had shared an important piece of united history that represented the culmination of centuries of ambition. Even before the dramatic happenings of 1989–90 there were signs of a developing *rapprochement*. Under cover of West Germany's economic interest, East Germany emerged as almost the thirteenth member of the European Community (EC). East German viewers became addicts of West German TV. And there was obviously a great East German popular longing to taste the prosperity of their West German kinsfolk. When it became clear to East Germans—as to the other peoples of Eastern Europe—that Gorbachev had lifted the embargo on change, they began to escape to the west by roundabout routes through Poland, Hungary, Austria, and Czechoslovakia and finally decided to flood over the Berlin Wall in November 1989. In the wake of these developments and the East German elections in March 1990 it was a short road to the unification of the two Germanies in October. With the joint blessing of the four powers which had presided over the Cold War division, East Germany passed out of East European history where it had sat a little uncomfortably. And Germany again became a single nation and leading power not only in Europe but also in the world at large.

OLD EAST EUROPEAN NATION STATES AND
NEW ONES

The GDR was not only the one new State to come into existence in Eastern Europe after 1945; it was unique also in not emerging as the result of a national movement using some change or other in the international situation to achieve independence. All the others came into being before or at the end of the First World War around an ethnic consciousness that subsequently gave them immense internal strength and the will to survive internationally. In the face of German and Italian aggression before and during the Second World War survival proved difficult, but after 1945 the international order was, at least in theory, increasingly based on the principle of one independence-minded nationality, one State.

In this context, independence had a limited meaning—a separate and distinct State organization, not necessarily without dependence in whole or in part upon other States. This kind of distinctiveness was reinforced at the end of the war with a series of population transfers—especially the expulsion of German minorities—and a number of frontier changes—notably the return of Poland's Ukrainian and White Russian territories to the USSR and its acquisition of former lands in what had been the east of the German Reich, the cession of Sub-Carpathian Ruthenia from Czechoslovakia to the Ukrainian Republic, and the *de facto* acceptance by Romania of the Soviet Union's wartime reconquest of Bessarabia. On the whole, this made the East European States more cohesive and therefore less likely to have their integrity impaired. Romania was left with a Magyar (Hungarian) minority of some two millions, equal to about a fifth of the population of Hungary; and under Ceauşescu it treated them abominably. But he initiated this policy for largely personal reasons, to maintain himself in power and to secure the succession for his family; and he could not entertain any idea of swallowing up Hungary. Equally, Hungary was too small and too beset with economic difficulties to contemplate action to reincorporate its compatriots and their territory.

Elsewhere in Eastern Europe small stranded minority groups were not the occasion of threats to territorial integrity. The Magyars in Czechoslovakia, for example, had grievances, and they were also the subject of complaints; but they did not seriously strain relations with Hungary. Bulgaria's treatment of its Turkish minority during Zhivkov's regime did produce calls for war from the Turkish side; but this crisis passed even before his fall in November 1989; and if it had come to fighting, neither community would have gone out of existence. But there were nationality strains of a different kind threatening the unity of one State. In 1969 Czechoslovakia became a federation of Czechs and Slovaks. Differences went back to the founding of the State in 1918, and went much deeper than, say, the feelings of some Scots and some English. But the basic cohesion of Czechoslovakia was never in doubt from the expulsion of its Germans in 1945 down to its 'velvet revolution' in 1989; and the federation that was allowed to proceed under Soviet tutelage was intended as a sop to the Slovaks who had been among the most vociferous in demanding economic and political reforms before the Soviet invasion in 1968. But the situation changed after 1989. Left to their own devices with the disappearance of Soviet-maintained communism, the Czechs and Slovaks—or some of them—could afford the luxury of disagreeing more profoundly about the policies of the reforming State and indeed about the existence of the State itself. If the election of June 1992 did not produce an overall popular majority in favour of its dissolution, it did return Czech and Slovak governments committed to a separation that came about within six months. The ethnic case may be less than convincing; but historical grievances, divergent economic interests, and personal political rivalries added all the extra weight that was required to produce distinct Czech and Slovak nation-states.

In the far more extreme case of Yugoslavia there is no doubt that the federal State is dead. The only question remaining is how many nation or nearly nation-states will emerge from the carcass. Yugoslavia was essentially a multi-ethnic State whose creation in 1918 resulted from the fusion of two opposing ideas: that propounded by the already independent Serbia and envisaging essentially a Greater Serbia; and the South Slav concept put forward by the newly liberated Croats and Slovenes who did not wish to be subservient to the Serbs but felt unable in the prevailing local and international situations to stand on their own. From 1929 the State was held together only by a royal dictatorship; and in the early years of the war there was more fighting between Serbs and Croats than between either group and the Germans or Italians. It was Tito's triumph to forge a fighting and working nation in the face of Hitler and then of Stalin. But even his charisma began to lose its effectiveness as the external threat declined in the 1960s and 1970s, and as the constituent nationalities rediscovered their rivalries in the midst of an experiment in economic devolution designed to raise living standards. Following Tito's death in 1980 a generally but unevenly deteriorating economic situation, coupled with the dramatic demographic growth of the non-Slav Albanian minority and the opportunity that provided for a reassertion of Greater Serbian aspirations, set nearly all the nationalities at one another's political throats, and raised the possibility of one or more groups seceding from Yugoslavia to form a new State or States.

What prevented such an outcome before 1990 was the fairly general fear that it might be worse than the existing situation, however bad. But exogenous developments intervened. Following the East European revolution in the winter of 1989–90 the Yugoslav League of Communists collapsed into ethnic factions at its spring congress; and multiparty elections held in the course of 1990 returned noncommunist governments in Slovenia, Croatia, Bosnia-Herzegovina, and Macedonia, committed to seeking independence. The demise of the CMEA was not quite enough to encourage the dissident republics to take the final step, particularly in face of European Community resistance to the unsettling effect of further drastic change and uncertainty about the possible reaction of the Soviet Union. However, with the latter's collapse in 1991 and an about-turn in the EC's position, the way was open for successive declarations of national independence. In theory, Serbia, with Montenegro, is no longer communist. But their ostensibly socialist governments are essentially Greater Serbian, trying by all possible political and military means, including the ghastly policy of so-called ethnic cleansing, to retain as much of Yugoslavia as they can as a Serbian nation-state. But by the time the various wars are over it seems certain that, whatever their frontiers and whatever their internal ethnic dispositions, there will be at least five independent entities where there was formerly one.

EASTERN EUROPE AND THE SOVIET UNION

The post-1945 relationship between Eastern Europe and the Soviet Union was one of increasing dependency. No State, of course, is totally free. But there are degrees of dependency that can vary from State to State and, with one State, from time to time. Thus although the Soviet Union had more power than all the East European States put together, it was never free of the threat presented by the USA, its responsibilities to other socialist States, and the challenges of the Third World. Yet these limitations varied with its military and economic strength relative to the outside world—perhaps its strength was greatest in the 1970s—and with changes in international behaviour—possibly most striking in the 1980s. Immense power with varying limitations was also rather an apt characterization of the specific Soviet link with Eastern Europe.

Stalin's attitude during and after the war was originally rather pragmatic. His first and obsessive task was to defeat Hitler, and he was therefore prepared in 1943, for example, to conclude a mutually advantageous alliance with President Beneš's 'bourgeois' Czechoslovak government-in-exile in London. But by 1944 his attitude was harder; his troops were fighting their way successfully towards Berlin and he was less inclined to be accommodating towards a far more right-wing Polish government-in-exile. In any case, he wanted to recover the lands occupied by Poland in 1921–2. He also had scores to settle with Romania (which switched from the Axis to the Allied side only at the very last moment), Bulgaria (which spent the war theoretically neutral but for all practical purposes on Germany's side), and Hungary (which withdrew from the Nazi invasion of the Soviet Union only as it began to go wrong); and he made sure that he bolstered the Communist Party in all three as he liberated them in 1944–5. But he was quite prepared to allow a loyal communist like Tito to free Yugoslavia on his own.

When it came to considering the future of Eastern Europe, Stalin retained some of his pragmatism. At Yalta, for example, he indulged in some give-and-take; and he was subsequently quite receptive to Churchill's proposal for dividing their influence among the individual Balkan States on a percentage basis. His overall aim seems to have been to share some kind of informal condominium in Europe with the Western powers to prevent a resurgence of Nazism in Germany. But as it became clear that he was not welcome in the West, he began to dig himself in in the East. In 1947 he rejected the Marshall Plan, as he was clearly meant to, and forced Poland and Czechoslovakia to do so as well. He also established the Cominform as his political and propaganda centre. From then on, with varying support from the local communists, he took over complete political and economic control of Eastern Europe. Whatever his original intention, there was no doubt about his ultimate achievement. By 1949 he was indulging all his paranoiac whims, staging bogus trials to dispose of anyone, communist as much as non-communist, who might be in the slightest degree hostile or simply have had Western exposure, and forcing all his new satellites to replicate exactly the objectives and methods of the Soviet model of socialism. The countries of Eastern Europe might appear to have enjoyed equal status with the Soviet Union, but they were in fact totally subservient to it.

It was as a propagandist response to the success of the Marshall Plan in Western Europe that Stalin established the CMEA in 1949.

But the reality of the Soviet–East European relationship was quite different. All the satellite States were instructed to plan their economies in the Soviet way, to develop heavy industry, and to collectivize agriculture, irrespective of their needs or resources. Some of them had been forced to pay reparations after 1945; with the outbreak of the Korean War in 1950 they were all told to produce for the North Korean and Chinese war efforts. The 'economic assistance' was all in one direction; and there was no system of multilateral agreements. The one exception in the whole system, of course, was Yugoslavia. As Stalin's mood changed in 1947 he could no longer applaud Tito's independent wartime achievement; he could certainly not tolerate Tito's free-lance diplomacy in trying to establish a Balkan federation with Bulgaria; and he would not brook opposition to collectivization or any other tenet of his personalized socialism. When he expelled Yugoslavia from the Cominform in 1948, he expected Tito to be overthrown and the country to return to the East European fold. There were many factors he failed to reckon with, including unconditional Western aid to Tito; but above all, he failed to appreciate that the Yugoslavs preferred a homespun dictator they knew to one who might be more distant but was also more powerful, more hostile, and downright brutal. Yugoslavia's continued exclusion from what came to be called the Soviet bloc was clear evidence of its dictatorial character. And the problem ever after was to find an alternative relationship that would allow the East European States not simply to exist but to have some say in their own destiny.

Relations with the socialist States of Eastern Europe were not the main preoccupation of Stalin's successors following his death in 1953. But as they dealt with priority domestic issues they frequently became all too painfully aware of the two-way connection between internal and external policies. When Khrushchev made his secret speech to the Twentieth Congress of the Soviet Communist Party in February 1956, his attack on Stalin was mainly against his dictatorial behaviour at home. But quite apart from references to various roads to socialism, his message was understood throughout Eastern Europe as an invitation to expect less dictatorship from Moscow and to tolerate less in the East European capitals. The belief that the nightmare of Stalinism might be over encouraged some communists to press for reform and many ordinary working people to expect it. There was a struggle within the Polish Communist Party and, in June 1956, street riots and deaths in Poznań. Fortunately in October the party found in

Gomułka, a victim of the purges, someone who could negotiate a settlement with Khrushchev that gave Poland freedom of manœuvre— for example, to decollectivize—in return for a promise not to do anything that would threaten the unity of what in its new guise came to be called the socialist commonwealth. Hungary was less fortunate. Its reforming communist, Nagy, was pushed out of office before popular discontent spilled over on to the streets in October 1956; and when he was swept back into power by the crowds, it was to announce the impossible—that Hungary would become a multiparty State and leave the recently formed WTO. Khrushchev might wish to get rid of Stalinism, but not of communism or of his socialist commonwealth. Nagy was a threat to the reforming establishment in the Soviet Union as well as in Eastern Europe. So he had to be disposed of—he was eventually executed in 1958—and someone more compliant put in his place. Kádár followed the Soviet tanks into Budapest, if not to reimpose Stalinism, at least initially to establish a fairly good imitation.

Czechoslovakia had been murmuring in the summer and autumn of 1956, but after the Hungarian disaster it quietened down. There was no subversive movement elsewhere; the local Stalins survived. Khrushchev then put considerable effort into trying deliberately to find a happier relationship with the East Europeans. He had to do this partly for internal reasons since his enemies to right and left were quick from opposing points of view to condemn his Hungarian action. He also had to do it to try to keep an increasingly assertive but ideologically old-fashioned China at bay. What emerged at the Communist Conference in Moscow in 1957 was a declaration supporting 'the principles of complete equality, respect for territorial integrity and State independence and sovereignty, and non-interference in one another's affairs'. This, in words at least, represented a considerable advance on the gut-reaction philosophy that had sent the tanks into Budapest. Yet it was not acceded to by the Yugoslavs since it also contained references to 'fraternal mutual aid' and 'socialist internationalism' and referred to everyone everywhere 'safeguarding from enemy encroachments the historic political and social gains effected in the Soviet Union—the first and mightiest socialist power'. A similar conference in 1960 reinforced these principles but went on to disparage national differences in the approach to communism and was thus not accepted by China. Yet Khrushchev could claim some kind of progress.

All the time, of course, he had to keep his eye on the home front, particularly the economy. Stalin had built and, after the war, had rebuilt an extensive industrial and agricultural undertaking. What was now needed was intensive development to improve productivity, and to introduce new industries, from chemicals to consumer goods. Much the same was true of Eastern Europe. The two notions came together in the years 1959–62 when Khrushchev attempted to breath fresh life into the CMEA, in part as a reaction to the establishment of the Common Market, but mainly to take advantage of the economies of scale offered by the East European connection and simultaneously to improve further the Soviet–East European relationship. But his Charter and his Basic Principles misfired. Stalin had built autarchy into CMEA membership, and the East European States were reluctant to give up their own planning mechanisms and therefore paid only lip-service to the idea of integration or even of co-operation. Indeed, Romania took up an openly hostile attitude since the suggested socialist division of labour seemed to prescribe for it an essentially sub-servient agricultural role; and from that time onward its co-operation with the CMEA was minimal.

In the 1970s Brezhnev revived and improved on Khrushchev's plans with a so-called Complex Programme in 1971, a Concerted Plan in 1974–5, and subsequently a series of Long-term Target Programmes. But little more emerged than a number of bilateral or multilateral joint ventures that frequently seemed to be predominantly to the advantage of the Soviet Union. Admittedly Eastern Europe got its energy supplies cheaply; but it put a lot of scarce investment into mining Soviet raw materials. However, the trouble was also that Brezhnev blotted his copy-book by invading Czechoslovakia in 1968. The Czechoslovaks had lost the opportunity to ease their bonds in 1956, but they slowly began to make up for that in the early 1960s. To some extent they were spurred on by the Hungarians who, under Kádár of all people, employed the relaxations of the later Khrushchev and early Brezhnev years to introduce genuine economic changes that made them comparatively prosperous. In 1968, taking advantage of the Moscow Declarations of 1957 and 1960, the Czechs and Slovaks embarked on a reform programme that was suddenly swept too far by the popular mood into demanding what the Soviet Union would not concede. It was neither independence nor greater autonomy. It was the proposed division of the Czechoslovak Communist Party into separate national parties and the tentative suggestion of a political pluralism in which communists would have to compete in free elections and could lose. Both of these ideas might destroy communism in Eastern Europe and, worse still, in the Soviet Union; and at the very least Czechoslovakia might vote itself out of the socialist commonwealth. So in went the troops, and out came the Brezhnev Doctrine:

There is no doubt that the peoples of the socialist countries and the Communist Parties have and must have freedom to determine their country's path of development. However, any decision of theirs must damage neither socialism in their own country nor the fundamental interests of the other socialist countries nor the world-wide workers' movement ... This means that every Communist Party is responsible not only to its own people but also to all the socialist countries and to the entire communist movement.

This was a distinct retreat from what might be called the Khrushchev Doctrine. It was clear enunciation of severely limited East European sovereignty. And even if the forces that invaded Czechoslovakia in 1968 theoretically represented the WTO, nobody in Eastern Europe had any doubt that the limitation on sovereignty was the whim of the Soviet Union itself. It was little wonder that grandiose new schemes for CMEA co-operation got nowhere.

In fairness to Brezhnev it must be conceded that he developed a more regular system of consultation with East European leaders than had existed before. The summer pilgrimage to his Crimean resort became standard practice; and more frequent meetings of the Political Consultative Committee of the WTO discussed important international issues. Even though he had quickly clamped down on economic reform in the Soviet Union, he allowed Kádár to introduce and develop his New Economic Mechanism; and he did not prevent Gierek in Poland borrowing too heavily in the West. Neither action, of course, really challenged the Brezhnev Doctrine. But it was different when Solidarity emerged in Poland in 1980. For one thing, the Polish party was disintegrating; for another, it looked as if a political trade union was about to take over and commit unpardonable sins such as allowing genuinely free elections and introducing market forces throughout the economy. The major advisory role of a revived Catholic Church was another worry. But on this occasion Brezhnev did not invoke his doctrine directly. Under the special relationship agreed with Gomułka he gave successive communist leaders the opportunity to produce a Polish solution—which in December 1981 General Jaruzelski did by declaring martial law. But this was not Soviet charity. In part, Brezhnev was afraid of coming into conflict with what was not just a popular revolt, but a nationalist rising; and more important, fully conscious of Soviet economic weakness and overburdened with the weight of the war in Afghanistan, he was simply in no position to intervene militarily. The Poles did not enjoy martial law; but the imposition of that particular form of restraint marked a turning-point in the Soviet–East European relationship. The infamous doctrine had become directly unenforceable.

When Gorbachev finally made it to the top in 1985, his focus was traditionally narrow—the Soviet economy. But the disaster he uncovered was even greater than he had imagined; and his reaction had to be along a much wider front. It was not just a combination of political embarrassment and humanitarianism that drove him towards reducing Soviet commitments abroad and seeking arms reduction and control. It was the burden of military expenditures on the budget and the effect of that on the standard of living of the Soviet people. Yet one consequence of arms reduction was a lessening in the importance of Eastern Europe for Soviet defence. Some troops and weapons were withdrawn. And in July 1989 Gorbachev went so far as to predict the termination of both NATO and WTO: 'It is likely that we shall come to resolve the final task, the break-up of military blocs', he told a Soviet television audience. Shortly afterwards both Czechoslovakia and Hungary negotiated the phased withdrawal of Soviet troops from their territory. Gorbachev went on to say that WTO 'will probably transform itself from a military-political alliance to a political-military one'. This was not quite the same thing. By implication the Soviet Union would continue to have the kind of political link with Eastern Europe that would enable it to spring its forces back at any time. And in any case the WTO was always thought of much more in political than in military terms, a means of aiding general co-operation rather than of organizing a joint military force—the East European armies were merely appendages of the Red Army. For all that, Gorbachev's statement represented a considerable shift in Soviet thinking, a loosening of the East European link.

He loosened it in another way. After taking over the general secretaryship of the Soviet Communist Party he was quick to follow the Khrushchev and Brezhnev lead in attempting to make something worth while out of the CMEA. In 1985 he launched a new Complex Programme for co-operation in science and technology. It was a technocratic leader's dream and in principle excellent; it would bring all the considerable inventive skills of the organization together to match and surpass the high-tech of the West. But in practice it achieved little, just one or two joint enterprises and a plethora of fresh committees. Gorbachev also set in train a serious discussion on integration, a genuine common market with free movement of investment and labour, and convertible currencies; but it could not surmount the obstacles of all members thinking first of themselves and of the East European members fearing Soviet dominance. So Gorbachev's fertile mind began to move in other directions. In June 1988 he finally accepted what his predecessors had resisted, an umbrella agreement with the European Community that would allow individual CMEA countries to make their own commercial deals with no more than a nod in the direction of their parent organization. Hungary and Poland were immediately off the mark; and the Soviet Union itself successfully concluded an initial agreement. This did not mean anything like the end of the CMEA. Countries doing at least two-thirds of their trade with one another could not immediately change markets, especially when producing so many inferior goods; and they also profited quite handsomely from some of their shared activities. But it did mean a gradual weakening in the Soviet–East European economic connection.

For many years there was a debate among Western scholars about the economic advantages and disadvantages to the Soviet Union of the East European connection. Gorbachev clearly decided that the loss was greater than the profit—yet another argument reinforcing his WTO and CMEA policy changes. This conclusion influenced a more political change of direction. He paid a series of visits to Eastern Europe and received its leaders in return, urging them to follow his lead by adapting his perestroika to their needs. One reason was obviously to reform their economies to their own advantage and to his. But just as at home he had found it increasingly necessary to pursue political changes to effect economic reforms, so he preached the same conclusion to the East Europeans.

The end-result was undoubtedly more far-reaching than Gorbachev expected. In the course of 1989 the Hungarians edged their cautious way towards a mixed economy and began to dismantle the Communist Party's monopoly. Lech Wałęsa entered into negotiations with General Jaruzelski, won the subsequent elections, and installed Solidarity as the first non-communist government in Eastern Europe since Stalin's time. Towards the end of the year, East Germany went west,

Czechoslovakia became pluralist, and Bulgaria deposed its hardline communist leaders; and in its closing days the Romanians murdered Ceauşescu and descended into a kind of democratic chaos. None of the new governments was immediately or violently anti-Soviet, and connections with Moscow were not broken. But the whole relationship was soon to be different on both sides.

From Gorbachev's point of view there was a general principle of international behaviour involved. For reasons already suggested he had adopted a less aggressive, less imperialist stand everywhere, and he had several times enunciated the right of every State to conduct its own internal affairs without interference. But there was also a more local point. The Brezhnev Doctrine had become virtually unworkable even in Brezhnev's time. How could it be enforced in a period of military reduction—not to mention international *détente*? And was Eastern Europe worth it? In addressing the Council of Europe in Strasbourg in July 1989 Gorbachev more or less buried the doctrine: 'Any interference in internal affairs, any attempt to limit the sovereignty of States—both friends and allies or anybody else—is inadmissible.' But once the new East European revolution had taken place in the second half of the year and Gorbachev had recognized the new governments one by one, the Soviet–East European relationship was hardly in need of elaboration by him or anyone else. In so far as it existed, it was entirely voluntary.

THE SOVIET UNION TOWARDS DISINTEGRATION

It was the assertion of Marx that the international proletarian revolution would overcome the destructive national divisions of mankind. When the world revolution failed to materialize in 1917 it was still the preaching of Lenin that the same happy outcome could be achieved within the new Union of Soviet Socialist Republics. And both before and after the Second World War it was the policy of Stalin to ensure by force as well as by propaganda that no nationalist thought should be allowed, never mind separatist movement. As Khrushchev relaxed slightly his predecessor's grip there were stirrings in the Ukraine and elsewhere. But Brezhnev was quick to restore central Russian control; and until some time after his death the likelihood even of one of the constituent republics exercising its theoretical right to secede seemed so remote as to be laughable. This was as true of the Baltic republics as of the others.

At the end of the First World War Estonia, Latvia, and Lithuania emerged out of the chaos of the Russian Revolution. They had not been Russian by language, religion, or heritage, only by conquest. In 1940 they disappeared again, annexed by Stalin in agreement with Hitler but also in defence against him; and in 1945 they were not permitted to reappear. But one of the many consequences of Gorbachev's attempt to open up society and get it working more effectively was a surge of grievances and aspirations from the more offended or frustrated nationalities, not least the three Baltic peoples. Their complaints were directed both at the party and at the Russians. Gorbachev gradually made important concessions, particularly the right of Union republics to economic autonomy, but this did not reduce the privileges of the Russians who comprised a fifth of the population of Lithuania and as much as two-fifths that of Estonia. Following republic elections in 1989, there were well-supported demands for actual independence.

It was difficult, at least from outside, to refute the case for independence in a world that had so many small and even mini-States of far more recent vintage. But while anxious to liberate energy and initiative in the Soviet Union, Gorbachev certainly did not wish to hive off new nations. Perestroika was not about reducing the country to its Slav core—still less its smaller Russian core. Independence granted to the three Baltic republics could scarcely be denied to the eleven other Soviet republics. The chain reaction would clearly not spread to all of the Soviet Union's approximately one hundred nationalities; but it might get to the twenty so-called autonomous republics or even to the eight autonomous regions. Under extreme pressure at the turn of 1989–90 Gorbachev agreed to prepare a secession mechanism for the Union republics. But his objective was still to make it difficult so that either it would not happen or that it would lead to a new form of intimate association with the rest of the Soviet Union.

Republican aspirations apart, it was impossible in the late 1980s not to be aware of ethnic disputes which frequently resulted in violence. But the situation was immensely complex. One of the most publicized and longest-running controversies centred on the Autonomous Region of Nagorno-Karabakh. But there the issue was not whether a particular small territory could raise its constitutional standing, still less secure its independence; nor was it particularly a matter of Caucasians against Slavs, except in so far as the ultimate decision-making authority in Moscow was Russian-dominated. The Region was one in which both Armenians and Azerbaijanis lived, distinguished from one another by language, religion, and predominant occupation. The Armenians were in the majority, but the Region was within the Union Republic of Azerbaijan which naturally enough supported the minority. However, equally naturally, the Union Republic of Armenia next door advocated the transfer of the Region to itself, an idea that hardly appealed to the generality of Azerbaijanis, poorer than the Armenians but with a far higher rate of reproduction. So in many ways the dispute was a local internal ethnic one unlikely, on the face of it, to produce a new State.

On the other hand, the likelihood was that such minor fires might in the end contribute to a major series of nationalist conflagrations. The territories comprising Armenia and Azerbaijan only came into tsarist Russian possession during the first half of the nineteenth century; and in the course of the civil war that followed the Bolshevik Revolution they were not reconquered and given their Union status until 1920. There were also many other factors stoking Armenian and Azerbaijani resentment against government from Moscow. The conspicuous and powerful presence of Russians in Yerevan and Baku and the tendency of the capital to envy the economic success of the two republics and to classify it, not always with justification, as the consequence of corruption were only two examples. Gorbachev's decision at the beginning of 1990 to send troops to Azerbaijan to prevent a massacre of Armenians was clearly forced upon him by the need to prevent inter-ethnic violence. But its effect was to turn the Azerbaijanis' minds to thoughts of independence, at least as a long-term aim. Similarly, in the case of the Union Republic of Georgia, it was the fighting within the Autonomous Region of Abkhasia that more often captured the headlines. But this violence resulted in large measure from the concern of the Abkhasis, who were actually a minority within the Region, that the rising tide of Georgian nationalism would sweep them away in the course of its campaign against what it conceived to be the ills of government from Moscow. And if anything, Georgia had a more distinguished history than Armenia and Azerbaijan.

Latterly another *cause celebre* was the effort made by the so-called Crimean Tatars, deported to Uzbekistan by Stalin in 1944, to clear their name of the charge of treason that he trumped up against them and to secure their return home. The injustice was recognized; but nobody wished to have more than a few of them back in the Crimea, while Uzbeks began to attack them not merely as an alien people in their midst but as a symbol of Moscow's rule. In short, a minor if nasty ethnic issue was swallowed up by a much greater and potentially more significant phenomenon, the emergence of strong nationalist feelings throughout Soviet Central Asia. It was not until the end of the nineteenth century that the last stretch of this area was incorporated in the tsarist empire, and it was 1924 before it was all won back by the Soviet Union. In this instance, however, the most frightening characteristic from Gorbachev's point of view was that its population, other than the Russian incomers, was almost entirely Muslim. Partly for this reason its reproduction rate was well above that of European Russia; a fifth of the Soviet total in the 1980s, it was clear that it might constitute a third by the end of the century. To sincere Muslims intermarriage remained undesirable; and more importantly, communism became anathema. Added to this was the example of the many successful Islamic-based national movements to the south, increasing the likelihood of a strong separatist movement or movements throughout Soviet Central Asia. At the turn of 1989–90 this was not a prospect that Gorbachev relished.

As developments elsewhere in the post-war period also showed, it did not need a viable economic base to make a new nation-state; a combination of adequate local feeling and a weakening of surmountable imperial power had frequently been sufficient. But all the Union republics so far mentioned did have economies that, subject to development, would ultimately be adequate for independent statehood—from the industrial skills of the Baltic republics to the agricultural prosperity of Transcaucasia and the mineral resources of Central Asia. Conversely, the two factors that most threatened the cohesion of the Soviet Union were its continuing economic failure, which caused different groups to think about alternatives, and the process of change designed to produce economic success, which positively encouraged them to do so. Neither the reforming Gorbachev nor his political enemies to the left or to the right wanted to destroy the Union; but if they wished to save it, they had to achieve a rapid turnaround in the economy to the point where a very much better standard of living would offset the lure of separatism. They also had to deal with the exogenous threat from developments in Eastern Europe.

The final collapse of the Brezhnev Doctrine and of any kind of Soviet hold over Eastern Europe meant that developments there could influence the course of events in the Soviet Union. From the spring of 1990 to the summer of 1991 Gorbachev swung between left and right and failed to rescue, let alone revive the economy. Inevitably, those who wanted change took up the cries of the East European reformers—an end to single-party rule and an end to Moscow's control. Pressure towards the first built up particularly strongly in the Russian Republic, and towards the second among the others. The failure of the August coup let both pressures succeed; and by December 1991 the Soviet Union had disintegrated. The count of fully independent successor States is currently fifteen; but it would need a very perceptive person to foretell how many it will be in the future. The Moldovan Republic may not survive intact, for instance, nor may several others. But come what may, the Marxist-Leninist-Stalinist fantasy about the inevitable triumph of class over nationality has been exploded, and the nation-state has come into its own in what was the Soviet Union as much as in Eastern Europe.

REGIONAL RELATIONSHIPS AFTER THE COLD WAR

The period 1990–1 marked the end of the Cold War that had done so much to reduce the independence of nation-states in Eastern Europe and to retard their emergence from within the Soviet Union. Gorbachev played his part in bringing it to its conclusion. He continued successfully the process of arms reduction and arms control; and in European terms a landmark was his negotiating the so-called Conventional Forces in Europe treaty that secured satisfactory cutbacks in non-nuclear weaponry. Another was his making Germany's membership of NATO conditional upon a sizeable reduction in its own military strength and that of allied forces stationed on its territory. However, he also had to accept the collapse of WTO, the accelerated withdrawal of all Soviet forces from Eastern Europe, and the demise of the CMEA. And it might be said that he signed the death-warrant for possible regional co-operation.

That the majority of the new East European governments then sought to take their countries into NATO and the EC appeared to be a further nail in its coffin. Yet Gorbachev himself had been building up a friendly relationship with NATO through his arms talks and was anxious to improve his economy through closer ties with the EC. What therefore emerged was a movement towards a kind of pan-European organization—perhaps not unlike whatever was his concept of a 'common European home'—but with extra-European participation. NATO established NACC, the North Atlantic Consultative Committee, which stopped short of accepting ex-WTO States as full NATO members but gave them considerable influence. Simultaneously the EC devised a form of association for Poland, Czechoslovakia, and Hungary, fashioned as a model for all of Eastern Europe and at least by implication for some of the ex-Soviet States. More significantly, the Conference on Security and Co-operation in Europe (CSCE), the body born of the Helsinki Final Act, began to assume a pan-European, even extra-European role in promoting and maintaining peace. This process accelerated with Gorbachev's resignation, as the Soviet Union collapsed, Yugoslavia began falling apart, and Europe as a whole had to face up to a new series of post-Cold War challenges. It began to look as if the old tie between Eastern Europe and the former Soviet Union was disappearing forever.

But this is not necessarily so. The Vishegrad Triangle, the economically motivated association of Hungary, Poland, and Czechoslovakia (or its successor States), is one fresh form of co-operation in Eastern Europe. The existence of a Commonwealth of Independent States is evidence of a perceived need to collaborate within the greater part of the former Soviet Union at least at the level of interstate trade. On a wider plane there is talk of filling the commercial void left by the abandonment of CMEA. Of course, the whole area is determined to integrate with the world economy. Yet it has a distinctiveness that will mark it out for a long time to come. It is not only the Cold War that has ended, but Soviet-style communism as well. Its deep industrial, agricultural, and environmental scars disfigure all the nation-states, old and new; and it is an interesting thought that their attempts to overcome the impoverishment, with or without outside help, may well bring them together voluntarily in a more lasting way than did their compulsory association under Stalin and Brezhnev. The nations have arrived, but the region is not dead.

FURTHER READING

Batt, J., *East Central Europe from Reform to Transition* (London, 1991).
Cviic, C., *Remaking the Balkans* (London, 1991).

Fritsch-Bournazel, R. (ed.), *Europe and German Unification* (New York, 1992).

Kozloz, V., *The Peoples of the Soviet Union* (London, 1988).

Light, M., *The Soviet Theory of International Relations* (Brighton, 1988).

Merritt, G., *Eastern Europe and the USSR* (London, 1991).

Narkiewicz, O., *Eastern Europe 1968–1984* (London, 1986).

Wallace, W., and Clarke, R., *Comecon, Trade and the West* (London, 1986).

White, S., *Gorbachev and After* (Cambridge, 1991).

6

The Middle East and North Africa

SIR ANTHONY PARSONS

The constellation of States in the contemporary Middle East and North Africa has developed over the past seventy years out of the centuries-old rivalry between Europe and the Islamic Empires which, in varying forms, stretched from the Atlantic coast to the Indian subcontinent for over a millennium. The kaleidoscope was given a violent shake by the First World War, but Arab aspirations for independence were set aside by the Great Powers who dictated the post-war settlement, the Levant world being carved up into artificial entities which reflected European interests rather than local desires. In the immediate aftermath, only one effectively independent Arab State emerged, the Mutawakkilite Imamate of the Yemen, abandoned by the defeated Turks. By the beginning of the Second World War in 1939, however, the pattern had evolved to some extent. The Kingdom of Saudi Arabia had been created in the 1920s following the overthrow of the Sharifian power in the Hejaz by the Al Saud family from the Najdi interior of the peninsula. Iraq had achieved independence in 1932 and Egypt in 1936, both, however, circumscribed by restrictive treaties with Britain. In Iran Reza Shah Pahlavi had seized power from the exhausted Qajar dynasty and was embarked on a modernizing programme analogous to that of Kemalist Turkey.

But France still controlled Syria and Lebanon, while her dominance in North Africa and Britain's along the Arabian peninsula littoral were unchanged. In a nutshell, the whole region was still in the hands of Britain and France, while American commercial interests had joined the competition for oil concessions in the Arab world—discoveries in exploitable quantities had been made in Iraq, Bahrain, Kuwait, and Saudi Arabia.

The Second World War ushered in the age of decolonization and the struggle amongst the newly independent nations to free themselves from foreign domination. At the creation of the United Nations in

1945, there were seven States from the region amongst the founding membership, namely Egypt, Iran, Iraq, Lebanon, Saudi Arabia, Syria, and Turkey. With the exceptions of Saudi Arabia and Turkey, their independence was more apparent than real, as Britain and France retained abnormal influence, with the USA looming on the horizon as a successor to the old European imperial powers.

Twenty-six years later, a further sixteen States had taken their seats in the regional roll of United Nations membership, namely Afghanistan (1946), Yemen Arab Republic (1947), Israel (1949), Jordan (1955), Libyan Arab Jamahiriya (1955), Morocco (1956), Sudan (1956), Tunisia (1956), Mauritania (1961), Algeria (1962), Kuwait (1963), Democratic Yemen (1967), Bahrain (1971), Oman (1971), Qatar (1971), and United Arab Emirates (1971). In 1990, this total was reduced by one when the two Yemens voluntarily united.[1]

This bald statement of facts conceals a history of turbulence, instability, dispute, political violence, and open warfare probably un-equalled in any other region of the world in the past forty years. The States of the Middle East and North Africa have experienced liberation struggles, internal rebellions and revolution, civil wars, interstate conflicts, aggression, militarism, the problems of the growth of State nationalism bedevilled by universalist movements such as Arab nationalism and Islamic revivalism, the intervention of external powers including the superpowers, the implantation, as the Muslim people of the region see it, of an alien colonizer (Zionism), violent social change arising out of oil wealth, and by far the largest transfer of conventional armaments to a non-industrialized area in the history of the world. On occasion Middle East crises have threatened world

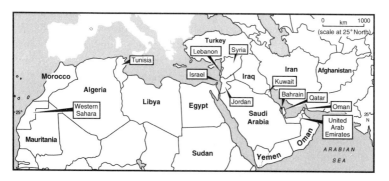

F IG. 6.1 North Africa and the Middle East

peace to a greater extent than events in any other region of East–West competition including Central Europe. Economically, the oil price rise of the 1970s, originating in the Arab–Israeli War of October 1973 and the ambitions for his country of the Shah of Iran, had an unprecedented impact on the financial and economic structures of the industrialized world. In the past thirteen years the Iranian Revolution of 1978–9 has released forces which have altered the configuration of the region, culminating in the Gulf crisis of 1990–1, one of the largest expeditionary military operations since 1945.

THE ARAB WORLD 1945–1971

In February 1947, the British government referred the question of Palestine to the newly created United Nations. For twenty-five years Britain had tried unsuccessfully to reconcile the irreconcilable parts of the 1917 Balfour Declaration, namely the creation of a Jewish National Home and the safeguarding of the rights of the Palestinian Arabs. At that date Palestine was fairly heavily populated—between 600,000 and 700,000 Arabs as well as 60,000 Jews. Obviously, significant Jewish immigration could not take place except at the expense of the Palestinians who, with the rest of the Arab world, rejected the idea of a Jewish National Home on what had been, for centuries, Arab territory. Between the wars Britain tried various expedients, none of which was acceptable to both sides: with the Hitlerian persecution of the Jews from 1933, pressure to emigrate to Palestine mounted and a serious Arab rebellion broke out between 1936 and 1939. After the massacres of European Jews during the war, pressure for the survivors of the holocaust to be allowed to go to Palestine and for the establishment of a Jewish State, supported by the USA, became irresistible and Britain faced a major campaign of Jewish political violence in Palestine. Again, no solution proposed found universal acceptability and, of all the peoples in the mandated territories created in the post 1914–18 settlement, the Palestinians alone were to be denied their independence.

In November 1947, the UN General Assembly adopted by a slender two-thirds majority the recommendation of a UN Commission that Palestine be partitioned into a Jewish State and an Arab State with Jerusalem under international trusteeship (ten years previously Britain had rejected the partition option). The Jews accepted the resolution, the Arabs rejected it. Fighting broke out immediately and, by May 1948 when the State of Israel was proclaimed, many Palestinians had been forced to flee their homes. In the subsequent war between Israel and the Arab States, the former was generally victorious and, by the time armistice agreements were concluded under UN auspices in 1949, Israel had expanded its borders beyond those allotted to the Jewish State in the partition plan. The Arabs refused to make peace or to recognize the existence of the State of Israel: only King Abdullah of Jordan was disposed to do so but he was blocked by a combination of Israeli inflexibility and Arab opposition. Meanwhile about 700,000 Palestinians had become refugees. The Arab–Israeli dispute was well under way.

The humiliation at the hands of the Jews accelerated changes in the Arab world which were already waiting in the wings. The independence of the Indian subcontinent in 1947 had a strong impact on the non-decolonized world, including the Middle East. There was an emotional tide flowing in the direction of full independence and freedom from foreign tutelage, however benevolent its ostensible purpose. By the same token Arab aspirations for unity (the League of Arab States was created in 1944–5) were burgeoning. Dissatisfaction with existing regimes, most of which owed their existence to foreign support, was widespread. There had been three military *coups d'état* in Syria by 1951. In 1947 the constitution of the pan-Arab Baath Party was proclaimed in Syria.

The gross mismanagement, corruption, and incompetence of the Egyptian regime in its conduct of the Arab–Israeli war of 1948–9 brought matters to a head. In 1952 a group of 'Free Officers', led by Lt.-Col. Gamal Abdel Nasser, overthrew the monarchy and embarked on a programme which came to proclaim positive elements (Arab unity, socialism, republicanism) as well as negative (anti-imperialism—mainly British and French, anti-Zionism, and non-alignment in foreign policy). Nasserism swept the region like a forest fire, especially amongst the urban, educated younger generation of Arabs who were especially susceptible to the propagandist outpourings emanating from the Cairo press and radio.

By 1956 deep splits had appeared in the region. Nasser was opposed to foreign military pacts and bases but, in 1955, the Baghdad Pact had been created, comprising Iraq, Turkey, Iran, Pakistan, and Britain with the USA a member in all but name. Britain saw the pact as a convenient means of modernizing her archaic treaty with Iraq and maintaining her military bases in northern and southern Iraq; America as a northern tier against Soviet penetration. Bitter hostility erupted between Baghdad and Cairo: Syria sided with Egypt, Jordan was torn, an unsuccessful attempt to persuade King Hussein to join the pact leading to violent rioting in Amman. In 1955, Nasser, having been unsuccessful in securing fresh arms supplies from the West (to resist Israeli aggression as he saw it, to enable Egypt to resume the struggle to eliminate Israel as the West perceived it), turned to the Soviet Union and a major arms contract was concluded between Egypt and Czechoslovakia. At a stroke the Soviet Union had overleapt the northern tier and both superpowers had become engaged on opposing sides in the Arab–Israeli dispute.

In 1956 Britain, the USA, and the World Bank withdrew from a project to construct the Aswan High Dam on the River Nile (sub-sequently built by the Soviet Union). In retaliation Nasser nationalized the Suez Canal Company, precipitating a major international crisis. At the end of October, British, French, and Israeli forces invaded Egypt and Israel occupied the Sinai peninsula. World pressures, especially from the USA, forced their withdrawal and replacement by a United Nations peace-keeping force (UNEF I—the first major operation of its kind). British and French prestige and power in the region was shattered and Nasser was seen to have scored a mighty victory against 'imperialism'.

The decade 1956–67 saw the apogee and the decline of Nasserism. For a time it looked as though the political map of the Arab world would be redrawn. In the Maghreb, Nasser gave open support to the Algerian rebellion against French rule (the exile government was situated in Cairo together with leaders of national liberation movements from all over Sub-Saharan Africa), which culminated in Algerian independence in 1962 after a war which cost hundreds of thousands of lives and precipitated a savage domestic crisis in France itself. In 1957 Nasserist officers tried unsuccessfully to overthrow King Hussein of Jordan. In 1958 Syria merged with Egypt in the United Arab Republic, to be joined in a federation, the United Arab States, by the Imamate of the Yemen. As a countermeasure Jordan and Iraq joined forces in the United Arab Kingdom. The dream of at least partial Arab unity seemed to be getting closer. In July 1958, the Western-supported construct in the Eastern Arab world collapsed. In a bloody *coup d'état*, Brigadier Abdel Karim Qasim and a group of 'Free Officers' overthrew the Iraqi monarchy, killed the king (Faisal

II, great-grandson of Sharif Hussein of Arab revolt fame), and proclaimed a republic. Iraq left the Baghdad Pact and, for a short time, it looked as though Iraq too might join the UAR. But, after an internal power struggle, the Nasserists among the conspirators were driven off and the historical Baghdad–Damascus–Cairo rivalry resumed. Throughout the Arab world, traditional and patriarchal regimes, especially those in 'imperialistic' relations with Britain, shook in the wind. The vision of a loosely federated, or confederated, Arab entity stretching from 'the Atlantic to the Gulf' ceased to appear totally chimerical, along with the full retreat of the old imperial powers of Europe and their replacement in terms of external influence by the USA (Israel's champion) and the Soviet Union (the champion of the Arabs).

The tide turned in the 1960s. Syria, the 'beating heart of Arabism' as it likes to think of itself, grew discontented at being a junior partner, the 'Northern Region' of the UAR. The last straw came with Nasser's massive programme of economic nationalization in 1961, something deeply offensive to the entrepreneurial tradition of Damascus. A military coup took Syria out of the Union. A year later the old Imam of the Yemen died and his successor was overthrown by an army colonel, Abdullah Sallal. The seizure of power was incomplete and a bitter civil war began with Saudi Arabia backing the monarchists and Egypt sending substantial forces to support the republicans. Meanwhile the British treaty of protection with Kuwait had been terminated at the request of the latter: Iraq, which had a long-standing claim to the emirate, threatened invasion. Ironically Nasser acquiesced in the despatch of British troops to safeguard Kuwaiti integrity pending the mobilization of an Arab League contingent. By that time revolutionary Egypt and revolutionary Iraq were on the worst terms: the dream of Arab unity was receding.

A crucial turning-point came in 1967. Early in that year tension had risen between Israel and Syria and armed clashes had taken place, especially in Syrian air space. The Syrians feared a major Israeli build-up and appealed to Egypt. Nasser, who had come under criticism for hiding behind UNEF I which was patrolling the demilitarized Sinai peninsula, felt obliged to respond. In May, he demanded the withdrawal of the UN force, reoccupied Sinai (although a large proportion of his army was still bogged down in the Yemen), and closed the Straits of Tiran, thus barring Israeli access to the port of Eilat. Warlike emotion rose to fever pitch throughout the Arab world and King Hussein of Jordan concluded a military pact with Egypt. On 6 June, in a brilliant pre-emptive strike, the Israeli Air Force destroyed the Egyptian Air Force on the ground and Israel invaded Sinai. Jordan opened fire from the West Bank. In six days Israeli forces had occupied the whole of Sinai (including the Gaza strip) up to the Suez Canal, had driven the Jordanians off the West Bank, and had occupied the Syrian Golan Heights. The disaster for Arab arms was total and, unlike 1948 and 1956, there was no excuse of corrupt and treacherous regimes or the collusion of Britain and France to lessen the blow. Moreover, the revolutionary regimes now needed to preserve, rather than overturn, the status quo in the oil-rich Arabian peninsula so that the flow of oil would continue uninterrupted, providing the finance necessary to rebuild shattered war machines. Overnight the campaigns led by Cairo and Damascus to subvert Arab regimes which had not adopted Nasserist or Baathist models of government and which had retained close relations with the 'imperialists', ceased. Arab solidarity replaced unity as the rallying cry and all States became free to choose their own path so long as they supported the Palestinian cause. Nasserism faded and the balance of influence shifted to the wealthy patriarchates of the Arab peninsula.

Simultaneously, and for the first time, autonomous Palestinian nationalism emerged from the wreckage. Until 1967 the Palestinians had delegated the conduct of their struggle to the Arab League which was in effect little more than an agency of the Cairo government. The Palestine Liberation Organization (PLO) had been created in 1964 but had remained under firm Arab League control. Now the disillusioned Palestinians took matters into their own hands under the PLO leadership of Yasser Arafat. Guerrilla attacks were mounted across the Jordan river and, by 1970, the Palestinians had become a 'State within a State' in Amman—as they later became, having been bloodily driven out of Jordan, in South Lebanon between 1971 and 1982. As in 1948 and 1956, the Arab–Israeli conflict had exercised crucial influence over Arab domestic politics, intra-Arab relations, and the whole process of national evolution. Even in far-off Libya the military coup of 1969 which brought Colonel Qaddafi to power had its origins in the discontent of middle-rank officers at the supine attitude of the monarchy during and after the 1967 war. Equally, Saudi Arabia and Egypt composed their differences over the Yemen and the civil war ended in 1970 without the restoration of the Imamate. Further south, the decline of Nasserism had not come soon enough to save the British plan for a federation comprising the Aden

Colony and the sultanates and shaikhdoms of the Protectorates in the hinterland. Egypt had been supporting a 'liberation struggle' since the early 1960s: in the summer of 1967 the Marxist-Leninist National Liberation Front seized power and Britain withdrew. The only communist State in the Arab world, the People's Democratic Republic of the Yemen (PDRY), had come into being. It was to last only twenty-three years.

In 1971, the last bastion of British imperialism in the Arab world fell. In 1968, the then British Labour government was in financial crisis and, notwithstanding earlier assurances given to local rulers, announced unilaterally that the protective treaties with the Southern Gulf States of Bahrain, Qatar, the seven shaikhdoms of the Trucial Coast (Abu Dhabi, Dubai, Sharjah, Ajman, Umm al Qawain, Ras el Khaimah, and Fujairah) would be terminated by the end of 1971. The incoming Conservative government confirmed this decision in 1970. Contrary to the Aden experience, and in the new atmosphere created by the 1967 war, all Arab States, except the PDRY, were ready to ease the path of the shaikhly rulers to full independence. The Shah of Iran too co-operated in an internationally endorsed settlement of the historic Iranian claim to Bahrain. In 1971, Bahrain, Qatar, the United Arab Emirates (formerly the seven Trucial States), and Oman were welcomed into the Arab League and the United Nations under their existing patriarchal regimes, a consummation which would have seemed inconceivable only five years previously.

The process of creation of the sovereign State in the Arab world, which had been evolving since the early nineteenth century, with major leaps forward in 1918 and in the post-1945 period, was complete. During this evolution, only the statelets of the Western and Eastern Protectorates in the Eastern Arab world had died (in the arms of the PDRY) and, of Arab peoples, only the Palestinians had been denied self-determination: since 1967 all the Palestinians in the world, perhaps as many as 4 million, have been living as Israeli citizens or in refugee camps, under Israeli military occupation, or in exile: this outcome cannot have been envisaged by the authors of the Balfour Declaration or the framers of the British Mandate for Palestine.

THE REGION 1972–1992

These two decades have witnessed convulsions and changes in regional political configurations which no forecaster could have anticipated.

In 1973, the consequences of the Arab–Israeli dispute gave another violent shake to the kaleidoscope, affecting not only inter-Arab relations but the whole world. On 6 October, Egyptian forces crossed the Suez Canal and Syrian forces attacked simultaneously on the Golan Heights. The Arabs gained initial advantage but the war ended as a draw advantageous to Israel. In the closing days a superpower confrontation on the battlefield was narrowly avoided and hostilities were terminated with the deployment of a UN peace-keeping force (UNEF II) separating the combatants.

For some years previously the discontent of the Middle East oil-producing States with the concessionary system and the fixing of oil prices by foreign oil companies had been rising: companies were being nationalized and prices were increasing as regional governments, in particular Libya, introduced independent oil companies to compete with the majors.

The October war boosted this process. Arab oil had been embargoed to certain Western destinations including the USA. With shortages developing, spot prices began to rise steeply. At an OPEC meeting in December, the price of crude oil was more than trebled to over $11 a barrel. The industrialized world was thrown into recession. Inflation soared and unprecedented quantities of money flooded into the producing States. A developmental spending spree ensued in Algeria, Libya, Saudi Arabia, the Gulf States, Iraq, and Iran. The Middle East became overnight one of the principal export markets in the world. The regional influence of the oil-rich States grew and fundamental social and economic changes took place. Oil wealth was used to fund the Arab confrontation States with Israel and the Palestinian cause. The poorer States such as Egypt fell deeply into the debt of the richer but more thinly populated States of the Arabian peninsula. By the end of the decade, the boom was over and, by 1981, there was a world-wide glut of oil: the price dropped. But the Middle Eastern scene had been irrevocably changed. Even demography was affected. The boom in the East had attracted hundreds of thousands, if not millions, of Arabs to the peninsula from Egypt and Jordan as well as nationals of States further east such as Pakistan, India, Bangladesh, Sri Lanka, Thailand, and the Philippines. Remittances from these 'guest workers' were a significant factor in the foreign exchange earnings of the non-oil producers. Internationally the Arab world was on the map and courted by the industrialized and non-aligned world as never before.

In the late 1970s, the solidarity which had characterized the Arab League States since the 1967 war was shattered. During the disengagement negotiations between Egypt and Israel, stage-managed by the US Secretary of State in the wake of the October war, President Asad of Syria had been growing increasingly suspicious that President Sadat of Egypt was being tempted into breaking the Arab front. In 1977 Sadat electrified the world by flying to Jerusalem and addressing the Knesset. A year later President Carter had mediated the Camp David Agreements which, in early 1979, culminated in a full-scale peace treaty between Egypt and Israel (now led for the first time by the Likud Party with Mr Menachem Begin at its head, the first break in the supremacy of the Labour Alignment since the Israeli State was created). The majority Arab view, orchestrated by Syria, was that Egypt had betrayed the Palestinian cause in order to recover the Sinai peninsula and that this 'separate peace' had fatally weakened the Arabs by eliminating Egypt from the military equation. Egypt was expelled from the Arab League the headquarters of which was transferred from Cairo to Tunis. Diplomatic relations were broken, only Oman, Morocco, and the Sudan remaining loyal to Cairo. An Arabic 'rejectionist front' was created with Syria in the lead.

In the 1980s, the region was racked by fresh spasms, some of which threatened the integrity of parts of the existing structure of States. The principal shock waves derived from the Iranian Revolution of 1978–9 and the Iran–Iraq war of 1980–8, the Soviet invasion of Afghanistan in 1979, and the Israeli invasion of Lebanon in 1982—which precipitated the final collapse of Lebanese governmental authority and the fragmentation of the country for nearly a decade into a mêlée of warring factions.

The Iranian Revolution, a cumulative mass uprising which overthrew a powerful, military-based regime in the name of traditionalist Shi'a Islam, was one of the major events of modern history, comparable to the French and Russian revolutions. For the previous thirty years, Pahlavi Iran had been a close ally of the West, a rapidly modernizing State, regarded by the USA and Britain as an important strategic, economic, and political asset in the region. The revolution overturned all these notions and the spectacle of an unarmed Muslim populace overthrowing a monarchy which was backed by a superpower, had its impact throughout the area.

To the East, Afghan traditionalists were encouraged to resist the Communist government which had seized power in 1978. By late

1979 the government was in such difficulties that the Soviet Union felt obliged to send in over 100,000 troops to maintain its protégés in power. By 1989, with 15 per cent of the Afghan population having taken refuge in Pakistan and Iran, after heavy Soviet casualties and even more massive losses among the Afghan resistance fighters and innocent civilians, Soviet troops had withdrawn, leaving Afghanistan to an uncertain future.

To the west, Iranian attempts to export the revolution to the Shi'a Muslim majority in Iraq led to acute tension between the two States. In the summer of 1980 scuffles broke out on the frontier. On 22 September Iraqi forces invaded South West Iran: President Saddam Hussein had decided to take advantage of the post-revolutionary chaos in the Iranian armed forces to 'teach Khomeini a lesson'. He had miscalculated. The war lasted eight years. For a time the very existence of the Iraqi State was threatened by the prospect of disintegration following an outright Iranian victory. By 1987 outside powers had been drawn into the conflict on the waters of the Persian Gulf where American, Soviet, British, French, Dutch, Belgian, and Italian warships were operating in protection of shipping on the Arab side. The 1988 cease-fire, brought about by the exhaustion of the combatants and the realization of the Iranian government that they were taking on half the world in arms, had yet to be translated into a peace treaty by the end of the decade.

The Iran–Iraq War had its effect on the wider Arab constellation. The traditional States of the Arabian peninsula (Saudi Arabia, Kuwait, Bahrain, Qatar, the UAE, and Oman) drew together by creating the Gulf Co-operation Council which, although far short of an Arabian NATO, gave greater cohesion to subregional security policies and enhanced Saudi leadership over the smaller States. Further afield the majority of the Arab world supported Iraq, the major exceptions being Syria and Libya, the former because of detestation of the fellow Baathist regime in Baghdad and need to secure Iranian support for Syrian policies in Lebanon, the latter because of its ties with Syria.

The repercussions of the Iranian Revolution were felt as well in the turmoil of Lebanon, intensifying the violence of the civil war which exploded in 1975. From the mid-1970s the Shi'a Muslim community, discontented with their position at the bottom of the power structure, had been mobilized by an Iranian-born religious leader. In 1982, Israel invaded Lebanon in order to destroy the power of the PLO which, on its expulsion from Jordan in 1970, had (as indicated) established a State within a State in South Lebanon; and to establish a Maronite government which would conclude a peace treaty, thus securing Israel's northern border. Israeli forces swept through the screen of a UN peace-keeping force (UNIFIL) which had been established following a previous Israeli invasion in 1978. PLO resistance was overcome and the Israelis penetrated to the outskirts of Beirut inflicting heavy civilian casualties. What remained of Lebanese governmental authority collapsed: the PLO fighters were dispersed to various Arab countries but Israeli expectations of a Maronite government were disappointed. Indeed, as the Israelis withdrew to a 'security zone' close to its southern border, Lebanon became a battleground of sectarian militias. The Druzes fought the Maronites and the Shi'a fought for control of West Beirut. A multinational force led by the USA moved in and US warships bombarded Druze positions in the mountains behind Beirut. Meanwhile Maronite militiamen had massacred Palestinian refugees in the Sabra and Chatila camps on the outskirts of the capital while the Israelis were still in occupation of the area. Through 1983, the disintegration of Lebanon continued and the Americans and French suffered heavy casualties at the hands of suicidal Shi'a truck-bombers. The multinational force withdrew in 1984 and the fighting continued with the additional hazard of terrorism in the form of the seizure of foreign hostages, a nightmare which did not end until 1991.

Throughout this period the Iranian government gave active support, including the despatch of Revolutionary Guards, to the Shi'a militias: in future the other confessional elements in Lebanon will know better than to treat the Shi'a, the largest Muslim community, as an unimportant underclass. The inspiration generated by the Iranian Revolution in Shi'a Muslim communities in Iraq (although the great majority of Iraqi Shi'as fought in the war against Iran as loyal Iraqis, perhaps to the surprise of the Iranian leadership), Lebanon, and the Gulf, coincided with the wave of Islamic revivalism which is still sweeping the Middle East. This phenomenon, with its connotations of rejection of Western materialism and cultural domination, has manifested itself in different ways in different States. It took the place of pan-Arabism as the transcendental movement of the 1980s, but it has so far posed a threat to the policies of governments rather than to the integrity of States.

Islamic revivalism has been countered in certain instances by violent repression, as when the Muslim Brotherhood attempted to overthrow the secular Syrian regime in the early 1980s, but Islamic parties have made substantial gains wherever elections have been held, Algeria and Jordan being the prime examples. Fear of Islamic government led the army to abort the Algerian elections in 1992 when the Islamic FIS gained a majority. At the time of writing the FIS was being persecuted and neighbouring Tunisia was acting similarly with regard to the Tunisian Islamic Al Nahda movement. In Egypt also, the regime's policy has become harsher in direct proportion to the spread of militant political Islam. Islamic revivalism has also been matched by a corresponding upsurge of Judaic fundamentalism in Israel, thus adding a dangerous new dimension of religious confrontation to what had hitherto been a struggle between opposing nationalisms. Indeed, the Islamic faction HAMAS is exercising increased influence over the Palestinian uprising (the *intifada*) in the Israeli Occupied Territories which has been rumbling on at varying levels of intensity since December 1987. A further consequence of the Palestine problem, the Iranian Revolution and Islamic revivalism has been the growth of international terrorism, so much so that the phrase has become conterminous in public opinion in the West with 'the Middle East'.

The events of 1990–1 have radically altered yet again the political and military conjuncture throughout the region. In August 1990 Iraq decided to resume its quest for hegemony over the oil-rich States of the Arabian peninsula, which had been interrupted by the war against Iran. Angry because of Kuwaiti refusal to cancel a large debt incurred in the war, to cede part of an oil-field plus two disputed islands, and to reduce oil exports in order to drive up prices, Saddam Hussein invaded and annexed (the first time that one UN member State had forcibly annexed another) the emirate. The Arab League, which had shortly before returned to Cairo, split but the UN Security Council, in the glow of post-Cold War co-operation, reacted quickly and decisively, imposing mandatory economic sanctions and, in November, authorizing the use of force by the large American-led Coalition (including Egyptian, Syrian, and GCC forces as well as British, French, and others) which had deployed to defend Saudi Arabia against Iraqi aggression. In January and February 1991 Coalition air attacks destroyed much of Iraq's infrastructure and Iraq's armed forces were routed in a 100-hour ground assault. Kuwait was liberated but Iraq had in the meantime directed Scud missiles at civilian targets in Israel and Saudi Arabia and had fired about 700 Kuwaiti oil-wells. As soon as the fighting was over, serious rebellions broke out in the Shi'a Muslim area of Southern Iraq and in Iraqi Kurdistan. Both were savagely suppressed by the remnants of Saddam Hussein's armed forces using helicopter gunships, the use of which the Coalition had not forbidden as it had with fixed-wing aircraft.

Iraq now lies under the most stringent cease-fire regime ever imposed by the United Nations—a peace-keeping observer group in a demilitarized zone straddling the Iraq–Kuwait border, mandatory economic sanctions excluding only essential food and medical imports, the monitoring and destruction of Iraq's weapons of mass destruction and near-nuclear capability by UN inspection, an arms embargo, reparations, and compensation as well as other constraints. In addition, the Coalition intervened militarily in northern Iraq to protect the Kurdish population from Saddam's attacks and to persuade them to abandon their mass flight, costing hundreds of thousands of lives, into Turkey and Iran. Most of Iraqi Kurdistan is now controlled by Kurdish freedom-fighters with an uneasy stand-off in place between them and the Iraqi armed forces south of the 36th parallel.

This gargantuan upheaval has had profound consequences region-wide. Days after his invasion of Kuwait, Saddam conceded all the Iranian demands, principally for a return to the 1975 Agreement dividing the Shatt-el-Arab waterway between the two countries and withdrawal of Iraqi forces from Iranian territory occupied in the last days of the fighting. The 1988 cease-fire has in effect been translated into peace. Within the Arab world, Iraq has been excluded from the diplomatic dialogue and can exercise no influence on a divided Arab League. The States which joined the Coalition—principally Egypt, Syria, and Saudi Arabia—have increased their influence correspondingly. Most important, the crisis revealed that the Soviet Union was no longer a significant power in the region and that the USA was the only superpower world-wide. The regional governments, with the expertise of two centuries of playing off external powers against each other, realized that a new phase of history had opened and that support for their causes lay with the USA alone. Syria, with American acquiescence, was thus able to bring the Lebanese civil war to an end by establishing its hegemony over the greater part of the country. Israel learnt that, with the Soviet threat removed, it was no longer a 'strategic asset' to the USA. By being perceived as having backed Saddam in the war, the PLO, whose influence had been on the decline since the dispersal following the Israeli invasion of Lebanon in 1982 and the autonomous nature of the Palestinian *intifada* since 1987, lost further credibility and most of its regional support.

This unforeseen new configuration has introduced a fresh spirit of moderation amongst leading governments especially in regard to the Arab–Israeli–Palestine problem. In November 1991, after months of strenuous negotiating, the US Administration succeeded in convening in Madrid an international conference attended by Israel, Syria, Jordan/Palestine, and Lebanon with the USA and what used to be the USSR as co-chairmen. This was an historic breakthrough in that, for the first time, Arab governments (with the exception of Egypt) were prepared to sit down with Israel in direct bilateral discussion, Israel was prepared to recognize and talk directly to a Palestinian delegation (drawn from the Occupied Territories), and the Palestinians were ready to negotiate transitional arrangements for local autonomy rather than demanding immediate Israeli withdrawal and Palestinian statehood. Hence 1991 closed with a faint hint of optimism in the air over the core problem of the region, for the first time since the Camp David negotiations of 1978. In June 1992, the defeat of the Likuud Party in the elections and the accession to power of a Labour-led coalition created further optimism. The new Prime Minister committed the government to restricting the growth of settlements in the Occupied Territories, to swift negotiation of Palestinian internal autonomy, and to the principle of an exchange of territory for peace. However, by the end of 1992 the faint upsurge of optimism had evaporated.

OTHER QUESTIONS

There have been other conflicts which had nothing to do with the interlocking causes adumbrated above, but which have relevance to the birth, existence, and death of States in the Middle East and North Africa. In the nearly sixty years of British rule in the Sudan, little had been done to integrate the mainly Christian and animist Southern provinces with the Arabized North; nor had it been practicable to lump the Southern Sudanese with their more natural associates in the emergent States of Sub-Saharan Africa. Almost from the date of independence in 1956 a civil war has intermittently been raging in the South. The probability is that the Southern rebels want genuine autonomy rather than a clean break to sovereign independence. Some years ago there was a settlement, but more intensified warfare has broken out since Islamic revivalism influenced the government in Khartoum into imposing Islamic law on the whole country. By 1989 the economy of the Sudan was in ruins, war and famine had taken probably hundreds of thousands of lives, The refugee problem was intense, and the future dark.

At the Western extremity of the region, on the withdrawal of Spain from the Spanish Sahara in 1975, Morocco and Mauritania divided the old colony between them. The indigenous inhabitants, led by the Polisario Front, declared the independence of the Sahrawi Democratic Republic and they have been engaged in guerrilla warfare with Morocco ever since. (Mauritania soon withdrew from its share of the territory which was promptly occupied by Morocco.) This dispute has split the Organization of African Unity—many of whose members have recognized the Sahrawi Republic—and has brought Morocco and Algeria close to open warfare. At the time of writing there was a fresh prospect of a settlement based on a referendum under UN auspices.

Another *sui generis* uprising of indigenous people took place in the Sultanate of Muscat and Oman. In 1965, the people of the Western province of Dhofar, who are of different ethnic origin from the inhabitants of the remainder of the Sultanate, revolted for reasons of local grievance. However, with the support of the neighbouring People's Democratic Republic of the Yemen, the insurrection took on a left-wing ideological coloration, and for some years posed a threat to the regime in Muscat. The rebellion was suppressed in 1975 by the Sultan's armed forces with British and Iranian military assistance. Since then the Yemen has desisted from subversive activity and the Sultanate has put in hand major development plans for Jebel Dhofar in order to eliminate local discontent and to weld the Dhofari people to the State.

Throughout this history of tumult, much of which has been a consequence of the collapse of the Ottoman Empire and the division of the spoils between the European victors, Republican Turkey has, so far as practicable, kept its eyes fixed firmly westwards, towards Europe. Turkey is a member of the Council of Europe, an aspirant to membership of the European Community, and has been the pillar of the eastern flank of NATO since 1951. In the region, Turkey has maintained diplomatic relations with Israel and supported the Western-inspired construct of the Baghdad Pact and its successor, the Central Treaty Organization (which died with the Iranian Revolution in 1979). Turkey has however been drawn closer to the region by the magnetic force of events on her southern border and has been touched by Islamic revivalism to an extent which would shock its founder, Kemal Ataturk. However, for all its domestic vicissitudes— democracy punctuated by military intervention since 1960—Turkey has broadly maintained the direction set by Ataturk, i.e. a secular State, more closely tied to Europe than to the Middle East. Its strategic importance to the West was emphasized by the key role it played in the Gulf crisis of 1990–1. Moreover following the involuntary decolonization of the Soviet empire Turkey began vigorously projecting its influence into the newly independent (Turkic) republics of what used to be Soviet Central Asia.

SUMMING UP AND CONCLUSIONS

The pattern of contemporary States stretching from the Atlantic to the borders of Pakistan emerged from varied origins, principally nineteenth-century European imperialism, falling just short in many cases of outright colonialism, combined with the collapse of the Ottoman Empire leading to the post-1918 settlement. With the exception of the Palestinians and the people of the Western Sahara, the formal process of decolonization/self-determination is now complete. The region comprises eighteen States members of the Arab League plus Israel, Asiatic Turkey, Iran, and Afghanistan. The Arab League has proved to be more of a diplomatic forum for the co-ordination of policies than a focus for greater unity.

Transcendental movements such as pan-Arab nationalism, the Palestine cause, and Islamic revivalism have swept through the area, some of which have threatened the integrity of the State structure. However, in the Arab world, State nationalism has thrown down deeper roots since the 1960s; the State of Israel is no longer under serious military threat—Israel has become in effect a regional military superpower; and there is little likelihood of the disintegration of Iran in spite of the disparate nature of the population of the old Empire. Afghanistan has demonstrated its resolve to remain independent by its resistance to the Soviet invaders and Turkey is a State imbued with fierce patriotism.

When one considers the disparity of power amongst the States members of the Arab League with, say, Qatar at one end of the scale and Egypt at the other, combined with the artificiality of some of the post-1918 settlement creations (Jordan in particular comes to mind), and in the light of the cultural and political pressure for greater Arab unity from the 1940s to the 1960s, the most surprising phenomenon has been the durability of the pattern of Arab States. There are many reasons for this. As suggested in the narrative, the tide of pan-Arab nationalism ebbed with extraordinary rapidity following the catastrophe to Arab arms of the June War of 1967. Solidarity behind the Palestine cause, based on the geopolitical *status quo*, replaced unity as the guiding slogan. Secondly, oil wealth (from the late 1960s onwards) provided the smaller and weaker States with a degree of independence which offset the military power of the larger States. Thirdly, a sense of divergent local interests began to develop within States widely separated by geography and facing different challenges. For example, the Iranian threat stimulated a sense of nationhood within Iraq (with the exception of the Kurdish provinces) which had been relatively shallow before the Iran–Iraq War. Even before that war, which led to the establishment of the Gulf Co-operation Council (GCC), the patriarchal regimes of the Arabian peninsula had moved towards forming an informal subgroup within the Arab League based on regional interests far removed from those of, say, Tunisia or Morocco.

With the collapse of Soviet power, there is now for the first time since Napoleon landed in Egypt in 1798 only one external power with influence over the regional States—the United States of America. The centuries-old game of playing off competing external powers against each other has ended. This is bound to affect the international relations of the region: indeed it has already done so positively in the Arab–Israeli context. Furthermore the revelation of Iraq as an unambiguous aggressor has reduced local inhibitions about invoking external military assistance even in intra-Arab quarrels. There will be no genuine tranquillity in the Eastern part of the region while Saddam Hussein and the Baath Party remain in power in Iraq, but Iraq's current weakness is a positive factor enabling the GCC States to recover from the shock of crisis and the Iranian regime to concentrate on economic recovery. Meanwhile the civil war in Afghanistan has wound down to an uneasy *modus vivendi* between the disparate Mujahadin factions.

Although prospects for the region look less dark than they did in the summer of 1990, there are no grounds for complacency. First there will be no secure peace in the region until the Arab–Israeli dispute is settled and it is too early to be more than cautiously optimistic in the extreme about the prospects for future negotiations. Secondly, although pan-Arabism is now dormant, there are hegemonic tendencies in certain areas. Baathist Iraq has for the moment been neutralized but Saddam Hussein is unregenerate. In the rival capital, Damascus, no Syrian leader has forgotten that the Ottoman definition of Syria embraced as well what is now Lebanon, Israel, and Transjordan. Thirdly, although existing regimes in the Arab world have proved remarkably enduring over the past two decades in comparison with the changing patterns of the 1950s and 1960s, the region will remain basically unstable until the majority of States devise some method of enabling their people to participate in decision-making and to change governments peacefully without resort to mass protest or violence, civilian or military.

At present only Israel and Turkey (for the moment) are democracies in the Western sense. The revolutionary regime in Iran came to power through the will of the majority of Iranians but it has become increasingly repressive. In the Arab world, there are no more than three States in which change of government could be theoretically brought about through the ballot box. For the rest, traditional monarchies, dynastic patriarchates, police States, and military dictatorships make up the total. This means that sudden change is always possible at any time. Moreover, in the Arab world, a common language and a shared sense of history mean that radical change in the more influential States does not take place in isolation: the violent overthrow of the Saudi regime would spread like wildfire through the Gulf States. Radical change in Syria or Jordan, let alone Egypt, would release political fall-out throughout the neighbouring States, and so on.

It is true that the public reaction in the Arab world to the American-led Coalition's assault on Iraq was far less violent than anticipated: only in Algeria, Morocco, and Jordan did governments face serious protest at street level. But the Arab world is still to some extent in shock at the dramatic nature of those events and a popular backlash against regimes perceived to be subservient to overbearing 'American imperialism' cannot be excluded, particularly if the Arab–Israeli negotiations founder and Israel is left in unchallenged possession of the Occupied Territories. Even in the Arabian peninsula which was quick to call on the USA to guard it against further Iraqi thrusts, reluctance to allow 'infidel' forces to remain in the area was by 1992 already apparent—particularly in Saudi Arabia.

For all the above reasons, the imponderables are such as to make speculation fruitless. It is fair to say that it is as impossible to predict the state of the region in the year 2022 as it would have been to predict the actual state of affairs in 1992 from the vantage point of 1959 when Nasserism was sweeping the region, traditional regimes were trembling in their shoes, and the Shah of Iran was riding high. It can only be stated that, so long as world-wide social and economic infrastructures are based on oil, the area which contains 50 per cent of the known reserves of that commodity will continue to be of abiding importance.

NOTES

1. The dates represent dates of UN membership and the designations those at present in use; e.g. the British mandate over Transjordan was terminated in 1946 but Jordan did not achieve UN membership until 1955. British protection over Kuwait ended in 1961 but the Iraqi claim to Kuwait blocked the latter from full membership of the international community for two years. When the Yemen was admitted to the UN in 1947 it was still the Imamate. This was overthrown by a military coup in 1962. Libya was a monarchy in 1955. And so on.

FURTHER READING

Brown, C., *International Politics and the Middle East* (London, 1984).
Chubin, S., and Tripp, C., *Iran and Iraq at War* (London, 1988).
Kyle, K., *Suez* (London, 1991).
Lacey, R., *The Kingdom* (London, 1982).
Laqueur, W., and Rubin, B. (eds.), *The Israel-Arab Reader* (London, 1984).
Louis, W. R., *The British Empire in the Middle East 1945–51* (Oxford, 1984).
Wilkinson, J. C., *Arabia's Frontiers* (London, 1991).

7

Sub-Saharan Africa

ROBERT H. JACKSON

POLITICAL BACKGROUND

In 1945 there were three sovereign States in Africa south of the Sahara: Ethiopia, Liberia, and South Africa. Only Ethiopia had unbroken connections with the pre-colonial African past owing to the fact that it was the sole indigenous State able to resist European imperialism. Liberia was founded in 1847 as a haven for liberated slaves who were 'repatriated' to the windward coast of West Africa with the active assistance and support of the American government. Although formally independent it was for all intents and purposes a colony of the USA. South Africa originated in 1652 as a Dutch settlement, was subjected to British imperialism at the start of the nineteenth century, and eventually acquired independent statehood in 1931 in the same evolutionary manner as Canada, Australia, and New Zealand. The rest of Sub-Saharan Africa was a colonial world.

1960 is widely regarded as marking the advent of African independence: in that year the entire French African empire was dissolved and thirteen new Francophone States became independent as well as Nigeria, Zaïre, and Somalia. European decolonization accelerated from this time and by 1980 only Namibia (the UN Trust Territory of South West Africa which was under the control of Pretoria in defiance of the United Nations) was still subject to alien rule. It became independent in 1990 at which time the Sub-Saharan region comprised forty-five States: about one-quarter of UN membership. Almost every existing Sub-Saharan State is the direct descendant of a jurisdiction which was drawn on the map, occupied, and for a time governed by a European imperial power. The geographical shape of South Africa was determined partly by European (mainly Dutch) settlers and partly by British imperialism.[1] Even the boundaries of Ethiopia were determined by the partition of Africa.

The links of existing Sub-Saharan States with pre-colonial political systems are in most cases slight or non-existent. Nor could there be such an inheritance because traditional Africa was not politically organized on a sovereign State basis. Prior to the partition and colonization of the continent launched at the Berlin Conference of 1884–5 neither the region at large nor its hundreds of component traditional political systems were members of the family of nations. Indeed, they were explicitly excluded on nineteenth-century positive legal grounds which deemed them unqualified for plenary political recognition. Nor were they members of their own regional system: there was at that time no African States system and very few territorial political systems with determinate boundaries under central governments which were easy to recognize as sovereign States. Old Africa was a political world far more recognizable to anthropology than to international law and diplomacy—it was not organized and did not operate on the basis of sovereign statehood.

That the vast interior of the continent was not subjected to European colonization before the late nineteenth century was owing primarily to its geographical remoteness and inhospitable climate. When at the

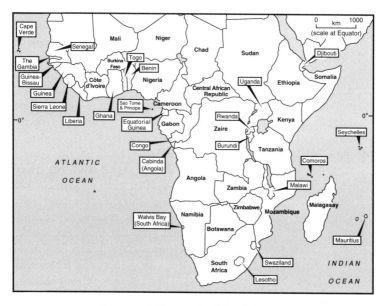

FIG. 7.1 Africa south of the Sahara

end of the nineteenth century modern technology could overcome these natural obstacles and European powers engaged in the scramble for African territories, they encountered few political systems which were able to act like modern States. Military resistance was credible in a few places, sporadic in some, but ineffective or non-existent in most. By this time European powers were equipped with rapid-firing weapons, electric communications, mechanical transport, pharmaceuticals, and other technologies which gave them an enormous military advantage. They could now effectively project their power into the interior of the continent and occupy it. Only the Emperor of Ethiopia was able to forestall European conquest permanently and eventually acquire full recognition and membership in the League of Nations. Every other indigenous government was subjected to colonial domination.

The foundations of a States system did not exist in pre-colonial Africa: the military and administrative means of large-scale and permanently organized territorial government and corresponding political and legal ideas were completely absent in most places. Africa was a continental archipelago of loosely defined political entities of which many were little more than extended kinship systems without any discernible central government whatsoever. Most societies were pre-literate. Technology was rudimentary. Monetary economies were rare. Even more centralized African political systems had boundaries that were vague and governments whose authority and power disappeared at the periphery.[2] The situation is characterized by Adda Bozeman in the following terms: 'African States were fluid and *ad hoc* creations that did not require a fixed human or territorial base . . . each is best understood as a system of more or less autonomous parts, held together by a dominant personality, family or lineage.'[3] Even the Islamic kingdoms—perhaps the most developed indigenous States—which rose and fell in the Sahel belt immediately south of the Sahara are described by Jacques Richard-Molard as 'the hastily assembled empires of Muslim adventurers'.[4] There often were no firm borders and tribute could be paid to more than one suzerain at the same time.

The modern State with a central government capable of routinely enforcing a ban on social violence and regularly mobilizing public revenues within a clearly defined territorial jurisdiction is a novel political arrangement brought to Africa by Europeans along with other social and physical technologies. Their colonies differed radically from the traditional suzerain-State systems: they were not based on tribute and personal rule. They were more ambitious political enterprises which routinely endeavoured to enforce law and order, impose regular taxes on their subjects, and introduce entirely novel ideologies and modes of production which in origin and operation were Western and not African. Partition of the continent established the first internationally recognized boundaries within which this new kind of State could be built. Colonization fostered centralized governments based on continuous bureaucratic administration, literacy, education, and modern communications and transportation infrastructure which began to orientate Africans away from their traditional societies, and towards the intruding colonial State and the external world that sustained it.

Although they usually did not have difficulty imposing their dominion on what were in the main rather simple, preliterate societies, the territorial governments established during the colonial era were themselves not very substantial or elaborate. In most cases they were little more than elementary bureaucracies with limited personnel and finances and were more comparable to rural county governments in Europe than to modern independent States. They governed large territories and populations with tiny staffs and finances: probably the most cost-effective governments of modern times. And they usually did not and could not alter fundamentally the underlying political culture of the small-scale traditional African societies in their jurisdiction which continued to shape the understanding and behaviour of most Africans. However, it was these foreign structures Africans would claim and inherit when the time came for independence. The colonial jurisdictions and organizations rather than the traditional political systems became the new States of Sub-Saharan Africa and therein perhaps is the root of the very great difficulty Africans in all parts of the vast continent have had in adjusting to the States system. In short, the modern State in most cases operating on a scale greater than anything that existed hitherto was superimposed upon the continent from outside. It is still in many respects an alien institution.

Africa became an overseas extension of European sovereignty. One could now speak in general of European Africa and specifically of the British, French, Belgian, Portuguese, Spanish, Italian, and—for a time—German African Empires. Indigenous African political systems and their rulers became subjects and sometimes agents of European colonial governments. In Sub-Saharan Africa this political reorientation occurred in a period of only sixty or seventy years. Exposure to the modern States system was rather superficial and the underlying traditional political culture continued to be defined by perceptions of tribute or clientage. In the framework of the sovereign State, this manifested itself as patronage, nepotism, and corruption, which persisted throughout the colonial era and expanded enormously after independence. In sum, Africans were catapulted by the rush of events into the States system of the later twentieth century with very limited preparation for large-scale self-government and still attached to indigenous practices and institutions of which most were rooted in kinship duties and clan or tribal (ethnic) identities that were contrary to the obligations and other requirements of modern sovereign statehood.

BIRTHS AND BIRTHRIGHT

When the time came for Sub-Saharan Africa to acquire independence the only logical candidates were the territories established during the colonial era. They already existed as determinate jurisdictions and their borders were registered on the political map of the world. Only a handful of the numerous traditional political systems emerged from colonialism as sovereign States: Madagascar, Zanzibar (which quickly united with Tanganyika to become Tanzania), Swaziland, Lesotho, Burundi, Rwanda, Botswana, and Somalia (the latter was a homogeneous linguistic and religious entity but was riven by clan divisions among a mostly nomadic population and was never an integrated political system). However, hundreds of indigenous political systems remained submerged beneath ex-colonial State jurisdictions either resigned to their subordinate fate, indifferent to it, or frustrated by it—such as Buganda (in Uganda) and some other traditional kingdoms.

I. M. Lewis thinks 'it is a remarkable irony that the European powers who partitioned Africa in the late 19th century when the idea of the nation-state was paramount, should have created in Africa a whole series of Hapsburg-style States, comprising a medley of peoples and ethnic groups lumped together within frontiers which paid no respect to traditional cultural contours.'[5] But was there any alternative? The political scale of traditional Africa was usually far too limited to be workable internationally. The alternative would have been a continent of pygmy jurisdictions and statelets which could not have succeeded in fitting into the world of sovereign territorial States as we know it. Colonialism expanded political scale in the continent on average by a factor of fifteen at least.[6] For example, if the documented pattern of ethnicity (tribal divisions) is used as a basis of jurisdiction instead of the present forty-five States there would be approximately 700 and possibly more.[7] Another way of putting this is to say that African States encompass on average about fifteen distinctive ethnolinguistic groups or what in Europe would be referred to as nationalities. In other words, on average each Sub-Saharan country is as complicated ethnically as the Balkans. What was gained in scale was of course lost in unity—unless the new jurisdiction could find some workable method of political integration which usually was not the case. Indeed, the new territorial African States—like the former Yugoslavia—can in almost every case be defined as posing a fundamental problem of ethnic division, tension, and not infrequently conflict which sometimes registers as civil war or secession movements.

Despite the remarkable increase in political scale during the colonial era, there was nevertheless some dissatisfaction at the time of de-colonization that by accepting the colonial frontiers as international boundaries the continent would still be 'Balkanized'. Kwame Nkrumah, the first President of Ghana, urged his African colleagues to unite to form a single pan-African State.[8] But his dream was totally unrealistic: the continent of Africa was not and still is not organized to sustain one territorial jurisdiction. The institutional and physical infrastruc-ture to support such a vast jurisdiction did not exist in 1960 and still does not exist more than three decades later. The infrastructure of Sub-Saharan Africa was and still is based on the colonial map: roads and railways, posts and telegraphs, towns and cities, ports and harbours, trade and commerce, government administration, education, language, and much else were adapted to connecting the individual territories to the overseas metropoles. African colonies were appendages of European States. Their successors were also outward-orientated and consequently somewhat isolated from each other and there usually were at best only minimal linkages and transactions between them. In the last decade of the twentieth century Sub-Saharan Africa is still only at an early stage of integration between its constituent States.

Even 'Africa' as a political idea and name was created by outsiders. From time immemorial inhabitants of the continent had conceptions of themselves as members of distinctive groups but not as 'Africans'. 'Africa' and 'Africans' were geographical and racial concepts which went back at least as far as the Romans. But it was only during the colonial era that African intellectuals, one of whom was Nkrumah, turned the idea of 'we are all Africans' into a political tool.[9] As indicated, the basis of Africa as a single State was then and is still largely non-existent. And this does not take account of the more immediately compelling political motivations that work against such a possibility: what African leader would sacrifice his opportunity to remain or become president or prime minister of an independent country (with all the power and privileges involved in being able to travel around the world as a head of State and/or government) for the alternative of being (presumably) a provincial governor unknown outside his parish? On the other hand, the desire to possess the perquisites of international status is an important force driving some African leaders who cannot become rulers of existing countries to achieve it by organizing secessionist movements aimed at creating new States under their control.

Among the illuminating features of the birth of African sovereign States is uniformity: they all emerged at more or less the same time. This characteristic is shared with some other parts of the ex-colonial world but it contrasts with the usual pre-twentieth-century sequential birth and death of States based on wars of conquest, colonization, or independence. This changed in 1919 when frontiers in Eastern Europe were determined more or less at one time not only by the outcome of the First World War but also by the ideology of national self-determination fostered by President Woodrow Wilson of the USA, which attempted to define territorial sovereignty according to the principle of freedom of nationalities.[10] The attempt was not wholly successful and most of the newly formed States of Eastern and Central Europe were divided internally along ethnonational lines. The principle of national self-determination nevertheless became the usual ground for claiming the right to sovereignty against imperial powers who were still occupying huge territories outside Europe.

Uniformity is also disclosed by political geography: African boundaries, for reasons already given, consist less of indigenous ethnolinguistic frontiers and more of straight lines or landforms, such as rivers and mountains. They resemble internal borders in the USA, Canada, and Australia.[11] Because they originated as arbitrarily defined subordinate jurisdictions the geographical logic of African States is closer to that of many Canadian provinces than to the international jurisdictions of Europe and some other parts of the world. That this is so should not be surprising in so far as the borders were drawn by the same sort of nineteenth-century people—European colonialists with a utilitarian outlook—engaged in more or less the same project—creating subordinate jurisdictions which would be militarily advantageous and (it was hoped) commercially profitable. The colonial enterprise (whether in Canada or in Africa) was significantly if not fundamentally utilitarian, and so it is perhaps to be expected that inconsequential indigenous institutions and jurisdictions in occupied territories were ignored or pushed aside—unless (as in the case of British indirect rule) they proved useful to the colonial power.

The concurrent birthdays and uniform ex-colonial frontiers of African States are connected to a changed doctrine of international legitimacy which occurred in the latter half of the twentieth century and was based on the categorical and unrestricted right of overseas colonies to become independent States: colonial (as distinguished from national) self-determination. This is essentially a doctrine of birthright: territories formed by European colonialism are considered to have a right to become sovereign with no questions asked if their inhabitants desire it. This ideology eventually prevailed against all contrary justifications of overseas metropolitan jurisdiction. The sudden and multiple births of African States was heralded by the celebrated 1960 UN Declaration on the Granting of Independence to Colonial Countries and Peoples, which reads in part: 'all peoples have the right to self-determination'; and, 'inadequacy of political, economic, social or educational preparedness should never serve as a pretext for delaying independence'. The quotation implies that many jurisdictions were not equipped for self-government—which was often the case in Sub-Saharan Africa. Nevertheless, it was adopted by a vote of 89 to 0, with 9 abstentions and is considered by many Third World States to be a revision of the UN Charter on self-determination.

This right is limited to ex-colonial peoples and does not extend to the numerous ethnonationalities which were subordinated by colonialism and remain subordinated by successor African States to this day. The Declaration can be read as a compact of ex-colonial States to promote the international *status quo* and their survival by making it impossible for non-colonial entities within their jurisdictions rightfully to claim sovereignty. It is emphatic that 'any attempt aimed at the partial or total disruption of the national unity and the territorial integrity of a country is incompatible with the purposes and principles of the Charter of the United Nations.' The 'country' is of course a former colony, and the 'attempt' at 'disruption' refers to ethnonational groups. (This doctrine of *uti possidetis* is discussed further in Chapters 16 and 17.)

The sanctity of ex-colonial frontiers in Sub-Saharan Africa was reiterated by the Organization of African Unity (OAU) which was founded in 1963 largely to preserve the ex-colonial territorial *status quo*. The July 1964 meeting of the OAU passed a resolution which stated that 'the borders of African States, on the day of their independence, constitute a tangible reality' which 'all Member States pledge themselves to respect'.[12] The only State in Sub-Saharan Africa that opposed and also defied this principle is the traditional ethnolinguistic entity of Somalia, which lost territory as a result of colonial partition and has on several occasions attempted to regain it by force and has justified its actions on the grounds that it was reclaiming territory inhabited by Somali people and therefore rightfully its own.[13] The multi-ethnic ex-colonial States which are the vast majority of OAU members naturally rejected Somalia's claim and condemned its use of force to regain territory from Ethiopia and Kenya. To do otherwise would, as A. C. McEwen puts it, 'plunge the continent into a readjustment of frontiers that would in effect be a new scramble for Africa'.[14] With the decolonization of Namibia all the former colonies are now sovereign and there is no possibility of any additional births on this basis. Henceforth new African State jurisdictions can emerge only if ex-colonial frontiers are changed.

The persistence of the present pattern of State jurisdiction since the end of colonialism is not due to any lack of disintegrating conditions or conflicts in the region. Many Sub-Saharan States if not most are still far from united. In many there are disaffected regions—usually based on an important ethnolinguistic group—whose leaders and populations do not identify with the new ex-colonial State or feel that they owe allegiance to its government, especially if the government consists of members of other such groups. If these alienated groups had the opportunity to form their own State many of them might very well seize it.

The disintegration of Sub-Saharan States is revealed most vividly by internal warfare or its threat which is a marked continuing characteristic of the region. Since independence wars in Africa have mainly been civil wars, of which the most significant have involved outside powers. Instances of the latter are the civil disruptions in Zaïre (1960–5), the Ethiopian civil war (1961–91), the Nigerian civil war

(1967–70), the Angolan civil war (1975–90), the recurrent conflict in Chad (1965–), and at the time of writing (1992) current wars in Liberia (1989–), Mozambique (1984–), and Somalia (1991–). The Angolan civil war drew in the Soviet Union and Cuba on the side of the government, and the USA and South Africa in support of anti-government rebels. The war in the Horn also became entangled in the Cold War and involved the Soviets and the Cubans on the side of Ethiopia with the USA aligning itself with the Somali Republic.

But there have been very few wars between Sub-Saharan members of the OAU and almost none of any significance. Two noteworthy exceptions occurred in the later 1970s: the 1977–8 conflict between Somalia and Ethiopia for control of the Somali-populated Ogaden region of the Horn of Africa, and the 1978–9 Tanzania–Uganda War which resulted in the overthrow of Idi Amin. Neither disrupted the inherited ex-colonial pattern of sovereign statehood in the region. Another exception was the civil war in Liberia (1989–) which involved military intervention by the Economic Community of West African States (ECOWAS) under the leadership of Nigeria and resulted not only in the overthrow of the incumbent ruler of Liberia, General Samuel Doe, but also the installation of one of the rebel groups as the new government. It is still too early to know whether this episode might have set a precedent for intervention by African States and international organizations in African civil wars—in the summer of 1992 there were reports that civil war had again broken out in Liberia.

THE RULES OF THE GAME

International law and diplomacy has to date obstructed the partition of even the most marginal and politically disunited State jurisdictions in Sub-Saharan Africa. The territorial legitimacy of existing frontiers has held fast and the political prospects of separatists, irredentists, and all others who desire to change post-colonial international boundaries by force and without the consent of the State(s) involved have been minimal. The perhaps unintended but inevitable consequence has been the emergence of an international region which consists pre-eminently and uniformly of empirically weak governments if not indeed 'stateless' jurisdictions.[15] This political reality determines the overriding preoccupation of international relations in Sub-Saharan

Africa: preserving ex-colonial jurisdictions which probably would not be independent in a less accommodating international environment. The UN and OAU Charters uphold the requirement that ex-colonial frontiers can only be changed by consent of the sovereign governments involved. Such consent is not likely to be granted if it resulted in loss of territory. Thus, every African country registered on the political map of the continent in 1960 is still in its appointed place despite the fact that what goes on inside the ex-colonial boundaries of many often bears little resemblance to effective central governance, much less democracy.

The desire to retain sovereignty and not to surrender it or even share it—for example, within a federal arrangement—is a powerful motive perpetuating the ex-colonial *status quo* in Sub-Saharan Africa. Sovereignty gives a relatively small number of people control of State positions which confer enormous palpable advantages and privileges available to nobody else in the country. In other words, it is essential to their high life-styles. Sovereignty makes a life of privilege possible by giving African rulers (and their collaborators) privileges and advantages unavailable to anyone else: management of foreign aid receipts; income from the movement of goods within jurisdictions and between them, for example through issuing tariffs and licences; borrowing and taxing powers; the right to set official exchange rates; the opportunity to participate in international organizations; unrivalled opportunities for corruption, and so forth. Sovereign rulers can also commandeer State or parastatal assets, such as aircraft from the national airline to fly them (and their retinues) around the world. Alternative sources of power, privilege, and wealth are few or non-existent in most Sub-Saharan countries, which are as a group the least developed in the world. Ruling élites literally live off sovereignty and most live very well indeed—as long as they live. They fight to keep it and others fight to take it from them—as is all too evident from recurrent coups and countercoups. If the experience of the past three decades of independent statehood is an indication, any arrangement that would require the sacrifice of sovereignty by leaders of existing countries almost certainly would not be entered into freely.

Preoccupation with sovereignty is strongly evident in the OAU Charter whose basic principles (enunciated in Article III) emphatically affirm the inviolability of African ex-colonial boundaries and condemn political assassination and any other subversive activities by any African statesmen against any others. At the second annual meeting of the OAU in 1965 a 'Declaration on the Problem of Subversion' was adopted in which member States 'solemnly undertake' 'not to tolerate' any subversion against other members originating either inside Africa or outside and 'not to create dissension within or among member States by fomenting or aggravating racial, religious, linguistic, ethnic or other differences'.[16] These classical rules of the sovereignty game— *cujus regio, ejus religio*—are the basic regional obligations of African States and arguably reflect problems of starting up and operating a brand-new States system along frontiers which never existed before colonial times and which encapsulate deeply divided populations within novel States which by twentieth-century standards are often disorganized and in some cases even chaotic (Zaïre, Chad, Angola, Ethiopia, Mozambique, Liberia, Somalia).

The OAU rules are an explicit acknowledgement of the weakness of African States and their vulnerability to international destabilization and possibly even disintegration. They clearly imply that disruptive groups exist which would welcome external intervention in their support, and that foreign powers could exploit such weakness. Owing to their extreme underdevelopment most Sub-Saharan governments are powerless to prevent this. They are therefore driven to forestall it by the only available means: reaching a consensus among themselves on regional norms governing foreign intervention which can discourage external *divide et impera*. Such a consensus among States whose domestic ideologies and policies are often highly divergent indicates that the problems of insecurity the OAU rules address are widely shared. The great majority of existing African States (and their ruling élites) consequently are real beneficiaries of the Charter. Few can gain from violating its basic principles.

Sub-Saharan Africa, contrary to what some Africanists are inclined to tell us, is not a strategic region and consequently the necessities or temptations of outside powers have not been as great as—for example—in the Middle East, South East Asia, or Central America. As indicated, great power interests in the region faded fast following the end of the Cold War. But even before there was less reason to intervene arbitrarily to preserve or restore the balance of power because Sub-Saharan States could not and still cannot affect that balance to any significant degree. Sub-Saharan Africa has always been somewhat off the beaten path of international politics. The strategic minerals which certain Sub-Saharan States possess can usually be obtained without going to the trouble of intervening. Bribery will work as well at far less cost—if past relations between Washington and the regime of President Mobutu in Zaïre are anything to go by. Indeed, it suits the pattern of African politics which is characterized by clientelism and corruption: the neopatrimonial State. There is also a legacy of paternalism in relations between the West and Sub-Saharan Africa which suggests that it would be unworthy of a Western power to impose its will on a weak African State by force. The ideological background for this is the universal taboo against colonialism. But this taboo is not incompatible with bribery of African personal rulers by foreign powers.

Although the OAU cannot prevent or suppress the domestic conflicts which provide the opportunity for military intervention by non-African powers, it has largely succeeded in securing the compliance of those powers with a basic norm of international law concerning such intervention: it must be solicited by a State for its own security and for deployment within its own frontiers. It must not be imposed from outside Africa or be solicited by a non-sovereign. This has been achieved for two main reasons: (1) the rule is consistent with the UN Charter, and (2) there have been few overriding strategic interests in Sub-Saharan Africa to tempt unsolicited intervention by major outside powers.

With the end of the Cold War the military interests of the West and the successors of the former Soviet Union in Sub-Saharan African conflicts has sharply declined and might soon disappear. On the other hand, the supply of arms from Middle Eastern, Latin American, or Asian States might continue and even increase. And the arms manufacturing industry of Russia (and some other States of the former USSR) might for domestic economic reasons be sorely tempted to participate in clandestine export of arms to the Third World. If the supply of arms to Africa is channelled through such pipelines (the international 'arms bazaar') it could end up supplying anti-government rebels as well as governments and could exacerbate both domestic and international political instability in the region. It could also encourage so far quiescent ethnonationalists to mobilize and launch armed struggles for independence. Other scenarios are also conceivable. But such arms transfers could not by themselves alter the formal rules of the sovereignty game in Africa or make it easier for separatists or irredentists to secure international recognition. That would require a change of those rules which could only be made by sovereign States and other international legal persons, such as the UN. Any such changes are unlikely.

PATRON AND CLIENT STATES

The extreme weakness and vulnerability of Sub-Saharan States can be expected to and does in fact result in bilateral clientage relations with non-African powers. All Western industrialized countries and also some of the high-income oil-exporting countries as well as (some of) the former Soviet bloc States, China, and one or two others have in the past provided Sub-Saharan States with international development assistance. Although foreign assistance is a small fraction of the resources of donors it represents in most cases a very significant supply of finances (and other resources) for recipient governments. Foreign aid is particularly attractive to ruling élites who actively solicit it from donor countries. Getting or keeping such aid is one of the main activities of African ambassadors to OECD States.

International clientelism has also manifested itself in organizational terms. Developed States and Sub-Saharan States have become jointly involved in a variety of what Peter Lyon aptly terms 'post-imperial ordering devices: practical testaments to continuing but freshly defined cordialities between erstwhile colonizers and colonized after the demise of empires'.[17] These include the Commonwealth, Francophonie, the Lomé Convention with the EC, and various UN bodies; during the Cold War they also included Soviet friendship treaties with African Marxist regimes. One cannot overlook links between certain oil-rich Arab States and African Muslim countries. Such arrangements are based on formal equality but there is little doubt that patron–client ties and motivations characterize many relations among their substantially unequal members.

The irony of this situation at least with regard to developed OECD States deserves comment: they (at least many of them) have been pursuing clients with as much evident enthusiasm as the underdeveloped States have been seeking patronage. A significant patron and a (somewhat) new kind of power is one with a retinue of clients which are sovereign States and not colonies. The latter are not able to contribute significantly to the power or wealth of the patron, which is what is new about the relationship. Indeed, the relationship is far more likely to cost the patron something. But it also contributes to his international prestige and influence. France has been cultivating patron–client relations with its former colonies in Africa at considerable expense but also with great success since 1960. Indeed, the French president is the grand patron at the head of a retinue of Francophone African heads of States: a relationship somewhat reminiscent of feudal fealty. Britain has been active but far less assiduous; but the British monarchy has in relation to the Commonwealth played a somewhat similar role to the French presidency. The USA, China, the former USSR, Cuba under Fidel Castro, and other powers have also engaged in patron–client relations in the Sub-Saharan region, although obviously not with the same historical advantage. Since patrons are bidding for their support, clients may be strongly tempted to accept the offers of more than one. A client may be on retainer to several patrons. The game gets tricky if a client finds himself in the awkward situation where his patrons are competing to call on his support which can only go to one or the other—for example in a vote at the UN. But such clear-cut conflicts arise too seldom to discourage the search for multiple patrons.

Canada, which never had colonies and therefore has no residual ex-colonial interests, has nevertheless spent very substantial effort and money to cultivate influence among Sub-Saharan members of the Commonwealth and Francophonie—evidently seeking to rival Britain and France. Since the latter have historical advantages which derive from the colonial era, Canada must assert its role. It has done this in the Commonwealth by rivalling Britain in its allocation of foreign aid and also following the African and Third World line on sanctions against apartheid South Africa (when in the past that was a major African international issue). It has been less successful within Francophonie where France continues to enjoy paramountcy and places great emphasis on its patrimonial role. However, Canada's position has nevertheless been that of the number-two patron. Canada also has attempted to act as a spokesman for African States—for example, registering their desire for debt relief—in exclusive international organizations dominated by Western capitalist powers—such as the G-7—to which it belongs. Sub-Saharan States consequently present a middle power like Canada with the opportunity to increase its international standing beyond what might otherwise be possible if it were determined by economic or military clout alone. A clientele can be valuable even if it consists for the most part of insignificant States—which most Sub-Saharan members of the Commonwealth and Francophonie are—because their support can be registered in elections in the UN and other international organizations. For example, Canada's success in competing periodically for election to a non-permanent seat in the UN Security Council is not unconnected with its ability to canvass votes from its numerous Third World 'friends' in the General Assembly.

How are we to characterize international relations such as these? They obviously are not colonialism, in so far as both clients and patrons are equally sovereign States. They must be characterized by interdependency rather than dependency, in so far as each partner has what the other wants and there is some choice of partners. There also clearly is some kind of exchange between them: patrons offer substantial aid and virtual representation in major power circles in exchange for the approbation and—when circumstances arise—the votes of clients. What we appear to have is a curious form of suzerainty. It is not suzerainty properly speaking: the clients are not in a tributary relation to their patron(s). Instead of weak States paying tribute to powerful patrons in exchange for protection and continued existence— the practice in a traditional suzerain-State system—Sub-Saharan States are pursued by developed suitors who are attempting to enlarge or maintain their prestige and influence in the States system by increasing the size of their international clientele. In our democratic age the weaker or poorer can evidently expect to be sought after by (some of) the stronger or richer in a reverse suzerainty relationship in which tribute flows ironically from the centre to the periphery. It is a relationship brought about by the international enfranchisement of numerous juridically equal but substantially very unequal States. Sub-Saharan Africa especially in its relations with the developed OECD States has since independence been marked by such patron–client linkages.

ARE THE RULES OF THE GAME CHANGING?

Since the revolution of 1989–91 we have been witnessing dramatic changes in international relations. The USA and Russia are no longer competing for supremacy in world politics and consequently they have withdrawn from regional conflicts by which they carried on their global struggle in the past. In Sub-Saharan Africa the civil conflicts involving the superpowers and their clients were by early 1992 largely wound down: the civil wars in Ethiopia and Angola were settled and the outlook for regional peace was better than it had been since the end of the colonial era. This development can hardly be regarded as anything but a positive consequence of the end of the Cold War.

However, from the perspective of African governments, there may also be a negative consequence. The Cold War encouraged African decolonization by opening a political space between East and West which manifested itself in the emergence of a non-aligned Third World. This turned the East and the West into suitors and invited a competition between them for the support and approbation of Third World statesmen which generally increased the significance and freedom (not to mention the wealth) of the latter. The end of the Cold War may reduce the international freedom and influence of African governments and indeed Sub-Saharan Africa may become relatively neglected by major outside powers. This decline of interest and involvement has already occurred on the part of former East bloc States and it could happen in Western relations with the region. In this scenario Sub-Saharan States might be left more on their own than they have been for a long time. They might even begin to revert to a position in world politics that is reminiscent of the era before colonialism—what Arnold Wolfers calls the pole of indifference.[18] African statesmen have been worried that if the West takes major steps to develop the run-down economies of Eastern Europe and the former USSR it will translate into a decline in Western foreign aid for them.

Other future scenarios are also conceivable. One is that the West will not turn away from Africa in its allocation of foreign assistance but will attach more demanding conditions now that the rivalry with the former Soviet bloc has ended. Whereas in the past African statesmen had some latitude to play off the Americans and the Russians, now that the latter have withdrawn from the game the West is in a position to set higher conditions for its financial and technical aid to Sub-Saharan Africa. There is evidence to suggest that this has already happened. During the 1980s the IMF and the World Bank increased the economic conditions for African (and other Third World) borrowers. They were required to move away from State subsidies and adopt free-market policies: structural adjustment. In a 1989 report the World Bank warned that little foreign aid would be forthcoming in the future 'unless governance of Africa improves'.[19] In 1990 British foreign secretary, Douglas Hurd, said that Africa's resources had been dissipated by war, bad management, and—in some countries—corruption.[20]

By 1991 certain Western donors were also talking about 'democracy' and 'human rights' as conditions for further economic aid—the same conditions that were being applied to Eastern Europe by the newly founded European Bank for Reconstruction and Development. A 1991 Report of the [British] House of Commons Foreign Affairs Committee spoke of a 'new "wind of change"' ... blowing through the political and economic structures' of African States.[21] And following the Gulf War which involved a major humanitarian intervention by Western powers in Iraq, comments by both African and Western spokesmen for humanitarian NGOs questioned the rights of non-intervention of abusive or incompetent Sub-Saharan governments. At the 1991 Commonwealth Heads of Government Conference in Harare, Zimbabwe, Canada put member governments on notice that henceforth their domestic conduct would be a matter of concern if it resulted in serious humanitarian abuses, in which case a reassessment of Canada's foreign aid to them would be considered.

These statements (and others like them) suggest that Sub-Saharan Africa will be affected by the end of the Cold War in a way that is more likely to reduce than enlarge the freedom of its sovereign governments. By early 1992 many Sub-Saharan governments were adopting or considering multiparty constitutions and there were signs that one-party States and personal dictatorships could no longer be justified. Those which remained defiant appeared to be fighting a rearguard battle. If this scenario were to become a reality it would be a more intrusive involvement of the West in Sub-Saharan Africa than anything we have witnessed since the end of colonialism. South Africa at the same time was abandoning apartheid and attempting to move towards a multiracial democracy. This development was brought about in considerable measure by a successful international campaign to isolate South Africa from the international community which was promoted by Black African States more than by any others. Their success in bringing about political reform in South Africa ironically may have awakened international and domestic demands for similar reforms of their own governments most of which have until recently been personal autocracies or ethnic oligarchies rather than democracies.

Finally, there were noteworthy developments concerning sovereign statehood in Sub-Saharan Africa. In Ethiopia a thirty-year civil war was brought to an end in 1991 by the defeat of the central government which had been heavily supported by Soviet military aid and was left vulnerable when that aid was withdrawn. The new government formed by the victorious Ethiopia People's Revolutionary Democratic Movement indicated they were prepared to recognize an independent Eritrea if that was what the Eritrean people desired in a referendum. In neighbouring Somalia the new era has been marked by an outbreak rather than an end of civil war between rival clan leaders seeking to control the State following the overthrow of a dictatorship. In northern Somalia the former British Protectorate of Somaliland declared itself independent in 1991 as the Republic of Somaliland but failed to secure international recognition. In Liberia ECOWAS under the leadership of Nigeria intervened in that country's civil war without being invited by its government. This was a new development which called into question important OAU and UN rules against foreign intervention and overthrow of governments. The recognition of Eritrea and even more so the Republic of Somaliland would be important developments should they occur. But they would not be a complete break with African international norms because both are former colonies; moreover the Ethiopian government would (presumably) have consented to the secession of Eritrea. In late 1992 the UN Security Council authorized a major humanitarian intervention in Somalia by armed forces of the USA and other Western powers. Because they were not invited by Somali authorities to intervene this UN action set a precedent which may have changed the rules of the game.

To sum up: the game of sovereign statehood in Sub-Saharan Africa has two main dimensions. The first dimension is the absolute inviolability of international boundaries declared in the Charter of the OAU to which all Sub-Saharan States are signatories (except South Africa which is likely to become a signatory once its own Constitution is reformed). There is little evidence to suggest that the rules of this sovereignty game will not continue to be generally observed in the future as they have been in the past. The second dimension is the patron–client relationship of (mainly) Western States and Sub-Saharan countries. African governments very likely will continue to be subjected to economic requirements by the IMF and the World Bank and also increasingly to political and humanitarian standards of conduct which may be more demanding than any they have been required to observe since the end of colonialism. If the end of the

Cold War reduces the freedom of manœuvre of African clients and increases the intrusiveness of Western patrons—recalling aspects of colonialism—it would suggest that a significant international change had occurred and perhaps that a new era in relations between Africa and the West had dawned. It is too soon to say whether this will happen. If it does happen it is certain to alarm African rulers but it may very well delight many ordinary Africans who have suffered under some of the worst governments to be found anywhere.

NOTES

1. 'Sub-Saharan Africa' includes all the continental countries of tropical Africa and also the offshore States of São Tomé in the Atlantic Ocean and Madagascar, Comoros, Seychelles, and Mauritius in the Indian Ocean. Sudan and Western Sahara are considered part of North Africa which is excluded. This chapter deals mainly with the continental States excluding South Africa.

2. J. Vansina, *Kingdoms of the Savanna* (Madison, 1966), 156. Also see L. Mair, *African Kingdoms* (Oxford, 1977), ch. 1.

3. A. B. Bozeman, *Conflict in Africa* (Princeton, NJ, 1976), 143.

4. Quoted by Bozeman, *Conflict in Africa*, 133.

5. I. M. Lewis, 'Pre- and Post-Colonial Forms of Polity in Africa', in I. M. Lewis (ed.), *Nationalism and Self-Determination in the Horn of Africa* (London, 1983), 73.

6. See the classical study by G. and M. Wilson, *The Analysis of Social Change* (Cambridge, 1945), ch. 2.

7. G. P. Murdock, *Africa: Its Peoples and their Cultural History* (London, 1959).

8. K. Nkrumah, *Africa Must Unite* (London, 1963). For an excellent overview of this subject see A. Ajala, *Pan-Africanism* (London, 1973).

9. See the intriguing attempt by A. Mazrui to define African international jurisdiction in terms of 'racial sovereignty', in *Towards a Pax Africana* (London, 1967), ch. 2.

10. See A. Cobban, *The Nation State and National Self-Determination* (New York, 1969), chs. 4 and 5.

11. The border between USA and Canada along the 49th parallel was formed the same way.

12. Quoted by A. C. McEwen, *International Boundaries of East Africa* (Oxford, 1971), 24.

13. The North African States of Morocco and Libya have also defied the principle: the former invaded and annexed large territories of the Western

Sahara and the latter occupied northern Chad. Recently Somalia has fallen into the usual pattern of internal conflict, in this case between warring Somali clans.

14. McEwen, *International Boundaries of East Africa*, 11.
15. See R. H. Jackson, *Quasi-States: Sovereignty, International Relations and the Third World* (Cambridge, 1990).
16. Repr. in Brownlie, *Basic Documents on African Affairs*, 17.
17. P. Lyon, 'New States and International Order', in A. James (ed.), *The Bases of International Order* (London, 1973), 47.
18. A. Wolfers, *Discord and Collaboration* (London, 1962), 81–102.
19. The World Bank, *Sub-Saharan Africa: From Crisis to Sustainable Growth* (Washington, DC, 1989).
20. 'Background Brief' (London, Foreign and Commonwealth Office), 5.
21. Quoted by ibid., 1.

FURTHER READING

Bozeman, A. B., *Conflict in Africa* (Princeton, NJ, 1976).

Bull, H., 'European States and African Political Communities', in H. Bull and A. Watson (eds.), *The Expansion of International Society* (Oxford, 1984), 99–114.

Jackson, R. H., *Quasi-States: Sovereignty, International Relations and the Third World* (Cambridge, 1990).

Lewis, I. M. (ed.), *Nationalism and Self-Determination in the Horn of Africa* (London, 1983).

McEwen, A. C., *International Boundaries of East Africa* (Oxford, 1971).

World Bank, *Sub-Saharan Africa: From Crisis to Sustainable Growth* (Washington, DC, 1989).

8

South Asia

W. H. MORRIS-JONES[1]

Even after the cataclysmic upheavals of 1990–1 in Eastern Europe and beyond, it remains true that each world region has its own parochialism, not least South Asia where each country's foreign policy is shaped far more by domestic and regional issues than by global concerns.

History and geography have played a large part. The seven very unequal States (India, Pakistan, Bangladesh, Sri Lanka, Nepal, Bhutan, and the Maldives) constitute the most imperialized of all regions[2]— only Nepal and Bhutan are partial exceptions—and although it was the first decolonized region in the modern period, its common experience of a single imperial domination was long and far from superficial. That commonality could build on geographical foundations: the region is self-contained by the Indian Ocean and the Himalayan chain so that, while each country is distinctive, types of landscape, soil, produce, villages, and towns extend easily across national boundaries, as do societal characteristics such as food and dress, community ties, and status distinctions.

One consequence of such commonality is that the region's distinctiveness from neighbouring regions is underlined. Despite several links in the past, East Asia, South East Asia and South West Asia all see South Asia as a very separate world—and are so seen by it. Yet at times events in certain countries—Afghanistan and Tibet more than Burma—in adjacent regions have caused anxieties in South Asia. Moreover, interactions between South Asia and its neighbour regions have tended to heighten tensions within South Asia. Thus in the 1950s India enthusiastically took the hand of the new China, but when those relations soured into actual border war it was Pakistan and China who grasped hands on the basis of one's enemy's enemy being a friend. Again, although Pakistan would have been in any event, and especially after its loss of Bangladesh, drawn by Islamic ties to South West Asia, it was American concerns about Soviet moves in that zone that committed Pakistan to a key conduit role for the Afghan resistance and thereby to further distancing of itself from India.

The commonality shared by the States of South Asia has further limitations: what is shared is divisive, what is common is contested. There are borders for a start, especially when India as the largest country has common frontiers with all the others except two, Sri Lanka and the Maldives. Along with borders, river waters are also shared, with consequent painful disputes. Again and above all, the common experience of the region, which might be expected to bring views together, works differently because its impact was differentiated. It has often deposited folk memories and images which, so far from being common, are divergent, inimical, conducive to distrust or worse; it is only necessary to consider the contrasted imprints of 1947 on Pakistan and India or of 1971 on Bangladesh, Pakistan, and India. But not only are minds and hearts set apart by the same events; actual sets of similar peoples are located in different States—more Muslims in India than in Islamic Pakistan, Bengalis in India as well as in Bangladesh, Tamils in India but also in Sri Lanka.

That reference to communities within nation-states points to a feature nowhere more salient than in South Asia. Such communities may be based on religion or sect or caste, on language or tribe. India contains every kind of subdivision; the more compact Pakistan has Sindhis, Punjabis, Baluchis, and Pathans, as well as the Islamic Shi'a–Sunni division; smaller States like Nepal and Bhutan contain distinct peoples; even Bangladesh has tribals in its Chittagong Hill Tracts who see Bengali incomers as strangers. Such communities have marked identities which suffer little erosion and can create lines of fracture within a State. Moreover, when sufficiently agitated, they can reach out to affect international relations—as when Sikhs in rebellion shelter in Pakistan and Sri Lankan Tamils take refuge in Indian Tamiland.

Thus although South Asia is a distinct world with its own commonalities, it is scarcely a harmonious one, less so perhaps than ASEAN or OAU. Hence the late creation of SAARC, the South Asian Association for Regional Co-operation; only after five meetings at foreign secretary level and one at ministerial level during 1981–3 was the first summit meeting achieved in 1985 at Dhaka.[3] This location at the capital of Bangladesh was not accidental, for indeed the initiative towards SAARC had been taken by the country which

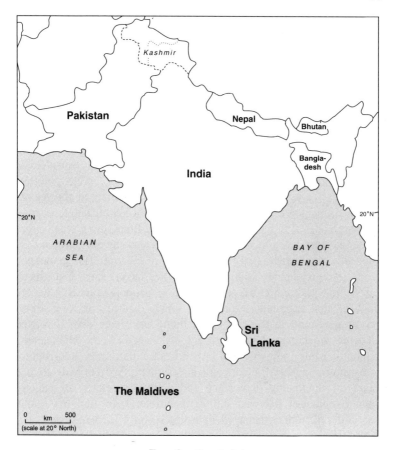

FIG. 8.1 South Asia

was new, middle-sized, and in some degree politically equidistant between India and Pakistan, the larger confronting powers of the region. Given the hesitation and caution (especially of India, fearing perhaps a setting for ganging-up against her) in the creation of SAARC, it was not surprising that the agreed ground-rule in the founding charter was the exclusion of bilateral disputes and contentious matters.[4] Accordingly the business of the summits consists of two extremes: agreements to fairly bland general statements and reviews of very particular fields for co-operation (such as health, agriculture, and telecommunications) which are examined by technical committees. Latterly, more mention has been made of developing intra-regional trade. Up to now the main links of trade and investment of the bigger countries have been extra-regional, those of the smaller three mainly with India. It is not easy to see that this pattern will be significantly altered; even the likeliest beneficiary, India, might be reluctant to press the point.[5] Overall, there is no doubt that the most important contribution of SAARC to date has been to furnish regular occasions for informal bilateral discussions at the highest levels.

To say that the establishment of SAARC was a considerable achievement and yet that its impact has been quite modest points to the delicacy and even difficulty of interstate relations in the region. The starting-point to an explanation has to be the disparate sizes of the seven States, in particular the bigness of India, three times larger (in area, more in population) than the other six put together, and its centrality too, which makes the others peripheral. But geography alone seldom dictates politics; three other factors have had crucial roles. First, the region has witnessed two partitions, that is, a double dose of that traumatic experience which deposits its own set of resentments and distrust. Second, there have been several regime changes which have had significant distancing effects on interstate relations: while India endured only a brief authoritarian interruption to its (however flawed) democratic government, Pakistan had very few years of functioning democracy and a quarter-century of military rule, Bangladesh followed suit in its briefer span, and Sri Lanka has suffered both a damaged democracy and a drift into civil war. Third, in recent years awareness in the region of India's predominant position has grown—for several reasons: her midwife role in the emergence of Bangladesh damaged Pakistan's morale and status (if not so obviously her power); her own economic development was sustained if undramatic; her defence capability has greatly increased during the past two decades. Not less important has been a change in India's own perception of its role; it has since the late 1960s turned from addressing a global audience on large issues of international morality towards dealing in a practical manner with the ample variety of more local difficulties, in effect making its weight felt where it really counts—within the region where it is dominant.

It will be useful first to set out some of the more salient phases in the relations of States of the region both *inter se* as well as at the supra-regional and sub-state levels.

1947. At the midnight hour on 14–15 August British rule on the subcontinent ceased, marking the beginning of the end of all European colonial rule and the entry on to the international scene of the Third World. At the same moment, through partition, two independent States of India and Pakistan came into existence.

The two States stemmed from two separate political movements in British India: the Indian National Congress (1885) purporting to speak for all Indians and the Muslim League (1906) purporting to speak for all Indian Muslims.[6] From the late 1930s the latter was indeed the spokesman for most Muslims living in the predominantly Hindu parts of India, while Congress was supported by most non-Muslim Indians. In 1940 the League passed a resolution which quickly came to be called 'the Pakistan resolution' even though the word did not appear in it; it made the claim that 'the areas in which the Muslims are in a majority, as in the north-western and eastern zones of India, should be grouped to constitute independent States'.[7] Whether Jinnah, the League's sole leader, seriously aimed at a separate State or intended to use it as a dramatic bargaining counter to secure the goal of equally shared power in a united India may never be certain.[8] In any event, by 1946 it was difficult for leaders to hold back followers, and by mid-1947 no answer was acceptable to both, except partition. With rival political passions rising and distrust turning to fear and hatred, with British power and will rapidly evaporating, partition was rushed through as an emergency-style and bloody operation.[9]

The very process, entailing perhaps some one million killings and ten times that number of refugees in the two-way flow, was a trauma which left a legacy of intense bitterness on both sides. Two aspects have to be noted as productive of special grievance and enduring consequences. Both, it may be added, represent outcomes of neglect and distraction attendant upon the speed of the complex operation. The first relates to Kashmir. It was only in July, a month before the final transfer, that it was made clear to the over 500 rulers of Princely States that they were required to sign instruments of accession to whichever of the two new sovereign States they would find themselves in. All but a handful quickly obliged, once they were persuaded that they had no alternative. But Kashmir bordered on both India and Pakistan and its Hindu ruler governed a Muslim-majority population. By 15 August he had failed to accede to either State and within a few weeks there were reports that Pakistan was first allowing and then encouraging the infiltration into Kashmir of armed Pathan tribesmen from the NW Frontier Province. As they neared Srinagar, India flew in its soldiers to halt the incursion—in exchange for the signature from the frightened ruler which sealed accession to India. A signal Pakistan grievance was born.[10] A second grievance arose from the need to divide the armed forces. A Joint Defence Council had been set up but the task was virtually left to a now powerless British former Commander-in-Chief who was to aim at a two-thirds to one-third split. The personnel sorted themselves out in such proportions fairly easily, simply by religion; Muslim officers and men moved over to constitute a new Pakistan Army. But arms, equipment and stores were not so easily shifted—and these were located preponderantly in India. By October the two armies were facing each other in Kashmir and the mediation-and-award task of the British general became impossible. The outcome was that Pakistan received only a small part of its one-third. To make matters worse it received only 19 per cent of the cash balances and 17 per cent of the sterling balances of the government of (undivided) India. Pakistan saw itself at the outset of its independent existence as cheated of the means to defend its territories against an unfriendly neighbour.[11]

The legacy of partition includes a couple of less tangible inequalities. One is 'merely' a question of names. Pakistan was clearly new and had therefore a new name. Since British India was dead and divided, Pakistan considered that the other new State needed a new name too, so as to make plain that there were two (equal in status) successor States. But India was, on grounds of principle as well as of convenience, determined to reject 'Hindustan' with its non-secular Hindu sound and to retain 'India'. Thus one successor State emerged a little more equal than the other, the successor to the Raj, no mere breakaway. A psychological point had been scored and, perhaps in the eyes of the world too, parity, even of esteem, had been denied to Pakistan. It is also worth adding that Pakistan suffered comparatively by being from its very conception doubly flawed. Its western and eastern wings were separated not only physically by over a thousand miles of India but also by large differences of language, social patterns, and culture; to compound the difficulty the capital and the dominant leadership were firmly located in the west, the east being virtually colonialized. Created solely on the basis of a shared adherence of the majority of the populations to Islam, only a dedicatedly Islamic ideology in both wings could conceivably have overcome the gulf between them; paradoxically a tendency in that direction in both wings became discernible only after they had broken apart in 1971.

A second handicap inherent in the design of Pakistan is less obvious but not less important. As already pointed out, Pakistan was built by the Muslim League on the foundation of Muslim grievances which were (except in Bengal) most marked where Muslims were a minority. But Pakistan's territory had to be defined as Muslim-majority areas. It followed that Pakistan's main leaders, moving in 1947 to West Pakistan, came as strangers to the promised land they were to rule. It was little wonder that elections were not readily embraced: within half a dozen years, aided certainly by the death of Jinnah and the assassination of Liaquat, democratic perspectives faded and a norm of authoritarian military-cum-bureaucratic rule came to be established with only brief exceptions. This distinctive type of regime constituted a further distancing factor in Indo-Pakistan relations.

1954. This year witnessed the signing of a Mutual Defence Assistance Treaty between the USA and Pakistan. This should not have been surprising as Pakistan, since its birth, had been begging the USA desperately for military aid to remedy its defencelessness *vis-à-vis* India. Initially the USA was otherwise concerned but by 1950–1 the relevance of South West Asia in terms of the Cold War became manifest and, in the wake of ties with Turkey and Iran, Pakistan soon came into view as a worthy cause. Moreover, Pakistan's security was strengthened not by arms alone but also by the new ties with the USA through SEATO and CENTO. An incidental consequence of these links was that Pakistan's Islamic eyes began to turn towards the Iranian and Arab worlds; closer diplomatic relations paved the way— especially after the Bangladesh break-up of Pakistan in 1971—for a variety of strong links, from military collaboration to the economic benefits of remittances home from some three million Pakistanis.

For India this new line-up was a most disagreeable shock. Apart from being a boost for a troublesome neighbour and an unwelcome distraction (despite some mollifying US economic aid) from domestic development programmes, a substantial superpower boot was now inside the door of the subcontinent and the fervently proclaimed cause of non-alignment was badly damaged. However, India was able to derive a little comfort from two other directions. First, this was the peak year of India–China friendship. It was a lonely peak because it had been preceded by the unease caused by the new Com-

munist regime's take-over of Tibet in 1950 which had eliminated
a buffer and brought China up to India's borders, thus unsettling the
Himalayan States of Nepal, Bhutan, and Sikkim and bringing a
potential power threateningly close to India's centres of population
and wealth. It was India's rather joyless recognition (*de facto* in 1950,
formally in 1954) of Tibet as a part, albeit with some autonomy, of
China which now led to the Nehru–Chou En-lai Joint Declaration of
1954 based on the 'five principles' of peace and friendship. But
already in 1956 a full-scale revolt in Eastern Tibet against the Chinese
met with repression and eventually the escape to India of the Dalai
Lama in 1959. The second comfort was of no great moment at the
time: a modest trade agreement had been signed with Moscow in
1953. This was unexpected because under Stalin the main Soviet
attitude to India had been a mixture of disregard and dismissal of
India as irredeemably bourgeois nationalist and Western-leaning. Yet
it presaged a Soviet reappraisal and was soon followed by aid for
building India's first giant steel plant.

1962. This was the year of high Himalayan drama when Chinese
forces made substantial incursions into North West India (the Aksai
Chin area between China, Tibet, and the Ladakh region of Kashmir)
and North East India (in Arunachal and adjacent to Bhutan). The
Indian Army held its ground well in the desolate Aksai Chin but
was severely mauled and surrounded in the north-east, eventually
escaping through Bhutan. The Chinese declared a cease-fire and
withdrew from the north-east, having taught India a Chinese lesson.

India was no doubt humiliated but not left without encouragement
from friends. Most speedy was the aid rushed in by the USA and
UK; most reassuring for the longer term were the fresh commitments
of arms supplies from the Soviet Union. India was able to observe not
only that both superpowers had come to India's aid but also that they
seemed to share the same view of China as a prime danger to
peace. Before long, however, India began to detect an even stranger
coming together of ideological opposites: Pakistan, a US client, was
developing friendly relations with China. Later fighting was to take
place between what seemed like ideological friends—on the Sino-
Soviet borders. In that double context the Soviet Union offered India
a treaty of friendship and co-operation; at that stage the offer was not
taken up. As regards India–China relations, the freeze proved very
long-lasting: an Indian approach in 1976 was sharply rebuffed; intermittent and rather laboured talks on the border resumed later; only

twenty-six years after their war did a top-level meeting take place at the end of 1988.

1965. In August Pakistan made an attempt to repeat in more systematic style its 1947 effort to solve by force its grievance against India over Kashmir where the 1949 UN cease-fire line had left all but the western fringe of the State in Indian hands. Pakistan infiltrated its own (mainly Kashmiri) commandos across the line—they received, contrary to Pakistan expectations, little support—followed by the Pakistan Army. The Indian Army responded by opening a second front across the Indo-Pakistan international boundary—another un-expected development—and heading convincingly for the Pakistan Army base at Sialkot. A UN cease-fire call met with a speedy response. These particular miscalculations apart, Pakistan (i.e. Ayub, advised by Bhutto) may have made two misjudgements: first, they may have thought that after Nehru's death there was no firm grip at the top, whereas Shastri was India's only underrated prime minister; second, they had gathered that there was anger in Kashmir at the arrest of the popular Shaikh Abdullah, thereby confusing anger against Delhi with love for Pakistan.

The Soviet Union emerged with some glory as an international peace-maker, moving the UN resolution and itself hosting the con-ference of the two sides at Tashkent (which broadly restored the 1949 line). Pakistan was as humiliated and Ayub as weakened as Nehru had been in 1962. But consolations came to both sides: while the USA placed an arms embargo on both contestants for a while, India received substantial arms from Moscow while Pakistan accepted its first weapons from China.

1971. During a crowded year South Asia witnessed the most striking birth of a new sovereign State since the end of European decolonization. Conception took place in the previous year when, for the first time in its twenty-three-year life, Pakistan held nation-wide elections. It was fully expected that in East Pakistan the Awami League led by Mujib-ur Rahman would perform well; even so, the massive scale of its victory on a bold manifesto of substantial autonomy for the province created unprecedented enthusiasm and high expectations among the Bengalis. By March 1971 lengthy and detailed talks between Islamabad and Dhaka on the degree and forms of autonomy finally broke down. Against a background of rising Bengali passion and a near breakdown of order in the eastern wing, the Pakistan government now under Yahya Khan decided to apply the force necessary to end disorder and preserve Pakistan by rein-forcing the army in the east (largely via Sri Lanka to avoid overflying India). The (mainly Punjabi) army was far from gentle but the popu-lation was far from submissive. The outcome was a large flow of refugees outwards and a resistance movement within. India gave the former shelter and let the world (which also shared the cost) know all about it; it also gave the latter a base from which to rest, recoup, and gather world support. India sensed that Pakistan's Army, with a virtual war of national liberation on its hands, yet with no line of retreat available physically or, seemingly, politically, could only become more desperate. So it was: air-raids on Indian territory on 3 December were the signal for an Indian offensive (though the Indian Army had quietly crossed the border, perhaps in exploratory fashion, some days before). Pakistan's third war with India was over in seven-teen days and Bangladesh was born. Pakistan's loss of status in the eyes of the world was considerable; whether it lost in political and economic terms is less clear, for the eastern wing was in any case becoming so highly intractable that even its value as a foreign exchange earner was likely to fall.[12]

In August, half-way through Pakistan's agony, India had signed the earlier offered and comprehensive Treaty of Peace, Friendship and Co-operation with the Soviet Union. It is easily seen as a valuable step for India in the context of the breakup of Pakistan, for its timing was good from the point of view of checking any 'tilt' towards Pakistan on the part of the USA and China. In fact already in April 1970 India had reached an agreement with Moscow that Tashkent even-handedness (including modest arms supplies to Pakistan) would cease and that India would shortly sign the full Treaty. Nor was the timing wholly related to the civil war in East Bengal. India already noted in July that Pakistan used its good connections with Beijing—where it was referred to as 'China's foremost ally'—to facilitate the visit of Kissinger to China which could pave the way for a Nixon visit. This caused considerable anxiety in Delhi where defence interests perceived a USA–Pakistan–China chain which could not only com-bine quantity and sophistication in arms supplies to Pakistan but also give China access to India in the North West (where the Khunjerab Pass road was soon to be completed with Chinese labour). Given such nightmare scenarios, the matching alliance with Moscow seemed a much-needed deterrent.

1974. A single event of a moment prompts the inclusion of 1974 as one of the nodal points. India exploded a nuclear device in the Rajasthan desert, ten years after China's similar test. That Pakistan too has been active in the development of a nuclear capability is confirmed by intense secrecy and clandestine procurement of necessary components. Also clear is the shared disregard and hostility in principle of both India and Pakistan to the Nuclear Non-Proliferation Treaty.

1979. In the previous year the classic buffer State of Afghanistan experienced a successful coup by leftist political leaders with the aid of elements in the armed forces. In early 1979 a momentous regime change took place in neighbouring Iran when the seemingly powerful government of the Shah crumbled to turmoil and was replaced by the rule of the Ayatollahs. At the end of the year Soviet armed forces entered Afghanistan to establish a government which would be both friendly and stable.

India had grave reservations about the Soviet intervention (and was more than a little upset that its treaty partner failed to consult or even inform it about the move), but it took a quietly understanding view and a decade later had greater unease at the prospect of an Islamic fundamentalist regime in Kabul closely allied to Pakistan and supported by the USA. The US position was initially, under Carter, cautious and chiefly exercised about the Gulf area. However Iranian events (which dealt a grievous blow at CENTO) coupled with those in Kabul certainly made Pakistan a key actor in American eyes. When Carter's offer of a grant of $400 million (half in military aid) in one budget year was dismissed rather pointedly as 'peanuts' by Zia, it is possible that he could see Reagan coming; soon the offer was raised to $3.2 billion over six years along with the right to purchase the precious F-16 aircraft. In exchange Pakistan coped with some 3 million Afghan refugees, served as a base for seven sets of Afghan guerrilla groups, acted as a conduit for arms to those forces, and saw itself become more than previously a gun- and drug-running society. Despite these travails, there were still funds left over to invest in Pakistan's own armed forces.

India certainly monitored Pakistan's gains and losses through the period of Afghanistan's Soviet presence. The US involvement in the Gulf entailed a stepping-up of its naval presence in the Indian Ocean centred on the Diego Garcia base. India had not only been for some years steadily building up its overall defence capability; it had also been paying increasing attention to its naval strength. While it was not displeased that the Soviet Navy in some measure kept up with the Americans, it focused too on its own navy and was gratified when Moscow let India have one of its nuclear-powered submarines to add to its strength in 'its own' ocean.

When after a decade of military support, the Soviet forces withdrew from Afghanistan in 1989, the expected collapse of the Kabul regime did not follow; indeed, Najibullah was well received in Delhi. The anti-Kabul guerrilla resistance groups continued sporadically to attack at strategic points but seemed at the same time to be devoid of all earlier semblance of cohesion—as well as any concerted USA–Pakistan sustenance.

1987. In July was signed the remarkable Indo-Sri Lanka Accord designed to bring to an end a virtual state of civil war begun some four years earlier between the Tamil and Sinhalese peoples of the island. The Accord affirmed, to Sinhalese satisfaction, 'the unity, sovereignty and territorial integrity of Sri Lanka' but conceded towards the Tamil demand for a separate State of 'Tamil Eelam' that provinces would become significant units of government and that the Northern (heavily Tamil) and Eastern (tripartite mixture of Tamils, Tamil-speaking Muslims, and Sinhalese) provinces would be merged into one—with the important proviso that one year after merger a referendum of Eastern province citizens would decide whether to continue merged or return to separation. The Accord additionally envisaged an immediate cease-fire to be enforced not by the Sri Lankan army (which was to quit the north-east) but by the Indian Army. Also attached to the Accord was an exchange of letters which stated that Sri Lankan security relations of significance with foreign governments would be modified or terminated—a provision ignored by Sri Lanka a few years later.

The Indian peace-keeping force initially succeeded in restoring order so that a coalition of Tamil and Muslim parties could form a North-East Joint Council. But the Liberation Tigers of Tamil Eelam declined to surrender arms and carried out bloody attacks on Sinhalese, Muslims, and collaborating Tamils, eventually retreating to their core area of the Jaffna peninsula. There they stayed, virtually in command; with local support, good terrain knowledge, and kamikaze methods, they held the IPKF (at times over 80,000 strong) and inflicted heavy casualties. By 1990 Sinhalese disenchantment with the Indian presence and Indian despair at lack of success came together in an agreed withdrawal of the IPKF. By then also the elimination of the JVP Sinhalese terrorists in the south had been achieved, so that Sri Lankan forces were freed to take the Indians' place—with, however, as little success. The reported involvement of the Tigers in the 1991 assassination of Rajiv Gandhi may however have damaged their Madras haven beyond repair.

What Sri Lanka has suffered from ethnic conflict for a full decade has, rather more recently, been matched by India. (Pakistan has suffered less but in Sind sporadically violent confrontations between Mahajir incomers—immigrants from the partitions of 1947 and 1971 —and Pathans and between both and the local Sindhis have become endemic.) The Indian Army has been notably engaged in Assam and even more saliently in Punjab and Kashmir. Assam is geographically at once somewhat isolated from core India and adjacent to five relatively new quasi-tribal States. Conflict therefore occurs within the general region and between it and Delhi. But it is also a frontier zone; neither the porous Burma border to the east nor the Chinese border to the north give Delhi peace of mind. Punjab has endured turmoil for a decade with an annual death toll of about 2,000 for much of the period. Militancy within the distinctive, majority Sikh community, was initially sparked by ill-advised Congress party politicking and then consolidated towards aspirations for a Sikh State of Khalistan by the shocking use of the Army to shoot its way into the Golden Temple in 1984. Mrs Gandhi paid for that decision with her life and her assassination prompted Hindu mobs in Delhi to a mass slaughter of Sikhs. Both political solutions and anti-terrorist war have been attempted and have failed to take the problem out of the category 'intractable'.[13]

Deserving of the same term is the nearby Kashmir problem. Although the Sikh war has a slight international component—the militants are alleged to have found haven and help from across the Pakistan border—Kashmir is more patently an Indo-Pakistan confrontation: the Indian Army has since 1989 been heavily engaged against Kashmiri guerrillas who have got the scent of Islamic fundamentalism as well as arms and training from the other side of the cease-fire line, in Pakistan-held Kashmir and Pakistan itself. In Kashmir, before and after 1947, the majority Muslim community had lived peaceably with the Hindu minority, sharing a strong sense of Kashmiri identity. Now most Hindus have fled to Hindu zones or to Delhi and most Muslims support their fighters.[14]

What does this sketch of key episodes over the past half-century tell us about the States of South Asia?

The once 'new States' are no longer new but age scarcely dim-

inishes jealous regard for their status and powers. Whether large or
small, each State of the region is acutely aware of inequalities both
inter se and in relation to greater powers beyond. A time there
was when India from its central position preached to the rest of
the subcontinent and even to the world. Its message was that the
superpowers—some more than others—were to be distrusted as
perniciously destabilizing influences, that new States should avoid
alignment with them in their collision courses, and that India's neighbours should heed advice from an elder brother. Pakistan early
closed its ears; the others kept their own counsel and tended their
fences. Fifty years on, the preaching has stopped but India's centrality
has become more markedly hegemonic. Accordingly mutual wariness
persists.

Meanwhile the wider world from the late 1980s has experienced a
transformation which even South Asia has to recognize. The breakup
and crumbling away of ideological cement in the Soviet Union and
Eastern Europe has set in motion a certain dismantling of armed
forces and an emergence of new nationalisms and even some new
nation-states. Furthermore, the emergence of the USA as the sur-
viving great power—China has for its own reasons turned inwards
and come to focus on matters in its own vicinity—at once revealed
and underlined the presence in the Soviet Union of more than a
collapse of a doctrine: an economy in ruins. The effect was at once to
make more salient than ever the economic relations of States. There
are still three great powers, but they are a different three—the USA,
an integrating Europe of uncertain scope, and Japan—and their
greatness is economic. Their interest will be in trade and investment,
anywhere opportunity beckons. At least one possibility could be the
further marginalization and dependence of the Third World.

Given that scenario, South Asia may be less easily marginalized
than Africa but less well equipped than much of South East Asia. Its
main components, India and Pakistan, may well find themselves
differently placed: Pakistan will surely cultivate further its economic
links with South West Asia; India has no comparable entrée to South
East Asia but, apart from being itself a large world, it may be big
enough to secure fruitful ties with the USA and Europe, especially if
its recent radical policy changes, away from governmental ownership
and controls towards a more welcoming view of foreign investment,
become firmly established.

Indeed the question is: how far, within the now changed world, will South Asia itself be able to change? The answer will have to be given mainly by the bigger countries, notably India—who may not find it easy to shake off her old image of great powers as obsessively 'interventionist'[15] and bent on the creation of 'client States'. And the answer has very largely to take the form of the prescription, 'doctor, heal thyself'. For as things stand, the perception held of South Asia by most of the world is one of a fractured region of fractured States, an unenticing world of little cohesion. Repairs are needed at both levels: relations among the States and between the component communities within each State (excepting only the minuscule Maldives).

Of the interstate relations, India–Pakistan remains central. The big power connections of each have been loosened: Pakistan, no longer a key instrument in America's Afghanistan concerns, yet persisting in its nuclear weapons programme, suffered in 1990 a sharp cut-off of US aid; India, though never so dependent on the Soviet Union, has discovered that there is now only a void to lean on. But shared disillusionment with their respective friends brought no friendship between themselves; the outside ties had been aggravations to underlying mutual distrust. Nor did the advent of civilian governments in Pakistan from 1988 bring real *rapprochement* nearer; regime similarities may ease discourse but perceptions of conflicting interests hold, especially since Pakistan's long periods of military rule could return.[16] India's regional pre-eminence—in size, centrality, defence capability, undramatic but substantial economic development, and political stability—is a perpetual irritant and challenge to Pakistan, from which armed conflict has thrice ensued. However, latterly their confrontations have related less to past legacies than to current Indian failures of internal conflict management.

Indeed the truth is that interstate fractures and intrastate fractures can be mutually aggravating. India's internal wars in Assam and Punjab have had only a marginal interstate component; rather, essentially domestic dissent has been either incompetently handled (as in Assam where admitted complexities were poorly grasped and allowed to fester) or culpably mishandled (as in Punjab where central interference crippled a moderate Sikh leadership and so created an extremist monster). Kashmir's war, however, is in a different category. It was contested territory from the start. But the absence of a clear welcome for the Pakistani forces when they invaded in 1965 showed Kashmir to be still essentially its own individual self. It is hard to believe that some further enhancement of its distinctive status could not have checked the inroads of Islamic fundamentalism. However, instead of seriously seeking a political solution, Delhi set the army to work.

Why it did so relates to a different and newly significant intrastate fracture in India: the recent rise, so far mainly in Northern India, of what has perhaps to be called Hindu fundamentalism. The term is partly misleading in so far as it suggests similarity with the Islamic form whereas, while Islam is spread internationally and is doctrinally relatively coherent, Hinduism is virtually confined to India and is doctrinally extremely multifaceted. Nevertheless in recent years it has acquired an almost unprecedented revivalism at both sophisticated and popular levels—plus a sharply political thrust spearheaded by the Bharatiya Janata Party and even more extremist organizations. It expresses through symbols and rituals pride in the ancient history and colourful forms of Hinduism; it constitutes an assertion of national identity and a rejection of Nehru's striving for a secular State. Hindu India has probably never been moved as it was in 1990 when the call went forth to build a temple to the mythological god Ram at the supposed site of Ram's birth, occupied since the sixteenth century by a mosque built by the Moghul Emperor Babar; the party's leader in a Hindu chariot undertook a six-week *rathyatra* (pilgrimage procession) and thousands of sanctified bricks were carried towards the site; communal violence flared and the army had to move in. While it is true that Hindu and Muslim were always both side by side yet distinct and sometimes in confrontation, now a deepening divide appears. How far the Kashmir (and perhaps Punjab) fighting spurred or was spurred by the new fundamentalism is uncertain; that the latter stands firmly in the way of a political resolution of the former is sure. It has to be added that India's contribution to the management of relations with Pakistan is weakened by uncertainties in its political system. With the assassinations of both Indira Gandhi and her son Rajiv, rather more happened than the end of the 1947–91 Nehru dynasty; the party system itself has lost clear shape and coherence.

By comparison to Indo-Pakistan relations, all others on the subcontinent are almost peripheral and mainly centred on India. Bangladesh had handy support from India at the time of its birth but that created no substantive gratitude. If anything, a sense of a common culture between the two Bengals has been eroded by separate statehood and increased Bangladeshi (Gulf-assisted) stress on Islam, while awkward problems of shared river waters and cross-border population movements produce accords only with difficulty. Nor can Bangladesh look to its former dominant partner and then enemy for support, least of all when Pakistan shows no interest in accepting responsibility for the mainly Bihari Muslims stranded in Bangladesh.

A not dissimilar mixture of caution and distrust obtains between India and Sri Lanka, despite both the removal of the former's peace-keeping force and India's disenchantment with the Tamils (especially the Tigers) of Sri Lanka. The distance across the twenty-mile Palk Strait appears to be widening, but to the Sinhalese the Indian brother still looks big. For both Bangladesh and Sri Lanka friendly hands from a safe distance are not easily found.

Of the three remaining States, Nepal and Bhutan are land-locked and the Maldives sea-locked. Of the last no more need be said than that the government there will remember with gratitude India's speedy dash across the ocean to snuff out an attempted coup. The Kingdoms of Nepal and Bhutan are more complex and have called for delicate handling.[17] Bhutan's *de jure* status was left a little unclear by the British who had accorded it internal sovereignty in 1910 but provided that its external relations were to be conducted under advice from Delhi. India confirmed this position in 1949 but at once became anxious when China first entered Tibet in 1950. Bhutan for some time resisted Indian pressures with spirit and skill, but when the revolt in Tibet was crushed and the refugees had to escape to India in 1959 and even more when three years later China attacked India in the vicinity of Bhutan's borders, the tune changed. Bhutan was content enough to accept from India economic aid, a road-building programme, and army training. However, subservience was never comfortable and in 1971 Bhutan secured India's sponsorship of its UN membership and it has been able, and allowed, cautiously to show its independence.[18] Even tiny Bhutan, however, has room for an internal fracture: a Nepali minority in the southern areas chafes at its lack of adequate representation.

The larger Nepal, despite its being a Hindu Kingdom and also because of its unambiguously independent status, has been a con-tinuous problem for India—and vice versa. Each country has sub-stantial minorities from the other; India has assisted dissident critics of autocratic royal rule; treaties relating to trade and transit, so vital to land-locked Nepal, have to be regularly and painfully renegotiated with an India which holds the screws. India has not been ungenerous but Nepal did cause India angry anxiety when it accepted an offer from the Chinese (for their own reasons) to build a road through to Kathmandu from Tibet. Nepal's hopes for Chinese trade and arms were however not much realized. Latterly, after the turbulent replacement in 1990 of nearly absolute royal rule by a democratically elected government, relations with India improved.

What prospects emerge from this survey for South Asia in the run-up to the next century? The region will no doubt seek to adapt to the changed world-scene in its own distinctive fashion. Put most generally, it will continue to be greatly self-absorbed—for the reason that each country's problems are pressing and because their relations with their neighbours are difficult. At the same time, and precisely for those very reasons, there will be some striving by each at once to escape from the local deadlocks and find succour through links with friendly powers outside their immediate vicinity. Whether they will find takers for their propositions is uncertain; the circle may have a vicious quality in that outside perceptions of the region's attractiveness may await clear improvements within the region. India's hegemony within the region will remain, even if it fails to do more than contain its internal stresses. Acknowledgement of that hegemony by the others will not come easily, least of all by Pakistan. Overall, the obstacles to peaceful advancement of the region appear substantial. Yet the energies and talents of its peoples are so manifest that such appearances may well prove deceptive.

NOTES

1. This chapter began its life as a paper for the Institute of International Relations at Geneva. It has been improved by comments from Anirudha Gupta, Peter Lyon, James Manor, Norman Palmer, and Leo Rose.
2. The Caribbean is also a candidate, but so much smaller and fragmented; also with a population whose base was of uprooted incomers rather than inheritors of successive civilizations of the area.
3. The story of the unrealized vision of Sir Stafford Cripps, seeking in 1947 to establish Indo-Pakistan 'bridges' in the form of joint authorities at the time of partition, is told in my 'Transfer of Power, 1947', in *Modern Asian Studies*, 16 (1982).
4. The seven-member composition of SAARC has been mainly non-problematic. However, the question of Afghanistan's admission to SAARC was, somewhat surprisingly, raised by India at the 1987 summit but, seemingly on Pakistan's initiative, the matter was not pursued.

5. Trade expansion within South Asia is extensively discussed in an issue of *South Asia Journal*, 1/2 (Oct.–Dec. 1987). One of the articles, by Abid Hussain of the Indian Planning Commission, gives useful figures showing the region's 'insignificant' share of world trade and the 'marginal character' of intraregional trade.

6. That the movements were separate owed something to British attempts at understanding the composition of Indian society by identifying constituent 'communities', something also to their later perception that 'counterweights' could ease pressures on them as rulers. Above all, separateness stemmed from the slower rate of adaptation and modernization among Muslims in the late 19th century.

7. The plural last word, 'States', is interesting and reflects in part no doubt Jinnah's inadequate central control of the League in 1940. More curious, however, is the fact that most Bengali leaders of the League remained silent on the point in 1946–7; the focus by then was on the break with India (once the brief life of a 'United Bengal' proposal had been ended).

8. The latter view is well argued in A. Jalal, *The Sole Spokesman: Jinnah, the Muslim League and the Demand for Pakistan* (London, 1985).

9. Who can with certainty hold that delay would have cost less?

10. Allied to this grievance is another, namely the Pakistan conviction, now essentially untestable, that the final Boundary Commission award was 'fixed' to provide India with its only easy road access to Kashmir.

11. See A. Jalal, 'India's Partition and the Defence of Pakistan', *Journal of Imperial and Commonwealth History*, 15/3 (May 1987). Gandhi protested to the Indian government and soon was assassinated by a Hindu extremist.

12. I may here relate a curious episode experienced at some date in the early 1960s. A young Pakistani naval officer (who understandably wished to remain anonymous) on a brief service visit to the UK asked for a private appointment at a quiet off-peak time in a Pakistani restaurant in London. He claimed that younger officers in the armed forces were disenchanted with Ayub Khan's leadership and a group was planning a coup. Once successful, an urgent priority on their agenda was to seek a deal with India: the province of E. Bengal, which they saw as not really a fitting part of Pakistan, would be offered in exchange for the whole of Kashmir which Pakistan prized profoundly. Would the Indian Government be likely to agree? I said I considered it most improbable.

13. See G. Singh, 'The Punjab Problem in the 1990s', *Journal of Commonwealth and Comparative Politics*, 29/2 (July 1991).

14. However the fighters are not unified and agreed about goals: one group looks to join Pakistan but the other seeks independent statehood.

15. Nehru may have initiated the theme but Indira made several dark references to 'foreign hands', only to be outdone in that by her son.

16. Correlations between army uniforms and belligerency are not secure; it was Mr Bhutto, not General Zia, who spoke of 'a hundred years war with India'.

17. See L. Rose, *Nepal: Strategy for Survival* (Berkeley, Calif., 1971) and the same author's *The Politics of Bhutan* (Ithaca, NY, 1977), esp. ch. 2. A distinction at least of degree can be drawn between Bhutan and Sikkim. Although the British found both areas obstructive in the 19th century and fought wars against them, British paramountcy was formally and in practical terms clear in Sikkim, where a Political Officer was appointed (as if in an Indian Princely State) and a Ruler was removed, interned, and replaced. In 1974 elections brought a demand for full accession to India and an end to the Ruler's power. A year later Sikkim became the 22nd State of the Indian Union. See N. Sengupta, *State Government and Politics: Sikkim* (New Delhi, 1985).

FURTHER READING

Barnad, W. J., *India, Pakistan and the Great Powers* (London, 1972).

Buzan, B., and Rizvi, G., *South Asian Insecurity and the Great Powers* (London, 1986).

Duncan, P. J. S., *The Soviet Union and India* (London, 1989).

George, T., *Security in Southern Asia: India and the Great Powers* (London, 1984).

Hussain, N. A., and Rose, L. E. (eds.), *Pakistan-US Relations* (Berkeley, Calif., 1988).

9

South East Asia

R. S. MILNE[1]

Old Societies and New States, a truly magnificent title, indicating major social transformations in South East Asia, but subject to some qualifications.[2] What of the old States and the new societies? Some new States can clearly be seen to derive from old ones (or at least from mythical versions of them).[3] Many new States in this region have been around for thirty or forty years. By now, we have grown quite accustomed to their shape. The question is: given the vast disparities in their sizes, populations, and resources, how have they managed to survive?

There are ten States conventionally treated as comprising South East Asia. Nine were formerly colonies or protectorates—Burma, Malaysia, Singapore, and Brunei (British), Indonesia (Dutch), the Philippines (American), and three Communist Indo-Chinese countries, Vietnam, Cambodia—for a time known as Kampuchea—and Laos (French). Thailand was never a colony. Indonesia is the largest and most populous (about 185 million). Vietnam, the Philippines, and Thailand have populations ranging from 60 to 75 million each, while Brunei has the smallest population (about 0.2 million), and is the second smallest in territory, Singapore being the smallest at 240 square miles. Per capita income is lowest in the three Indo-Chinese States and in Indonesia, and is highest in Brunei, followed by Singapore.

In this chapter 'survival' is used in a restricted sense, to refer to the persistence of boundaries. The nature of the regime inside these boundaries may undergo drastic transformations, while the State's appearance on the map remains the same—Cambodia is a case in point.[4]

COLONIAL BOUNDARIES AND BOUNDARIES
AFTER INDEPENDENCE

Generally speaking, the boundaries of South East Asian States follow previous colonial boundaries—decolonization was not co-ordinated by the colonial powers. It is easy to imagine other possible boundaries, if the circumstances had been slightly different, e.g. if the Spaniards had arrived a few years later than they did in what they christened the Philippines, the Visayas or even Southern Luzon might by then have been under Muslim occupation. Objections to the boundaries of the new States came from two main sources, although Great Powers which were not the former colonial power sometimes also became involved, especially in Indo-China. Some objections came from another new South East Asian country, e.g. the Philippines' claim to Sabah. Other objections came from (often ethnic) groups inside the newly created States. Because, upon independence, colonial boundaries were followed quite closely, antagonistic ethnic groups might live close together in a single State. (It should be noted that *any* conceivable borders would leave a sizeable number of people on the 'wrong' side of 'their' ethnic boundary.) Additionally, in Vietnam and Indonesia the claims of dissenting groups became associated with the struggle for independence and led to the alignment of groups either with or against the colonial power. Some internal disputes were resolved fairly rapidly. Others, however, still persist.

Just how closely were colonial boundaries followed? The general pattern was that: (1) at the time of independence the new State inherited all the administrative domain of the colonial power; (2) where adjacent territories *were* divided, this usually reflected status/ administrative divisions already existing under the colonial power; and (3) with one exception—East Timor—subsequent additions to independent States consisted of nearby territories belonging to the *same* colonial power.

The first case (1) is exemplified by Burma and the Philippines. Under (2) there are three sets of examples, the colonial powers being Britain, The Netherlands, and France. Singapore was separated from Malaya in 1946, later acquiring control over its own internal affairs, and the post-war (1946) Crown colonies of Sarawak and North Borneo retained their status for a time, as did the protectorate of Brunei—until 1984 when it became independent once more. For the French and Dutch colonies the process was more complex because

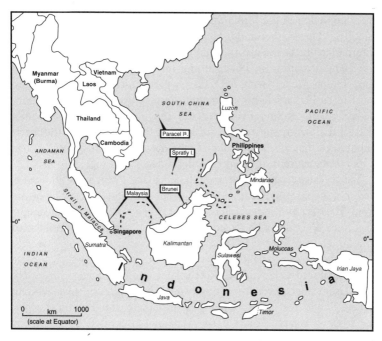

FIG. 9.1 South East Asia

full independence was denied by the colonial power, and armed conflict followed. In each case the colonial power attempted to make distinctions in the degree of independence accorded to its former possessions, to its own advantage—'divide and differentially quit', as it were. As far as Vietnam was concerned, the transition to independence in the form of a single State was prolonged by the agreeme ts arrived at during the Geneva Conference (1954), by the emergence of South Vietnam (quite widely recognized as a sovereign State), and by warfare until the proclamation of a united Vietnam in 1976. The other new States concerned, Cambodia, Laos, and Indonesia, achieved independence more quickly from their respective colonial rulers, in the 1950s.

Under (3), Sarawak, North Borneo (Sabah), and, temporarily, Singapore, joined Malaya in Malaysia (1963), and Indonesia 'incorporated' West Irian in the same year. The exception under this heading is that in 1975–6 Indonesia took over East Timor, a former Portuguese colony. The incorporation of West Irian could be seen as the completion of the formation of Indonesia, because both had been ruled by The Netherlands. However, there was greater opposition, internationally, to the incorporation of East Timor in 1976. Following the 1974 revolution in Portugal and the collapse of colonial rule in East Timor, the left-wing FRETILIN party emerged as the strongest local force. After lengthy negotiations and a declaration of independence by the Ruling Front for the Independence of East Timor (FRETILIN), Indonesian troops entered the territory and Indonesia announced that, in the absence of effective Portuguese control, it had a moral obligation to guarantee orderly decolonization.

These categories do not include Thailand (which, as indicated, had not been colonized). Also, Singapore's non-violent departure from Malaysia and independence (1965) constitutes the only example of a State's coming into existence which had previously formed part of a larger new State.[5]

The post-1945 balance sheet therefore is as follows. No State which achieved independence lost it later on. Two States, Singapore and Brunei, acquired/reacquired it—ironically, not just without having fought for it, but actually against their will! For the former, the loss of a larger market (in Malaysia) presented an economic problem. For the latter, the loss of a protector (Britain) constituted a security problem.

(In the foregoing type of analysis, the temptation to use terms such as the 'birth' or 'death' of States should be resisted. People differ too much from States for such analogies to be apposite.[6] Sometimes they could even lead to absurdities. It would be hard to describe Brunei's 'resumption' of sovereignty in 1984 in human terms except by saying that it had been born again—incongruous in view of the country's ethnic composition.)

BOUNDARY CHANGES AND CLAIMS

Less dramatic alterations in the catalogue of States are boundary changes and claims not affecting the number of States. Sometimes there are claims because an area of special value is disputed. One of these concerned Cambodia and Thailand who contested an area where a temple was located. In 1962 the International Court of Justice supported Cambodia's claim, a decision accepted by Thailand. If boundaries are in sparsely populated and in remote areas, there may be little concern expressed, unless the territories are important strategically or have rich resources. Water boundaries may be hard to enforce and may be conducive to smuggling or piracy, as in the areas between Sabah (Malaysia) and Sulu (Philippines), Singapore and Sulawesi (Indonesia), or Singapore and the (Indonesian) Riau Islands. Recent changes, or claims for change, in maritime boundaries afford increased potentialities for conflict.[7]

Foremost among territorial claims has been the Philippines' claim to part of Sabah, based on the contention that in 1878 the Sultan of Sulu had leased, not ceded, the territory to the predecessors of the North Borneo Company, from whom it passed to the British Crown.[8] Endemic for years, it regained prominence in 1962, and has still not been entirely laid to rest. In 1988 agreement was retarded by Malaysian arrests of Filipino fishermen, which led to mutual re-criminations of violating each other's waters, exacerbated by defective map reading on the part of a Filipino naval officer.[9]

In the late 1960s Brunei revived a claim to Limbang (Sarawak, Malaysia), which had been seized by Sarawak in 1890. In May 1987 it was alleged—but denied by the Malaysian government—that Malaysia might return the territory to Brunei in exchange for financial compensation.

Finally, there are claims by several countries to portions of the Spratly Islands, inhabited only by soldiers, whose name suggests their minute size but underrates their strategic (and mineral resources) potential. The islands are close to the path of the vital sea routes that link the Indian and Pacific oceans. Chinese sovereignty was challenged in the 1930s, and now five countries have opposing claims —China, Taiwan, Vietnam, Malaysia, and the Philippines. In July 1991 the first three of these and the Association of South East Asian (ASEAN) States agreed not to use force on the issue.

The fighting in Indo-China has produced, or revived, surprisingly few boundary claims. One was Laos's historical claim to areas in north-east Thailand, which led to border clashes in 1984 and 1987–8.[10] However, the Chatichai government's 1988 move towards *rapprochement* with Vietnam and Laos led to efforts to resolve these boundary disputes.

INTERNAL REVOLTS

South East Asia has been characterized as a 'region of revolt' and has had almost fifty post-independence armed rebellions.[11] Yet there have been only two major revisions of the map (apart from those arising from the creation or abolition of States), and both have been on the periphery of the region (the inclusion in Indonesia of West Irian in 1963 and East Timor, 1975–6). Strictly speaking these were not solely the consequences of internal revolt but were shaped substantially by external intervention. Many of the revolts (proper) no longer constitute grave threats to security, and certainly not to boundaries, notably revolts in Indonesia soon after independence which assumed 'regional' or 'religious' forms, and communist revolts in Malaysia and Thailand.[12]

Two important considerations affect the number of revolts and their strength. On the one hand, some rebel movements are pacified by provisions for autonomy which stop short of secession. On the other hand, although some rebels do not win independence, neither is the government able to suppress them, which results in a stalemate. Consequently, some *de facto* autonomy is achieved, as in Burma and the Philippines.

Currently, the major revolts are in the Philippines, Thailand, Burma, and East Timor. The Philippines suffers from two revolts, one (currently less serious) in the southern island of Mindanao, led by the Muslim National Liberation Front (MNLF), and another carried on by the New People's Army (NPA) all over the country.[13] The MNLF was founded in 1968 and has been operating, on and off, ever since. Religion has been a binding force, but the revolt was based mainly on economic distress, and by Muslims' eviction from their land by a large influx of Christian immigrants. Marcos had considerable success in weakening the force of the revolt, from time to time, by buying off some of its leaders. There was a cease-fire agreement with the Aquino government in 1987, although some fighting still goes on.

The NPA is the military wing of the Communist Party of the Philippines—Marxist-Leninist (CPP)—a breakaway movement from the pro-Soviet Communist Party, which had conducted a major part of the resistance against the Japanese but had been largely subdued by the government during the 1950s. Attempts by the Aquino government to reach a *modus vivendi* with the CPP failed, and the revolt continues, although its impetus has slackened.[14]

Thai ethnic revolts have been on a much smaller scale. Before 1985 there were four principal Muslim secessionist movements, all operating in the south of the country, where in some parts about 40 per cent of the population is Muslim. In 1985 three of them formed a coalition. Recently, the thrust of the revolts has been greatly blunted by measures giving autonomy to areas in the south and providing more opportunities for upward mobility for educated Thai Muslims.

In Burma, minority ethnic group disaffection has existed since independence, the Burmans having played the major part in the nationalist movement which obtained it.[15] Dissidence was intensified after the 1962 military coup, and further confirmed by the, in effect, unitary constitution of 1974. Nearly every ethnic group has its own movement and its own army, sometimes more than one. Even the Communist Party of Burma (CPB) is overwhelmingly non-Burman ethnically. Many of the ethnic movements finance themselves by smuggling, through levies on goods passing through their territories, and by participating in the opium trade, particularly in the notorious 'Golden Triangle', where Burma, China, and Laos meet. Revenue-raising has often become their chief concern.

Since Indonesia took over East Timor, 1975–6, the main armed resistance has been conducted by FRETILIN. Originally quite intense, resistance dwindled (as did opposition from the Melanesian Free Papua Movement in Irian Jaya). However, in November 1991 Indonesian troops shot into a crowd in Dili, East Timor's capital, killing or wounding hundreds and producing an international outcry.

By their very nature, 'ethnic' revolts are likely to have sectional objectives. Their most ambitious aim would be secession, not taking over the entire country. In fact, only the Thai groups in revolt seem to be consistently in favour of secession, which may partly account for their small degree of support. The MNLF in the Philippines went through a series of switches on the choice between secession and autonomy before agreeing to settle for autonomy in 1986–7. In Burma, similar switches along the secession–autonomy spectrum have occurred. Not only do 'ethnic' revolts in a country vary in their objectives, the groups themselves are often ethnically antagonistic. Ethnicity, therefore, is at the same time a basis for revolt but also a hindrance to *co-ordinated* revolt. Even if there were some measure of co-ordination, the State is too strong for revolt to prevail.

WITH A LITTLE HELP FROM MY FRIENDS

Internal revolts quite often have external links, although intervening countries usually operate with circumspection. The MNLF, for example, is believed to have received aid (in finances and in material) from Libya, and possibly from Iran, as well as from Islamic Conference member States. Until 1976 some help came from, or via, Sabah (Malaysia). The Malaysian government behaved with propriety. It has also refrained from supporting rebel movements in Thailand, although devout Muslim parties and movements in Malaysia have expressed support for these movements. They have also had help from Libya.

The Communist Party in Burma has received help from China. Thailand, because of ethnic affinities, is sympathetic towards the Shans. However, in 1988 Thailand started a new and profitable relationship with Burma. It obtained concessions in timber, minerals, and fish, which improved the Burmese government's shaky finances and weakened Thailand's support for the Shans. In Kampuchea, there has been help from outside for the various factions of the tripartite coalition opposing the Heng Samrin regime, from China for the Khmer Rouge, and from the USA for the two non-communist components of the coalition. The regime itself received external support from the Soviet Union.

However, when considering giving aid to rebels, countries are inhibited by the same considerations which apply to their policies on territorial expansion—their own fragility and the desire not to endanger stability. Also, their sources of external aid may differ, because the providers have varying ethnic contacts or preferences.[16]

DISINCENTIVES TO TERRITORIAL EXPANSION

The survival of States and the limited impact of territorial claims and internal revolts is especially surprising when two other circumstances are considered: the importance generally attached to territory and the extreme weakness of some of the States in the area. Possession of territory is an essential element in the definition of a State. The amount of territory available is limited, hence the fierce devotion of governments to their territory, and sometimes to the acquisition of more territory.[17] Contemplation of land or territory stimulates the emotions, as when President Sukarno is reputed to have said that even a child could look at a map and see the natural unity of Indonesia.

Some States may be so weak[18] that they seem almost to present an easy target for aggression. This might be because of their small size, or because they lack control of large portions of their territory— Burma and the Philippines are good examples—arising from a failure to penetrate and influence society. Although sovereign in respect of their relations with other States, internally such States are neither fully effective nor fully legitimate.[19]

In spite of these considerations, there are several disincentives to territorial expansion, and to encouraging revolts in other countries. Some rest on self-interest, on a State's consciousness of its fragility and overriding desire to secure its own stability.[20] 'Consequently, there has been more interest in securing authority within one's own State than in promoting instability in others.'[21] This is one reason why Islamic Conference members have limited the amount of help they have given to the MNLF. In addition to the requirements of financial prudence, each member has actual or potential forces inside its own State which threaten its stability.[22] It is understood that it is in the interest of all concerned not to 'rock the boat', especially if there is doubt about its ability to meet minimum safety standards. A second disincentive is that frequent meetings of a group of leaders (e.g. in ASEAN) may develop a 'club' atmosphere, in which gentle-men's agreements are possible, and in which conflicting interests may be more easily resolved on the basis of established and valued personal contacts.

Other disincentives have been suggested, but they seem to lack much effect. One is based on the premise that, if a territorial claim were effectively established, the territory acquired would probably be hard to govern. However, there is no evidence that, say, the Philippines has ever seriously thought about this with regard to the Sabah claim. Similarly, so deep is the attachment of States to their territory that they are loath to abandon even territories which are obviously difficult to govern. Burma constitutes a rather special case, because, although its government's capabilities are low, its power-ful neighbours China and India do not threaten it. The existence of numerous dissident ethnic groups would pose problems for any country that wanted to invade and govern it. Neither China nor India is much interested in it, and both appreciate its value as a neutral, isolationist, and autarkic buffer State. Neither has a historic unfulfilled territorial claim on Burma.

The nature of the disincentives may be spelled out in more detail by referring to ASEAN and the ways in which conflicts between its member States have been reduced. '[The] ASEAN States hang together in part from a common awareness that conflict among them would be more likely to exacerbate their domestic political fragilities than to override them.'[23] This attitude was implicit in the Declaration of ASEAN Concord signed in Bali in February 1976. Clarifying rules on which the members were already acting, and reaffirming commitment to the UN Charter, the Declaration required them to respect each other's territorial integrity, settle their disputes peacefully through the organization's good offices, and co-ordinate views and policies on international and regional issues through regular contacts and consultations.[24] Thus, differences were to be resolved internally if possible, and outside States and other organizations were to be given minimal opportunities to intervene.

In a wider context, ASEAN demonstrated its strongest support for the principle of territorial integrity after Vietnam's invasion and occupation of Cambodia. By upholding the tripartite coalition—whose leading element was the notorious Khmer Rouge—ASEAN affirmed the view that the Pol Pot regime's gross human rights transgressions could not be put forward as an excuse for the violation of Cambodia's frontiers. ASEAN-wide agreements are often supplemented by bilateral ones. These mostly have to do with defence, through arrangements for training, weapon-testing, etc.

An important exception was a 1978 pact between Singapore's Prime Minister Lee Kuan Yew and Malaysia's Dr Mahathir (even before he became Prime Minister). The two countries agreed that they would not meddle, interfere, or support opposition groups in each other's home ground. Good personal relations are vital, especially in Asian diplomacy, and require building up over a long period. Mr Lee Kuan Yew was assiduous in cultivating rapport with President Suharto, in view of Indonesia's major role in ASEAN and the need to bridge the two countries' different cultural orientations.[25] Lee made a point of having the younger generation of Singapore leaders meet their opposite numbers from the other ASEAN countries.

ASEAN has certainly followed energetically the injunction to make contacts and hold consultation. There are about four hundred official ASEAN meetings a year. As a general rule, new ASEAN leaders make their first visits abroad to the other ASEAN countries. Where ASEAN countries send representatives to meetings with a wider membership, they are likely to have frequent contacts and consultations among themselves. It is also the practice that when a high-level diplomat from another ASEAN State passes through Singapore, his (approximate) counterpart in Singapore will go to the airport to have a brief conversation with him. If disputes do arise between ASEAN members, there are 'hot line' techniques which permit almost instant contact to be made at the highest level. Such procedures were used to deal with the situation resulting from allegations of (maritime) border infringements and the arrest of forty-nine Filipino fishermen by Malaysia (August–September 1988).

ASEAN's practice of maintaining contact and consultation extends even to the Indo-Chinese bloc in South East Asia. There were some contacts in 1978, which were interrupted by the Vietnamese invasion of Cambodia, but later revived. Although perceptions of the threat from this direction have differed among the ASEAN States (Thailand and Singapore believing that Vietnam constitutes the main immediate threat, while Indonesia and Malaysia lay more stress on the longer-term threat from China), a workable procedure was devised. Indonesia, as the largest ASEAN member and the one most favourably inclined towards Vietnam, sometimes functioned as an 'interlocutor', a sort of diplomatic point man, in dealings with Vietnam during the 1980s, although occasionally Thailand took the lead.

Much of ASEAN's success is attributable to its informal functioning, as in the example just cited. Its security arrangements—mostly bilateral or trilateral[26]—are not likely to be formalized much further. However, in 1991 its secretariat was enlarged and strengthened. Economically, little was achieved until the early 1990s when there was a flurry of new initiatives and initials. Some of these related to intra-ASEAN issues, such as free trade. Others, partly a reaction to the formation of European and North American economic blocs, had to do with ASEAN States' membership in larger Pacific Rim groupings.

THE GREAT POWERS: INTERNATIONAL ORGANIZATIONS: REGIONAL POWERS: MNCS

In the 1980s, converging agreement among the Great Powers, especially the two superpowers, constituted another disincentive to boundary changes. This situation contrasted sharply with the era of colonization and with post-Second World War interventions, especially in Indo-China. The *détentes* between the USSR (preceding its dissolution) and the USA and China, respectively made it more likely that boundaries would be maintained. These *détentes*, plus the China–Vietnam *détente* promised to find expression in a viable agreement on Cambodia.[27]

However, recent speculation about the effects of a two superpower system being replaced by a multipolar system,[28] suffered a shock when the USSR disintegrated in 1991. The question now is whether there will for a time be a 'single superpower system' or a more rapid transition than expected to a multipolar system? The latter may come about because of the reduced threat from the USSR and the closing of the US bases in the Philippines in 1992. US ships and aircraft, however, would still be able to make some use of Philippine installations. Arrangements had also previously been made that Singapore would provide 'services' for US ships and aircraft. Nevertheless, in spite of such agreements, there were signs of some degree of US withdrawal from the region.[29] Demands that the US economy needs help, even at the expense of the defence budget, would tend to accelerate withdrawal. Fear of Japan militarily in South East Asia, vital as its investment is for the region, can be allayed only if the USA remains as a controlling force, in exchange serving Japan's interests by helping to protect its sea-lanes. Closer to the region than any of these, and possibly viewing it as an area for ultimate expansion, is China—the most feared long-term threat.[30] However, in the short- and medium-term, unless there is a precipitate US withdrawal, the prospects for stability in the region are good.

The United Nations may also be regarded as a stabilizing force. It is an arena where resolutions tend to recognize existing and, ironically, often colonial boundaries and condemn any changes to them that are not based on consent all round. Similar norms are followed by other bodies, such as the Non-Aligned Movement. The United Nations has undoubtedly helped to freeze the *status quo* and to ensure that territorial predation is no longer recognized as part of the game of international politics. However, the United Nations is not a self-starting force for peace. 'It is in the first instance a forum in which the great powers compete or co-operate, as they choose, in the Third World. Their readiness in the last few years to experiment in the ways of co-operation has revived the UN.'[31] The horses precede the cart. Although the UN was an impressive forum during the Gulf War, this assessment remains valid.

The United Nations' limited influence in South East Asia was illustrated by the failure of its annual resolutions to unseat the *de facto* government in Cambodia. Also, although Indonesia has not managed to eliminate the East Timor issue from the UN agenda, or to persuade it to accept the annexation, in 1988 the Speaker of the Indonesian House of Representatives affirmed that the sixth (unopposed) postponement of discussion on the subject was proof that Indonesian diplomacy had been successful.[32] However, this evaluation may need revision in the light of events in 1991. In this respect, the United Nations is a 'club' where members tend to receive support as against non-members.

Membership of the Commonwealth adds somewhat to the stability of Malaysia, Singapore, and Brunei. Malaysia and Singapore are members of the Five-Power Defence Arrangement (1971), which also includes Britain, Australia, and New Zealand. The five States' defence forces hold joint exercises from time to time. Lee Kuan Yew, one of the Commonwealth leaders longest in office (1959–90) made use of Commonwealth Conferences for presenting his statesmanlike views on the future of the world. The Prime Minister of Malaysia, Dr Mahathir, initially did not seem to be strongly committed to the Commonwealth idea, believing perhaps that Britain played too dominant a role. Later he came round to the view that Commonwealth conferences were a useful forum for the presentation of Malaysia's policies and the 1989 leaders' conference was held in Kuala Lumpur.

Ranking below the Great Powers are the major powers in the region. Each of the two major groups, ASEAN and the Vietnam–Laos (and previously Kampuchea) group, contains a country which is at least *primus inter pares*, Indonesia and Vietnam, respectively.[33] Each has the largest territory, population, and armed forces inside its bloc. Perhaps each is too weak economically to merit applying the term 'hegemony' here. Yet a contrast is apparent between the two leading countries. Vietnam is more than a leader, and plays a role equivalent to a traditional suzerain. It bound Laos to it by treaties of friendship, and attempted to integrate Laos with it economically, although Laos blocked its efforts to set up a joint Indo-China economic commission. Vietnam actually installed the Heng Samrin government in Cambodia, and encouraged Vietnamese to settle in that country, although it made substantial troop withdrawals in 1989. It also stationed troops and advisers in Laos. It has been paternalistic, tending to identify its own interests with those of Indo-China.[34]

Within the ASEAN constellation, power is not so concentrated. ASEAN takes the form of a regional club which supports the jurisdictional *status quo* by observing norms of reciprocity, mutual respect, and non-intervention—at least if economic power is considered. Singapore and Brunei, by far the least populous, are also far and away the most prosperous in per capita terms. Indonesia's predominance might be courteously denied by its leaders and representatives, who would, however, equally properly, express doubts that any other ASEAN country was predominant. Yet the ASEAN secretariat is located in its territory and its foreign minister has recently stated that its internal consolidation and progress now equip it to play an even more active part diplomatically.[35] It also exercises a Malay (used in a broad sense) or Islamic 'leadership'[36] over Malaysia and Brunei and even over Singapore. An increasingly multipolar balance among the Great Powers would enhance its influence greatly.

The existence of bloc leadership permits the would-be classifier of States to use gradations intermediate between 'State' and 'Great Power'. It also may provide a 'functional substitute' for expansion and aggression. A State is enabled to exert leadership and influence areas beyond its own boundaries without the costs and unpopularity attendant upon seeking to extend its territories.

By definition, Multinational Corporations (MNCs) also operate at the international level. Foreign investment by MNCs is keenly sought after by the ASEAN countries, particularly by Singapore whose economic survival is predicated on a high level of external investment. Until recently, the isolationist policies of Vietnam, Laos, and Burma have inhibited these States from striving to attract such investment, but they now warmly welcome it. Unequal relations between MNCs and Third World countries are the subject of a voluminous literature. The conventional wisdom is that MNCs' activities tend to undermine the independence of Third World States. The bargaining power of a country *vis-à-vis* the MNCs is obviously crucial in this regard, and perhaps only Singapore can match the MNCs' bargaining power, mainly because it offers an efficient infrastructure and services and an absence of corruption. However, it is also relevant to note that MNCs rate stability as a prime requirement in choosing countries in which to invest.

This preference is obviously conducive to reinforcing the ASEAN countries' existing inclinations to avoid territorial adventurism. Similar reasoning influences the operations of the International Monetary Fund and the World Bank,[37] as well as those of the Inter-Governmental Group on Indonesia, which constructed a loan package for the Suharto government in Indonesia soon after it came to power in 1965.

SMALL STATES' STRATEGIES FOR SURVIVAL

Disincentives to territorial claims will be strengthened if potential victims plan intelligently and fight hard to resist them. Singapore[38] and Brunei[39] are the two smallest States in the area, yet both have survived and more. They are wealthy, but also vulnerable to threats if stability in the area is weakened. Common problems have brought them close to each other. Their relations have been good, long preceding Brunei's independence. They co-operate militarily, are important trading partners, and the Brunei dollar is pegged to its Singapore counterpart. To be sure, their cultures are very different. Also, while Brunei has had a long (although interrupted) history as a State, Singapore has enjoyed full independence only since 1965. Yet, since then, it has constructed a world-wide network of investment and trading links, and was a foundation member of ASEAN. It managed to strengthen its defences and to assert its identity in international forums, thus reinforcing both physical and psychological disincentives to aggression.

Both Singapore and Brunei have built up defence forces which are small but of high quality. Singapore has aimed at presenting the image of a 'porcupine', as a deterrent. Brunei, just before independence, bargained successfully to retain one of its advantages while a protectorate—its battalion of Gurkhas. In addition to their own forces, Singapore and Brunei have benefited from the Five Power Defence Arrangement and both have been helped by bilateral agreements and security arrangements inside ASEAN.

However, the two countries' armed forces and the purely *military* advantages provided by ASEAN are only one component of their security. At least equally important are the enlistment of coinciding interests with other countries, and the ability to profit from the team spirit and solidarity inside ASEAN. Because of its international economic links, Singapore has been able to attract a large volume of foreign investment, which has given industrialized countries a vested interest in its survival and prosperity. Its offer of military facilities (not bases) to the USA in 1989 was accepted. At the same time, it has tried to accommodate its immediate neighbours, thus minimizing cultural differences, and defusing in some measure their possible envy of its more rapid development and technically more sophisticated economy. For example, it declined to enter into diplomatic relations with China before Indonesia did (1990), and was patient and conciliatory in the protracted negotiations with Malaysia over its water supply, eventually concluded in 1988.[40] In the aftermath of Vietnam's invasion of Cambodia, it was a very active player in the ASEAN team. Consequently, it is now an accepted and valuable member of ASEAN, greatly strengthening its security—at least under the present Indonesian and Malaysian leaders, or like-minded successors.

There is, perhaps, only one issue which Singapore ranks as a higher priority than the cultivation of good-neighbourly relations— upholding the principle of the independence of small States. In the Cambodian example these considerations were reinforcing rather than conflicting. In denouncing the Vietnamese invasion of 1978 Singapore was both deploring a shift in the power balance adverse to the ASEAN States and also supporting the territorial integrity of small States—a bulwark of its own survival. But when the UN General Assembly voted initially on a resolution condemning Indonesia's actions in East Timor, Singapore risked incurring Indonesia's displeasure by abstaining.[41] Later, it supported the Indonesian position in the UN. True to form, it was more forthright in denouncing the Iraqi invasion of Kuwait than ASEAN fellow-members.

Brunei encountered a difficult period in the late 1960s and early 1970s after reviving its claim to Limbang, when Malaysia (with Indonesian backing) challenged its status in the UN. (Predictably, Malaysia was supported by Indonesia, the Philippines, and Thailand, but not by Singapore.) However, in 1976, the new prime minister, Dato Hussein Onn, abandoned interventionist policies—possibly in order to avoid international opposition similar to that which resulted from Indonesia's annexation of East Timor in 1976. A reconciliation between Brunei and Malaysia (along with Indonesia) was made public in 1978, and when Brunei attained independence in 1984 it entered the safe, internationally legitimizing haven of ASEAN. It passed, almost without a break, from one protector to another.

Small States benefit greatly from the shelter of an 'umbrella' association which will provide protection against outside threats. The reason why they are *given* shelter seems to be that the stronger powers in the association prefer to exercise influence, or some degree of hegemony, by indirection rather than by incurring the costs of brashly altering boundaries. This reasoning also helps explain the continued survival of Laos. Its existence is due, not to its power, but, rather, to its lack of power, and to accurate cost-benefit analysis by Vietnam. The situation resembles a modern version of indirect rule.

CONCLUSION

Relations among the Great Powers (and inside the former USSR) are now changing so rapidly that their future influence is hard to discern. An interesting possibility is that, if the Cambodian conflict is peacefully resolved, Vietnam, Laos, and Cambodia might seek to join ASEAN. Their desire to do so (and Burma's) may be re-enforced by their recent attempts to shift towards more open economies. However, an enlarged organization would be subject to additional economic and security strains. Also, how long would it take for the new members to merit, and be accorded confidence and trust? (A similar problem exists for the EC with regard to the admission of East European States.) Additionally leadership in ASEAN might be hard to resolve and might even be shared by Indonesia and Vietnam on some kind of bipolar basis.

Boundaries are still relevant. Indeed, they have become more so in the sense that, apart from the aberrant case of Iraq's attack on Kuwait, they are increasingly respected as effective barriers to territorial invasion. At the same time, recognition as a State is a poor indicator of the location of power. This is partly because some States cannot exercise effective control inside their borders. Even if they do, some are more powerful than others. The sanctity of boundaries may deter invasion but can do little to arrest permeation by external forces. The key roles of great and regional powers, MNCs etc., have produced a curious resemblance to the situation in South East Asia before European expansion in the area. Suzerain countries, such as China, exercised influence over, and were paid tribute by, otherwise 'autonomous' realms.[42] The main difference today lies in the proliferation of suzerains and the increasing difficulty of predicting the outcomes of their sometimes conflicting influences.

NOTES

1. The author is indebted, for funds, to the Social Sciences and Humanities Research Council of Canada and, for ideas, to Bruce Burton, Chao Tzang Yawnghwe, Kal Holsti, Robert Jackson, Johan Saravanamuttu, Michael Leifer, and Diane Mauzy.
2. C. Geertz (ed.), *Old Societies and New States* (New York, 1963).
3. B. R. O. G. Anderson, 'Old State, New Society: Indonesia's New Order in Comparative Historical Perspective', *Journal of Asian Studies*, 42 (1983), 477.
4. M. Leifer, 'The International Representation of Kampuchea', *Southeast Asian Affairs*, 53 (1982).
5. R. S. Milne, 'Singapore's Exit from Malaysia', *Asian Survey*, 6 (1966), 175–84.
6. B. Buzan, *People, States and Fear: The National Security Problem in International Relations* (Brighton, 1983), 36–8.
7. Buzan, *People, States and Fear*, 64.
8. See L. G. Noble, *In Pursuit of the National Heritage: The Philippine Claim to Sabah* (Tucson, Ariz., 1977).
9. *Straits Times*, 16 Sept. 1988.
10. See N. Chanda, *Brother Enemy: The War After the War* (San Diego, New York, and London, 1986), 11–13, 32–3, 56, 97.
11. M. Osborne, *Religion of Revolt: Focus on Southeast Asia* (Harmondsworth, 1971); Chai-Anan Samudavanija and Sukhumbhand Paribatra, 'Development for Security, Security for Development: Prospects for Durable Stability in Southeast Asia', in Kusuma Snitwongse and Sukhumbhand Paribatra (eds.), *Durable Stability in Southeast Asia* (Singapore, 1987), 3–4.
12. R. McVey, 'Separatism and the Paradoxes of the Nation-State in Perspective', in J. J. Lim and S. Vani (eds.), *Armed Separatism in Southeast Asia* (Singapore, 1984), 9–11. Anderson has commented that only one of the Indonesian rebellions, 1950–64, aimed at actual separation—the abortive revolt of the South Moluccas: B. Anderson, *Imagined Communities* (London, 1983), 20.
13. See D. Wurfel, *Filipino Politics: Development and Decay* (Ithaca, NY, 1988), 154–65, 223–31, 264–70, 292–4, 311–15. See also *Asiaweek*, 19 Aug. 1988, 21–2.
14. D. G. Timberman, 'The Philippines in 1989', *Asian Survey*, 30 (1990), 171–2.
15. D. I. Steinberg, 'Burmese Domestic Politics and Foreign Policy Towards ASEAN', in K. Jackson (ed.), *ASEAN in Regional and Global Context* (Berkeley, Calif., 1986), 259.
16. Wurfel, *Filipino Politics*, 183–5.
17. McVey, 'Separatism', 13, which only slightly exaggerates the point. She

adds that in pre-modern South East Asian politics the opposite principle prevailed—that power was identified with control over population.

18. Buzan, *People, States and Fear*, 66–9, 97.
19. See Sukhumbhand Paribatra and Chai-Anan Samudavanija, *Internal Dimensions of Regional Security in the Third World* (London and Sydney, 1986), 5.
20. H. Bull and A. Watson, 'Conclusion', in Bull and Watson (eds.), *The Expansion of International Society* (Oxford, 1984), 460.
21. McVey, 'Separatism', 19.
22. Interview with a diplomat from an ASEAN country, Manila, Sept. 1988; Wurfel, *Filipino Politics*, 164.
23. B. Buzan, 'The Southeast Asian Security Complex', *Contemporary Southeast Asia*, 10 (1988), 12–13.
24. Quoted in M. Leifer, *ASEAN and the Security of Southeast Asia* (London, 1989), 165. The book also reproduces the Treaty of Amity and Co-operation in Southeast Asia (Bali, 1976), 170, which amplifies the point.
25. *Straits Times*, 15 Aug. 1988.
26. M. Alagappa, 'Regional Arrangements and International Security in Southeast Asia: Going Beyond ZOPFAN', *Contemporary Southeast Asia*, 12 (1991), 269–305.
27. According to Lee Kuan Yew, implementing the so-called 'accord' on Cambodia will not be easy because disarmament of the opposing factions may not be enforceable (*Asian Wall Street Journal*, 6 Nov. 1991). Implementation has still not occurred—8 Jan. 1993.
28. See McVey, 'Separatism', 18; Buzan, 'Southeast Asian Security Complex', 8; *Jakarta Post*, 24 Sept. 1988 (Soedjatmoko).
29. *Asian Wall Street Journal*, 21 Oct. 1991; *San Francisco Chronicle*, 2 Jan. 1992.
30. R. O. Tilman, *Southeast Asia and the Enemy Beyond* (Boulder, Col., 1987), 84–105.
31. *Washington Post*, quoted in the *International Herald Tribune*, 28 Sept. 1988.
32. *Jakarta Post*, 27 Sept. 1988.
33. Chai-Anan and Sukhumbhand, 58–9.
34. D. Pike, 'Vietnam and its Neighbors', in K. Jackson (ed.), 245.
35. *International Herald Tribune*, 29 Aug. 1988.
36. Sukhumbhand and Chai-Anan, *Internal Dimensions*, 58.
37. On their efforts to stabilize the unstabilizable Marcos regime, see Walden, *Development Debacle: The World Bank in the Philippines* (San Francisco, 1982), 95, 97, 100.
38. R. S. Milne and D. K. Mauzy, *Singapore: The Legacy of Lee Kuan Yew* (Boulder, Col., 1990), ch. 8.
39. M. Leifer, 'Decolonization and International Status: The Case of Brunei', *International Affairs*, 54 (1988), 240–52.

40. On the breach in Singapore's relationship with Malaysia, occasioned by the visit of the president of Israel in Nov. 1986, see M. Leifer, 'Israel's President in Singapore: Political Catalysis and Transnational Politics', *Pacific Review*, 1 (1987), 341–52.
41. Obaid ul Haq, 'Foreign Politics', in J. S. T. Quah *et al.* (eds.), *Government and Politics in Singapore* (Singapore, 1985), 297.
42. H. Bull and A. Watson, 'Introduction', in Bull and Watson (eds.), 3.

FURTHER READING

Brown, D., 'From Peripheral Communities to Ethnic Nations: Separatism in Southeast Asia', *Pacific Affairs*, 61 (1988).

Buzan, B., 'The Southeast Asian Security Complex,' *Contemporary Southeast Asia*, 10 (1988).

Leifer, M., *ASEAN and the Security of Southeast Asia* (London, 1989).

Lim, J. J., and Vani, S. (eds.), *Armed Separatism in Southeast Asia* (Singapore, 1987).

Kusuma, S., and Sukhumbhand, P. (eds.), *Durable Stability in Southeast Asia* (Singapore, 1987).

10

North East Asia

GERALD SEGAL

North East Asia[1] has it all. It is the backyard of Russia and an area of primary interest for the USA. It is the home waters of the world's second largest economy (Japan) as it is for the fastest-developing economies (South Korea, Taiwan, and Hong Kong). Its total GDP has just passed that of the combined West European States. It is the location of the first cases of post-war decolonization (Korea and Taiwan) and the first of the major wars in the developing world (the Korean War). North East Asia has also been the only place where two nuclear powers have fought (Sino-Soviet border).

Thus, apart from the European theatre, no other piece of the post-1945 political map is as important for the global balance of power or prosperity. North East Asia is also notable for playing host to some of the most interesting trends in post-war international relations. It has seen the decline of the importance of the superpowers, the destruction of the concept of the Third World, and the great split in communist ideology.[2] Needless to say, these significant trends have had an important bearing on the subject of this book—the meaning of independence in the post-war world.

BIRTH

The difficulty with the term independence is obvious when assessing the very birth of States in North East Asia. Of its nine States, there are still question marks over the formal sovereignty of five of them. In fact, it is still difficult to use the term 'State' to describe Hong Kong, Macao, and perhaps even Taiwan and the two Koreas. Taking the four most straightforward cases, it is easiest to begin with Mongolia.

The Mongolian People's Republic was born in 1921. It was not involved in the Second World War, and thus continued after 1945 as a notionally sovereign State. But as will become apparent below, 'independent' Mongolia has never been anything but heavily linked to the Soviet Union, at least until the second Russian revolution of 1991.

Then there is Russia, the precursor and successor to the Soviet Union. During the Second World War the Soviet Union never lost any territory in Asia, although as a result of its attack on Japan in 1945, it did acquire new territory from Japan and for a time the Soviet Union had aspirations of taking territory from China. Prospects for formal border accords with both China and Japan were unsettled by the disintegration of the Soviet Union in 1991.

In 1945 China was a sovereign State, but vast parts of its territory were occupied by Japan during the war, and the Western imperial powers still controlled enclaves in Hong Kong and Macao. The defeat of Japan left the European empires in place and more importantly left China to get on with its civil war between communists and non-communists. It was only in 1949 that Mao Zedong's forces took control of mainland China, but the communists were unable to take the offshore island of Taiwan which was held by Chiang Kai-shek's forces, along with various small islands in the region.

The fourth independent State was Japan. Although defeated in the war, and occupied by the USA, it was never the American intention to absorb Japan. Thus formal sovereignty was never fully snuffed out, although for all intents and purposes the USA ruled Japan until April 1952 when the peace treaty came into force.

Japan had ruled Taiwan and Korea as colonies and both were surrendered as part of Japan's defeat. Taiwan was returned to Chinese control but became part of the civil war. Korea was split by the two superpowers into zones of occupation, and like the two Germanies, formal sovereignty was granted as the superpowers disengaged from direct rule. North Korea, otherwise known as the People's Democratic Republic of Korea, was established in September 1948 and South Korea, alias the Republic of Korea, was formed in August 1948. Neither Korean State saw the division of the country as anything but temporary and North Korea tried to take over the South in June 1950.

The final political units in North East Asia were the European colonies of Hong Kong and Macao. Britain and Portugal returned to control after the defeat of Japan with the clear expectation that they would retain control of their territories.

FIG. 10.1 North East Asia

Therefore, in 1945 there was really only one fully independent State, the Soviet Union. But if the rules of sovereignty are relaxed to include the Soviet-dominated Mongolia, then there were two sovereign States. By 1950, using some peculiar categories, one could add the Chinas and Japan to the list of independent States. By bending all the usual rules in 1953, the two Koreas could be added when they agreed to an armistice. The count stood still at seven, loosely defined independent States.

DEATH

No States apart from the Soviet Union have died in the region. But five of the nine units can be said to be in some kind of serious risk of ceasing to exist. Repeated proposals for unification of the two Koreas have been as fruitless as the periodic attempts at military 'persuasion'.

It can be argued that both Koreas are gradually evolving towards the German model of cross-recognition which is then followed by unification. But there are stark differences between the Korean and German cases and the route to Korean reunification may well prove to be more dangerous.

When the USA caught up with the sentiment of its Western allies, it bestowed full recognition on mainland China. Taiwan lost the formal recognition from most States as the government of China during the 1970s. Of course, the Republic of China (to give it its proper name) has not ceased to exist as a government in control of territory, even though some tiny offshore islands were lost to China in 1955. All that changed was formal international recognition and as will be argued below, Taiwan shows no signs of losing all the effective implements of independence and sovereignty.

The same cannot be said for Hong Kong and Macao. As laid out in an Anglo-Chinese agreement in 1984, Hong Kong will be returned to China in 1997. Macao will be handed back by Portugal in 1999. While these two colonies were never independent States, Hong Kong at least has had more effective independence than most States and far more economic success. Nevertheless, by the turn of the millennium there will be two fewer political units in North East Asia.

LIFE

There are huge disparities between the States of North East Asia. If measured in terms of the relatively unchanging feature of geographic size, China is the largest State in the region and Russia a close second. The next largest unit, Mongolia, is 16 per cent the size of China and Japan is 4 per cent the size of China. The two Koreas together constitute 2 per cent the size of China but South Korea alone is 64 per cent larger than Taiwan.

In terms of population, the disparities are somewhat different but still vast. With 1.1 billion souls China is clearly in a class by itself. Japan, with 122 million is the next largest with the two Koreas having a combined total of 63 million. The 42 million in South Korea is far larger than the 2 million people of Mongolia, the 5 million people of Hong Kong and the 20 million people of Taiwan.

In terms of size, China is the only powerful power broadly defined. Russia and Japan are mirror images of each other's strengths and weaknesses. The two Koreas and Taiwan can fit into a middle range of relatively balanced size and population. Mongolia, like Russia is sparsely populated, and the micro-units of Hong Kong and Macao are in a class by themselves.

In terms of wealth, there is more of a trend towards real equality. Japan has the world's second largest economy and a 1987 GDP of $2,664 million, many times larger than the $286 million GDP of China and the $118 million of South Korea. Measured in per capita terms, Japan is by far the richest State in North East Asia, but Hong Kong is more than half the Japanese figure and Taiwan and South Korea are coming up fast. Mongolia, Russia, and to some extent North Korea are in another class, with roughly one-sixth of the Japanese per capita figures. China, with the region's second largest total GDP, is still by far the poorest State on per capita calculations.

BETWEEN FORMALITY AND REALITY

No State in the region has been without a challenge to its sovereignty since 1945. The types of challenges were myriad, as indeed have been the responses. For the entities varied enormously in the extent to which they had effective control and could decide policy despite the pressures from markets, allies, and enemies. It is most revealing if the types of challenge to real sovereignty are divided into those that relate to the main dimensions of sovereignty: defence policy, economic policy, and ideology and culture. The list of countries that follows is more or less in (an avowedly subjective) order from least to most sovereign.

Mongolia may have more formal exchanges of diplomatic relations than most States in the region, but in reality it has been severely circumscribed.[3] The Mongolian predicament was a product of history and geography. It was caught between the often rival powers of China and Russia. Mongolians have only been able to act relatively independently at times when the Chinese Empire was weak. The Mongolian State of the twentieth century could only have emerged because everyone else was picking the bones of the fading Chinese Empire. As China reasserted its imperial claims, Mongolia sought protection from its only other great neighbour, the Soviet Union.

Thus Mongolian defence policy was totally dependent on the Soviet Union.[4] In order to remain outside the Chinese Empire,

Mongolia had to agree to become an informal member of the Soviet empire, being dependent on Moscow for arms and training, and even having Soviet troops on its soil to deter China. Mongolia was the Soviet Union's closest ally.

In economic policy, Soviet influence was equally direct and pervasive.[5] Mongolian domestic policies, not to mention its foreign trade was dominated by links with the Soviet Union or the Soviet-dominated COMECON States. When Moscow shifted its own internal models, as it did after the death of Stalin or under Gorbachev, Mongolia followed suit. With its tiny population, Mongolia stood no chance of developing more economic independence unless it developed ties with China. But even if it could overcome its historical fears, the degree of independence could not be vast given the already sharp orientation of its economy in response to the needs of the Soviet Union.

As has already been suggested, in ideological terms, Mongolia was closely tied to shifts in Soviet policy. In the broader domain of culture, Mongolian distinctiveness is clear. But to some extent it had little more freedom to experiment with new ideas and self-definitions than did some of the Soviet Asian republics. In the age of glasnost the freedom of manœuvre was somewhat greater, but Mongolia found that any attempt to develop a more specific Mongol character would upset China and therefore restrained what limited options the Mongolians already had in making foreign policy.

The broad picture was one of real inequality and dependence. What was more, this was an old, established picture and one that showed few signs of changing. Unlike any other of the Soviet Union's allies, Mongolia has nowhere else to go. With the demise of the Soviet Union in 1991, Mongolia became more free to pursue its own domestic policies and the communist system was gradually abandoned. But the geopolitical reality of Mongolia being squeezed between China and Russia remained much the same.

Hong Kong and Macao may be in a different league of sovereignty from Mongolia, but more importantly, they are in different political and economic worlds. Both will be returned to China before long, largely because they are so clearly vulnerable to Chinese pressure. For this reason, both units are taken together, although Macao is even more dependent than Hong Kong and its future has always been closely linked with the fate of the far larger colony next door. Nevertheless, because both have been long-standing colonies of

Western States, and both are on the coast, they have had far more options than Mongolia. Formal sovereignty and defence of Hong Kong were officially vested in Britain, but since 1945, British power has gradually retreated east of Suez. Moreover, it had been clear since the triumph of communism in China in 1949 that China had the power to take Hong Kong if it so chose.[6] That China chose not to do so said more about the other priorities of Chinese foreign policy, and the deterrence that came from the determination of Western powers to defend Western interests in Korea and Taiwan. The 'independence' of Hong Kong, albeit as a formal colony of Britain, was ensured by the broadest possible definition of post-war deterrence—the sense that territory would not easily change hands between East and West. As will be seen, China also received economic benefits from letting Hong Kong serve as an entrepôt for its foreign trade, as well as the diplomatic benefits of appearing to be a sensible neighbour.

Thus Britain and Portugal, as colonial masters, defended their colonies only in the sense of being part of the broader Western alliance and having sent troops to fight in Korea. Hong Kong and Macao did not formally defend themselves, but then they were colonies and would not normally be expected to do so. So what makes them more independent than formally independent Mongolia?

The answer lies in the root of Hong Kong's startling success—its economy. It is only a bit of a caricature to say that Hong Kong has been the only truly free-market economy.[7] It certainly has been British policy to have virtually no policy beyond providing some rudimentary features of economic management. This free port has been allowed to find its own niche in the global market-place, relatively unhindered by government intervention. Certainly there has been relatively little intervention from London.

The result has been one of the most penetrated, interdependent economies in the world.[8] Hong Kong traders have literally served the nations of the world. In their turn, American and Japanese business came to take a major role in the Hong Kong economy, bringing investment and foreign contacts. Markets for Hong Kong products were found around the world. Thus the basic levers of economic control in the hands of the colonial authorities were rarely used. The market determined prices, and hence wages and even rates of currency. Hong Kong was one of the first States to demonstrate that despite the absence of formal independence, real economic

independence brings genuine interdependence, and—therefore—
loss of control. The pay-off was a high standard of living and
continued growth.

Although North East Asia accounted for 46 per cent of Hong
Kong's trade in 1987 (up from 33 per cent in 1981), it was China
that was regularly the largest single factor in the local economy.[9] In
the days before China's open door in the late 1970s, China earned
large portions of its foreign exchange simply by selling food and water
to Hong Kong. In return, China obtained a window on the capitalist
world and expertise in such services as banking. When China eventually did open its doors to the capitalist world, its investments and
practice in Hong Kong allowed it to rapidly learn how to play the
capitalist game and prosper. Hong Kong became a valuable re-export
and re-import point for Chinese goods travelling to such difficult-to-
trade-with-states as South Korea, Taiwan, Israel, and some Gulf
States. Thus it was hard to judge the full nature of Hong Kong trade.
But in the pragmatic world of East Asia, Hong Kong clearly had a
niche as the pragmatic meeting-place.

Given such frenetic toing and froing in Hong Kong, it is not
surprising that it became one of the earliest places to find its culture
deeply affected by the trends towards a global mass culture.[10] The
British colonial base was always a small one in comparison with the
pervading sense of being in an outpost of the great Chinese civilization.
Hong Kong's population remained over 95 per cent Chinese. But the
post-war period saw the spread of 'Coca-colonization', especially in a
tiny colony that thrived on the global market economy. The non-
ideology in Hong Kong, apart from *laissez-faire*, ensured that the
territory would see a mixing of cultures.

The American influence, at least superficially in the form of food
and life-style, was the most obvious. But Japanese money and influence
brought yet another flavour to the mix, as did the communities from
elsewhere in Asia who did business in Hong Kong. The product is
not an American clone, and certainly it is quite different from anything
one finds in China. There are some resemblances to Japan, or more
accurately to Taiwan, in the sense of modernity and Confucian
culture. But the mix is more volatile and varied in Hong Kong. The
result is a distinctive colony, although one that has prospered by
becoming clearly interdependent with the global market economies.

Taiwan shares a number of features with Hong Kong, but yet
constitutes a different, and indeed quite unique case. Because of its

circumstances of birth as part of the Chinese civil war, there has always been an ambiguity about whether Taiwan is a province of China or an independent State.[11] Both communists and capitalists alike argued that Taiwan was a part of China, but for much of the 1950s the rulers of Taiwan felt there was a chance they would return to power on the mainland. When it became increasingly clear that such dreams were far from being fulfilled, Taiwan settled down to creating economic prosperity. The larger segment of the population that was Taiwan-born was reluctant to demand formal independence, especially as long as they had no real domestic power. It was only in the late 1980s when the generation of leaders born on the mainland died out, that *de facto* Taiwanese independence became more likely and democratization began to draw Taiwan further away from the dream of returning to the mainland.

In the meantime, Taiwan's international position had altered. In the opening days of the Korean war, the USA had sent its 7th Fleet into the Taiwan Straits in order to keep China from attacking Taiwan. As the primary military guarantor of Taiwan, the USA then became drawn into a series of offshore island crises when China tried to test American resolve in defending Taiwan. Although there were risks of major escalation and possibly even nuclear war, the USA agreed to deter China while holding the Taiwanese back from antagonizing the Chinese.[12] At this time, Taiwan was heavily dependent on the USA for arms and deterrence of the communist adversary.

If China was to have any hope of regaining control of Taiwan, it eventually came to see that it would have to be peacefully and with tacit American co-operation. During the visit by President Nixon to China in 1972, China obtained recognition as being the one China. But it was not until the full normalization of Sino-American relations in 1979 that the USA demoted Taiwan to the limbo it is presently in. The USA, like most Western States, has a representative in Taibei in the guise of an 'interest section' or 'trading organization'. But the representatives are diplomats in mufti and operations are all but normal diplomatic relations.

Taiwan does not like its second-class diplomatic status, but it takes what it can get while seeking better treatment. Formal sovereignty would give Taiwan enhanced status and some benefits of expedience in diplomacy, but not much else. Real sovereignty was far more important. Taiwan has gradually come to accept that it can go to the Olympic games or join international organizations as 'China, Taibei' or some such ruse. The result is an evolving *de facto* independence for Taiwan, although not formal sovereignty.

Such pragmatism is evident in the area of Taiwanese defence policy. Most arms still come from the USA despite a Sino-American agreement that the flow of arms should be reduced. While formal arms sales are cut, co-production deals and transactions at the company-to-company level ensure Taiwan can retain sufficient military capability to deter China. All Taiwan needs to do is to make the expected cost of occupation so high that China will not attack.

There is also a continuing, unspoken American deterrence of China's use of force against Taiwan.[13] The Chinese have recognized that they stand less chance of obtaining the benefits of an integrated and prosperous China including Taiwan if force were used. Certainly it would do major damage to China's international standing even if it blockaded Taiwan. For their part, the Taiwanese recognize that a declaration of independence or the open acquisition of nuclear weapons might make it easier for China to get away with a blockade.

Thus Taiwan can be said to have grown more militarily independent because of its grudging willingness to play the pragmatic game of deterrence. It has certainly survived the trauma of formal abandonment by the USA and has made it decreasingly likely that China will be able to take control of Taiwan.

This more independent defence policy also owes a great deal to Taiwan's ability to develop economically and play an important part in world trade. The success of the Taiwanese miracle, like that in Japan, owes a great deal to state-directed capitalism. The so-called capitalist development State (CDS) thrives on access to the global market economy, but it is often built on the basis of heavily state-directed strategies.[14] Taiwan is not quite as dependent on trade as is Hong Kong, but its ratio of trade volume to GDP of 123 per cent (up from 93 per cent in 1981) still means its economy is heavily dependent on global trade.

Taiwan does not fit the CDS model as well as South Korea, if only because of the multiplicity of its small entrepreneurs who thrive below the level of big, State-directed business.[15] But broadly speaking the model fits. As a result, and unlike Hong Kong, Taiwan is not quite as penetrated by foreign firms. It is true that Taiwan is crucially dependent on markets in the developed capitalist economies, but these are more global markets.[16] Some 30 per cent of Taiwan's trade is with North East Asia (up from 23 per cent in 1981), half the degree of regional dependence as in the case of China.[17] A growing percentage of production for these markets is directed by foreign, even American and European firms, seeking production bases in Taiwan for export to the home country of the multinational. More than 30 per cent of Taiwan's trade imbalance with the USA, and more than half its imbalance in high technology goods is attributed to American-owned corporations buying or making things in Taiwan and exporting them back to the USA.[18] Increasing percentages of so-called international trade is really intra-company trade.

To speak of economic independence in these circumstances is meaningless. Like Hong Kong, independence and wealth have been achieved through extensive interdependence. The price is close integration to global capitalist market forces. When the USA and other G-7 nations decide that Taiwan's currency should be revalued, it is. To an increasing extent, trends in the global market make Taiwanese economic policy, as is common in most developed economies.

In ideological and cultural terms, as has already been suggested, Taiwan is evolving a distinctive character. With a firm Sinic base, there are overlays of American and essentially global Western ideas and habits. The search for a pragmatic type of independence has helped encourage greater domestic democratization within the confines of a basically Confucian political culture. Moderated authoritarian government seems likely to remain.

The character of Taiwan changes with the new waves of change in the global culture of the capitalist system. Japan, as the former imperial power, left an especially strong base in Taiwan. With the resurgence of Japan in the global market, Japanese influences return to thrive very easily in the soil of Taiwanese culture. American influence is of course powerful, while the Chinese dimension remains predominant. But what is a Sinic culture? As Taiwan, Hong Kong, and even Singapore show, China is not the definition of what is Sinic. Each has a distinctive definition in keeping with its particular pressures. None is fully independent of global influences. But Taiwan, like Hong Kong, shows that wealth brings greater cultural self-confidence and to that extent a more equal fight with larger States. Yet it remains the paradox of independence through interdependence that shapes the character of Taiwan.

North and South Korea are perhaps most similar to Taiwan in that they were unlikely to have survived if not for the military power of their Great Power patrons. Like former West Germany, South Korea depends on the Americans for arms, troops, and deterrence. The American determination to fight the war in Korea, 1950–3, ensured the survival of the non-communist forces. Continued American support kept North Korean adventurism at bay. The USA has still not withdrawn all of its troops, and the conflict is merely controlled not ended.

Yet unlike Taiwan, there are increasing calls, even from South Koreans, for the withdrawal of American troops.[19] Both a deficit-strapped USA, and an increasingly confident South Korea, see less need than ever for the American contingent. To be sure, the defence of South Korea is in part still provided by American deterrence of North Korea. American deterrence of China and the (former) Soviet Union long ago ceased to be necessary as both powers came to see the virtue of a negotiated settlement.[20] If the main problem is really deterrence of North Korea, then the South is increasingly able to provide it on its own: hence the possibility of reducing the number of American troops. Of course, at least the presence of some American troops makes it even less likely that the North would attack, if only because it would force its allies to rein in the North Koreans.

But it is economic factors which again make a big difference in the changing nature of defence policy. With a far faster rate of growth, the South is able to sustain defence spending at less cost. Time is against the North Koreans. The South Korean economy is the classical CDS, with a key dependence on foreign trade. Its ratio of trade to GDP of 74 per cent in 1987 (69 per cent in 1981) was higher than the average in the region.[21] Its large firms have become multinationals and are increasingly involved in global markets. Even those markets supposedly closed to South Korea, such as China and Russia, have opened up in the 1980s. The prosperity of the economy depends on the ability to sell in the global capitalist market-place and the South Koreans have shown they are increasingly successful at the game.[22] After being a heavily indebted country on Latin American levels, in the 1990s South Korea became a creditor nation.[23]

South Korea is also closely integrated in the global economy by virtue of foreign investment in South Korea itself. The Americans and then the Japanese have been the major players.[24] As in the case of Taiwan and Hong Kong, many of these investments are for export to the home market of the multinational. The same patterns exist that render conventional discussions of formal economic control largely obsolete.

The North Korean economy is a striking contrast. It has a small foreign trade sector and most of that is dominated by China and Russia. The North Koreans have had more room for manœuvre than Mongolia, if only because Pyongyang has been adept at playing off its two communist patrons when they were rivals for favour. But with Sino-Soviet *détente* and simultaneous *détente* with the West in the late 1980s, North Korea found its leverage, and independence, severely circumscribed. Neither power was as willing to compete in giving aid to North Korea and both urged Pyongyang to engage in reform.

That North Korea, unlike any other communist State in Asia, is able to hold out against the pressures for economic reform, owes a great deal to the distinctive rule of Kim Il Sung and the fear about his succession.[25] Neither China nor Russia seems prepared to push very hard when they know the door will soon be opened by the death of the elder Kim. China and Russia feel free to develop pragmatic contacts, and more recently even official links with South Korea instead of browbeating North Korea into accepting the new reality. North Korea's economic independence seems secure for the moment, but at the cost of internal decay and loss of international support. All can be reversed, although not all regained, by reform. But reform will bring greater economic interdependence.

In cultural and economic terms, the contrasts between North and South are also clear.[26] North Korea can lay claim to being one of the most ideologically independent States in the modern world. As in communist Albania or Burma, distinctive, if ludicrous ideologies for the modern world can survive behind self-imposed isolation. North Korean radios can tune to only one station and the ideological indoctrination makes Stalinism seem like soggy pragmatism. But the death of Kim Il Sung is expected to change all that, much as it did in post-Mao China. Greater integration with the reform-minded strands of modern communism seems inevitable.

South Korea resembles the other CDS cases with its powerful local culture overlaid with the ideas from the global market-place. The American influence is perhaps stronger here than anywhere else in the region, but as in the case of Taiwan, it fades with the complicating influence of Japan and the greater local confidence that comes from prosperity. Democratization has been hard to achieve and gains have regularly been replaced by slides back into military rule. Yet much of the country is governed in a relatively natural form of Confucian authoritarianism and the Western standards of democracy are certainly not applicable in South Korea.[27]

Japan and the other two powers in the region are in a class by themselves. Unlike China and Russia, Japan has a major, if dubious, distinction of being a very wealthy and populous State but also a vulnerable one. Despite having become the world's third largest spender on defence, Japan remains indefensible without the American nuclear umbrella. Whereas the West Europeans could mount a credible independent deterrent if they chose, Japan cannot as long as it remains a non-nuclear power.

The close Japanese–American relationship in the defence field developed naturally out of the post-war reconstruction of Japan, directed by the US occupation authorities. Although the USA did give up the territory it controlled in Japan, American troops remained in bases in Japan and American ships and aircraft patrolled the area. To this day, Japan acknowledges its dependent relationship.[28]

Whether Japan can be considered a 'full ally' of the USA is a difficult question to answer. Allies need not be equal and Japan does bear an increasing burden of defence of the North East Asian region. But Japan itself is not defensible without American aid, much as West Germany could not have defended itself without NATO assistance. Thus Japan has grown more independent in that it bears an increasing portion of the burden of the regional and national interests. But it remains fatally flawed as a great power because of its undue dependence on the USA.[29]

Japan's increasing ability to bear a greater share of its defence burden is due entirely to its growing economic power. It is not that Japan is spending a greater percentage of its GDP on defence, but rather the impressive growth of its total GDP which produces so much more firepower.[30] But as we have seen elsewhere, economic power when it is based on closer integration with the global economy, brings more interdependence. But unlike most countries in the region, the ratio of Japanese trade to GDP has fallen in recent years to 14 per cent (in 1987) from 27 per cent (in 1981).

The Japanese–American economic relationship can perhaps be described as one of mutual assured destruction. Japan has ceased to be solely dependent on US investment and access to American markets. Japan now is the world's largest creditor nation and is the creditor for large swathes of the American budget deficit. Neither the Japanese nor the Americans can push a trade dispute too far for fear of doing basic damage to their own economy. Japanese firms are increasingly investing in the other economies of the capitalist market-place (18 per cent in North East Asia in 1987, 13 per cent in 1981) in order to reach local markets and even re-export to Japan.[31] Some 40 per cent of the late 1980s Japanese trade surplus with the USA was accounted for by American-owned corporations' sales to the USA from Japanese bases.[32] Such intra-company trade is part of the general process of capitalist interdependence. American-owned companies in Japan sold more goods in Japan than the total of the American trade deficit with Japan in 1985. Japanese firms are able to weather currency revaluations because of their heavy investment elsewhere around the world.[33]

Thus Japanese growth and international economic profile is part of the complex process of interdependence. The analytical division between international relations of States and that between multinational corporations and States is useless in this world of interconnected and multilevel trade.[34] And much as the USA and then the West Europeans showed the way in this international business world, now Japan is following with impressive performances. Japanese capital and corpor-ations are flooding into global markets, including and perhaps even especially the NICs of North East Asia.[35] Although Japan has been cautious about China and Russia, there exists large potential for closer integration with its immediate Great Power neighbours.

In cultural and ideological terms, Japan has perhaps retained greater independence than many had thought possible. Like China, Japan had before the nineteenth century long kept the outside world at bay. But unlike China, Japan quickly adapted to Western ways and even made many of them its own. At present, there is perhaps far too much talk of Japan's uniqueness and the lessons that the rest of the world ca. learn from Japanese culture and ideology. Certainly some of this much-vaunted uniqueness is recognizable as 'Victorian values' or a stage of development.[36]

Yet it remains true that Japan has retained to a remarkable degree its own version of Confucian ethics and local culture, despite the close contact with the USA and the related global culture of capitalism. The number of English words in Japanese, the interest in baseball and American films, are often cited as evidence of American influence. But the flow is now increasingly two-way as Japan takes a more confident part in the global culture it helps underwrite. The language barrier still divides Japan from the mainstream yet clearly the level of

interconnections has grown between Japan and the outside world and
the nature of Japanese culture and ideology has been modified by it.
One need merely look at the Japanese political system to see how
Western form and traditional practice are sometimes uncomfortably
mixed.[37] But such discomforts and ironies are the stuff of the modern
global economy.

China is, as always, another special case. By virtue of its size, place,
and past, it has been the dominant actor in North East Asian international relations. But this dominance, like the importance of Japan,
has been skewed by the unequal size of its economic and military
power. In military terms, defending China has been an arduous and
bloody business. But by and large it has been done without the need
of other powers as allies.[38]

Therefore China, like Russia, is one of the few genuinely independent States in the region. The Chinese communists came to
power under their own steam. They fought the Korean War with
Soviet arms, but they also fought in part for Chinese objectives. China
certainly proved it could defend against the threats it perceived, even
though it failed in its more ambitious objective to throw the Americans
off the Korean peninsula. In various Taiwan Straits crises in the
1950s, China also proved it could conduct its own defence and
compellence policy, even if it was not always successful.

In 1962 China successfully whipped the Indians in war, again
without outside aid. In the mid-1960s China assisted North Vietnam
in its war with the USA, an effort in part carried out in tacit co-
operation with the Soviet Union. But in 1969 when China and the
Soviet Union fought brief border skirmishes, China was humiliated.
Nevertheless, China did not seek foreign assistance.

In the 1974 and 1988 operations in the South China Sea, China took
territory from South Vietnam and then from a united Vietnam. But in
an equally independent operation against its communist neighbour in
1979, China failed to teach Vietnam a lesson. Thus the Chinese
record is one of independent defence and offensive policy, and one
with a mixed record of success. To that extent, China is a great
power like only two other countries: Russia and the USA.

In economic terms, China has been less independent. In the period
of reconstruction in the 1950s there was large-scale Soviet aid in all
sectors of the Chinese economy. Although China claimed it had to
pay back all the aid, it is still true that the Soviet Union made real
sacrifices in extending the assistance. Given the precarious state of

the Chinese economy at the time, the relative importance of Soviet aid was high. Yet China's foreign trade never accounted for more than 5 per cent of GDP at that time. Given the continental dimensions of the Chinese economy, foreign economic relations were never as central for its prosperity as it was for any State in the region save for the Soviet Union. Nevertheless, when the Soviet Union withdrew its aid to China in 1960, the action made an already serious Chinese economic crisis even worse.

In the two decades following the Sino-Soviet split, China cut itself off from most foreign contacts that could have a comparable influence on the Chinese economy. In the 1980s, contacts with the West developed to the extent that some reports suggested more than 10 per cent of the Chinese economy depended on foreign trade. The ratio of trade to GDP rose from 16 to 29 per cent between 1981 and 1987.[39] Certainly the open-door policy allowed coastal regions to flourish and this had more than a superficial impact on the direction of the Chinese economy. Nevertheless, China was still able to turn the taps on and off in response to foreign trade problems, even with Japan. China chose the road of multiple paths to the open door, thereby ensuring it was not unduly reliant on one partner. Even the door to the Soviet Union and Eastern Europe was reopened in the late 1980s. Chinese independence was guaranteed by keeping its options open, a strategy made possible by the basic realities of continental China.

Similarly, cultural and ideological independence has been largely maintained, despite periods of relatively close ties to various States. The closest affiliation was with the Soviet model in the 1950s, including Soviet direction of ideology, education, and even some aspects of cultural policy. The backlash that culminated in the Great Proletarian Cultural Revolution was xenophobic in the extreme and was eventually abandoned.

With its traditional sense of being the 'middle kingdom', China has rarely seen the value of exporting its culture to the outside world. Emigrants took the culture abroad in large numbers, leaving a lasting impression on South East Asia. But Chinese immigrants in these communities showed few signs of acting as a fifth column for China, even at the height of official Chinese government support for revolutionary movements. In any case, these issues were more important for South East Asia and not relevant in North East Asia.

In the 1960s China showed it could go it alone in cultural and

ideological terms, although clearly not to the benefit of its people.
The result was the reforms of the Deng Xiaoping era and the open
door. Despite the wilder Western claims that China had adopted
capitalism and the Coca-Cola culture, the reality was more complex.
China did reform its ideology in order to implement what it prag-
matically called 'socialism with Chinese characteristics'. After the
Gorbachev reforms began, it became clear that China was clearly
operating within the confines of the new reformist trends in communism and not adopting capitalist ideology.[40] The Chinese had led
the way in economic reform, but were always more backward in
political reform. The brutal events of June 1989 in China, coming
just after the Sino-Soviet summit, were clear evidence of the deep-
rooted problems raised by such reforms.[41]

In broader cultural terms, China did open its doors to Western
influences. But the door remained on a swinging-hinge that swung
shut when 'bourgeois influences' and 'spiritual pollution' threatened
the rule of the party. The imposition of martial law in May 1989 was
only the most violent of the swings. What is more, China learned
from various sources, including Japan and Eastern and Western
Europe, thereby spreading the risk. By the late 1980s, even Soviet
culture was making a comeback in some circles.

This robustness of the Chinese political culture is no surprise.
After all, Chinese culture had long been dominant in the region.
Even though this dominance was lost outside China by the post-1945
period, it endured inside China. To be sure, China had still not
decided precisely what it wanted to borrow from the outside world,
but it was proud and conscious of its cultural heritage. China had
aspirations, albeit unofficial ones, to become a major power in the
world. It would not do so as anything but a modernized Sinic culture.

Russia is similar to China in its ability to remain independent in
North East Asia, although the process of transition from the Soviet
Union back to Russia will undoubtedly mean a major reassessment of
the precise type of role the Russians may play. The Soviet Union was
a superpower, but in East Asia it was always more vulnerable than in
Europe. The demise of communism may well allow Russia to evolve
into a power more naturally involved with the regional economy, but
the process of transition is bound to be prolonged.

In defence policy, the Soviet Union acted as independently as any
power.[42] It rumbled over Japanese troops at the end of the Second
World War and seized island territory off northern Japan. It also

rolled into Korea and set up a client State. The Soviet Union helped push China into the Korean War and Moscow ended the war in 1953 when it chose. It aided Vietnam in its struggle with America and eventually triumphed. China was trounced in border skirmishes in 1969 and eventually forced to the negotiating table. The Soviet Pacific fleet became bigger than its Atlantic fleet in the 1980s. Of course, it can be argued that many of these operations were mistakes. But they were mistakes the Soviet Union made and its use of force was entirely its own decision. At least in this respect, the Soviet Union was a superpower, even in East Asia.

In economic terms, the Soviet Union was always notable for its relative isolation from the international capitalist economy. The ratio of foreign trade to GDP hovered around 8 per cent in the 1980s and trade with North East Asia remained around 6 per cent of total Soviet trade in the same period. But given the relative economic weakness of the Soviet position in East Asia, its prosperity was dependent on economic ties with North East Asian neighbours. When relations with China were good, up to 100,000 Chinese worked in the Soviet Far East and goods crossed the border relatively freely. The Sino-Soviet split ended this interdependence with the Chinese economy.

In the 1970s the Soviet Union improved relations with Japan and sought Japanese investment in Siberia. Most of the dreams were unfulfilled, but it was made clear to Soviet planners that a serious degree of prosperity for the Soviet Far East depended on opening contacts with the capitalist Pacific.

The reforms of the 1980s in the Soviet Union began to explore both the Chinese/socialist and capitalist routes to interdependence.[43] The death of communism in the Soviet Union in 1991 meant that Russia would, in the medium term, be more able to seek closer integration with China, Japan, and the NICs. Even before the demise of communism the Soviet Union admitted that real reform required real interdependence. Given the small Russian population in East Asia and the vast distances from European Russia, it is clear that Russians will not be able to take anything like a leading role in North East Asian politics. Unlike China, Russia has fewer reserves of local culture and economic power to protect it from the influence of the international global economy. The old paradox returns, real power will require real interdependence and less real sovereignty. Thus only China may remain a truly independent power in North East Asia.

CONCLUSIONS AND THE HEREAFTER

The conclusions are obvious. *De facto* independence is becoming increasingly eroded, although at a faster pace for those States most closely involved in the global economy. The interdependence in the security field, most apparent in arms control, has not yet come formally to North East Asia. But there has been informal arms control that suggests even in this respect there is a growing recognition of the fading ability to guarantee national security.[44]

In the European context, it is arguable such interdependencies have gone on longer and have taken more formal shape. This is unlikely to happen in the same way in North East Asia. The balance of power is more complex and the political traditions more diverse. Informal arrangements are more likely to be developed in the tested pattern of pragmatism which has been seen in recent years.

NOTES

1. The region designated by the editors as North East Asia is arbitrary and in no way based on geographic, political, or economic logic. At a stretch it is the Sinic or Confucian zone, plus or minus some peripheral people. Its membership of nine includes Russia, China, Mongolia, North Korea, the three Newly Industrialized Countries (NICs, otherwise known as Newly Industrialized Economies if you prefer the Chinese term) of Taiwan, Hong Kong, South Korea, and not least Japan, one of the world's most developed States. Tiny Macao is counted as the ninth unit.
2. These themes are developed in G. Segal, *Rethinking the Pacific* (Oxford, 1990).
3. A. Sanders, *Mongolia* (London, 1987).
4. R. Rupen, *How Mongolia is Really Ruled* (Stanford, Calif., 1979).
5. Sanders, *Mongolia*, ch. 4.
6. M. Yahuda, *China's Role in World Affairs* (London, 1983).
7. 'A Survey of Hong Kong', *The Economist*, 3 June 1989.
8. In 1987 the ratio of trade volume to GDP reached 230 per cent, an increase on the already astounding figure of 187 per cent in 1981.
9. *Financial Times*, 6 Jan. 1989, and more generally M. Yahuda, *China's Foreign Relations After Mao* (London, 1983). See economic details in A. J. Youngson (ed.), *China and Hong Kong: The Economic Nexus* (Hong Kong, 1983); E. Chen, 'Foreign Trade and Economic Growth in Hong Kong', in C. Bradford and W. Branson (eds.), *Trade and Structural Change in Pacific Asia* (Chicago, 1987).

10. See a more general discussion in Segal, *Rethinking the Pacific*.
11. L. C. Harris, 'Towards Taiwan's Independence', *Pacific Review*, 1 (1988).
12. G. Segal, *Defending China* (Oxford, 1985).
13. Chiao Chiao Hsieh, *Strategy for Survival* (London, 1985) and M. Lasater, *The Taiwan Issue in Sino-American Relations* (Boulder, Col., 1984).
14. R. Wade, 'State Intervention in Outward Looking Development', in G. White (ed.), *Developmental States in East Asia* (London, 1988).
15. C. Schive, 'Trade Patterns of Taiwan', in Bradford and Branson (eds.), and S. Kuo, *The Taiwan Economy in Transition* (Boulder, Col., 1983).
16. K. Grosser and B. Bridges, 'Economic Interdependence in East Asia', *Pacific Review*, 1 (1990). See also *Far Eastern Economic Review*, 16 Mar. 1989.
17. See further details in *International Herald Tribune*, 7 Feb. 1989; *Far Eastern Economic Review*, 2 Feb. 1989; *Financial Times*, 3 Mar. 1989; and *The Economist*, 25 Mar. 1989.
18. R. Reich, 'Corporation and Nation', repr. from *The Atlantic in Dialogue*, 1 (1989).
19. For example A. Jordan and W. Taylor, 'Cut US Troops in Korea Now' in *New York Times*, 2 Dec. 1988.
20. G. Segal, 'The New Agenda for Sino-Soviet Relations', *The World Today*, May 1988.
21. R. L. Neurath, 'State Intervention and Export-Oriented Development in South Korea', in Gray, *Developmental States*.
22. Wontock Hong, 'Export-Oriented Growth and Trade Patterns of Korea', in Bradford and Branson (eds.).
23. *Financial Times*, 11 Jan. 1989.
24. 'Japan Survey', *The Far Eastern Economic Review*, 8 June 1989.
25. B. Bridges, *Korea and the West* (London, 1986).
26. Byung Chul Koh, *The Foreign Policy System of North and South Korea* (London, 1984).
27. C. Johnson, 'Democracy and Development', *The Pacific Review*, 1 (1989).
28. F. Langdon, 'Is Japan Ready to become a Full Western Ally?', *The Pacific Review*, 1 (1988).
29. R. Drifte, *Japanese Foreign Policy* (London, 1989).
30. M. McIntosh, *Japan Rearmed* (London, 1986).
31. 'The Yen Bloc', *The Economist*, 15 July 1989.
32. Reich, 'Corporation and Nation'.
33. *The Economist*, 4 Mar. 1989.
34. See generally D. Julius, *Global Companies and Public Policy* (London, 1990).
35. *Far Eastern Economic Review*, 8 June 1987.
36. Discussed in Segal, *Rethinking the Pacific*.
37. K. van Wolferen, *The Enigma of Japanese Power* (London, 1989).
38. Segal, *Defending China*.

39. M. Lockett, 'The Economy', in *The China Challenge* (London, 1987).
40. H. Harding, *China's Second Revolution* (Washington, DC, 1988).
41. For background see the special issue of *Pacific Review*, 2 (1989) and *China in Crisis* (London, 1989).
42. D. Zagoria (ed.), *Soviet Policy in East Asia* (New Haven, Conn., 1982); G. Segal (ed.), *The Soviet Union in East Asia* (London, 1983); and R. Thakur and C. Thayer (eds.), *The Soviet Union as an Asian Pacific Power* (London, 1987).
43. G. Segal, *The Soviet Union and the Pacific* (Boston, 1990).
44. G. Segal (ed.), *Arms Control in Asia* (London, 1987).

FURTHER READING

Drysdale, P., *International Economic Pluralism* (London, 1988).
Elegant, R., *Pacific Destiny* (London, 1990).
Haggard, S., *Pathways From the Periphery* (London, 1990).
McCord, W., *The Dawn of the Pacific Century* (London, 1991).
Mack, A., and Keal, P. (eds.), *Security and Arms Control in the North Pacific* (London, 1988).
Rozman, G. (ed.), *The East Asian Region* (Princeton, NJ, 1991).
Segal, G., *Rethinking the Pacific* (Oxford, 1990).
Shibusawa, M., *Pacific Asia in the 1990s* (London, 1992).
White, G., *Developmental States in Asia* (London, 1988).

II

Oceania

J. D. B. MILLER

Oceania (by which is meant here the South Pacific Islands, together with Papua New Guinea, Australia, and New Zealand) is the home of the archetypal mini- and micro-State. Here the gap between status and power is perhaps greater than anywhere else. Nauru, with an area of 8 square miles and a population of 9,000, seems as small as a State can get; yet it has a rival in Tuvalu as the smallest of the small: Tuvalu also has about 9,000 people. Both of these entities are sovereign States. The other island States have bigger populations, but most of them are still absurdly small by European or American standards. It is true that there are bigger countries near by—Papua New Guinea, Australia, and New Zealand, which will be given their due here; but the emphasis in this chapter will be on the island States, their relations with each other and with the regional powers just mentioned, and their place in the world.

It cannot be said that the islands have been of major importance to the outside world, or indeed to anyone but themselves. Apart from being caught up in the major powers' scramble for colonies in the nineteenth century, and (for some of them) being fought over in the Second World War, they have lived enclosed lives. They have not figured prominently in world trade, except for Fiji sugar, Nauruan phosphate, and copra from a number of islands; they have not captured any headlines with struggles for independence (except for the non-independent New Caledonia); and it can be questioned whether they have been important in strategic terms, although a naval strategist with an eye to base facilities can make them appear to be so, as happened when the USA obtained a 'strategic trusteeship' over the Micronesian islands from the UN.

To the Western world they have since the late eighteenth century been islands of romance in the South Seas, and the abode of the noble savage and the sexually indulgent.[1] In the twentieth these images were coarsened by the movies. Dorothy Lamour, Bob Hope, and Bing Crosby were more in the way of symbols of the islands to the English-speaking countries than anything or anyone indigenous, until *South Pacific* appeared; even then, the indigenous element was subordinated to the French and American. Gauguin's paintings gave Europe a romantic picture of Tahiti, but the interest proved to be more in Gauguin than in the people he painted. The same was true of the various romantic versions of the mutiny on the *Bounty*: the emphasis was on the Europeans.

To some extent, this indifference towards the island peoples arose from their situation as inhabitants of tiny dots on the world's biggest ocean. Clearly, they had something in common in terms of their distant origins and the kinds of society which they had developed. But they were mostly so far apart that there was little contact between them, their outside connections were very much with colonial powers (though education and migration did give their peoples some knowledge of one another), and their economies were not adjusted to the modern world. There were exceptions resulting from foreign investment, such as the sugar and phosphates already mentioned, and gold in Papua New Guinea; but these did not bulk large for the islands as a whole. When sovereignty came to them, it came suddenly and to peoples largely unprepared for it.

That was not true of Australia and New Zealand, which must have been amongst the most reluctant of ex-colonies to accept statehood. Founded in the late eighteenth and early nineteenth centuries as settlements of people from the British Isles, they preserved a 'British' quality, and a determination to follow Britain in all respects, until the 1930s and 1940s. Even the passage of the Statute of Westminster in 1931, which established 'dominion status' as a matter of formal independence from Britain, passed them by: it took some time before they ratified the Statute, and even then they were sometimes disinclined to declare their independence. To this day it is impossible to point to definite dates at which they achieved sovereignty, though it is now universally accepted that they are sovereign States.

That fact has been established by such actions as their alliance with the USA (and by New Zealand's defiance of American attempts to berth US naval ships in its harbours without affirming their non-nuclear character); their joint participation in the Vietnam War while Britain remained neutral; Australia's treatment of British people as foreign nationals; and their willingness to pursue their own interests

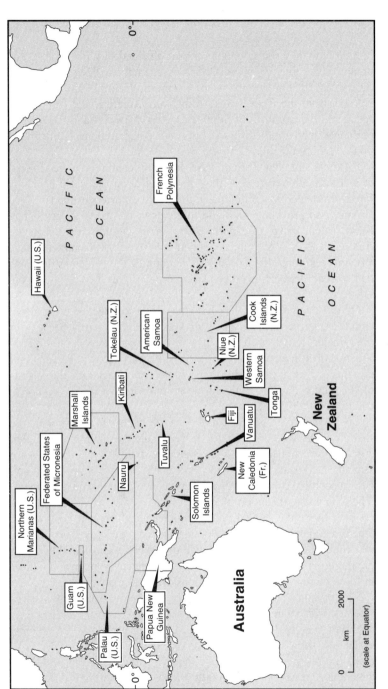

FIG. 11.1 Oceania

in international forums, whether these coincided with British interests or not. Since the 1940s, Australia's population has been increasingly diversified by immigrants from Northern, Central, and Southern Europe, from the Arab States, from South America, and from Hong Kong and the countries of South East Asia. New Zealand has not experienced such a wide diversity, but has had its traditional 'Britishness' diluted by immigration from the South Pacific.

Australia and New Zealand have, however, continued to be affected to a considerable degree by their dependence on the world economy for their prosperity. Traditionally, they were exporters of foodstuffs to Britain, also providing wool and minerals to the world at large. The New Zealand range of exports, always more circumscribed than the Australian, was especially dependent on the British market. Since Britain's entry into the European Community, the two countries have had to seek markets in other places, especially in East Asia and the USA.

Of the two, Australia has had the closer connection with Asian countries, partly because of its greater proximity, partly because of the greater range of its exports (especially minerals), and partly because of a more intensive effort on the part of its politicians and diplomats. New Zealand has been more concerned with the islands of the South Pacific. Both, however, have long-standing economic connections with these.

To what extent Australia and New Zealand will proceed in the shadow of major Asian States is very much a matter of opinion. There is no compelling reasons why they should. Their cultures are strongly European in character, and likely to remain so. They still have substantial connections with Europe in both trade and investment. There is little likelihood that any Asian power would attempt to conquer them: the gains would be problematical, and the costs heavy. There are richer pickings in South East Asia. Yet it is clear that the two countries' future prosperity will depend to a considerable extent upon mutual trade with Asian countries, particularly Japan and China; in these circumstances good relations are a necessity.

The relationship between Australia and New Zealand themselves (the first with 16 million people, the second 3,500,000), requires little attention. The two countries' political systems and attitudes, accents, social structure, and institutions of various kinds are so similar as to make the two peoples more alike than any others one can find. This generalization has not been greatly affected by either their differential immigration in recent years or the considerable intermarriage between Maoris and whites in New Zealand. Migration between the two countries is continuous, at present being very largely from New Zealand. The fact that New Zealand was frozen out of the ANZUS Pact with the USA because of the Lange government's approach to nuclear issues has made no noticeable difference to relations between Australia and New Zealand. They are steadily becoming a single free-trade area. They rarely differ on major international questions, and are very much alike in their approaches to the island States.

To the South Pacific island States, Australia and New Zealand are patrons whom it is desirable to cultivate so that aid will continue, along with opportunities for trade, investment, and migration. The differences in living standards between the two settler countries and the island States, so largely indigenous in their economies and populations, mean that the two will give and the others take.

BIRTH

The island States are, in descending order of population and with their dates of achieving independence:[2] Papua New Guinea (3.9 million) 1975; Fiji (736,000) 1970; Solomon Islands (320,000) 1978; Western Samoa (161,000) 1962; Vanuatu (145,000) 1980; the Federated States of Micronesia (100,000) 1990; Tonga (98,000) 1970; Kiribati (73,000) 1979; the Republic of the Marshall Islands (43,380) 1990; Tuvalu (9,000) 1978; Nauru (9,000) 1968.

It is important in terms of the international politics of the region to list also the territories which, while still affected by colonial powers, have been granted varying degrees of self-government. They include: New Caledonia (164,173); French Polynesia (188,000); American Samoa (46,638); Cook Islands (18,000); Tokelau (1,690); Niue (2,000). There is also American Micronesia, which comprises countries in varying stages of self-government: Guam (132,726); the Northern Marianas (43,345); and the Republic of Palau (15,000).

The colonial connections of the various territories have had a considerable effect on the development of their institutions and upon their orientation towards the outside world. Of the sovereign States, Fiji, the Solomon Islands, Tonga, Kiribati, and Tuvalu were British dependencies; Papua New Guinea was Australian, and Vanuatu an Anglo-French condominium under the name of the New Hebrides;

Western Samoa was successively a New Zealand mandate and trust territory, while Nauru was held jointly as a mandate and then a trust territory by Australia, Britain, and New Zealand, but administered by Australia. Of the non-independent territories, New Caledonia and the islands of French Polynesia, centred on Tahiti, are French; the Micronesian territories and American Samoa are American (in spite of US disclaimers); and the Cook Islands, Tokelau, and Niue are still linked with New Zealand.

Some of the island territories were once ruled by Germany and some by Japan; but the two world wars altered the situation, providing Australia, New Zealand, and the USA with the opportunities reflected above. The German and Japanese legacies are now paying dividends in the form of development aid. Linguistically, the division of the islands between Anglophone and Francophone means that there are two kinds of regime in the South Pacific. The point is elaborated below.

Independence came easily to the islands which are now sovereign. The principal influence was not local demand but, in the case of the former British dependencies, the obvious desire of the British government to get rid of its remaining colonies once it had disposed of those in Africa and the Caribbean. Whatever the reasons why the island colonies had been acquired in the first place (and they ranged from missionary pressure to the need for coaling stations), they had disappeared by the end of the 1970s. Britain had ceased to be a naval power in or near the Pacific; there was very little British investment in the islands, Australia being the principal source of capital and expertise; and there were no British settlers to constitute the sort of problem they had created in Kenya and Rhodesia—unless one counts the fewer than 100 descendants of the *Bounty* mutineers on Pitcairn Island, whose sparseness in numbers has not prevented their coming under the notice of United Nations committees. No aspect of British external policy could be said to be affected by the Pacific islands. Nevertheless, there have been some signs lately of a revival of British concern based upon considerations of alliance with the US and France, rather than upon specifically British interests.

The only problems of decolonization which Britain faced were in Fiji, where there were two somewhat incompatible peoples, indigenous Fijians and immigrant-descended Indians, and in the New Hebrides (now Vanuatu) where it was necessary to end the condominium with France. Both were successfully surmounted, and difficult internal consequences in the two territories were not encountered until the 1980s, long after British responsibility had ended. By the time the South Pacific islands gained their independence, the British had extensive experience in framing post-colonial constitutions, and were not averse to some changes in the Westminster system if this would please the people who had to operate the new arrangements.[3]

The need to determine a basis for self-determination, which had sometimes been difficult to identify in Africa and Asia where tribes and communities often extended across land boundaries, and where in some cases the 'self' could be visualized only in administrative terms (as, for example, in Nigeria), was much less evident in the Pacific. An island has a natural boundary; so usually has a group of islands. Such conditions applied to all the island territories, but not to Papua New Guinea, which had an extensive land boundary with West Irian, a part of Indonesia, and which was also close to the Solomon Islands (one of which, Bougainville, is part of Papua New Guinea), and to the Torres Strait Islands, which are part of Australia.

In general, the islands' selves were already determined before independence became an issue. British policy was simply to give up control of entities which were already in existence and did not require definition, though they might call for a change of name. The policies of Australia and New Zealand towards their dependencies were, like the British, part of the general decolonization movement of the 1960s, though somewhat in advance of Britain's. Papua New Guinea was given independence by Australia notwithstanding its strategic and economic significance: the will to go on governing three million alien people was not present amongst the 15 million Australians, and there was no support for its becoming Australia's 'seventh State'. New Zealand's interest in Western Samoa, Niue, and the Cook and Tokelau Islands also had strategic and economic aspects, and there were, too, ethnic links between their people and New Zealand's Maoris. But these considerations did not stop the territories' advance to independence or self-government. New Zealand's relationship with them is more familial than Australia's with Papua New Guinea. In addition, New Zealand was (and is) able to act as a big fish in a small pond.

Colonial powers' policies, rather than local agitation, were thus the reasons for the creation of sovereign States in the South Pacific. It is a colonial power's policies that stand in the way of further independence there. France has reasons for denying independence to New Caledonia and French Polynesia, in the first case because of resistance from French settlers and other non-Melanesians, in the second because of the value of Mururoa and other atolls as nuclear test sites, and in both because of reluctance to give in to pressure from all the sovereign States of the region. There have been calls for independence in French Polynesia; in New Caledonia the Kanaks have campaigned for it with some success. In both the territories, France's subsidies—far greater than Britain's ever were—provide an argument against going it alone, especially in French Polynesia.

The fact that all the sovereign States in the area have criticized the continuance of French colonialism is no more important than is their opposition to French nuclear testing. They have little or no chance of marshalling massive resistance to France; in any case, they get little response from the local peoples, except for political activists. As suggested above, one can regard the South Pacific as divided into two separate international regimes. On the one hand there are the former British, Australian, New Zealand, and (in practice) American colonies, all Anglophone, and nearly all represented in the South Pacific Forum along with Australia and New Zealand, which attract much of their attention, except in the case of the Micronesians. On the other there are the French territories, very much focused on France and built in its image so far as their élites are concerned. One regime is characterized by sovereignty, the other by colonialism; but perhaps the differing cultures acquired from the metropolitan powers are more important than the formal status of the territories in keeping the two regimes apart. In between them, in a sense, lies uneasy Vanuatu. As a result of the Anglo-French condominium, which established two education systems, one in each language and under Church control, Catholics speak French and Anglicans and Presbyterians English; there is an Anglophone–Francophone division in politics and in education.

The present pattern of independent statehood seems likely to persist, whether there is a change in the status of the French territories or not. None of the existing States shows any inclination to merge with any other. The normal attractions of statehood and the distances which separate most of them provide sufficient reason for them to stay as they are. Indeed, the fact that their Exclusive Economic Zones (EEZs) extend so far within these great distances is an especially cogent reason for retaining the existing territorial character of the island States. The sorts of States they are may well change as internal conflicts become sharper: the Fiji experience is instructive here. On the whole, however, the States are likely to preserve the *status quo* in respect of one another, and their joint arrangements—largely in terms of the South Pacific Forum—show no sign of change.

DEATH

The lack of change just suggested relates to change brought about by political forces and processes. There is another kind of change which could well affect the situation: physical change. The fact that a number of the States consist of small islands means that their futures can be greatly affected by an alteration in the global environment. If the 'greenhouse effect' has the consequences postulated for it, including a rise in sea-level, some of the low-lying atolls could disappear. Another physical factor threatens the future of Nauru, which may lose its viability when the phosphates run out in the next few decades.[4] Such physical changes could lead to wholesale evacuation of populations and perhaps an end to the States affected. There are also some Micronesian and Polynesian islands which may be so depopulated through voluntary emigration that very little of their society remains.

Thus, it may some day be quite correct to speak of the 'death' of some of the States, in the sense, not of absorption into other States, but of a closer approximation to the physical dissolution which occurs in animals and human beings. It may never happen in regard to the warming of the global climate, but is certain in the case of Nauru's present means of sustaining life. The effects of substantial emigration can perhaps be likened more to anaemia; but prolonged anaemia could well become living death.

LIFE

Internal contexts

The life which the island States lead within the international community is essentially that of minor figures in both politics and economics. None of them is big enough to affect other States' lives in any compelling fashion: even the biggest, Papua New Guinea, lives next door to Indonesia, the largest State of South East Asia, whose population, military forces, and position in the world economy far outweigh those of Papua New Guinea. It could perhaps lean heavily on its smaller island neighbours, the Solomons and Vanuatu; but it is difficult to see how anything positive could be achieved by doing so. None of the other States could do anything of the same nature. Similarly, none of the island States has either military force or an economy sufficiently strong, diversified, specialized, or strategic to cause difficulty to other States by refusing to co-operate in trade, investment, finance, or military activity.

Some of the island States' internal problems embroil them in international situations, and some impel them to look for international solutions or at least for some sort of help. Amongst the problems are the following: first, they lack resources with which to provide themselves with substantial military forces, especially the naval strength needed to police their EEZs. Papua New Guinea has 200 men in its navy, with five combatant vessels.[5] The others have none, though they expect to get patrol boats from Australia as a gift. Second, there is the vulnerability of all the islands to natural disasters such as hurricanes: when these occur, there are few local resources to provide food, clothes, and shelter for those rendered homeless; disaster aid from abroad has to be solicited and welcomed, though it often becomes the subject of argument about suitability. Third, there is the difficulty of making more efficient the export industries on which the islands' external trade rests, together with that of financing new industries. They have little prospect of trading with one another, so they look for international sources of funds. They urgently need to diversify their economies in order to provide further export income, but they are hindered by heavy transport costs, the lack of relevant skills, and the impossibility of achieving economies of scale.

A fourth problem is the pressure of population, not so obvious in Polynesia because of massive emigration, but very evident in Melanesia, and presenting a problem for more prosperous countries expected to accept immigrants: this in itself is an international problem, not unlike the reception of refugees. Fifth, there are frequent balance of payments deficits, leading to increased debt to foreign banks or the IMF to the extent that the deficits are not covered or reduced by foreign aid and remittances from expatriates. Sixth, there is the difficulty that in most cases the island States have inherited high standards of government provision in such fields as health, education, administration, and law and order; these have to be paid for. Continuing with these services is increasingly expensive, since the parliamentary representatives of different areas demand more of them. Local tax bases are often insufficient to meet that demand, especially since the élites who staff the services are adept at getting their salaries raised. This in itself accentuates the attractiveness of jobs in cities and draws attention away from the legitimate demands of agriculture, as elsewhere in the Third World. The effect is to divert aid from infrastructure and production to administration of various kinds. International organizations such as WHO and FAO are the obvious bodies from which to seek assistance, but Australia and New Zealand provide most of the funds.

Each of these problems draws the islands further into the international system. So do others. Those listed are generated by the physical and economic circumstances of the island States. They do not involve ideology in the sense of political belief; they are practical problems characteristic of Third World countries with simple economies. There is, however, a further dimension of questions in which ideology is deeply embedded and which impels the island States to take up attitudes within the international community. It involves two major issues which are in no sense confined to Oceania, but have special relevance there. They excite favourable reactions to the island States' protests when these are made in international organizations such as the UN. They are colonialism and nuclear weapons. In both cases the villain of the piece is France.[6] Whereas the other problems are intrinsically intractable and highly diffuse in practice, these two arouse strong emotions which are readily mobilized against France and sometimes against the USA. They are the stuff of political rhetoric; discussions at the South Pacific Forum are enlivened by them, while the socio-economic questions are likely to be regarded as routine. Since solutions to the latter problems would require complex and sometimes unwelcome action domestically, it is no wonder that the two ideological issues have come to dominate the international stance of the island States as a group.

External relations

Against this background the external relations of the island States since independence can now be examined. The main question is whether their sovereignty has been under threat. The answer is 'no', though this would not satisfy ideologues who maintain that any dependence upon foreign capital and foreign markets is a derogation from sovereignty. But in terms of continued formal independence, the States which became sovereign in the 1960s and 1970s have remained so: no foreign power has invaded them, attempted to take them over, or instituted subversion of their governments.

Because of the island States' meagre resources and small size, they have placed much reliance on their sovereignty as a means of enhancing their international status and protecting themselves against unwelcome intrusion, whether economic or political. David Hegarty writes that they 'hold to an acute notion of sovereignty', and that they argue that 'security is advanced ... when neighbouring States, friend or foe, "respect" their political independence, and are not "intrusive" and do not attempt to dictate or direct small States' foreign and domestic behavior.'[7] In pursuit of these aims, they value their membership of the UN and of the Commonwealth of Nations (where these apply), but even more, probably, membership of the South Pacific Forum. Here they can combine to deplore colonialism, nuclear testing, and the disposal of nuclear waste—and can exert some pressure on Australia and New Zealand, the nearest developed countries and those with which their relations are closest. In the UN General Assembly they are merely the latest addition to the Third World majority, which is dominated by the Arab and African blocs. No one takes much notice of them. In the Forum, however, they are the raison d'être: it was formed by them and has survived because of their energy and persistence, plus the conviction of Australia and New Zealand that it is worth while to be associated with them.

A notable example of the effects of sovereignty as a factor in Oceania was provided by the coups in Fiji in 1987. These involved the ousting by the army (composed of native Fijians) of a newly elected government largely, but by no means entirely, supported by Indians, and the likelihood of a new constitution which would place power firmly in the hands of native Fijians. Such events, unparalleled amongst the island States (though there was an unsuccessful attempt at an insurrection in Vanuatu in 1980, put down with the help of troops from Papua New Guinea), stirred the Australian and New Zealand governments to protest. They deplored what had happened and demanded that the ousted government be restored.

The effects of sovereignty manifested themselves at two levels. The first was in respect of Fiji itself. There was little protest from native Fijians against the coups; if anything, foreign criticisms increased local support for Colonel Sitiveni Rabuka, the military leader, though some of this has since faded away. The local Indians tacitly approved the demands for restoration, but were frightened to say much. The second level was that of the island States as a group. It became clear that Papua New Guinea, Vanuatu, and the Solomons saw the situation as one in which Fijians were trying to defend their control of their own islands against immigrant-descended Indians—and deserved support, not criticism. They did not share the indignation of the Australians and New Zealanders, whose utterances became more muted with their awareness of Melanesian opinion. For the same reason, and as another instance, the Melanesian States and their Polynesian counterparts were in favour of Kanak (i.e. Melanesian) control of New Caledonia.

The significance of sovereignty in such cases lies not in the exercise of power in any palpable sense, but in the inconvenience and embarrassment caused to the State which is being opposed. In the Fiji instance, Australia and New Zealand did not wish to experience opposition within the context of the South Pacific Forum. The goodwill of the island States was cherished by the governments of Australia and New Zealand. To alienate them could be highly inconvenient.

To say this is not to deny the point made earlier about the colonialism and nuclear issues—that the public opposition of the South Pacific Forum has not deflected France from its purpose, and that the island States have exerted little influence in practice, even though much of their criticism has had support from Australia and New Zealand. When a major power is determined to pursue a particular course, it need take little account of weaker neighbours, sovereign though they may be: it is a case of equal States, unequal powers. Only when the stronger power can see disadvantage in continuing to ignore the weaker ones is it likely to take some notice of them. Thus at first the USA ignored the complaints of the island States about the loss they suffered from the operations of American tuna boats in their waters, and actually cut off aid to the Solomons when a tuna boat was seized for illegal operations. When, however, the Soviet Union began to show interest in the South Pacific, the USA agreed that they had a case, and went on to reach an agreement with them in 1987.

The tuna boat issue illustrates the importance of sovereign status in terms of the islands' Exclusive Economic Zones (EEZs). These maritime zones are substantial. Kiribati has a sea area of 3,550,000 square kilometres in contrast with its land area of 690 square kilometres; Tuvalu has 900,000 to its land area of 26 square kilometres. The other instances are less striking, but still remarkable.[8] The EEZs represent tangible resources which only a sovereign State can claim (though it can also claim for its colonies: New Caledonia and French Polynesia have extensive EEZs negotiated by France). Sovereign status enables the island States to make common cause with other archipelago States; to act together in support of the extension of their jurisdiction beyond the traditionally narrow limits; and to indulge in mutual support when one of them is subject to infringement. All this, of course, flows from the fact that their status was fundamentally altered—from colonial subordination to independent statehood. As such, the essence of the island States' active foreign policy is embarrassment of major powers by the use of publicity, agitation, lobbying, and rhetoric.

The importance of outside powers

The external concerns of the island States can now be summarized, leaving aside such issues of individual importance as the West Irian issue as it affects Papua New Guinea. For the group as a whole, certain States are important, as follows.

Apart from the significance of the islands it controls, *France* is a symbolic presence in the South Pacific, a symbol of colonial power, disregard of others' interests, and determination to preserve a nuclear deterrent by tests far distant from metropolitan France. There is a basic contrast between France and *Britain* in their approaches to colonies and former colonies. France interferes, Britain does not. Britain has played no role in post-colonial Oceania, just as it has played only a minor role in post-colonial Africa. The promises made about aid have been kept, but that is all. Britain appears to have no interest in the area. Perhaps it never had more than an administrative concern superimposed upon the varying motives it had for originally acquiring the colonies.

It is difficult to distinguish between wishful thinking and fact in regard to the interest that *Russia* has in the South Pacific. Since the beginning of 1971, when Edward Heath enlivened a Commonwealth Heads of Government meeting at Singapore by telling them that Russian naval vessels were on their way through the Strait of Malacca and could be seen from the window, there was Western concern about what role the Russians wished to play in both the Indian Ocean and the South Pacific. The Soviet accession to the one-time US base at Camranh Bay in Vietnam, and uncertainty about the Philippines' attitude towards continued US occupancy of bases there, made for intensive propaganda from CINCPAC (the command structure of the US Pacific fleet in Hawaii) about the threat posed by a Russian presence in the South Pacific, and the need for the island States to give at least tacit support to the USA. Opinion is still divided about the significance of the Soviet fishing agreements with Kiribati in 1985 and Vanuatu in 1987. Those opposed to Russia became convinced that it wishes to infiltrate the island States in the interests of a major naval presence which might be a threat to the sea-lanes. Others maintain, as the now defunct Soviet Union itself did, that its concern is merely with fishing and will have no effect on local security. So far, there has been no obvious infiltration. It is certain that none of the island States wishes to be beholden to Russia; but they are also wary of the USA, and indeed of any States more powerful and more experienced than themselves. Contact with the Russians is still on a very small scale.

For those in the islands, the *USA* is represented primarily by the Pacific fleet and by its command, CINCPAC. CINCPAC's importance in determining US policy should not be underestimated. It has many friends in Congress, and can tap the deep wells of traditional American concern about the Pacific, fed by memories of Japanese perfidy and by the apprehensions of Californians, and now augmented by the importance of Japan, China, and Korea to the USA. Whether there were Russian intentions in the South Pacific or not, CINCPAC's conviction that its future depended on the worst possible construction of those intentions would register with Congress and with important sections of the public in the USA.

Nevertheless, the USA remains a magnet for many island people, and a possible source of munificence to their governments, most of which (with the possible exception of the regime in Vanuatu) have been broadly favourable towards the USA and concerned at the effect that any incursion by the Soviet Union might have on their peoples. In any case, American influence is firmly established in Micronesia and American Samoa, and is unlikely to decline.

The influence of *Libya* has been inflated beyond recognition by those in the islands and elsewhere who wish to capitalize upon it. Libyan policy is to cultivate malcontents in a wide range of Third

World countries in the hope of swinging those countries' governments against the USA, Israel, France, and other States which have attracted Libyan enmity. Vanuatu is the island State which has shown the most interest in Libya at the official level; the others have been more cautious. Any influence likely to be exerted by Libya would almost certainly be countered by Western countries through aid of various kinds. At the most, Libya could be only an exotic and distant player in the Pacific game.

It is *Japan* and to a lesser extent *China* which some observers of the South Pacific think might bulk large in the affairs of the island States in future. China would have a starting-point in the small groups of Chinese traders who have long been a feature of island life, notably in Papua New Guinea. It is difficult, however, to see what China would gain from spending money so far away on such insignificant countries, except perhaps to combat the influence of Taiwan. They have little or nothing to give that China does not have already. It is different with Japan. The islands have, in some cases, natural resources which Japan would find useful, such as timber, copper, and fish. They are also ripe for development by the Japanese tourist industry, with Japanese businessmen and honeymoon couples as the obvious consumers.

Since Japan began to amass large balance of payments surpluses, it has looked around for places where some of this money might be spent on economic aid, so as to improve the previously unimpressive Japanese record in this regard. The island States offer a useful area in which to operate. They are small and poor, peaceful and largely conservative by nature; it would not be necessary for Japan to spend much in order to cultivate a good reputation. Moreover, Japanese aid policy has usually concentrated on the infrastructure (roads, ports, transport, etc.) which would enable Japanese companies to develop such local industries as timber and fishing for the Japanese market. It is true that in the islands there are fading memories of the harsh practices employed by Japanese forces in the Second World War; this is a reason for Japan to be circumspect, but, as in South East Asia, the memories would be unlikely to affect local States' policies if enough Japanese aid and investment were forthcoming.

The island States' approach to *Australia* and *New Zealand* is equivocal, as is theirs to them. These are the States which the islands know best. When questions of migration arise in the island States, it is to these two countries (and to the USA) that people are most likely to want to go.

Australia is bigger and richer and has more substantial military forces than New Zealand, but both are involved in local security arrangements. 'Australia has a Defence Co-operation Agreement with the Forum island countries whereby patrol boats and other surveillance assistance are supplied, and the Royal New Zealand Air Force helps patrol the island countries' EEZs.'[9] Australia and New Zealand continue to play important parts in the islands' shipping and aviation services, and in the supply of consumer goods, and Australia has been prominent in the development of the tourist industry. Its trading houses are still of importance. All in all, there is considerable Australian and New Zealand influence in the islands' affairs. The difficulty which this entails is that Australia in particular is easily stigmatized as 'Big Brother' when something with which it has been connected goes wrong.[10] No matter how much Australian prime ministers may strive at Forum meetings to emphasize the sovereign equality which they share with the island leaders, there is still an unavoidable air of superiority and sometimes a touch of arrogance in what they say and do.

The issues arising from Australia's adjustment of its defence policy from 1987 onwards were more complex. Briefly, the Hawke government in Australia put aside the traditional Australian policy of sending forces abroad to support major allies (first Britain, then the USA) in distant theatres of war. Instead, a policy of home defence emerged, involving not only the Australian mainland, but also two zones of strategic concern. The first, of direct military interest, includes Indonesia, Papua New Guinea, New Zealand, and countries of the South West Pacific. The second, of broader interest, extends to South East Asia and farther into the Pacific.

The zone concept necessarily involves the island States, with particular emphasis on Papua New Guinea. It means that Australia will become more concerned about those States' military circumstances, through supply of equipment, joint exercises, sharing of intelligence, and the like. There is a fine line between this kind of co-operation between micro-States and a larger and richer one, and actual or perceived domination by the larger State. This writer, an unreformed Cobdenite, believes that any Australian attempt to police the South Pacific in terms of installing acceptable regimes and withstanding real or imagined inroads by external powers would be a failure; the example of the USA in the Caribbean is one to avoid. Others hold different views. It is certain, however, that some political elements in the island States are amenable to a policeman's role for Australia, while others are strongly against it.

This survey of the range of relations with particular countries of greater power and significance indicates that the island States have little to fear so far as their sovereignty is concerned. They do, however, require skilled diplomacy and effective administration if they are to distinguish between possible suitors, make the best use of available aid, and yet retain, as far as possible, their freedom of action. It is most unlikely that any power would attempt to annex any of them or subject them to military pressure; but that is not the only form of pressure, and weak States may have difficulty in withstanding the subtler forms—especially when these seem to promise more prosperity.

Pressure may come from foreign firms and multinationals as well as from foreign governments. The island States' freedom so far from assaults, real or imagined, by multinationals may be simply an index of their lack of resources and their small size. Where there are resources of obvious value, as with copper in the island of Bougainville, and gold elsewhere in Papua New Guinea, multinationals have shown an interest: in the Bougainville case, unusual in the amount of capital required and the massive nature of the mining enterprise, it was originally possible to arrive at arrangements taking account of the interests of the multinationals, of the Papua New Guinea government, and of the local people. One major instance of this kind can serve as a guide to future negotiations. The fact that the island States can call on official and unofficial advice from Australia and New Zealand, which are developed States with ample and varied experience of multinationals, is something of a safeguard for them.

As in regard to their relations with major States, there does not seem to be any threat from non-State actors to the sovereignty of the island States, though there may be an impact on their social cohesion through such activities as tourism. Most non-State actors, such as the multinationals, have bigger fish to fry; in any case, the days when fruit, rubber, and mining companies could hold small States to ransom appear to be over. It is lack of attention from major corporations, rather than too much attention, that the islands have to fear. Probably they should be more concerned about get-rich-quick operators who promise high returns for investment and have their eyes on quick profits before they decamp, or wish to use the islands' sovereignty for their own purposes. The islands' social and economic circumstances may well be affected by foreign financial influences, while their sovereignty remains unimpaired.

To see the island States' situation in this way is to emphasize the profound difference between them on the one hand and Australia and New Zealand on the other, where external investment is sedulously sought. The opposite is often true of the island States. They have, at one and the same time, more homogeneous societies and more fragile economies.

HEREAFTER

There is no prospect of integration between the island States. They are too far away from each other in most cases to make this practicable. By a stretch of the imagination one could envisage a Melanesian Federation comprising Papua New Guinea, the Solomons, and Vanuatu. But it is no more than a phantom. It can join other ghosts such as the federations which existed or were proposed in the Caribbean, East Africa, and Central Africa.

The island States have, however, provided themselves with a regional association, the South Pacific Forum, which, as has been seen, enables them to act together in matters on which they can agree. It also gives them special access to Australia and New Zealand. Formed in 1971, it comprises all the sovereign States of the area and some of the others. Originally composed only of countries with a background of British, Australian, and New Zealand colonialism, 'the inclusion in May 1987 of the Marshall Islands and the Federated States of Micronesia in the Forum has enormously extended the boundaries of Forum interest, while also increasing regional liabilities. The American defence connection with Micronesia is . . . an implied locking of the area into global interests.'[11]

The members' heads of government assemble once a year. In between these meetings the Forum has been served by the SPEC (South Pacific Bureau for Economic Co-operation) which has recently changed its name to Forum Secretariat, but continues to operate in much the same way. There is also the Forum Fisheries Agency which helps with managing fishing stocks and in negotiations with foreign countries which fish the area. The Forum was responsible for the Treaty of Rarotonga of 1985, which established a South Pacific Nuclear-Free Zone; this came into effect in December 1986, after eight of the Forum members had ratified it. Its protocols, designed to be agreed to by the nuclear powers, have been accepted by the Soviet Union and China, but not by the nuclear powers of the West. The Forum has also been active in protests against French nuclear testing, in comment on the New Caledonia situation, and in setting up SPARTECA (the South Pacific Regional Trade and Economic Agreement) which it was hoped would increase the flow of island products to Australia and New Zealand. It has had only moderate success.

The Forum appears to offer no threat to sovereignty. The Australian and New Zealand governments have been careful not to give any appearance of domination, and have been largely successful in this. The Forum's staff operates with a low profile. The emphasis is very much on the independence and formal equality of the member States. The annual meetings involve differences of approach but not at the level which would preclude practical co-operation.

There is another international organization in the region, the South Pacific Commission, originally constituted in 1947 with the colonial powers as members. Of these, the Dutch have since dropped out. As the island States became independent, they joined the Commission; but it was dissatisfaction with the lingering colonialist tone of the organization, especially the presence of France (the SPC's headquarters is in Nouméa) that led to the formation of the Forum. The Commission was in any case supposed to deal with economic and social questions and to eschew politics; this was unsatisfactory to the élites of some of the newly independent States. It still provides some technical services. In the island States' policies the emphasis is very much on the Forum.

In conclusion, one can say that the small States of Oceania have survived because they are really quite small and not the object of any major State's rapacity; because their economies are relatively simple; because, with one or two exceptions, their reliance on international trade has not been so great as to cause disruption (though this is by no means a permanent condition); because their societies have proved fairly easy-going and have not produced crises except for the coups in Fiji, the troubles in Bougainville, and various goings-on in Vanuatu; because their relations with major powers have been restricted, mostly cordial, and irritating rather than discordant; because Australia and

New Zealand, in spite of occasional grumbles, have not so far tried to rule the roost; and because the Pacific is so vast that they can still seem remote in spite of modern communications. Though they are so unequal with the major powers, their formal sovereignty has helped their size, their location, and their societies to keep them in being. A sovereign State, however small, is a formidable adversary in terms of publicity—much more so than a Goa or an East Timor. Sovereignty is no guarantee of security, but it helps. It has helped Australia and New Zealand to acquire a certain degree of dignity and influence in international affairs, and may do the same for the smaller States.

NOTES

1. It is difficult to imagine a more sensitive and understanding portrayal of these attitudes than G. Daws, *A Dream of Islands* (New York, 1980).
2. The figures for population are from *The Statesman's Year-Book 1988–89*. They are rounded off and are meant to be indicative at the best.
3. Some of the arrangements were unusual. See G. Fry, 'Succession of Government in the Post-Colonial States of the South Pacific: New Support for Constitutionalism?', *Politics*, 18 (1983), 48–60.
4. 'Viability' is an ambiguous term. If Nauru's royalties have been wisely invested, the islanders may still retain a different sort of viability—but for how long? And where?
5. *The Military Balance 1988–1989* (London, 1988), 160, 174.
6. This is true in terms of size and prominence; but there is an especially complex problem for Palau in respect of the USA and nuclear weapons.
7. D. Hegarty, *Small State Security in the South Pacific* (Canberra, 1987), 6.
8. Hegarty, *Small State Security*, 33.
9. M. Brookfield and R. G. Ward (eds.), *New Directions in the South Pacific* (Canberra, 1988), 10.
10. For a valuable description of Pacific Islands attitudes to the Australian connection, see R. G. Ward, 'Australia in the Pacific Islands', in D. N. Jeans (ed.), *Space and Society* (Sydney, 1987), 394–8.
11. Brookfield and Ward, 9.

FURTHER READING

Brookfield, M., and Ward, R. G. (eds.), *New Directions in the South Pacific* (Canberra, 1988).
Daws, G., *A Dream of Islands* (New York, 1980).
Hegarty, D., *Small State Security in the South Pacific* (Canberra, 1987).

Latin America

FRED PARKINSON

While the genesis of the bulk of States in Asia and Africa occurred shortly after the Second World War, the vast majority of Latin American States emerged much earlier from colonial rule—over a century and a half ago. The discussion of their birth and consolidation therefore reaches farther back into the past. These are not the only differences. In Asia and Africa after 1945, for instance, the metropolitan powers were by and large, within certain margins, willing to withdraw, even where such withdrawals were unconscionably long delayed. In Latin America, however, the tide of history at the beginning of the nineteenth century had not as yet turned the world public ethos against the imperial idea, as it was to do in the mid-twentieth century.

Latin America was an anomaly. From 1808 onwards the Iberian possessions in the Americas were suddenly cut off by developments in the Napoleonic Wars in Europe, with only Brazil retaining a direct dynastic link, and with the Spanish colonial territories plunged into anarchy. 'When in 1808 the Spanish sovereign was deposed by Napoleon, the fabric of the Spanish colonial empire in America fell apart.'[1] 'The peoples of Spanish America were unprepared for self-government. They were orphan children, not the adult heirs of imperial Spain. Colonial autonomy, relatively well developed in the British colonies, scarcely existed in the Spanish.'[2] Twentieth-century techniques of decolonization were unheard of, procedures for the orderly transition unknown, and the grooming for independence denied to Latin America.[3] The result was chaos, causing perplexity in all quarters, and Latin America finding herself thrown back on methods of crude trial and error in search of a way out. Time was pressing in hard on her as she grappled simultaneously with a host of problems related to sovereignty, legitimacy, organization, and international relations. A semblance of order had to be fashioned out of chaos, a process which was to take up more than half a century, and is not complete yet in all parts of the region even today.

What was involved was a long process of creating rudimentary States capable of raising taxes and recruiting troops in the hope that new bases of ensuring loyalty would emerge. In part this was done by converting existing administrative boundaries into international frontiers. Moreover, a consensus was formed that the territorial units so created should be respected—what came to be known as the principle of *uti possidetis juris*. What was uppermost in the minds of the governments of the gradually emerging successor States was to secure a framework of international legitimacy, with the element of unity in face of a possible reconquest running a close second. Accordingly, there was also a search for recognition of the new situation from beyond Latin America. In the event this was not a problem. For both Britain and the USA soon acted as if the separation of the Spanish colonies from the motherland was an accomplished fact.

There were some early fluctuations in boundaries, due to the failure of federal experiments. But this did not alter the fact that Latin America had been incorporated into international diplomatic society by formal recognition of its independence in the 1820s. There followed its gradual but firm integration into the international economic system by the mid-nineteenth century, and its reception into the universal political system—forerunner of the League of Nations and the UN—at the Hague Peace Conferences of 1899, when Mexico provided the vanguard, and 1907, when seventeen Latin American States were added. The only Latin American non-participants on the latter occasion were Costa Rica and Honduras.

The principle of *uti possidetis* was a great help in enabling the region to weather the storm of State succession. Subsequently, its experience was mixed. As the Industrial Revolution got under way and demand for certain raw materials soared as a consequence, some poorly mapped areas acquired a new economic significance, which in some cases led to frontier disputes. The obvious remedy for resolving disputes of that nature wherever negotiation had failed was arbitration. Scholarly opinion is divided as to how far arbitration succeeded in ironing out differences of that sort, with one line of thought contending that resort to arbitration was the norm in the nineteenth century, and on the whole proved to be successful, with another line of thought claiming that only relatively unimportant matters were referred to arbitration, leaving the bulk of frontier disputes unresolved.[4] The

Fred Parkinson

FIG. 12.1 Latin America

former can cite the sheer number of arbitrations that had taken place, while the latter is able to point to the large number of frontier disputes festering to this day.

Uti possidetis was wholly effective in keeping away unwelcome would-be occupants of alleged *terra nullius* who would have liked to invoke the universal principle of 'effective occupation', but it proved less useful in reducing tensions between Latin American States. Theoretically, *uti possidetis* presented the successor States with a legal criterion on which to base their claims and to allow the process of arbitration to settle political controversies by turning them into legal disputes. In practice, however, it was not relied on as a principle in any treaty contemplating arbitration of a frontier dispute before 1930. Instead, a pragmatic line was often followed.[5]

As regards present times, one prominent academic put the position thus: 'Arbitration has been invoked much less often in recent years than in the past, and no State would be well advised to go in for it unless prepared to accept some form of more-or-less artfully disguised compromise, instead of a true judgement of the merits of the case.'[6]

SUCCESSOR-STATE CONSOLIDATION

The search for political and diplomatic uniformity

Because of the understandably frequent changes of regime in a Latin America in perennial turmoil, the matter of recognition of *de facto* governments was to assume importance. While the rules of public international law concerning recognition remained ambiguous, and in any case tended to follow State practice, it was up to each government to adopt, and if so inclined, spell out its attitude toward new regimes in Latin America, or anywhere else, for that matter. No uniform practice evolved in the course of the nineteenth century, nor was any attempt made to co-ordinate policies of recognition. This would have been impracticable, considering that governmental instability in the region was caused by the same multiplicity of political choices that prevented the emergence of a uniform policy of recognition.

United States policy. The problem became compounded when, with the increasing sway of the USA over Latin America from 1880 onwards, the element of ideology as a criterion of recognition assumed growing importance. Until the turn of the century the prevailing norm in US recognition of Latin American governments tended to be factual. Thus, in an exchange of notes between the USA and Chile in 1835 the only difference between the two countries was the purely factual one of whether control of only three out of several provinces of Peru gave the revolutionary government sufficient status to conclude a treaty.[7]

It is a well-known fact that in times of tension with extra-hemispheric powers, US governments make the stability of Latin America the cornerstone of their policies in respect of that region.[8] The result has been the pursuit of cautious policies of recognition, hedged round in terms of constitutional conditionality, as best seen during the Mexican Revolution after 1911. President Woodrow Wilson, in particular, hitherto pragmatic but enraged by the conduct of some Mexican revolutionary leaders, swung round in 1914 to a line of 'teaching the Latin Americans to elect good men'. This may be considered a watershed after which US policy was heavily influenced, in times of war, or 'cold war', by ideological considerations. From 1936 onwards US decisions in matters of recognition were taken in the light of perceived overall considerations of hemisphere security dictating a maximum of political and diplomatic uniformity on an inter-American scale. The culmination of this trend was reached in the adoption of the Inter-American Alliance for Progress, first suggested by President Eisenhower but put into effect by his successor, President Kennedy in 1961, which made US economic aid uniformly conditional on the adoption of liberal political and economic reforms. None of these attempts succeeded, and since 1965 there has been a gradual but noticeable return to political and economic pluralism in matters of US recognition of Latin American governments outside Central America and the Caribbean—both continuing to be looked upon by the USA as falling unambiguously within its sphere of paramountcy.[9]

Latin American policy. The new phenomenon of conditional recognition was also practised by a number of Latin American governments, some of which may have been inspired by no more than gaining some short-term political advantages. Many such governments tried to have their policies—usually dignified by the term 'doctrine'—formally adopted and sanctioned by existing inter-American institutions. None succeeded in this endeavour, and Latin American political and diplomatic uniformity in matters of the recognition of fellow-Latin American governments has remained illusory. There have been no further attempts in that direction since 1961 when the traditional Latin American pragmatism of the nineteenth century was reintroduced.[10] It is useful, however, to sample a few such doctrines with a view to separating the long-term from the short-term elements.

The Tobar doctrine (1907) attempted to limit recognition to constitutional governments and those brought to power as a result of constitutional change. In practice, the problem arose only in the event of the latter condition. The doctrine was incorporated into the Central

American treaty of the same year.[11] It must be rated a well-intentioned, though unsuccessful attempt to stabilize Latin American governments.

Variations of the Tobar doctrine with less high-minded intention tended to contain a fair element of constitutional conditionality. Thus, the Guaní doctrine (1943) postulated recognition of governments in Latin America after inter-American consultation only.[12] Unlike the two preceding doctrines, the Rodríguez Larreta doctrine (1945) proposed that the principle of non-intervention within Latin America be tempered by the establishment of: (*a*) a parallelism between peace and democracy; (*b*) the indivisibility of peace; and (*c*) a minimum of human liberties. Representing the high-water mark of constitutional diplomacy, ostensibly to be applied throughout the region, this doctrine was in fact directed only against the Perón regime in Argentina.

If the Rodríguez Larreta doctrine was the high-water mark of constitutional conditionality, then the Betancourt doctrine (1961) turned out to be the most short-sighted and self-defeating. It called for a declaration or a treaty to be drawn up by the next Inter-American Conference (never held) to oust from the Organization of American States (OAS) governments not freely elected by the people of the country concerned.[13] This was a move clearly directed against the Castro regime in Cuba. The doctrine was put to the test in 1964, when there was a military coup in Brazil. Venezuela chose not to break with the new regime in Brasilia, however, and no more was heard about this doctrine.

The Estrada doctrine (1930) purports to be severely non-ideological. Provoked by numerous US attempts to influence Mexican policy by either granting or withholding recognition of Mexican governments, it postulates that there is no need for recognition always to be formal. Recognition of changes of government are immaterial once a State has been recognized, and States must therefore accept whatever regime is in power.

Suiting Mexico's requirements *vis-à-vis* the USA, the doctrine was none the less applied by Mexico in a discriminatory way. In 1939 recognition was withheld from the Franco government in Spain because the country had been 'invaded'. Trujillo's government in the Dominican Republic was shunned because of a decision taken by the OAS in 1961. By way of contrast no notice was taken of an OAS decision to break off relations with Castro's Cuba in 1961 or to impose sanctions in 1964. In November 1974 Mexico broke off diplomatic relations with Pinochet's Chile. The same fate befell

Somoza's government in Nicaragua in 1979 as a result of a joint Andean Group decision and on the interesting ground that 'dying dictatorships' produce instability. At this point the wheel had turned full cycle back to Tobar. Mexico's Estrada doctrine has been consistently applied only in relation to the USA.

Latin American doctrines of recognition of *de facto* governments in the region are at best attempts to produce political stability through the introduction of diplomatic conformity, and at worst a tactical device in furthering their own individual objectives in foreign policy. One must conclude, therefore, that regional attempts at the co-ordination of policies of recognition, though intrinsically desirable for purposes of general stabilization, are feasible only up to a point within the context of relatively close political integration. This is unrealistic on an all-Latin American scale.

The balance of power

South America. Though divided by numerous physical barriers, South America presents a high degree of strategic coherence. As the successor States of the area overcame the initial post-colonial chaos and began to consolidate the bases of their incipient sovereignty, so a balance of power emerged—impersonally, gradually, spontaneously, and almost imperceptibly—in response to the new strategic realities of the subcontinent. Whereas public international law tended to ensure formal equality between the successor States, and *uti possidetis* to guarantee the legitimacy of their succession, the balance of power superimposed itself on both of these, obeying solely the coldly mathematical logic of the symmetry of power, while taking scant account of the principles of formal equality and historical legitimacy.[14] That balance of power was made up of three components: (*a*) the West coast, with its solar plexus in Peru; (*b*) the East coast, with its epicentre in the River Plate area; and (*c*) a belt of three 'buffer' States acting as strategic pivots not only between the two coastal components of the balance, but also between Portuguese- and Spanish-speaking South America: Uruguay, Paraguay, and Bolivia. The last component was most important and merits comment. It was only in Uruguay that an attempt was made at the end of a war between Argentina and Brazil (1823–5) to impose a formal regime of neutralization as part and parcel of the peace treaty.[15] The idea was probably derived from Swiss neutralization of 1815, but, unlike Switzerland, Uruguay was neither protected by mountain barriers nor capable of defending her neutral status by her own military resources. It was for reasons like these that the Oriental Republic was never saved from further outside interference. Paraguay had previously acted as a buffer between the two Iberian colonial empires in South America, and this tradition was forcefully carried over into the era of independence. In those endeavours the country's leaders, unlike Uruguay's, could rely for their determined policies of isolation on the physical remoteness, as well as on her natural river boundaries. Under the dictatorship of José Gaspar Rodríguez de Francia (1766–1840) Paraguay was sealed off completely from the outside world. Originally called Upper Peru and under the jurisdiction of Lima in Spanish colonial times, Bolivia's desert, jungles, and mountain fastness assisted her independence. Each valley, each mountain, each village had its partisan group and its petty caudillo *republiquetas* where local particularism 'burgeoned into independence'.[16] Even more so than Paraguay, Bolivia looked the part of a 'buffer' State, and managed to retain its independence by making the most of its favourable strategic position.

The all-American balance. The South American balance of power proved an effective regulator of intra-South American relations during the half-century following independence, but[17] the massive intrusion of US power into Latin America after 1880 drove the South American balance underground, where it was to remain for the next eighty-five years, surfacing only occasionally to bear testimony of its continued existence. During that period the USA quickly imposed its authority in the shape of paramountcy in the Central American–Caribbean area, while having to be content with the exercise of mere hegemony—a much less burdensome type of domination—over South America.[18] The main difference between paramountcy and hegemony within the present context lies in the ultimate willingness on the part of the USA to resort to unilateral intervention in the case of the former but to abstain from such action in the case of the latter. The USA also attempted to institutionalize its predominance via the PanAmerican Union (1889) which was supplanted by the Organization of American States (1948) by using those organizations to align Latin American foreign policies as far as possible with her own and manipulate the balance of power in general. Latin America was by and large powerless to stem the advancing tide of US influence, which tended to curb Latin American freedom without ever squashing it altogether.

The South American balance re-emergent. After 1965, falling rates of economic growth and the weakening external payments of the USA have afforded South America a breathing-space in which the old, nineteenth-century balance of power has been resurfacing. Though retaining its structure after its prolonged period of hibernation, the order of magnitude within it has undergone some remarkable changes. For instance, Brazil's gross national product was now three times that of Argentina's as a result of an extended economic boom between 1964 and 1984 which enabled it to tower over every other Latin American country and aspire to major power status.[19] Mexico, on the other hand, appears to be locked in the economic grip of the USA, a conceivable candidate for inclusion in an extended US–Canadian Free Trade Area.[20]

Any illusions of grandeur entertained by Brazil have had to be dispelled in the 1980s.[21] Brazil, ranging eighth in the world league of industrialized countries as indicated by total GDP, should by rights be a member of the world industrial club of countries, the Organization for Economic Co-operation and Development (OECD), which includes as members countries of far less industrial status, such as Turkey and Greece. However, this is not feasible in view of the firm commitment to NATO of the bulk of OECD countries which Brazil is unwilling to make and it must be content for the time being with playing a prominent part in South America. Whether this will facilitate or exacerbate relations between her fellow-South American countries and lead to a strengthening or weakening of the South American balance of power remains to be seen. Some misgivings are voiced from time to time regarding Brazil's traditional tendency to spread its influence beyond its immediate frontiers. Consequently some of her actions, such as thrusting the network of her roads towards her frontiers, a normal function of infra-structural development, have been seen as strategic moves, causing alarm among her neighbours. A marked preoccupation with geopolitics at Brazil's military academies since 1964 has done little to calm those worries.

Economic sovereignty

Foreign investments. Whilst independence ended the Spanish colonial trading monopoly it tended to favour the commercially advanced countries outside Latin America. Thus, British businessmen swarmed into the River Plate region,[22] and pressures were exerted for the opening to all shipping of commercially significant rivers in South

America. The latter demand was fiercely resisted by both Francia of Paraguay and Juan Manuel de Rosas, Captain-General of Argentina (1793–1877), who both saw such a move as prejudicial to the economic independence of their countries. However, to be able to diversify their basically agrarian economies in the classical age of industrialization, Latin America needed foreign investments on a large scale.

Fear of being overpowered economically has consequently been a constant theme in the history of Latin America. The perceived propensity of foreign economic interests to call for diplomatic intervention by their home States on their behalf in redress of alleged wrongs has provoked resentment and legal attempts to curb it. This resentment, as articulated by Carlos Calvo (1824–1906), Argentine jurist and diplomat, maintained that no foreign investor should be allowed to appeal for diplomatic intervention without having scrupulously exhausted all local judicial remedies (Calvo doctrine). Specifically, Calvo recommended the insertion of a clause (Calvo clause) into contracts, legislative acts, constitutions, and, wherever possible, treaties, requiring an express undertaking on the part of foreign would-be investors to waive their right to diplomatic intervention.[23]

Calvo's appeals were widely disregarded at the time but the sheer magnitude of the mounting flow of capital into Latin America toward the close of the nineteenth century began to cause serious concern as threatening the hard-won political sovereignty of Latin American countries. Measures were consequently adopted for the containment and control of foreign investments in the strategically and economically vital sector of oil exploration and production, with State enterprises being set up and the appropriate supervisory legislation being passed.[24] The validity of Calvo's ideas was eventually vindicated in the largely Latin American-initiated and UNCTAD-sponsored Charter of Economic Rights and Duties of States passed by the General Assembly of the United Nations in the form of a Resolution in 1974.[25]

From 1937 onward further and more radical measures were taken in that direction through the outright nationalization of key sectors of the economy in foreign hands. In 1937 and 1938 Bolivia and Mexico nationalized foreign-owned oil enterprises, and in 1943 Venezuela imposed far-reaching curbs on her sizeable, foreign-owned and operated oil industry.

In 1945 President Juan Domingo Perón of Argentina nationalized the British-owned and run railways, and though an attempt to nationalize the well-entrenched United Fruit Company in Guatemala was

thwarted by US foreign intervention in 1954, a tidal wave of national-
izations followed in the wake of Fidel Castro's seizure of power
in Cuba in 1959. In 1969 Peru nationalized foreign oil concerns
and subsequently some foreign copper interests, and in 1971 Chile
nationalized the *gran minería* of foreign-owned and operated copper-
mines.[26]

From the late 1950s onwards, however, it was the purposive economic development through rapid and massive industrialization, rather
than the control of foreign investments that was identified as the key
that would open the door to the attainment of economic independence,
laying to rest at long last the fears of creeping alienation of Latin
America's sovereignty. The analytical and strategic thinking behind
this reasoning was the work of Raúl Prebisch (1900–85) who claimed
that the terms of trade of commercial exchange between industrialized
and substantially agrarian countries were permanently tilted against
the latter, and that this adverse condition was curable only by single-
minded policies of sustained industrialization, aided by complementary
measures on the international plane. Towards that end he recommended (*a*) the merger of Latin American markets; (*b*) the granting
of preferential tariff treatment by developed countries; and (*c*) the
stabilization of international commodity markets. The latter two recom-
mendations were intended to generate sufficient revenue with which
to finance Latin American industrialization.[27]

Prebisch's views were widely popularized in Latin America and
shaped the thought of the influential United Nations Economic
Commission for Latin America (ECLA/CEPAL) which influenced
various States in the region to sign treaties incorporating Prebisch's
doctrines. Few positive results were achieved through those brave
endeavours, however. For one thing, the discrepancies in the various
levels of economic development, and the consequent reluctance on
the part of the better-off to make short-term sacrifices for the sake of
long-term gains was never fully recognized. For another, the sheer
inability of political establishments, even where wholly committed to
those schemes, to enlist the support of vested interests for the common
cause was not appreciated. Above all, tragically, the overriding power
of world market forces to frustrate the designs of the planners was
nowhere properly gauged.[28]

Transnational corporations and 'dependencia'. If foreign investments in
the late nineteenth century were seen by Latin America's governments
as essential for the economic progress of their countries, then the

transnational corporations of the mid-twentieth century were regarded as the indispensable purveyors of newly developed industrial and administrative technologies.[29] Unlike foreign investments of the earlier period which were effected anonymously through the sale of bonds by financial institutions, present-day transnational corporations cannot help acting conspicuously through corporate implantation at local level, thereby arousing the misgivings of interested parties in the host countries, straining relations not only with the authorities of those countries but also with a broad range of interests in their home States. Transnational corporations have tended, therefore, to be seen as the latest potential threat to the economic independence of Latin America.[30]

The unpopularity of transnational corporations was deepened by their business methods practised at local level. Latin Americans were strongly critical of their inclinations to pre-empt local savings, local enterprise, and local managerial talent and thereby placing scarce indigenous factors of production under foreign control.[31] Though the 'spin-off' in terms of lasting benefits was also undeniable, this way of setting about corporate business affairs was bound to produce negative political reactions. Ultimately the question had to be asked whether the technological gains were worth the candle if they led, or were perceived to be leading, to a loss of *autonomy* and, possibly worse still, the extinction of cultural identity. In this way the transnational corporations were targeted as the chief antagonist in the struggle for Latin American economic sovereignty.[32]

On the political level it was soon realized that because transnational corporations were able to operate on a universal scale almost without let or hindrance, action to bring them under control also had to be on that scale. For the best part of a decade, therefore, United Nations agencies found themselves engaged in drafting a functionally suitable and universally acceptable code of foreign investment. The final outcome of those efforts was inconclusive since the document could never be completed to the satisfaction of the transnational corporations' home and host States alike. In the course of that decade, however, the practices of the transnational corporation got a thorough airing, which helped to cleanse the atmosphere, leading to modifications of some of their objectionable practices.

Latin America was the first underdeveloped ex-colonial continent in which the constituent parts acquired sovereign status. Having gained a headlong start in gathering experience in coping with fully developed countries in an unequal economic and political setting, Latin America took the lead in initiating attempts to eradicate the condition of *dependencia*, a term which betrays its Latin American origin. Milestones on that road on an inter-American level have been various but not strikingly successful attempts to start a fruitful dialogue with the USA and other developed countries.

Latin America fared notably better when having given up the ghost of establishing a special relationship with the developed countries it began to act in concert with the rest of the developing countries of the world in the relevant organs of the United Nations, such as the General Assembly, UNCTAD, and the UN Conference on the Law of the Sea (UNCLOS). In doing so Latin American delegates proved to be among the most resourceful and energetic representatives of economic diplomacy. They were also conspicuous in the 'Group of 77' developing countries (now swollen in number to over 120) set up during the first UNCTAD in 1964 to act as a ginger group.

Since the bulk of world debt is heavily concentrated in the Newly Industrializing Countries of Latin America, it was only natural that Latin America should find itself in the position of *de facto* spokesman of the world's debtors from 1982 onwards. Veering in its tactics from loyal fulfilment of its obligations to government and banker creditors alike to the somewhat unrealistic but politically frightening threat of collective default, the so-called Cartagena Group of Latin American and Caribbean countries set up after 1983 is constantly on call for consultation, the provision of economic intelligence, or—ultimately but improbably—for collective confrontation with the creditors of its members.

Whether the debt crisis has weakened Latin America's sovereignty is a moot question. After all, John Maynard Keynes once remarked that if someone owes a bank £100 and is unable to repay, the debtor is in trouble; but if someone owes a bank £100 million and is unable to repay, then the bank is in trouble. The implication for Latin America is plain.

EQUAL STATES—UNEQUAL POWERS

The problem of the antithesis between the formal equality of States and the informal inequality of powers in Latin America is *au fond* a question of the immanent tension between international law and international order.

International law

There has been a marked historical tendency away from the concept of an isolated Latin America developing her own regional-legal identity in favour of a gradual and spontaneous process of assimilating to universal principles of public international law. If there are divisive tendencies, they are now on functional rather than on regional lines, with Latin America pulling her weight with the rest of the developing countries of the world in an effort to create something like a universally valid international law of economic development. These are Latin America's new priorities in international law.

The problem that seems to be for ever defying solution in the region concerns the delimitation of frontiers. These frontiers are not so much fragile, though they are frequently that as well, as legally contentious. A traditional and persistent bone of contention, they might well cause the occasional fierce flare-up of arms, witness the eternal Peruvian–Ecuadorean dispute punctuated by intermittent armed clashes. Though varying in emotional intensity but invariably touching a raw nerve, those frontier disputes are, however, incapable *per se* of shifting power relations or, for that matter, bringing about more than marginal territorial adjustments.

A new and potentially disrupting trend made its appearance recently, however. The novel feature in this development has been the growing ethnic consciousness on the part of the once conquered Amerindians who never allowed themselves to be assimilated and are now taking their fate into their own hands. They are apt to claim autonomies, as well as title to land alleged to have been taken from them illegally. If this trend is allowed to work itself out to its logical conclusion it could result in demands for independent statehood, which would certainly involve a redrawing of frontiers on ethnic lines. At present there are no real prospects of this happening, but the outcome of persistent Amerindian agitation throughout the continent in the long run is quite uncertain.

Turning now to a different legal matter, the absence of an inter-American court of justice means that the World Court at The Hague has to serve as a substitute in inter-American disputes. Numerous Latin American international disputes have been resolved in that way.

Where such disputes have arisen between Latin American States and the USA, the picture has been different. The USA has proved adamant in its refusal to be taken to the International Court of Justice, certainly in disputes arising out of a Cold War or allegedly Cold War situation. Attempts by Mexico and Cuba to apply to the World Court for an Advisory Opinion were regularly blocked by the USA.[33] The most notorious instance of US obstruction, however, occurred when Nicaragua filed a complaint with the World Court about alleged aggression by the USA. Nicaragua felt safe in doing so in the knowledge that both States were parties to declarations made under Article 36.2 of the Statute of the International Court of Justice (the so-called optional clause) which obliged them to submit to the jurisdiction of that Court. Some fifty States had made such a declaration since the late 1940s, but most of the remaining members of the United Nations prefer to pick and choose in their dealings with the Court by way of *ad hoc* submissions. In October 1985, rather than face the Nicaraguan charges in that forum, the USA retreated from the former to the latter position by withdrawing its declaration under the optional clause. The USA also withdrew from the case altogether, which had to proceed without it. The action was blatantly political in character, having been taken in response to losing the first round of the proceedings brought by Nicaragua in 1984.

International order

In retrospect, confederalism experienced a theoretical flowering when it was propagated by Bolívar as a suitable mode of Pan-Hispanic American international order as an alternative to post-colonial chaos. It was given a fillip during the era of US predominance, when the latter pressed for co-ordination on an inter-American scale in foreign policy and defence. A high watermark of confederalism, thus defined, was reached during the Second World War, but the extensive cohesion achieved then could never be replicated during the ensuing Cold War period. The Río Pact of 1947, principal legal instrument of Cold War confederalism, proved nowhere near as effective as the wartime alliance, since few Latin American countries were willing to commit themselves to US foreign policy as wholeheartedly as they had done between 1941 and 1945. Latin America's position during the Cold War consequently contained a large measure of ambivalence. The Río Pact became not so much defunct as irrelevant after 1965.

The South American balance of power has undergone a substantial qualitative change of character, mirroring equivalent change in the world balance of power since 1945. Broadly, while before 1945 alterations in power relations internationally were registered in terms of territorial change, after the Second World War power was measured in stochastic, vertically intensive terms. The volume of all-round military might itself, rather than the extent of territory controlled, became the prime criterion. Since 1945, therefore, changes in military power in one Latin American country, particularly where reinforced by newly developed military technology, were seen as having to be offset by equivalent changes in other countries.

In South America, if not everywhere else, warlike actions to bring about adjustments in the balance of power have been unknown since the Second World War. Peaceful balancing, whether by traditional diplomacy or through periodic readjustment of armaments and military technology, including economic progress in strategically sensitive spheres, is now the order of the day. Thus, armaments in the widest sense have become a tool of diplomatic routine while military alliances as a mode of balancing are disdained as old-fashioned and counter-productive.

The international order in Latin America, and in particular in South America, is now both stable and mature, and can be maintained without the institutional aid of formalized, and largely discredited systems of collective security. Irrespective of internal social convulsions, chronic economic maladjustments, political dislocation, and external indebtedness, virtually all successor States to the Iberian colonial empire in the Americas have proved viable. Moreover, there are certain tacit rules of Pan-Latin American solidarity. Thus, no South American State has taken advantage of Colombia's horrific internal disruptions since 1948, even though successive Colombian governments have had to tolerate and live with guerrillero 'republiquetas' cheek by jowl in the midst of Colombian sovereign territory[34] demonstrating an underlying expectation that in the not altogether remote event of something similar happening to other Latin American States, equal restraint would be shown.

If we discount the collapse of the Gran Colombian (today's Venezuela, Colombia, and Ecuador) and Central American federations of the early nineteenth century as ill-conceived and unworkable *ab initio*, the Latin American ledger registers not one case of the extinction of a successor State. There have been two latecomers—

Cuba in 1898 and Panama in 1903[35]—both owing their independence to support received from the USA, and both now straining
to shuffle off the coils of US encumbrance. Only Castroite Cuba
from 1959 onwards and to a much lesser extent Sandinista Nicaragua
from 1978 onwards have succeeded with the help of the Soviet
Union in breaking the tight embrace of US paramountcy in the
Central American–Caribbean region.

In theory, something like a 'hegemonial integration' *de facto* might
occur in South America[36] if Brazil were prepared—which she is not
at present though she probably has the capacity—to throw the weight
of her fast-expanding and diversifying economy fully into the scales
of the regional balance of power. However, such an almost inconceivable move would be followed almost certainly by resistance from
the three regional 'buffer' States, Uruguay, Paraguay, and Bolivia.
Similarly, Mexico and Venezuela, acting jointly as they have occasionally done in the recent past, might conceivably attempt something
similar in the Caribbean, but they would quickly be checked by the
paramountcy of the USA.

As regards the colossus in the north, all indications suggest that it
is trying to compensate for the loss of hegemony in South America
and diminished status of paramountcy in Central America by further
tightening its paramount status in the Caribbean[37] where it is acting
as the successor State to the rapidly fading British colonial presence—
witness the wholly unauthorized and totally unsolicited invasion by
US forces of Grenada, a member of the Commonwealth, in 1983.
There is now a notable tendency on the part of Latin American
governments to undertake the management of crises on an *ad hoc*
basis and quite independently of the USA. This was most noticeable
in the manner in which the Contadora powers (Mexico, Venezuela,
Colombia, Costa Rica, and Panama), supported by Brazil, Argentina,
Uruguay, and Peru, and eventually by all Central American States,
were able to act as peacemakers between the warring factions of
Nicaragua between 1983 and 1988 in defiance of the wishes of the
US administration of the time.

Towards economic independence?

Joint measures of economic development in Latin America must not
be mistaken for determined drives towards regional or subregional
economic integration. Nowhere, with the possible exception of Central

America, has regional economic integration been seen as an end in itself. On the contrary, however ambiguous the logic behind the reasoning, the explicit and implicit goal of all schemes of economic development has been to strengthen the economic independence of the individual States involved in them. The teleological-multilateral schemes of the 1960s and 1970s have gradually been modified and in some instances abandoned *de facto*, giving way to cautious pragmatic steps of economic co-operation on a bilateral or multilateral basis—such as the Treaty of Asunción between Argentina, Brazil, Paraguay, and Uruguay in 1991 for a *mercado común del sur* (MERCOSUR)[38]—which often owe more to political inspiration than single-minded economic initiative. What is proceeding apace is physical-infrastructural integration (dams, railways, roads, bridges), as well as deliberate frontier integration with the emphasis on technical aspects.[39]

The upshot: from Bolívar to de Gaulle

With the growth of Latin America's industrial middle and working classes from the second half of the nineteenth century onwards and their partial incorporation into the political processes of their countries, the shafts of sovereignty have been cast deep down into the social fabric, *ipso facto* causing separation from other Latin American countries and increasing the political individuality of each. Merger of State jurisdiction is under those conditions as impractical as is the prospect of the extinction of States.

All this hardly squares with Bolívar's early image of Latin America as a 'nation of republics'. Consequently, with the exception of the notoriously unsettled state of its frontiers, the international relations of the region today differ little in kind from those of other continents in which States tend to pursue their own interests individually. In that sense, then, an adaptation of the late General de Gaulle's characterization of 'une Europe des patries' is applicable to Latin America, which has become 'una América Latina de patrias'. However, whereas in Western Europe internal integration long preceded regional integration, the Prebisch approach of seeking to strengthen individual sovereignty through regional economic integration suffered shipwreck largely because the requisite minimum amount of internal political and administrative integration was still palpably lacking.

In Latin America the contradiction between the formal equality of

States and the informal inequality of powers survives unabated, as the newly industrializing big three of Mexico, Brazil, and Argentina are stealing a march on the remainder, while US influence, though notably weakening, is still being felt throughout the region.

NOTES

1. J. Lynch, *The Spanish American Revolutions 1808–1826* (New York and London, 1986), 132.
2. R. A. Humphreys, 'Simón Bolívar: "Liberator"', *Listener* (12 Feb. 1959), 285–7.
3. As has been pointed out, by contrast: 'From India and Pakistan on 15 August 1947 to Brunei on 1 January 1984, a whole succession of sovereign States have been unambiguously born at precisely identifiable times', A. James, *Sovereign Statehood. The Basis of International Society* (London, 1986), 65.
4. L. D. M. Nelson, 'The Arbitration of Boundary Disputes in Latin America', *Netherlands International Law Review*, 20 (1973), 267–94. See also W. R. Manning (ed.), *Arbitration Treaties Among the American Nations to the Close of the Year 1910* (New York, 1924).
5. 'When the Spanish records violated the accepted facts, the principle of *uti possidetis* did not prevail.' Indeed, in two of the most important arbitrations between the successor States, those between Argentina and Chile in 1902 and 1966 respectively the principle of effective occupation was expressly invoked. See D. P. O'Connell, *International Law*, i (London, 1970), 426–7.
6. P. Calvert, *Boundary Disputes in Latin America* (London, 1981), 26.
7. W. R. Manning (ed.), *Diplomatic Correspondence of the United States Concerning the Independence of the Latin American Nations* (New York, 1925), 45–7.
8. Thus, Vice-President Dan Quayle of the USA told reporters on Air Force 2 that his government wanted to see 'stability in our hemisphere' because 'these countries are our backyard', *Guardian*, 3 Feb. 1989.
9. On US policy of recognition, see T. P. Wright, 'Free Elections in the Latin American Policy of the United States', *Political Science Quarterly*, 74 (1959), 89–112; K. A. Bode, 'An Aspect of United States Policy in Latin America', *Political Science Quarterly*, 85 (1970), 471–91; J. D. Cochrane, 'United States Policy toward Recognition of Governments and Promotion of Democracy in Latin America since 1963', *Journal of Latin American Studies*, 4 (1972), 275–91.
10. It is essential to distinguish policies of recognition of governments during the 19th century from those practised, since at least as early as 1856, of

refusing recognition of territorial change which was directed as much against peaceful conveyance as forcible seizure. See R. Langer, *Seizure of Territory: The Stimson Doctrine and Related Principles* (Princeton, NJ, 1969), ch. 7.

11. For details of the Tobar doctrine, see *Revue générale de droit international public*, 21 (1914), 482. For the text of the Central American Treaty of 1907, see *American Journal of International Law*, 2 (1908), Suppl., 229.

12. R. A. Humphreys, *Latin America and the Second World War, 1942–1945* (London, 1982), 90, 124, 166, 245.

13. See A. Thomas and A. J. Thomas, *The OAS* (Dallas, 1963), 238.

14. R. N. Burr, *By Reason or Force: Chile and the Balancing of Power in South America, 1830–1905* (Berkeley, Calif., 1967).

15. L. A. Herrera, *La Paz de 1828* (Montevideo, 1938).

16. Lynch, *Spanish American Revolutions*, 119.

17. For a closer analysis, see F. Parkinson, 'The World Powers and South America', in M. Morris (ed.), *Great Power Relations in Argentina, Chile and the Antarctic* (London, 1989), 176–96.

18. The system of paramountcy had its origins in imperial India by which the British *raj* reserved to itself a veto over a certain, more or less well-defined range of decisions by the princely States. See Percival Spence, 'The Right of Paramountcy', 629 ff. and 658 in V. A. Smith (ed.), *Oxford History of India* (1958). See also R. Bharati, *Hyderabad and British Paramountcy: 1858–1983* (London, 1988).

19. For details see F. Parkinson, in M. Morris, (ed.), *Great Power Relations*, 176–96.

20. See B. Mabire, 'México y Estados Unidos hoy', *Foro Internacional*, 28 (1988), 117–35; G. Vegas Canovas, 'El Acuerdo bilateral de libre comercio entre Canadá y Estados Unidos: implicaciones para México y los países en desarrollo', *Foro Internacional* (Jan.–Mar. 1988), 387–403.

21. D. Poneman, 'Nuclear Proliferation Prospects for Argentina', *Orbis*, 27 (1984), 858–80, and D. J. Myers, 'Brazil: Reluctant Pursuit of the Nuclear Option', *Orbis*, 27 (1984), 881–917.

22. Lynch, *Spanish American Revolutions*, 259.

23. D. B. Shea, *The Calvo Clause* (Minneapolis, Minn., 1955).

24. J. D. Wirth (ed.), *Latin American Oil Companies and the Politics of Energy* (Nebraska, 1985); G. Philip, 'PEMEX and the Petroleum Sector', in *id.* (ed.), *The Mexican Economy* (London, 1988), 229–48.

25. Doc. UN-GA 3281 (XXIX).

26. D. Rosenberg, *Le principe de souveraineté des états sur leurs ressources naturelles* (Paris, 1983); P. G. Casanova, *La ideología norteamericana sobre inversiones extranjeras* (Mexico City, 1955).

27. See Institute for Latin American Studies at Austin, Texas, *Development Problems in Latin America* (Austin, Tex., 1970), ch. 9, 257–78.

28. The political modifications rendered necessary in the course of operating

those schemes were reflected clearly in the altered legal provisions of the second Treaty of Montevideo of 1980 which, by setting up the Latin American Integration Association (LAIA/ALADI) codified the practice of its predecessor, the Latin American Free Trade Association (LAFTA/ALALC). See D. Tussie, 'Latin American Integration from LAFTA to LAIA', *Journal of World Trade Law* (1987), 399–413.

29. G. Ranis, *The Transnational Corporation as an Instrument of Development* (New Haven, Conn., 1974); United Nations, *Transnational Corporations and Technology Transfer* (New York, 1987).

30. On the intrinsic nature of transnational corporations as a species, see J. K. Galbraith, *The New Industrial State* (London, 1967).

31. On transnational corporations operating in Latin America, see J. P. Gunnemann (ed.), *The Nation-State and Transnational Corporations in Conflict: With Special Reference to Latin America* (New York, 1975); L. Martins, *Naçao e corporaçao transnacional: A política das empresas no Brasil e en América Latina* (Rio de Janeiro, 1975); K. R. Mirow, *A Ditadura dos Cartéis. Anatomía de um subdesenvolvimento* (Rio de Janeiro, 1978); D. C. Bennett and K. E. Sharpe, *Transnational Corporations versus the State: The Political Economy of the Mexican Auto Industry* (Princeton, NJ, 1986); J. Jenkins, *Transnational Corporations and the Latin American Automobile Industry* (London, 1987); and R. Parque, *Las Empresas Transnacionales en la economía del Paraguay* (Santiago, 1987).

32. The *dependencia* school is not associated with any single representative. Among a host of writers on the subject: H. Jaguaribe, *La dependencia político-económica de América Latina* (Mexico City, 1972); O. Sunkel, 'Big business and "dependencia"—a Latin American view', *Foreign Affairs*, 50 (1972), 517–31; T. Dos Santos, *El nuevo carácter de la dependencia* (Santiago, 1968); J. Sierra (ed.), *Desarrollo latinoamericano: ensayos críticos* (Mexico City, 1974).

33. F. Parkinson, 'World Powers and South America', 138, 190.

34. See E. Hobsbawm, 'The Revolutionary Situation in Colombia', *The World Today*, 19 (1963), 248–58. Also O. F. Borda, 'Violence and the Break-up of Tradition in Colombia', in C. Véliz (ed.), *Obstacles to Change in Latin America* (London, 1967), 188–205. See also four articles on 'Colombie: la paix desirée et violentée', in *Le Monde Diplomatique*, Jan. 1986.

35. The USA in 1903 justified its recognition of the newly created Republic of Panama within three days on 'political', not on legal grounds, and for the reason that international law does not fix the precise time of recognition, which is to be ascertained by a 'just sense of international rights and obligations' and the 'vast importance to the whole civilised world' of the interests (the Canal) involved, D. P. O'Connell, *International Law* (2nd edn., London, 1970), 134. Colombia in 1920 announced that her accep-

tance of Article 10 of the League of Nations Covenant did not imply recognition of Panama as an independent sovereign State. See *id.*, 156.

36. A theory of 'hegemonial integration' was developed by K. Deutsch in *Political Community and the North Atlantic Area. International organization in the light of historical experience* (Princeton, NJ, 1957).

37. D. F. Ronfeldt, 'Rethinking the Monroe Doctrine', *Orbis*, 28 (1985), 684–96 argues that so far as the Caribbean is concerned, the Monroe Doctrine is still valid.

38. See *International Legal Materials*, 30 (1991), 1041–2, 1044–63.

39. J. E. G. Velasco, 'La nueva política de fronteras en Iberoamérica', *Revista de Política Internacional* (Madrid), 138 (1975), 147–64.

FURTHER READING

Davis, H. E., *Latin American Diplomatic History: An Introduction* (Baton Rouge, La., 1977).

Hurrell, A., 'Latin America in the New World Order: A Regional Bloc in the Americas?' *International Affairs*, 68 (1992), 121–40.

Lynch, J., *The Spanish American Revolution 1808–1826* (New York, 1986).

Mecham, J. L., *The United States and Inter-American Security 1889–1960* (Austin, Tex., 1961).

Parkinson, F., *Latin America, The Cold War and the World Powers* (Beverly Hills, Calif., 1974).

Thomas, A., and Thomas, A. J., *The Organization of American States* (Dallas, 1963).

13

The Caribbean

ANTHONY J. PAYNE

The Caribbean exemplifies almost classically the tension between expanding statehood on the basis of equality of status and the actual inequalities of power which exist in the international society. Two observations establish the framework of the argument. First, the region has progressed from a situation in 1945 in which all its territories, with but three exceptions, were possessions of different colonial powers, to the complex contemporary reality of a political landscape made up of no less than sixteen independent States, two 'associated' States, and only ten remaining dependencies, variously defined. Second, the region is composed of States which are nearly all weak by any definition of power used in the analysis of international politics; and it is situated in the 'backyard', as the phrase has it, of the USA, the more powerful of the two superpowers of the post-war era and the only remaining superpower of the post-Cold War era. In a sense, this says virtually all there is to say: a sizeable number of new States, most of them small islands with tiny populations, have had to explore the limits of their sovereignty in the shadow of a huge State which has substantially shaped the economic and political character of the entire post-war world order. Nevertheless, looking back over the last forty years, the dichotomy between statehood and power—these two vital conditioning features of the international political life of the modern Caribbean—has been both intricate and absorbing, their different dynamics often unfolding in unexpected and contradictory ways.

BIRTH: ISSUES OF VIABILITY AND COLONIALISM

At the end of the Second World War, Britain, France, The Netherlands, and the USA were the remaining colonial powers in the

Caribbean, and the basis was thus laid for the four different processes of decolonization witnessed in the post-war period.

Britain

In March 1945, Oliver Stanley, the British secretary of state for the colonies, sent a dispatch to representatives of the various British possessions in the region inviting them to meet and discuss with him the possible creation of a West Indies federation. The official British view of that time held that it was 'clearly impossible in the modern world for the present separate communities, small and isolated as most of them are, to achieve and maintain full self-government on their own'.[1] Certain minimum criteria of size, measured in terms of economic resources, population, and territorial area, which countries as small as Jamaica and Trinidad, much less Barbados and the Leeward and Windward Islands, did not fulfil, were necessary for a colony to be 'viable' and thus able to claim and sustain sovereign status. Federation was, from this point of view, a means of increasing the effective size of the West Indian territories to a point where they became eligible for self-government as one unit. In the event, however, it proved to be an unconvincing vehicle in which to make the journey towards independence. By the time the Federation eventually came into being in 1958, the larger territories, the extent of whose commitment to the union was bound to be crucial, had been allowed to move closer to independence in their own right. This turned the politics of the Federation on end. As one observer put it, 'the desire for self-government now began to work against federation, instead of in its favour'.[2] The argument that the Federation was the indispensable prelude to the attainment of independence was finally invalidated in 1960 when the British government intimated that Jamaica was eligible for this status on its own. The little remaining political substance to the Federation was removed and it was wound up in 1962.

With its demise went Britain's original approach to the decolonization of its West Indian possessions. As in other parts of the empire, the policy in the Caribbean also became one of granting independence to territories as and when they asked for it. The four leading colonies— Jamaica, Trinidad and Tobago, Barbados, and Guyana—thus became independent between 1962 and 1966, and the concept of Associated Statehood (which granted internal self-government but preserved external and defence responsibilities in Britain's hands) was only

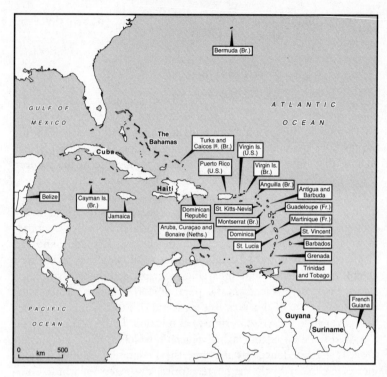

FIG. 13.1 The Caribbean

created in 1967 because the islands of the Leewards and Windwards
could not be persuaded to come together within an eastern Caribbean
federation and were still thought at the time to be too small to be
viable as independent entities. This perception was shared by the
islands themselves and they broadly welcomed their new status. The
only real difficulty attached to Anguilla's reluctance to accept the
continuing political dominance of the government of St Kitts, with
which it had previously been joined. Following its secession from the
putative Associated State and the subsequent intervention in 1969
of British paratroopers and London policemen, the problem was
eventually resolved by the reabsorption of Anguilla into full colonial
status.[3] For the other Leeward and Windward Islands, Associated
Statehood brought to light all manner of contradictions between
internal and external affairs, but did at least have the merit of buying
time for other constitutional options to be considered.

By the early 1970s the idea that there was some firm equation relating size and sovereignty had been widely exposed as mythical by sundry political developments in other parts of the world. As a result, the Bahamas felt sufficiently self-confident to request its independence, which was achieved in 1973, and even the tiny islands of the eastern Caribbean gradually began to consider the possibility of cashing the 'independence cheque' which the notion of Associated Statehood had given them from the outset. According to the terms of the West Indies Act which established these particular constitutions, all the island governments had to demonstrate was that they had the support of their people in wanting to move to independence, a condition which it had been intended should be met by the achievement of a two-thirds majority in a referendum. However, in 1972, Eric Gairy, the premier of Grenada, persuaded the British government—keen by then to withdraw from its responsibilities in the Caribbean—that victory in an election in which independence had been a key issue was sufficient. Grenada subsequently became independent in 1974, notwithstanding bitter local opposition, culminating in a general strike and violent disturbances, to the new powers being handed to Gairy.[4] The pattern was thus set and, in turn, the other Associated States followed suit: Dominica in 1978, St Lucia and St Vincent both in 1979, Antigua-Barbuda in 1981 and St Kitts-Nevis in 1983. Amongst the other British possessions in the region, Belize was a special case, attempts to decolonize being repeatedly thwarted by Guatemalan threats to invade the country if independence was granted before the settlement of the long-standing border dispute. Nevertheless, in 1981, Britain decided to press ahead with the granting of independence, accepting that it would have to maintain a defence commitment to the territory for what was described as 'an appropriate period'.[5]

This left, and still leaves, six continuing British dependencies in the Caribbean—Anguilla, Bermuda, the British Virgin Islands, the Cayman Islands, Montserrat, and the Turks and Caicos Islands. Totalling a mere 420 square miles and sustaining no more than 120,000 people, these are literally the rocks on which Britain's policy of decolonization and withdrawal from the Caribbean has foundered. British governments during the 1970s were keen enough to discharge their responsibilities and sporadically tried to build up public support for independence in the territories. The blockage was the unwillingness of the island leaders and their peoples to seize the independence option. In the mid-1980s a general review of British policy towards the dependencies[6] concluded that Britain 'would not urge them to consider moving to independence', but would 'remain ready to respond positively when this is the clearly and constitutionally expressed wish of the people' and, in the meantime, would implement 'a number of administrative measures to ... ensure the good administration ... of the dependent territories'.[7] For all the careful phraseology, the statement represented a significant shift of approach, which can best be described as reversing the balance of expectation. Whereas in the past the assumption had been that, sooner or later, the dependencies would progress to independence, in the future it was to be that they would remain under residual control. Independence was still there for the asking, but it was not to be a presumed outcome. A recent survey of politics in the Caribbean dependencies also reports that only in Montserrat and Bermuda is there a modicum of support for independence, although in neither case is it substantial or broadly based.[8] In other words, Britain has knowingly settled for remaining a colonial power in the Caribbean for at least the foreseeable future.

France

With the establishment of the Fourth Republic following the liberation of 1944, the decision was taken by the new government in Paris that some form of decolonization was necessary for France's 'old colonies' in the tropics. In keeping with the assimilationist philosophy which underlay French colonial administration, it was proposed that they should become integral parts of France with their citizens having the same rights as any other French person. Referendums were held in the Caribbean colonies of Martinique, Guadeloupe, and French Guiana (Guyane) to assess local political reaction to the idea, and in each case produced large majorities in favour. The Law of 19 March 1946 then formally conferred the status of overseas departments (*départements d'outre-mer*, or DOM) on the three territories. Unconcerned by the growth of independence movements in other parts of the colonial world in the aftermath of the Second World War, the French believed that they had successfully fulfilled their commitment to decolonization in what they called the Antilles.[9]

Since 1946, the policy of all succeeding French governments has been to maintain this arrangement as a permanent feature of the political structure of France itself. 'Modified departmental status', as it is known, was effected between 1958 and 1960 but served only to introduce a number of reforms of French administrative practice to the DOM. The subsequent, occasional emergence of discontent in the Caribbean departments has generally been met by the provision of financial resources to build schools and houses and institute welfare services, rather than by the granting of political concessions which might develop in the direction of independence. Indeed, in the French view, there were no such concessions which could constitutionally be made. In June 1967, for example, it was declared that the people of the French Antilles were bound by a contract to France: it was legitimate for them to seek to be free, but 'useless to demand to be independent' since departmentalization served to assimilate them to their compatriots of the metropolis.[10] Neither the events of 1968 in France nor the acquisition of independence by the British colonies in the Caribbean changed this view. When President Giscard D'Estaing visited Martinique in December 1974, he made just the same point. No adjustments were necessary to the political status of the French Caribbean, although he conceded that there was still room for progress in the social and economic fields.

That became the dominant emphasis of French policy and the independence issue did not again come to the fore until the early 1980s when violence in both Guadeloupe and French Guiana drew attention to the continuing potential for disquiet in the French Caribbean territories. Yet, despite charges by some Gaullist politicians that he had a secret plan to give them independence, President Mitterrand has, since his election in May 1981, remained true to tradition in his handling of the overseas departments, merely instituting a greater degree of decentralization. In fact, by appeasing some of the demand for autonomy which has existed in the departments for more than a decade, his administration may be said to have undercut the tiny pro-independence movements which exist in Guadeloupe, Martinique, and French Guiana and thus ensured the continuity of the DOM system into the foreseeable future.

The Netherlands

At the end of the Second World War, the government of The Netherlands did not favour independence for its Caribbean colonies, preferring when eventually it felt it had to act—following events in Indonesia—to incorporate them, rather like France, into the metropolitan political system. The Netherlands Antilles (which comprises the islands of Aruba, Curaçao, and Bonaire situated off the Venezuelan coast and the Windward Islands grouping, Saba, Eustatius, and half of St Maarten, 500 miles to the north of Puerto Rico) and Suriname were thus first granted internal self-government in 1950 and then, four years later, formally linked with Holland within what was called the Tripartite Kingdom of The Netherlands. Within this structure, their autonomy was constitutionally guaranteed and they were given the right to participate in the formulation of policies for the kingdom as a whole.[11] The UN General Assembly accepted this as evidence of decolonization in December 1955 and so too did the majority of the inhabitants of the two 'associated' territories. The main opponents were members of the Dutch Labour Party and other socialist groupings in the metropolitan Netherlands, who were aware that the arrangement was still viewed as neocolonial by many leading Third World figures.

However, the Tripartite scheme did not succeed in insulating the government and people of the metropolitan Netherlands from the problems of the two overseas parts of the kingdom. Extensive Surinamese migration to Holland was as unpopular as the request of the government of the Netherlands Antilles for Dutch military assistance in the face of prolonged rioting in Curaçao in 1969 was embarrassing. The attraction of being rid of such problems grew in The Hague, with the result that, from the early 1970s onwards, the policy adopted by the Dutch Labour government of Joop Den Uyl was to urge full independence on both Suriname and The Netherlands Antilles. The Surinamese government was responsive to pressure to move in this direction and agreement on independence was achieved quite easily, the final dissolution of the constitutional link coming in 1975. The government of the Netherlands Antilles, on the other hand, was more reluctant to have independence forced on it. The small size of the territory (only 383 square miles in area over all six islands), its unusual split location, its diverse ethnic composition and linguistic division, and its weak internal economic integration—all raised questions about the wisdom of breaking away from the protection of The Netherlands. There was also the prior need to agree maritime boundaries with Venezuela, but this was achieved in 1978.

In due course, a further obstacle arose—Aruban separatism.[12] Arubans, who are generally not of African descent but are mostly mestizos and whites, had long felt that the central government of the territory in Willemstadt, Curaçao, did not satisfactorily serve their interests and in the 1970s came openly to oppose participation in an independent Antillean federation. The Netherlands government was only willing to grant independence to all six islands together, but in March 1983, following talks to try to resolve the impasse, came up with proposals which allowed Aruba a separate status (*status aparte*) within the territory, from January 1986 onwards, and the option of independence on its own by 1996. Under the interim arrangement, the Dutch government remained responsible for defence and external relations and Aruba stayed part of a co-operative union with the other Netherlands Antilles territories in economic and monetary affairs. However, this plan has now been overtaken by a new proposal for a Dutch Commonwealth which emanated from The Hague in 1990, following a change of government in The Netherlands. This envisages an arrangement of four autonomous partners: The Netherlands, Aruba, Curaçao, and Bonaire in partnership, and the three Windward Islands. The Dutch have in effect given up their ambition to rid themselves of colonial responsibilities in the Caribbean. The Antilles, for their part, got what they wanted, which was further insularism and a continuing Dutch connection. Even Aruba has accepted the plan.

The United States of America

The US government also sought to extend self-government to its two Caribbean colonies after the end of the Second World War. The Virgin Islands were granted a measure of internal autonomy in 1954, but several subsequent attempts to increase this have all been rejected by popular referendums. Puerto Rico was similarly given an extension of internal self-government by President Harry Truman in 1947 when Congress approved a law giving the people of the island the right to elect their own governor. In 1950, in another move towards greater internal autonomy, Congress approved Law 600, allowing Puerto Rico to draft its own constitution. This process culminated in March 1952 when, in a special referendum, the people of Puerto Rico approved a new constitutional arrangement, under which the territory was styled as a 'Commonwealth', or *estado libre asociado*—'a State which is free of superior authority in the management of its own local affairs',[13] although remaining in association with the USA. This meant that Puerto Ricans could freely travel to and from the US, enjoy the benefits of the US social security system, participate in its currency and customs area, but could not take responsibility for their country's defence or foreign relations. On this basis, the US government nevertheless succeeded in persuading the UN General Assembly to remove the territory from its list of remaining colonies.

The establishment of the Commonwealth did not, however, end discussion in Puerto Rico about its constitutional status. Moreover the island's unusual constitutional position was further highlighted when, in 1972, Cuba formally placed it before the UN Committee on Decolonization, arguing that the Puerto Rican people had been denied the right of self-determination. The issue has since been regularly debated within that forum, with the Committee in 1981 going so far as to resolve that the General Assembly itself should consider whether Puerto Rico should be viewed in future as a 'non-self-governing territory', even though a motion to that effect was subsequently defeated in the Assembly.[14] The USA has consistently denied that Puerto Rico is a colony and maintains that the issue is an 'internal' one of no concern to the international community. However, demands for a reconsideration of the country's status surfaced again in Puerto Rico in 1989 and a referendum was conceded by the Bush administration in the USA, originally scheduled to be held in 1991. Although not binding, it was to have offered the people of Puerto Rico the three alternatives: maintenance of the current Commonwealth status, statehood, or independence. At the last moment it ran into opposition in the US Senate and the idea has been allowed to lapse.

DEATH: ISSUES OF SECESSION AND BOUNDARIES

The Caribbean has not witnessed the death of any of its States in the period since 1945. The West Indies Federation lasted only from 1958 to 1962, but it was never granted sovereign status; it may be said to have been stillborn. For the rest, two threats to statehood can be discerned, each of which has reared its head but without, as yet, achieving a victim. They are the issues of secession and boundaries, reflecting the two contrasting sides of the region's geographical character.

Secession

The secessionist threat does not derive from ethnic conflict within States: the two territories with the most obvious such divisions,

Guyana and Trinidad and Tobago, have seen racial conflicts between their African and East Indian communities, but this has not led to the emergence of a separatist nationalism yearning after statehood. Rather, where secessionist politics has emerged it flows from the multi-island character of some regional territories, parcelled together as they so often were for the administrative convenience of the colonial powers. Thus Anguilla rebelled and successfully broke from St Kitts-Nevis-Anguilla in 1967 and Aruba partly escaped from the Netherlands Antilles in 1986. Barbuda toyed with such a course for a period in the run-up to its eventual acceptance of independence in 1981 as part of the twin-island State of Antigua-Barbuda, and Nevis only acceded to the same status as part of St Kitts-Nevis in 1983, having secured certain guarantees of its autonomy.[15] All these movements took place, however, during the negotiation of independence. Once States had been created, 'outer island' complaints did not necessarily disappear—as Trinidad knows with regard to Tobago, St Vincent with some of the Grenadines, and the Bahamas with several of its constituent islands—but they were muted by the pull of State patronage, and no independent Caribbean State has so far lost any part of its territory by this means. Nor is any such possibility on the horizon.

Boundaries

By contrast, island character does at least help to establish boundaries with some degree of firmness. Trinidad and Tobago has had long-standing arguments with Venezuela over fishing rights in the Gulf of Paria, and Venezuela also has a claim to some of the islands in the Netherlands Antilles, but for the most part the islands have not faced disputes over or threats to their territorial integrity. Haiti and the Dominican Republic even share the same island of Hispaniola, not without some discomfort perhaps, but without overt boundary disputes. The same cannot be said for the mainland States of the Caribbean— Belize, Guyana, and Suriname. Belize has long faced a Guatemalan claim to nothing less than the whole of its territory which delayed its independence and still necessitates the presence in the country of a British garrison.[16] Guyana has similarly had to live throughout its period of independence with the fact that Venezuela claims about two-thirds of its territory in the Essequibo region. Guyana, in turn, has a border dispute with Suriname, although relations improved after 1979 following the restoration of diplomatic links and the growth of trade between the two countries.[17] In all of these cases, the boundaries of the States in question have not been altered by force or its threat, and it is not likely now that they will do so. The disputes, however, have been real and destabilizing, especially in the Belizean case, and they have shaped the foreign policies of the beleaguered States.

LIFE: ISSUES OF SOVEREIGNTY AND HEGEMONY

The life of Caribbean States within the international system has conventionally been understood in terms of the problems faced by small, poor, weak, dependent entities when confronted with more powerful States, notably the 'colossus to the north' on whose 'doorstep' they unavoidably reside. All analysts of international politics in the Caribbean draw a picture marked at heart by the notion of an inherently unequal struggle between forces of a different order and scale. Yet, within this broad metaphor, different specific accounts of regional politics emerge which reflect the different theories of power in the international system developed by the realist and structuralist schools.

Realism

What is immediately noteworthy from this perspective is that Caribbean States are poorly endowed with power-resources, however these are defined. States in the region are obviously small in a variety of senses. Their territory is limited in size: Guyana and Suriname are the largest (at 83,000 square miles and 63,251 square miles respectively), but substantial parts of their land-areas are uninhabited and unexploited. Of the islands, Cuba is the largest (44,218 square miles), but the norm is much smaller. Many eastern Caribbean States are no more than 100–200 square miles in size, the smallest independent State in the region, St Kitts-Nevis, being only 104 square miles in area. Their populations are also equally tiny by global standards. Cuba is again the most populous, with some 10 million people, followed by the Dominican Republic and Haiti with about 6.2 million and 5.4 million respectively. At the other end of the spectrum come St Kitts-Nevis (46,000), Dominica (73,795), and Antigua-Barbuda

(79,269).[18] As a consequence, the gross domestic products of Caribbean States are bounded. Taking 1978, more or less at random, as the basis for comparison, the range runs from Cuba ($US15,400 million), through the Dominican Republic ($US5,700 million), Trinidad and Tobago ($US3,896 million), and Jamaica ($US2,729 million), down to St Vincent ($US47 million), Dominica ($US36.9 million) and St Kitts-Nevis ($US35.2 million).[19] These are, even so, not the poorest States in the world, especially if economic well-being is measured in per capita terms. But what is clear is that by *comparison* with the large and indeed enormous extra-regional States with which they must reckon (the USA, Venezuela, Mexico, Brazil), the small States of the Caribbean do not possess much by way of natural resources (broadly defined) with which to pursue their interests in the international system.

This is reflected in the limited apparatus of international political action which the region's States have been able to assemble. Militarily, with the sole exception of Cuba, which is an obvious special case in this context, courtesy of its former alliance with the Soviet Union, they have not built up armies or navies of any strategic significance. Indeed, part of the anxiety generated in the eastern Caribbean at the modest development of Grenada's internal capacity to resist the threat of invasion during the period of revolutionary rule between 1979 and 1983 was precisely because that part of the region has no history of military prowess. For the rest, the armies of Haiti and the Dominican Republic are more dangerous to their own citizens than those of other States; the Guyana Defence Force could not hope to resist a Venezuelan invasion; and, as already noted, Belize has long needed the assistance of a British garrison to protect the country from Guatemalan incursions. Diplomatically too, Caribbean States have had to be highly selective in the extent to which they deploy overseas representatives. Some postings have been deemed essential (New York, Washington, London, and/or Brussels), but, in general, resources have been thinly spread and a good deal of reliance placed on the talent of a few. All of this means that the region has not been able to wield much power in the international system, as traditionally understood. Yet, from the point of view of the realist perspective, the sovereignty of the sixteen fully independent States in the region is one of their few power-resources. Given the centrality of the concept to the post-1945 organization of the international system, even small and weak States, like those in the Caribbean, are given a weapon they can use. It works for them both as a vote and a symbol. In the UN General Assembly, for example, the votes of just the former English-speaking Caribbean States count *numerically* for as much as the whole of continental Latin America, even though it is the case that their voices are heard with less attention. Nevertheless, this is one of the reasons why former Caribbean powers such as Britain are now paying renewed attention to the region as a part of the world which can actively assist the pursuit of British foreign policy.[20] The latter point emphasizes the attractiveness of sovereignty as the ideology which legitimizes the post-war international system. The argument in defence of sovereignty is one with which offending States can be brought to the bar of international opinion, and at least to some degree restrained. In this connection, it is significant, to say the least, that all Caribbean States have survived as States in the post-war era despite their proximity to the USA and their emergence into statehood during some of the most highly charged phases of the Cold War. The ideology of sovereignty can be said to have served them well.

Even so, there remains something deceptive about this situation, for the benefit which can be derived from the appeal to the legitimizing qualities of sovereignty may be more apparent than real. In the Caribbean context, this is well illustrated by the US invasion of Grenada in October 1983. For no amount of appeals to the shrine of sovereignty in international law—and the action was condemned in the UN General Assembly by an overwhelming vote of 108 to nine—could effect the removal of the marines or block the wider political purpose of the USA in reasserting its power over the Caribbean. Washington simply refused to play the new post-colonial game of respecting the sovereign rights of the weak, and got away with it.

Structuralism

From this perspective, what is important is the Caribbean's peripheral status in a world capitalist economy created and controlled by the hegemonic power of the USA in the post-1945 era. As the considerable literature of the Caribbean dependency school attests, the development of the region's economy has been conditioned by its integration into a system not of its making and not to its advantage. All such writers stress the dependence of the Caribbean people on the rest of the world: for markets and supplies, transfers of income and capital, banking and financial services, business and technical skills, and 'even for ideas about themselves'.[21] Clearly, multinational capital has flowed in and out of the region with few restraints. Regional States have vied with each other to offer the more attractive package of incentives to external investors in a competition to embrace what was once tellingly, and scathingly, referred to as 'industrialization by invitation'.[22] The particular terms on which each State has sought to make its peace with the capitalist system—'living with dependency', as it has been described[23]—naturally vary, but all have succumbed, with once more the single important exception of Cuba since 1959. Whatever may be the debate about the 'socialist dependency' on the Soviet Union with which revolutionary Cuba had to live until very recently,[24] it manifestly is a different relationship from that to which structuralists point in respect of the rest of the region.

The political aspect of this system is seen to be a willingness on the part of the USA, the State which exercises hegemony over the region, to 'defend' it against all forms of 'attack' from radical and socialist politics in whatever form they emerge. The instances of such a response in the Caribbean are many and varied: Cuba 1959–, the Dominican Republic 1965, Jamaica 1972–80, and Grenada 1979–83 are only the most notorious. The techniques of intervention are deemed to range from 'destabilization', involving economic and other threats to undermine the legitimacy and effectiveness of allegedly subversive governments, via the attempted assassination of key political opponents, to outright invasion if all else fails and opportunity arises. In all cases, local allies and regional supporters are required. Nevertheless, the way that the Caribbean's part in such a process of hegemonic management is described has to be carefully modulated. The region cannot be said to contain many key US economic interests, which means that a crude economic determinism is inadequate to explain the assertion of US power over the Caribbean. The region's significance is, as Sutton has argued, primarily 'political—as proof of American power'. The Caribbean matters, he has written, 'because of what it represents to the people of the USA and to the outside world . . . a belief that if the USA cannot deal effectively with events in its own sphere of influence it will not deal effectively with events elsewhere.'[25] President Reagan, from this perspective, was quite right to decry those who denigrated the importance he attached to Grenada because its best-known export was nutmeg. 'It is not nutmeg that is at stake down there,' he declared in March 1983, 'it is the United

States' national security.'[26] And, as this example shows, national security, understood in structuralist terms, is truly all-encompassing.

HEREAFTER: ISSUES OF ECONOMIC AND POLITICAL INTEGRATION

The Caribbean State system has engaged with the possibility of moves into the hereafter for as long as it has existed. Indeed, the debate about closer union, federalism both formal and functional, and many other forms of regional integration substantially predates the expansionary phase of State creation after 1945.[27] The establishment of the West Indies Federation in 1958 brought the different strands of the process together, at least in the English-speaking part of the region, but its swift demise ended such agreement as there was on the character of a future regional order and effectively fractured the movement into economic and political integration schools.

Economic integration

The first Caribbean political leader to recognize that federation was but one manifestation of the regional idea, and not necessarily the best available at that, was Dr Eric Williams, the first prime minister of Trinidad and Tobago. Even as the West Indies Federation was being laid to rest and his country was attaining independence in 1962, he was urging his party to consider 'the future establishment of a Common Economic Community embracing the entire Caribbean area',[28] within which he unquestionably included Puerto Rico, Cuba, Haiti, the Dominican Republic, and the French and Dutch Caribbean. There were obviously formidable obstacles in the way of such a scheme and Williams soon retreated into a proposal to organize a regular conference of the heads of government of independent and self-governing Commonwealth Caribbean countries, the first of which gathered in Port of Spain in July 1963. This body was inevitably preoccupied with matters of economic and functional co-operation within that subregion and, in August 1968, gave rise to the Caribbean Free Trade Association (CARIFTA), composed by that stage of all the leading States of the Commonwealth Caribbean, except the Bahamas. This organization presided over a limited experiment in regional free trade which lasted for five years before being transformed in 1973, in good part in reaction to Britain's accession to the European Economic Community, into a wider Caribbean Community and Common Market (CARICOM).[29] Its goals were considerably more ambitious, embracing deeper economic integration, expanded functional co-operation, and the co-ordination of foreign policy by the independent States of the Community.

CARICOM, however, still eschewed any commitment to the political integration of the region and thus contained no threat to the sovereignty of the State.[30] Notwithstanding its commitment to foreign policy co-ordination, the CARICOM treaty was quite deliberately designed to avoid any mention, any hint even, of supranationality. The Community is controlled by a series of conferences and councils, made up of territorial politicians, and is only serviced by its secretariat.[31] With the exception of a few relatively unimportant items, decisions have to be agreed unanimously by representatives of all the member States of the Community and then have to be legitimated by each State in accordance with its own constitutional procedures. In short, CARICOM was designed and has been run by men who remain in, as Stanley Hoffmann put it, 'the mental universe of traditional inter-state relations'.[32] In that sense, it cannot be properly described as an integration movement at all. What best describes the practice of CARICOM is the concept of regionalization, which I have previously described as 'a method of international co-operation which enables the advantages of decision-making at a regional level to be reconciled with the preservation of the institution of the nation-state'.[33] At the end of the day too, this is much more an artefact of the State than the integrated regionalist community, serving to reinforce, rather than replace, State action. Theories of neofunctionalist spill-over from economic to political integration have thus never had much applicability to the Caribbean.

The process of Caribbean regionalization has also remained confined to the Commonwealth Caribbean. The 'widening' of the Community has often been discussed, and Haiti formally applied to join in 1974, but that request was dispatched into the limbo of secretarial study and no adjustment of the Community's membership has ever taken place. Several countries, including Haiti, have been granted observer status on some CARICOM ministerial committees, but they have not yet been allowed to take the relationship further, although it is significant that the issue of 'widening' is again on CARICOM's agenda. The involvement of Puerto Rico and the French and Dutch islands is effectively eliminated for constitutional reasons, and Cuba for political reasons, despite the fact that in October 1972 Jamaica, Trinidad and Tobago, Guyana, and Barbados led the way towards the ending of sanctions against Cuba by jointly establishing diplomatic relations with Havana.[34] As yet, though, Dr Williams's original vision of a Caribbean-wide economic community remains unfulfilled.

Political integration

The notion of the political integration of the Caribbean disappeared from view for several years after 1962, but it did eventually re-emerge, albeit only, as before, amongst the English-speaking States. It has always been understood in a very formal sense by West Indians brought up in the British constitutionalist tradition—as a process leading to the formation of a political community or union between a group of States, in which some or all of their authority is transferred to a new supranational body. Authority is seen as an absolute, not a relative, concept, something which cannot be eroded, only extinguished. Whether the goal be a federation or a unitary State or some novel structure, political integration is envisaged as the change from inter-state society to the domestic political system of the new union. Defined in this way, it is easy enough to see why such schemes have all failed to win a response from governments. Sovereignty is perceived, especially by the political élites, to be too valuable a prize to give up. Sustained by the emergence of popular nationalisms even in the smallest of the States but alert above all to the vested interests, both domestic and international, involved in the preservation of separate statehood, territorial leaders in the Caribbean manifestly still want to be seen to possess the right to make policy on their own initiative, even if they lack the capacity to do so effectively.

It is interesting, though, that the idea of political integration does still keep on surfacing. One recent analysis reported that no less than seven such proposals were made between 1971 and 1976, ranging from the so-called 'Grenada Declaration' issued by the heads of government of Dominica, Grenada, Guyana, St Kitts-Nevis, St Lucia, and St Vincent to schemes advanced by regional technocrats, academics, and other professionals.[35] As Emmanuel's analysis indicates, they varied considerably in form, proposed powers, and territorial composition. For the most part, Jamaica was excluded in recognition of its relative separateness from the majority of the other States in the eastern Caribbean. Indeed, generally, it has been the smaller

States of the Leeward and Windward Islands which have been seen as the ripest for political amalgamation. Although they have been grouped since 1981 within the Organization of Eastern Caribbean States (OECS), an interstate body which has pursued co-operation in economic, functional, and security matters with some success, they agreed in October 1986 to seek a full political union. Within two years, however, the wider project had been shelved, with first Antigua-Barbuda expressing its opposition, followed by St Kitts-Nevis and Montserrat (which, although a British colony, is a member of OECS), leaving only the Windward States to see what they can produce between themselves. A number of regional constituent assemblies have met and made progress towards the preparation of a draft constitution, which when agreed will still have to be approved by each national parliament and by the people of the four islands in a referendum.[36] As can be seen, plenty of pitfalls remain, not least the electoral victory of opposition parties opposed to political unity in one or more of the States.

At the same time, the arguments which keep the political integration question alive in the region do not look like disappearing. At heart, they imply that independence for such small territories cannot be made meaningful in any other way. Within this rubric, the precise formulation of the case has then varied from advocate to advocate— building sometimes on the belief in a sense of West Indian nationhood, or the benefits of having a single voice in international affairs, or the need to complete the process of economic integration, and at other times on the advantages of ending wasteful duplication of administrative and political activity or being better able to entrench civil liberties at a regional, rather than national, level.[37] They are good arguments, no doubt, and they appeal to Caribbean intellectuals, but that does not mean that they have the sheer political clout necessary to override the hard-headed calculations of politicians holding power in States that already exist. The performance of these States in the international system as presently organized will have to worsen markedly—to the point where their very existence is imperilled by some external threat— before political integration becomes the natural response.

CONCLUSION

The arguments advanced in this chapter can be simply summarized. They assert that the basic architecture of international relations within the Caribbean are set in a relatively stable mould. No new independent States are in the process of creation, Aruba having seen the practical advantages of the new Dutch Commonwealth. Nor do many States face death, certainly not involuntarily by annexation or secession, or even voluntarily by amalgamation or union. Only Dominica, Grenada, St Lucia, and St Vincent are actively discussing political unity and they still have much work to do before their plans are ready to be implemented. Most Caribbean States will instead continue to co-operate, sometimes effectively, sometimes ineffectively, within regional organizations which do not threaten sovereignty. In short, the life of the region's States as it has been experienced thus far in the post-1945 era will remain the pattern into the immediate future, notwithstanding the ending of the Cold War. Small, weak, generally impoverished States will continue to grapple as best they know how with an international system in which they do not and cannot command much power.

NOTES

1. *Memorandum on the Closer Association of the British West Indian Colonies*, Cmd. 7120 (London, 1947), Pt. 2, para. 11.
2. J. S. Mordecai, *The West Indies: The Federal Negotiations* (London, 1968), 33.
3. See W. J. Brisk, *Anguilla and the Mini-State Dilemma* (New York, 1971).
4. A. E. Thorndike, 'The Concept of Associated Statehood with Special Reference to the Eastern Caribbean', Ph.D. London, 1979, 292.
5. 'Belize and the Dispute with Guatemala', Foreign and Commonwealth Office Background Brief, mimeo (London, Feb. 1983), 3.
6. See T. Thorndike, 'When Small is not Beautiful: The Case of the Turks and Caicos Islands', *Corruption and Reform*, 2 (1987), 28–35.
7. T. Eggar, parliamentary under-secretary of state, Foreign and Commonwealth Office, in House of Commons, Parliamentary Debates (*Hansard*), 124, Col. 574, 16.
8. T. Thorndike, 'No End to Empire: Prospects for the British Caribbean Dependencies', mimeo (Stoke-on-Trent, 1988), 13.
9. See G. Lasserre and A. Mabileau, 'The French Antilles and their Status as Overseas Departments', in E. de Kadt (ed.), *Patterns of Foreign Influence in the Caribbean* (London, 1972), 82.
10. 'Speech on 26th June 1967 by Pierre Billotte', in R. Preiswerk (ed.), *Documents on International Relations in the Caribbean* (Rio Piedras, 1970), 569.

11. See H. Hoetink, 'The Dutch Caribbean and its Metropolis', in de Kadt, *Patterns of Foreign Influence*, 103–20.

12. See R. Hofte and G. Oostindie, 'Upside-Down Decolonization', *Hemisphere*, 1/2 (1989), 28–31.

13. Excerpt from the Puerto Rican Constitution of Mar. 1952.

14. See J. Heine and J. M. Garcia-Passalacqua, *The Puerto Rican Question* (New York, 1983).

15. On Barbuda, see D. Lowenthal and C. G. Clarke, 'Island Orphans: Barbuda and the Rest', *Journal of Commonwealth and Comparative Politics*, 18 (1980), 293–307; and on Nevis, see J. Nesbitt and B. Gibbs, 'The Nevis Secession Movement: Its Origins and Prospects', *Bulletin of Eastern Caribbean Affairs*, 4 (1978), 20–2.

16. See A. Payne, 'The Belize Triangle: Relations with Britain, Guatemala and the United States', *Journal of Interamerican Studies and World Affairs*, 32 (1990), 119–35.

17. See R. H. Manley, *Guyana Emergent: The Post-Independence Struggle for Non-Dependent Development* (Cambridge, Mass., 1979).

18. All population figures are taken from *South America, Central America and the Caribbean* (London, 1987).

19. All GDP figures are taken from International Monetary Fund, *International Financial Statistics* (Washington, DC, 1982).

20. See 'Britain and the Caribbean: The Way Ahead', speech by T. Eggar to the Annual General Meeting of the West India Committee, 28 June 1988, mimeo (London, 1988), 4.

21. A. McIntyre, 'Some Issues of Trade Policy in the West Indies', in N. Girvan and O. Jefferson (eds.), *Readings in the Political Economy of the Caribbean* (Kingston, 1967), 165.

22. N. Girvan and O. Jefferson, 'Introduction', in Girvan and Jefferson (eds.), *Readings in Political Economy*, 2.

23. P. Sutton, 'Living with Dependency in the Commonwealth Caribbean', in A. Payne and P. Sutton (eds.), *Dependency under Challenge: The Political Economy of the Commonwealth Caribbean* (Manchester, 1984), 281.

24. See R. A. Packenham, 'Cuba and the USSR since 1959: What Kind of Dependency?', in I. L. Horowitz, *Cuban Communism* (New Brunswick, 1988), 109–39.

25. P. Sutton, 'The Caribbean as a Focus for Strategic and Resource Rivalry', in P. Calvert (ed.), *The Central American Security System: North-South or East-West?* (Cambridge, 1988), 39–40.

26. President Reagan's speech to the National Association of Manufacturers, cited in *Caribbean Contact* (Bridgetown, 1985), 3.

27. See J. H. Proctor, 'The Development of the Idea of Federation of the British Caribbean Territories', *Caribbean Quarterly*, 5 (1957), 5–33.

28. *The Nation*, 4 (1962).

29. For the early history of CARIFTA and CARICOM, see A. Payne, *The*

Politics of the Caribbean Community 1961–79: Regional Integration amongst New States (Manchester, 1980).

30. For a discussion of this point, see W. G. Demas, *West Indian Nationhood and Caribbean Integration* (Bridgetown, 1974), 44–55.
31. For a description of the organizational structure of the Community, see K. Hall and B. Blake, 'The Caribbean Community: Administrative and Institutional Aspects', *Journal of Common Market Studies*, 16 (1978), 211–28.
32. S. Hoffmann, 'Discord in Community: The North Atlantic Area as a Partial International System', *International Organization*, 17 (1963), 527.
33. Payne, *Politics of the Caribbean Community*, 286.
34. See R. E. Jones, 'Cuba and the English-speaking Caribbean', in C. Blasier and C. Mesa-Lago (eds.), *Cuba in the World* (Pittsburgh, 1979), 130–3.
35. P. Emmanuel, 'Political Unity in the OECS: New Approaches to Caribbean Integration', *Caribbean Affairs*, 1 (1988), 101–25.
36. See R. Sanders, 'Disunity in the OECS', *Caribbean Affairs*, 2 (1989), 114–24.
37. See Payne, *Politics of the Caribbean Community*, 270–7.

FURTHER READING

Braveboy-Wagner, J., *The Caribbean in World Affairs: The Foreign Policies of the English-speaking States* (Boulder, Col., 1988).

Bryan, A. (ed.), *Peace, Development and Security in the Caribbean* (London, 1990).

Deere, C. D., *In the Shadows of the Sun: Caribbean Development Alternatives and U.S. Policy* (Boulder, Col., 1990).

Dominguez, J. I., *To Make a World Safe for Revolution: Cuba's Foreign Policy* (Cambridge, 1989).

Heine, J. (ed.), *A Revolution Aborted: The Lessons of Grenada* (Pittsburgh, 1990).

Knight, F. W., and Palmer, C. A. (eds.), *The Modern Caribbean* (Chapel Hill, NC, 1989).

Payne, A., *The International Crisis in the Caribbean* (Baltimore, 1984).

—— and Sutton, P. (eds.), *Modern Caribbean Politics* (Manchester, 1993).

14

North America

DAVID G. HAGLUND AND RICHARD MATTHEW

AMERICAN – CANADIAN TENSIONS

Problems of sovereignty in North America do not take the form
of classical security dilemmas. The evolution of a durable security
community on the continent, benefiting from the ability and promise
of the USA to defend North America, has produced a region that
apparently has come to terms with its unequal distribution of power
in ways that assure the security, prosperity, and integrity of both
countries. This point is of course obvious to any political observer
who turns his or her attention towards Canada and the USA.
However this does not mean that questions of sovereignty do not
arise in the North American context or that those which do can be
dismissed as insignificant.

North Americans—Canadians and, to a lesser extent, also
Americans—face a number of challenges to sovereignty which one
could broadly categorize as contemporary dilemmas. How should
the State address the demands of certain groups—aboriginals for
example—to forms of 'self-government' within it? How should this
'quasi-sovereignty' be granted while still maintaining the primary
sovereignty of the State? In addition to these internal dilemmas, both
North American polities must also contend with external challenges
to sovereignty. How should economic interdependence and regional
co-operation within North America be managed? To what extent do
regional institutions like the (1988) Free Trade Agreement (FTA)
and the (1992) North American Free Trade Agreement (NAFTA)
with Mexico diminish the sovereignty of member States? These
sovereignty questions are of course not unique to North America and
have been debated in the context of European union as well. Finally,
how can sovereign States come together to address and resolve
outstanding issues such as environmental problems which by their

very nature do not and cannot respect human conventions like international boundaries. If air-borne pollution emanating from one State moves into another and produces acid rain, what does this imply about the sovereignty of the affected State?

While these questions affect both Canada and the USA, these two States do not assign equal importance to them. The USA is of course a hemispheric and indeed global power and its primary concern regarding security issues is necessarily directed far beyond its own North American hinterland. Furthermore, in so far as the USA is a great power and even a superpower it does not have to be concerned about its own sovereignty. Not so for Canada which despite its membership in the G-7 club of leading economic powers remains by and large concerned with regional issues many if not most of which are related to questions of sovereignty. Canada's world-view is overwhelmingly shaped by its experience as (at best) a middle power on the doorstep of the American superpower. This disparity, while certainly not a threat in the classical definition of sovereignty, nevertheless makes Canadians and their governments extremely sensitive to even the slightest hint of any trespass by the USA on Canadian sovereignty defined in the broadest terms. (In this respect, Canada is in much the same position as Mexico *vis-à-vis* America.) This sensitivity manifests itself in virtually every dealing the Canadian State has with its American neighbour from free-trade disputes to pollution of the Great Lakes. Hence, for example, the ongoing Canadian preoccupation with adequate Canadian content in television programming to protect Canada's 'cultural sovereignty' from American infiltration and domination.

These challenges to a common understanding of sovereignty are world-wide, and if they affect North America, there is no reason to suppose that they do so with greater force or significance than elsewhere. In what follows, we shall develop our argument that both North American States face challenges to their 'sovereign' status, of an internal as well as an external provenance. Moreover, for one of those States, Canada, there is a sense in which it can be said that, in spite of the existence of a North American security community, the USA constitutes a principal threat to its sovereignty. While it would be silly to reverse the formulation and see in Canada a threat to American sovereignty, it is our argument that even the USA confronts a growing number of challenges to its sovereign status which its undeniable power may be incapable of deflecting.

FIG. 14.1 North America

DOES THE USA HAVE A SOVEREIGNTY PROBLEM?

Perhaps the most glaring distinction that can be drawn between the two North American societies is the way each relates to sovereignty. In Canada, no other concept can be counted upon to inspire as much political debate as sovereignty. By contrast, to American audiences few concepts are as tedious, in spite of recent, strident claims that Japan is buying up California and other choice pieces of US real estate. Although Americans express concern about the foreign market for their national assets and foreign influence in their political system, they do not seem unduly worried about the continuing existence of the USA. To the contrary, the predominant debate in the USA has focused on concerns about its position in the international system—as one would expect given its superpower status. Yet arguably Americans themselves have a sovereignty dilemma, which though certainly not as acute as Canada's nevertheless does have an impact upon the bilateral relationship between the two countries.

Throughout much of the post-Second World War era America's hegemonic position in the system of States enabled Washington to promote both prosperity and security. But as America's standing in the world has eroded along with its ability to control its external environment, so has its people's confidence in its government declined.[1] Evidence of the erosion of competence can be seen in problems of foreign trade and investment, pollution, illegal immigration, and drug-smuggling. But does Washington's inability to resolve these problems derive from incompetence, or, in the contemporary era of uncontrollable global forces and increasingly permeable borders, is it rather that strategies are not available that will be both effective and consonant with liberal-democratic values? We cannot be sure of the answer, but as long as the US government is unable to deal successfully with such problems, tensions between it and the American people can be expected.

Potential implications of this dynamic situation can be illustrated with reference to the interrelated forces of ideology and trade that have long played a stabilizing role in North America. By some accounts, the USA seems to be reassessing the merits of existing liberal trade and investment arrangements—a development that has some intriguing parallels with the older debate within Canada over the costs and benefits of foreign direct investment and freer commercial intercourse. An example is an article by Felix Rohatyn, entitled 'America's Economic Dependence'. Rohatyn sounds some of the now-familiar cautions about the large US budgetary deficit (approximately $370 billion), the trade deficit (about $70 billion), the domestic government debt (around $3 trillion), and the foreign debt (of more than $500 billion). What makes his argument familiar to Canadian readers is his concentration upon the perils of foreign ownership.[2] 'In the long run, foreign control of a larger proportion of American business, coupled with our failing educational system, will have significant implications for innovation, product development and research, in addition to increasing the level of financial transfers abroad.'[3]

However, not all challenges to America's sovereignty from within (which are exacerbated by external forces), can be subsumed under economic categories or the tensions between popular self-determination and the imperatives of government competence. Before we begin our discussion of Canada's sovereignty dilemmas, we would like to point out two unrelated, although not entirely dissimilar, domestic features of the American polity with direct bearing on the theme of this volume: the cases of Puerto Rico and the aboriginal peoples of the USA. Unfortunately, space does not allow any more than a cursory glance at these issues within a chapter which must discuss Canada as well as the USA.

Unlike most of Latin America, Puerto Rico's long period of colonial tutelage did not culminate in independence.[4] Instead, in 1952 it negotiated a commonwealth status with the USA, which, after heated discussion, was given recognition by the UN, even though some member States deemed it an affront to Article 73 of the Charter. Since that time, Puerto Ricans have divided into three camps, seeking independence, American 'statehood', or the preservation of the *status quo*. The first objective has been strongly supported by Cuba, but the US government has acted to undermine this movement both in the UN and in Puerto Rico. The possibility of 'statehood' has been given lukewarm support from the past five US administrations, who have wanted to restrain Puerto Rico's anti-colonial impulses without alienating the American public, which would possibly oppose admitting Puerto Rico into the Union. In consequence, the *status quo* has been retained.

Two problems lie at the root of this history of debate and indecision: Washington is far from clear about its goals for Puerto Rico; and the Puerto Ricans themselves remain divided, unsure that they can survive on their own but wary of committing themselves to a perennially second-class status within the USA. The future may depend on the role Washington plays in dealing with Puerto Rico's current economic crisis, which may in turn depend in part on the extent to which this small island is perceived as strategically important.

While Puerto Rico has found itself at the centre of debates on decolonization and grand strategy, and unable to plot a clear course into the future, the native peoples of the USA have become increasingly concerned with their right to self-determination. (A comparable development has occurred in Canada, see below.) Their status has long been unclear, defined in some 4,000 often vague and contradictory official documents prepared over the past two centuries, and their lack of political and economic power has generally made political neglect the path of least resistance. None the less their history shows a pattern of evolution towards an increased recognition of their rights as 'sovereign' peoples, manifest in the Indian Civil Rights Act (1968) which imposed 'fewer legislative restrictions on tribal governments than the Constitution imposes on State and federal governments'.[5]

A concept of self-government has evolved, such that today the aboriginal peoples are regarded as possessing certain rights outside the legal framework of the USA. But what these rights are and how they can be protected and exercised is unclear, especially since Indians remain subject to acts of Congress. It is improbable that the US government will act quickly to clarify the status of native Americans who are, in the final analysis, largely powerless and easy to ignore for long periods of time. Thus while the act of recognizing some rights to be self-determining is certainly important and provides a crucial foundation for further and more concrete gains, the substance of this status remains unspecified and it is likely that the native Americans will continue to exist in a sort of netherworld on the margins of mainstream America for some time to come.

One conclusion to be drawn from the examples of Puerto Rico and the American aboriginals is that the principle of sovereignty is enmeshed in a matrix of power relations. The USA recognizes both groups as having some sort of valid claim to sovereignty, but until they can organize a viable power structure, which the USA, for obvious reasons, tends to discourage, sovereignty will be unattainable. Nevertheless, it is in part due to this principle that these groups are taken seriously at all.

CANADA AND THE CONTOURS OF INTERNAL
SOVEREIGNTY

In some ways Canada provides a mirror image of the American experience. The political history of Canada suggests a tendency towards decentralization internally and an increasingly dependent status—with regard to the USA—in external relations. However, because Canada's federal government has not had as strong a claim to either competence or popular consent as has its American counterpart, the provinces have assumed a greater share of supreme power and authority than have the States. Centralization has been a key ingredient of America's success. By contrast, in Canada decentralization has reduced some domestic tensions but works against a sense of shared fate. Canada has sought to distribute political competence and self-determination among distinct cultural groups and different levels of government, but this has frequently created tensions.

Perhaps the most puzzling question the student of Canadian politics faces is: Why has Canada endured? In view of strong regional and provincial identities, a weak sense of national unity, and perennial threats of secession, the potential for breakdown seems high. This has led to a now familiar pattern: a renewed interest in Quebec independence, widespread discussion of the unbridgeable differences within Canada, and a new round of constitutional talks. And yet, so far, Canada has not only survived but flourished.

It is commonplace to argue that what really holds Canada together is fear of the USA and the economic promise of an east–west corridor, coupled with a vague sense of a mission to develop the north. But Canada has also benefited from its geographical location, a large and forbidding wilderness which, since the American invasion in 1812–14, no country has had much interest in acquiring. Having as its immediate neighbour a superpower long committed to encouraging self-determining liberal-democracies and to protecting the Americas has also been to Canada's advantage. If Canada has no reason to worry about the military threat posed by the USA it need not fear any external threat to its security. Yet, perhaps a price has been paid for this military guarantee. In other words, external security underwritten by American power has perhaps made it possible for Canada to survive with only a weak sense of national unity and purpose.

The greatest threats to Canada as a sovereign State have, since 1945, come from within. It is Quebec that has posed and continues to pose the most serious challenge. In so far as Canada has been accepted by the French-speaking majority in Quebec, the price has been a strong provincial government and a special status for Quebec within a new constitution. In particular, Quebec has demanded security for the French language and culture—demands that have led to much confusion elsewhere in Canada over what exactly is threatened. Quebec's objectives were partially clarified following the election of the Separatist Parti Quebecois (PQ) in 1976. Although a referendum authorizing the PQ government to negotiate a quasi-independent status ('sovereignty association') was defeated in 1980, the alternative view, advocated by then prime minister Pierre Trudeau, of a bilingual and bicultural country, has not triumphed. Instead, equivocation has persisted and Quebec politicians have recognized the strength of their hand which derives from the persistent threat of separating from the rest of Canada.

Recent developments suggest that Quebec's goal continues to be the achievement of self-determining status, within Canada if possible, without if necessary. However the precise nature of this status remains largely contested both within Quebec and indeed the rest of Canada. Special status for Quebec could embody anything from the 'distinct society' vision of Quebec federalist premier Robert Bourassa to the older 'sovereignty association' ideal of former separatist premier Rene Levesque and his successor and current leader of the Quebec 'independists', Jacques Parizeau. This confusion results in no small measure from the fact that the sovereignty arrangements which are being proposed in Canadian constitutional politics are new and therefore do not have precedents within our classical under-standing of the concept.

Another internal sovereignty concern relates to Canada's aboriginal peoples. Recent developments suggest a willingness on the part of the Canadian State to elaborate a right of self-government. For example, the *1992 Report of the Special Joint Committee on a Renewed Canada* recommended the entrenchment of the inherent right of aboriginal peoples to self-government within Canada. However, as in the USA, the content of this right still remains to be specified. The general objective is for aboriginal governments to 'take the place in native peoples' lives that provincial and municipal governments take in the lives of other Canadians'. But to be successful, such a right must include access to essential public services, a secure land base, an adequate economic base, and strong native associations that encompass the many tiny communities scattered across the vast Canadian north. One obstacle lies in the federal and provincial governments' 'impulse to control everything of importance'.[6] And given the long history of defending jurisdictions that has characterized Canadian politics, it is unlikely that many agreements will be forged in the near future, especially with attention riveted on Quebec. But the future holds some promise. In late 1991 the federal government announced its intention to grant the Inuit (Eskimo) people a large tract of land in the north (approximately one-fifth of the Canadian land mass) and self-government. However, the actual form this will assume, and its implications for other native peoples seeking control over more widely valued territory, have yet to be determined.

CANADA, THE USA, AND THE NORTH AMERICAN 'DIALECTIC'

In this section we focus on two issue areas where external sovereignty considerations have been affecting Canadian–American relations in recent years: economics and the military.

The discrepancy between equal sovereignty and unequal power has not gone unregarded by students of Canadian–American relations. In an earlier age, before the principle of equal territorial legitimacy had fully evolved and been incorporated into acceptable codes of international behaviour, it was thought that what kept the USA from exercising its 'manifest destiny' over the entire northern half of North America was a prudential understanding of the potential risks associated with taking on the British. This is not to say that all or even most Americans were anxious in the nineteenth century to annex Canada; some were, but many clearly were not.[7] While the USA may originally have been deterred from expanding into Canada by a fear of European involvement, it is now held in check by not only international norms but also its own ideology, which supports friendly democracies and opposes territorial aggrandizement. Of course, this does not mean that fears about diminution or loss of sovereignty have disappeared in Canada.

Theorists of international relations and students of Canadian–American relations do not agree about the significance of sovereignty: we lack a scholarly consensus on the juridical equality–empirical inequality dialectic. On one side are writers whose approach is informed by a conflictual understanding of the relationship, while on the other are those who stress its underlying co-operative aspect.

The Canadian debate over economic independence demonstrates this analytical cleavage as clearly as it can possibly be displayed.[8] For much of the post-1945 period, Canadians have been arguing about the relative costs and benefits of foreign direct investment—a debate, as we noted above, that is only beginning in the USA. Lately, as the bitterness of the 1988 Canadian federal election campaign revealed, free trade with the USA, which Canada historically has opposed, re-emerged as a topic of controversy. The election was won by the

Conservatives who supported free trade. But many were disturbed by a prospect of Canada's eventual loss of autonomy, especially in areas like culture and social services. A few see the USA as launched on a longer-term project of imperialism that has been both advanced by and enshrined in the 1988 Free Trade Agreement (FTA). For those with this view, the USA is seeking what it has always sought from Canada, untrammeled and inexpensive access to Canadian raw materials and other economic assets.[9] It is feared that this will inevitably undermine Canada's cultural distinctiveness and Welfare State, by forcing Canada to adopt American free-enterprise norms regarding labour markets, government subsidies, privatization, and so forth.

The contrasting school holds that while international relations, including Canadian–American relations, are becoming more complicated, there is no necessary reason for Canada's sovereignty and other interests to suffer as a result of the spread and deepening of the processes of interdependence. Indeed, to some in this school, Canada has been doing much better in its bilateral dealings with the USA under conditions of 'complex interdependence' than would ordinarily be expected; in effect, Canada has resolved the dilemma associated with the juridical equality–empirical inequality dialectic by using the former to minimize the latter.[10] This does not mean that the sovereignty issue is irrelevant, only that with proper management Canadian economic relations with the USA can be as isolated from other aspects of Canadian domestic and foreign policy as could be expected in an interdependent world.

It is not our purpose in this survey to try to resolve this debate. But we do wish to add to the discussion by drawing attention to the manner in which some of the issues we addressed in our section on US sovereignty questions have an impact upon the Canada–USA relationship. A major contributory factor that impelled Canadian policy-makers to seek and obtain the FTA was their conviction that the world economic (mainly trading) order was becoming increasingly imperilled as a result of the formation of great economic blocs in Europe and the Far East which threatened Canada's trading economy. For many in Canada, securing access to the American market was sought less as a primary goal in itself than as a means of averting, *faute de mieux*, even greater economic problems if left entirely on its own.[11]

As regards Canada–USA military relations, two problem areas

have been identified. The first is the celebrated question of 'Arctic sovereignty'. The 1985 transit of an American Coast Guard vessel, the *Polar Sea*, triggered an intense barrage of opposition in Canada, and not just from the traditional sources of nationalist anti-Americanism.[12] What was at stake were conflicting claims made by Washington and Ottawa over the status of the waters of the Arctic archipelago (but not the islands themselves). Canada's position, stated rather casually in earlier years, is that the waters belong to it, and constitute what would legally speaking be internal waters. In November 1987 Washington and Ottawa reached an agreement that, at least for one category of vessel (ice-breakers), seemed to indicate American recognition of the Canadian claim; under the terms of the agreement, the USA would in future secure Canadian permission for transit of these vessels through the Canadian Arctic. Military vessels, however, are not covered by this agreement.

The military use of the Arctic leads us into the second, sovereignty-related strategic issue that has appeared in recent years. This is the question of the possible impact that American strategic defence measures might have on Canadian sovereignty. A discernible trend occasioned primarily by technological developments, such as the forward deployment of the US Navy's hunter-killer submarines, was engendering controversy in Canada during the late 1980s because of the effect on Canada's territorial legitimacy. However, the ending of the Cold War, and subsequent demise of the Soviet Union, might be expected to result in a decrease in the strategic value of Canadian real estate to the USA. If so, control of Arctic waters may revert to Canada simply from American loss of military interest in them.

The above does not exhaust the set of territorial disputes that occasionally strain Canada–USA relations. For example, the US refusal to pass legislation prohibiting its trawlers from exploiting Canadian fisheries, a refusal related to the US decision not to ratify the Law of the Sea Treaty, has left Canada with the delicate issue of how to protect its territorial waters when it lacks adequate naval capabilities and is anxious to avoid a confrontation with the USA. Another long-standing dispute concerns the problem of acid rain. Roughly half of the acid precipitation that affects Eastern Canada is caused by sulphuric and nitrous oxide emissions originating in the USA; due to prevailing wind patterns and the far lower capacity of a much smaller Canadian industry to produce pollution, the USA has not faced a comparable reciprocal problem. Concerns about air pollution, the disposal of toxic materials, and the quality and quantity of water supplies, together with many other environmental issues, will surely intensify in the years ahead testing the ability of Canada and the USA to co-operate for their mutual interest.

This raises interesting questions about national sovereignty in relation to global forces that one writer has labelled the menace of the 'four P's': pollution, poverty, population, and proliferation.[13] For those who share this perspective, 'the mounting problems of the earth as a whole no longer are amenable to attack with the ethnocentric conceptual equipment inherited from the nineteenth century.'[14] And among this outdated equipment, according to this view, nothing stands out as much as the concept of sovereignty.

CONCLUSION

We began this chapter by suggesting that, at first blush, North America appears to have been relatively immune to many of the classical problems that have plagued the State system since 1945. But on further analysis, North America has provided important insights into the contemporary dialectic between equal States and unequal powers in a complex and rapidly changing world.

For Canada, the traditional security dilemma has been largely resolved through the North American security community. Similarly, Canada has benefited from its continued participation in arguably the biggest regional economy in the world—the 'Europe 1992' project notwithstanding. But by pinning much of its security and economic well-being on the benevolence, co-operation, and competence of its much larger neighbour, Canada finds itself constrained in its defence and economic policies. Whether it is evolving into (or has reached) a neocolonial status, or instead is pioneering forms of interstate co-operation that could serve as models for the rest of the world, is a question that leads, as we have noted, to sharp disagreements among students of USA–Canada relations.

Nevertheless, it is essential to recall that three factors have worked together to produce a situation that has been extremely beneficial to Canada. First, the USA has been ideologically predisposed to respect Canada as a sovereign liberal-democracy; second, the countries have generally enjoyed mutually beneficial economic relations; and, third, the USA has tended to envision its own defence in extra-territorial terms in which Canada provided, as it were, the strategic foreground. These factors have proven not only compatible with, but by and large supportive of, the classical principle of sovereignty. Thus while this principle may have some marginal impact on USA–Canada relations, it has so primarily because of a larger ideological and pragmatic framework.

However, these factors may be undergoing a gradual erosion. Problems with the US economy have reanimated the debate over protectionism versus free trade (itself complicated by global trends not yet well understood), and the demise of the Soviet threat coupled with the promises of new military technology could make Canada less important to American grand strategy. This could leave room for greater Canadian sovereignty in the north, but at the possible price of Washington's indifference to Canadian concerns. Where these trends will lead, however, is far from clear.

In the case of the USA, sovereignty has hardly been an issue since the Civil War. Nevertheless, we see an important relationship between the decline of US hegemony and the internal tension between legitimacy and competence that has persisted since independence. Confidence in government is waning, a sense of its remoteness is growing, concern for liberal-democratic values may be mounting, and doubts about the economy are proliferating. At the same time the need for a powerful and rational State, unimpeded by domestic pressures, to chart a new course through stormy post-Cold War international waters is widely acknowledged. In the years ahead the extent to which Washington will be able to fulfil its traditional functions—the provision of security, prosperity, and avenues for political participation—may become a central political issue as America's position in the international system changes.

Finally, it appears that sovereignty is acquiring new connotations within the broad framework of Western thought as previously marginalized or exploited groups, such as North America's aboriginal peoples, seek to recover some control over the conditions of their lives. There is no evidence to suggest that this evolution is likely to be rapid; on the other hand, it is certain to be of interest to similar groups world-wide and may be an early sign of future changes to the contemporary world's ideal unit of political organization, the nation-state.

NOTES

1. There is substantial recent literature on the phenomenon of US 'hegemonic decline'. See e.g.: P. Kennedy, *The Rise and Fall of the Great Powers: Economic Change and Military Conflict from 1500 to 2000* (New York, 1987); D. P. Calleo, *Beyond American Hegemony: The Future of the Western Alliance* (New York, 1987); R. Gilpin, *War and Change in World Politics* (Cambridge, 1981); S. P. Huntington, 'The U.S.—Decline or Renewal?' *Foreign Affairs*, 67 (1988/89), 76–96; and P. Seabury, 'The Solvency Boys,' *National Interest*, 13 (1988), 100–5.

2. The literature on Canadian approaches to the foreign direct investment question is vast; for a summary of the major perceived costs and benefits of such investment, see J. A. Finlayson and D. G. Haglund, 'Oil Politics and Canada-United States Relations', *Political Science Quarterly*, 99 (1984), 271–88.

3. F. Rohatyn, 'America's Economic Dependence', *Foreign Affairs: America and the World 1988/89*, 68, 53–65.

4. Material in this section on Puerto Rico is drawn from R. Pastor, 'The International Debate on Puerto Rico: The Costs of Being an Agenda-Taker', *International Organization*, 38 (1984), 575–87; R. Carr, *Puerto Rico: A Colonial Experiment* (New York, 1984); A. M. Carrion, *Puerto Rico: A Political and Cultural History* (New York, 1983); and E. Melendez, *Puerto Rico's Statehood Movement* (New York, 1988).

5. D. Sanders, *Aboriginal Self-Government in the United States*, Background Paper no. 5 (Kingston, Ont., 1985), 38.

6. N. Lyon, *Aboriginal Self-Government: Rights of Citizenship and Access to Governmental Services* (Kingston, Ont., 1984), 68.

7. Two indispensable sources for the period albeit from differing perspectives are A. K. Weinberg, *Manifest Destiny: A Study of Nationalist Expansionism in American History* (Baltimore, 1935), and F. Merk, *Manifest Destiny and Mission in American History: A Reinterpretation* (New York, 1963). Also useful is M. S. Hunt, *Ideology and US Foreign Policy* (New Haven, Conn., 1987).

8. See, *inter alia*, K. Levitt, *Silent Surrender: The Multinational Corporation in Canada* (Toronto, 1970); J. Fayerweather, *Foreign Investment in Canada: Prospects for National Policy* (White Plains, NY, 1973); and I. A. Litvak, *Canadian Cases in International Business* (Toronto, 1984).

9. For a critical examination of this argument, see D. G. Haglund (ed.), *The New Geopolitics of Minerals: Canada and International Resource Trade* (Vancouver, 1989), ch. 6: 'Canadian Strategic Minerals and US Military Potential'.

10. This, of course, is the thesis advanced in R. O. Keohane and J. S. Nye, *Power and Interdependence: World Politics in Transition* (Boston, 1977).

11. This argument is developed further in D. G. Haglund, 'Unbridled Constraint: The Macdonald Commission Volumes on Canada and the International Political Economy', *Canadian Journal of Political Science*, 20 (1987), 599–624.
12. Although it is often claimed that one can be 'pro-Canadian' without at the same time being 'anti-American', there is a school of thought that sees anti-Americanism as being a (perhaps the) defining characteristic of English Canadian nationalism. See K. R. Nossal, *The Politics of Canadian Foreign Policy* (Scarborough, Ont., 1989), 157.
13. Kenneth N. Waltz, *Theory of International Politics* (Reading, Mass., 1979), 139.
14. George Modelski, 'The Promise of Geocentric Politics', *World Politics*, 22 (1969–70), 635.

FURTHER READING

Axline, A. W. (ed.), *Continental Community?: Independence and Integration in North America* (Toronto, 1974).

Doran, C. F. (ed.), *Canada and the United States: Enduring Friendship, Persistent Stress* (Englewood Cliffs, NJ, 1985).

Holmes, J., *Life With Uncle: The Canadian-American Relationship* (Toronto, 1981).

Jockel, J. T., *Security to the North: Canada-US Defence Relations in the 1990s* (East Lansing, Mich., 1991).

Lipset, S. M., *Continental Divide: The Values and Institutions of the United States and Canada* (New York, 1990).

McKinsey, L., and Nossal, K. R. (eds.), *America's Alliances and Canadian-American Relations* (Toronto, 1988).

Osherenko, G., and Young, O. R., *The Age of the Arctic: Hot Conflicts and Cold Realities* (Cambridge, 1988).

PART III
SIGNIFICANCE AND FUTURE

15

Economic Interdependence and Independent Statehood

STEPHEN D. KRASNER

INDEPENDENCE WITH INTERDEPENDENCE

Interdependencies have always been an inherent aspect of the States system: it is linkages and exchanges among a number of independent units that distinguish an international system comprised of States from a system made up of a single empire in which the very notion of 'international' becomes problematic because the imperial ruler claims universal authority. The crucial development in the consolidation of the modern State system was the triumph over that most formidable of transnational institutions, the Catholic Church. As opposed to empires, whose preoccupations were mostly inward-looking, sovereign States were always presented with external threats and opportunities. The essentially anarchic character of the State system meant that war was always possible and that States could be conquered and even dismembered. Military competition drove States to engage in economic competition as well because security depended not only on elements of physical size—number of subjects, extent of territory— but also on a State's relative economic and technological capabilities. Sovereign States have remained the only basic units of the Western-cum-global international system right down to the present time.

Sovereign statehood involves two basic principles: self-help and territoriality. Self-help means that there is no authority above the State; territoriality means that authority is exercised within a defined geographic area as opposed to being exercised, for instance, over a group of people who might move from one location to another. Sovereign States are in this respect independent geographically based political systems.

Interdependence is an inherent, a logically necessary, aspect of an international system composed of sovereign States. Interdependence, economic or otherwise, does not pose a direct challenge to *de jure* as opposed to *de facto* sovereignty—that is, it does not present some juridical alternative to the sovereign States system. It does, however, raise the question of whether *de facto* sovereignty—the ability of States to exercise effective control over issues where they claim to possess authority—is being eroded. Juridical sovereignty has never been frontally challenged, except perhaps in recent times by the European Community although even this experience is equivocal.[1] There have been occasional efforts to create an alternative form of political organization that would stand above or beside the sovereign State but, to date, all of these attempts have failed. There are still no entities other than States that can make final authoritative decisions—the litmus-test of organized political life.

The basic question posed by interdependence, therefore, is not whether juridical sovereignty has been supplanted by something else, but whether it has become an empty shell. This is the question I will address. It may be that State policy-makers still have the formal authority to make certain decisions but that these decisions are inconsequential. A State may, for instance, attempt to close its borders to certain goods, or all goods, and still be overwhelmed by smuggling; or, a State may attempt to conduct an independent monetary policy and yet be confounded by international capital flows. Policy-makers may see themselves as so constrained by the external environment that they simply do not attempt to act at all in certain issue areas.

Any judgement about the extent to which *de facto* sovereignty has been eroded must therefore examine not only the character of external pressures, both positive and negative, but also the ability of States to respond either unilaterally or collectively to such pressures. The competence of States to react unilaterally is a function of the resources that they possess relative to other States and the capacity of policy-makers to redeploy these resources. The ability of States to act co-operatively is a function of the distribution of costs and benefits and of their skill in constructing institutions that can overcome problems of collective action.

Finally, the pressures emanating from the international environment have increased in some areas because technological changes have reduced the costs of communication and transportation. For example, international capital markets are very highly integrated and billions of dollars, yen, or Deutschmarks can today be moved by computer around the world in seconds without stopping at international boundaries. Yet, on balance such international transactions have become less threatening because the relationship between economic exchange and political and military power has weakened considerably. Large, highly developed States with diversified economies, multiple trading partners, sophisticated domestic markets, and well-trained State bureaucracies can mitigate or adjust to pressures emanating from the international environment. Small underdeveloped States, however, remain extremely vulnerable; they are closer to the European States of the seventeenth and eighteenth centuries than they are to their more powerful and industrialized contemporaries.

STATE SECURITY AND THE GLOBAL ECONOMY IN HISTORICAL PERSPECTIVE

This dialectical process will be more evident if we glance briefly at the relationship of economic interdependence and State security in historical perspective, focusing on the crucial issues of trade and finance.

Medieval and early modern trade

Links between security and international economic transactions are anything but new. The world economy that emerged in Europe after the fall of the Roman Empire had by the tenth century included the extensive maritime area demarcated by Bruges, London, Lisbon, Fez, Damascus, Azov, and Venice. It was characterized by sea trade with little penetration of hinterlands.[2] From the outset political authorities claimed the right to control international trade and linked trade with political and military objectives. Economic activities outside of routine agricultural transactions were regarded as being legitimate concerns of the king. In what came to be England, State regulation of trade began as early as the seventh century. By the eleventh century English kings were imposing regular duties on trade. By the seventeenth century English merchants believed that it was necessary to get permission from the Crown to engage in foreign trade. Foreign trade had to be opened either by an act of Parliament or by the king.[3]

The English and the French used trade as an instrument of statecraft especially but not exclusively against each other. In the twelfth and thirteenth centuries English kings used wool supplies, a product in which England had an effective monopoly, to pressure France. France imposed control on wine sales to England near the end of the Hundred Years War, by which time the French monarchy had taken back from England the major wine-producing regions. Both England and France used State power to undermine the primacy of Dutch commerce in the seventeenth century. England's tactics included prohibiting its colonies from trading with the Dutch and stipulating that imports must be carried on English ships or the ships of the exporting country, thus cutting out the Dutch. The Staple Act of 1663 required colonies to purchase all of their European products from England.[4]

Such practices were rationalized by mercantilist theories of international trade which were the prevailing economic doctrine in Europe until the nineteenth century. These arguments were not naïvely and narrowly aimed simply at accumulating large stocks of bullion. Rather, they delineated general policies that could be used to improve the military position of States. Trade surpluses could provide the State with revenues. Controlling the movement of specific commodities, mandating for instance the import of military goods and prohibiting their export, could enhance the international power of the sovereign. Even as late as the nineteenth century trading relations were often closely tied to quite specific economic and security ambitions.

It was only with the appearance of Adam Smith's *Wealth of Nations* (1776), Ricardo's theory of comparative advantage, and the publications of the Manchester School in the middle of the nineteenth century that alternative conceptions of international trade, which supported openness and the unlinking of economic and political (and military) objectives, began to offer an intellectual alternative to mercantilism. The doctrine of free trade and derivative theories of international trade which dominate economic thought and heavily influences practices in the contemporary world virtually divorce international economic transactions from State security.

Early modern State finance

In finance, as in trade, the relationship between international economic transactions and national security has diminished over the long term.

In the early period of the modern States system—the seventeenth and eighteenth centuries—States' finances were driven by the preparation for and conduct of war. During the major wars of the eighteenth century, military expenditures accounted for between 61 and 74 per cent of public spending in Britain. During the Great Northern War, Peter the Great spent 90 per cent of Russia's revenues on the military. In the 1780s, France spent about 25 per cent of revenues on the military.[5] Yet, States or sovereigns were not able to finance their military efforts from domestic sources. International banking began in Europe in the late Middle Ages with banking houses that made loans primarily to European rulers who used these resources for military purposes. The development of a large supply of funds, however, required the existence of a market where negotiable securities could be sold. Such markets first developed in the seventeenth and eighteenth centuries, initially based upon the national debt of England, France, and Holland and the stock of merchant companies.[6]

Thus, before the Industrial Revolution there was a fundamental and persistent conflict between the fiscal demands of war, and the ability of States to raise money from domestic sources. In the medieval period kings were routinely expected to finance their needs from their personal properties, but this proved to be impossible if they became engaged in major conflicts with other sovereigns and they were forced to appeal to sometimes recalcitrant estates or parliaments for funds.[7] Even as late as the early modern period European States still were not able to secure a very large proportion of domestic economic resources. In England, which instituted the most efficient tax system in Europe, taxes as a share of GNP rose from 3.5 per cent in the 1670s to 11–12 per cent during the American Revolution. The share of taxes increased again by one-third during the Napoleonic Wars. The French monarch was able to secure only about half as much income in proportion to GNP as his English counterpart. Although domestic excise taxes were the most important source of revenue, customs duties accounted for 20–30 per cent of revenue in England cum Britain during the eighteenth century.[8]

European political leaders were thus compelled to resort to international financial markets to secure the resources they needed. Because defaults were frequent, high-risk premiums were placed on loans to States, which further increased the costs of lending. Debt service to both domestic and foreign lenders consequently buffeted and often overwhelmed State finances. Even in England cum Britain, about 30 per cent of revenue was used to service the debt after 1707. In France debt service had increased to about 60 per cent of revenue by 1764, and in The Netherlands the figure was even higher during the first half of the eighteenth century.[9]

Yet, as with medieval rulers, when early modern rulers attempted to escape from these pressures by increasing domestic taxation they often encountered fierce resistance. Philip IV of Spain touched off a major revolt when he attempted to get Catalonia to pay for troops that had been sent to protect the border. The American Revolution was precipitated by British efforts to raise revenues to pursue the war with France. The French Revolution was triggered by a series of wars that drained the State's reserves and forced the king to call the Estates General, which had been more or less moribund, in an effort to raise additional taxes. Before the nineteenth century, European States were thus locked into an interdependent financial and military nexus that was enormously constraining for statesmen.

While the changes of the nineteenth century, especially the Industrial Revolution and the rise of nationalism, increased the carnage of war, they also enhanced the ability of States to finance military activities. The bureaucratic and monitoring competence of governments increased. A much larger and more accessible domestic tax base came into existence. Financial markets became more secure. Lenders were more willing to provide funds to governments at lower interest rates because they were more confident about being repaid. During the nineteenth century material resources increased dramatically in Europe and North America and governments were able to tap a greater proportion of this wealth. The importance of international borrowing declined for the most advanced countries. They were able to finance a much higher proportion of their military activities from internal sources.

International finance beyond Western Europe

The situation was, however, very different for newly emerging peripheral countries in the nineteenth century. The pattern of high external debt and reliance on taxes on international trade, which had characterized Europe in the eighteenth century, was repeated in Latin America in the nineteenth century. Latin American countries initially entered the international capital market to finance the purchase of arms to pursue their wars of independence. They, like their European counterparts in the eighteenth century, were caught up in a nexus of international finance that was driven by military pressures. They hoped to pay off these loans using customs duties— which accounted for 50 per cent of Mexican and 80 per cent of Argentinian revenues in the 1820s.[10] Given that taxes were dependent on trade, and trade was dependent on economic conditions in Europe, this was not a very secure situation for the new governments of Latin America.

The history of Latin American debt has been one of repeated booms followed by financial crises. There were major defaults in the late 1820s, 1873, 1890, and 1931. Booms were the result of economic expansion in the advanced economies, which increased the availability of capital for international lending. Contractions in the economies of these same countries consequently led to increased capital costs and financial crises for Latin American borrowers. Furthermore, European States possessed blue water naval capability that could directly project power into Latin America. They were prepared to intervene to compel the repayment of loans. Britain, Germany, and Italy used force against Venezuela in 1902–3 to secure various foreign claims. Britain used the threat of force to facilitate the collection of a number of claims in the Caribbean. In 1913 a battleship was dispatched to Guatemala to compel the government to use coffee duties to repay bonds held by British subjects.[11]

Military intervention and the threat of force were by no means the only ways in which European powers, and later the USA, intervened in the affairs of borrowing countries in the nineteenth century. When States defaulted, foreign lenders would set up control committees to oversee restructuring of government finances, as happened in Bulgaria, Greece, Serbia, Persia, the Ottoman Empire, and Argentina. For example, the Ottoman Empire agreed in 1881 to put some of its revenues under the control of external creditors. A separate administration, controlled by foreign bondholders, was created to collect revenues. In return for the consolidation loan of 1895, Serbia created a monopolies commission that administered the revenue from the State tobacco, salt, and petroleum monopolies, liquor taxes, some stamp taxes, and some railway and customs revenues. These revenues were committed to paying off foreign loans and the receipts were never deposited in the Serbian treasury.[12] These are only a few of many examples one could cite that give an indication of the extent to which European international finance, usually with the backing of strong European States, penetrated and controlled the taxing jurisdictions of borrowing governments, reducing many of them to a virtually colonial status.

In sum, before the nineteenth century governments were heavily dependent on international loans because they could not secure from internal sources the financial resources that they needed to fight wars. Governments frequently defaulted and lost access to financial markets. At the same time, however, these largely private markets were not able to impose non-economic sanctions on defaulting lenders. In the nineteenth century financial markets were more closely tied to specific States. While the governments of Western Europe and North America were increasingly able to secure resources from domestic means, the weaker States of Latin America and the European periphery were compelled to resort to foreign markets, subjecting themselves not only to economic pressure but to the possibility of military intervention as well.

State supervision of international finance

In general, central government decision-makers in the major European lending countries—Britain, France, and Germany—maintained close control—direct or indirect—over international lending during the nineteenth century. This financial supervision was explicitly connected to and dictated by concerns about State security. The French State was particularly concerned about the relationship between international financial flows and political objectives and by the end of the century the foreign ministry was engaged in activities explicitly designed to link foreign policy and international finance. States that were perceived as potentially hostile, notably Germany, were denied access to the French capital market. The initial entente between France and Russia was cemented by allowing Russia to float loans on the Paris bourse. Foreign lenders seeking admission to the official list often had to offer political compensation.[13] In Germany the banks regularly consulted with the foreign ministry about foreign loans and rarely rejected the government's preferences. The level of loans to Russia from 1897 onwards closely followed political relations between the two countries. When relations cooled after 1906, all loans to the Russian government ended.

While there was little direct British government supervision of loans before the First World War, there was a great deal of informal interchange between the financial élite and the political leadership and bureaucracy. Private loans generally tracked Britain's political interests. When bank activities were out of line with official policy, public officials made their views known and banks generally accepted them.[14]

In the interwar period, international finance continued to be closely tied to political objectives—especially for France and Germany. The imposition of large reparations on Germany during the 1920s reflected not only the desire of French and British leaders to mollify their own populations but also—especially for France—to weaken if not cripple Germany. However, during the 1930s Germany developed trading and financial relations with the smaller countries of eastern and central Europe that were designed to maximize her political leverage.[15]

Western security, liberal internationalism, and LDCs

After the Second World War the relationship between international economic policy and national security objectives diminished for Western, non-communist States. At the same time, however, security issues preoccupied Cold War relations between the USA (and its Western allies) and the Soviet bloc. American policy-makers tried to insist that any and all economic interactions with the Soviet bloc be subordinated to Western political and security concerns. The Soviet Union, however, was too large and self-sufficient to be enmeshed in a web of American dominated economic relationships that could be used for political leverage. America's allies generally advocated more open policies. Once it had launched its policy of *ostpolitik* in the early 1970s, the Federal Republic of Germany was particularly anxious to demonstrate to the Soviet Union that a Western State could be a reliable economic partner. The basic objective for Germany was, however, still political: to keep the question of German reunification at least on the table, a policy that eventually succeeded beyond anything imagined.

Outside the Soviet bloc, the USA promoted the economic prosperity of its allies through capital transfers, such as the Marshall Plan, and by accepting free-rider policies on the part of Western Europeans and Japanese, such as restrictions on American exports and investment. At the same time, American leaders encouraged the long-term development of market relationships in which the State set the basic rules but was not an active player. Before the 1980s American policy-makers were almost oblivious to any security consequences that might result from economic interactions with allies. American leaders were concerned with enhancing the aggregate power of the West; they were not interested in the distribution of power within the Western alliance, or with using economic sanctions to secure political leverage over their allies.

American policy-makers acted as if there were no fundamental strategic or political conflicts within the Western alliance. They presumed that they could accomplish all of their core objectives—the promotion of economic development in the non-communist world, economic growth for the USA, and increasing utility for American consumers—by pursuing a policy of liberal internationalism.[16] Only recently has apprehension arisen over dependence on foreign, especially Japanese, producers for military components.

American policy-makers also supported the creation of the International Monetary Fund, the World Bank, and the GATT. These institutions were designed to discourage economic nationalism. The Bank and the Fund initially directed resources to more developed areas, but since the late 1950s, they have focused on LDCs. These and other international financial institutions, such as the Inter-American Development Bank and the Asian Development Bank, are part of a larger network of aid-giving organizations. The very concept of foreign aid—the notion that wealthier countries should contribute resources to poorer ones to promote their economic development rather than to further specific security and economic interests of the donor—is a novel concept of the post-war period. Small countries, such as The Netherlands and Sweden, give substantial amounts of international aid even though such contributions cannot possibly promote their specific interests. The statistical relationship between bilateral foreign aid and economic and security interests is weak for most countries.[17]

In the area of trade the USA strongly supported an international regime based on diffuse reciprocity, non-discrimination, and the elimination of barriers to the movements of goods and factors of production. These norms are embodied in the General Agreement on Tariffs and Trade (GATT). Such a regime reduces the leverage that can be exercised by any individual State.[18] Hence, by the late twentieth century international economic relations were separated from political and strategic calculations to an historically unprecedented degree. Within the West the close State supervision of loans to make sure that they promoted political and strategic goals—which had permeated French and German and to a lesser extent British activity in the nineteenth century—had almost disappeared. Gunboat diplomacy and direct collection of taxes by foreign creditors had been replaced by IMF stand-by agreements and Paris clubs of international creditors, far less stringent forms of external constraint.

THE INTERDEPENDENCE–INDEPENDENCE DEBATE

The argument presented in this chapter can be illuminated by a contrasting argument which emphasizes the importance of interdependence and the erosion of *de facto* and perhaps even *de jure* sovereignty. Many analysts believe that the international system has fundamentally changed in so far as the constraints imposed on national policy-makers by economic interdependence are so extraordinary that sovereignty no longer has any real meaning in practice. The following arguments of James Rosenau and of Jeffrey Frieden (reporting a conversation with Walter Wriston, a former head of Citicorp Bank) are typical:

The state-centric structure of world affairs, in which actions and interactions are dominated by nation-states, is now rivaled by a more complex, less symmetrical set of patterns whereby international issues arise and are managed. Many of today's crucial problems—such as currency crises, environmental pollution, and the drug trade—are transnational in scope, with the result that governments are less and less able to be effective within their own domains and must, instead, contend with a multiplicity of issues sustained in part by external dynamics.[19]

Money goes where it's wanted, and only stays where it's well treated, and once you tie the world together with telecommunications and information, the ball game is over. It's a new world, and the fact is, the information standard is more draconian than any gold standard . . . You cannot renounce the information standard, and it is exerting discipline on the countries of the world, which they all hate. For the first time in history, the politicians can't stop it. It's beyond the political control of the world, and that's good news.[20]

Such descriptions cannot be gainsaid: international economic activity has increased enormously; global communications have become virtually instantaneous. The following analysis gives only a brief overview of the subject.

Trade

In absolute terms there has been a tremendous growth in the level of world trade (exports plus imports) since 1950. This is a long-term historical trend and not just a phenomenon of the post-war period. For those countries for which data are available world exports as a percentage of world GNP increased from 4.6 per cent in 1830 to 11.4 per cent in 1913. During the interwar period, in reaction to global depression and world war, the relative importance of trade declined. In 1950 world trade was only 8 per cent of world GNP, but it more than doubled to 17 per cent by 1980.[21] The volume increased by a little more than 6 per cent per annum during the 1950s, by 9 per cent during the 1960s, by 6 per cent during the 1970s, and by 3 per cent from 1980 to 1987. These growth rates are all higher than the growth rate of world output.[22]

Trade as a percentage of output also grew for all of the major industrialized market economy countries with the exception of Japan during this same period. The USA experienced the most dramatic change with trade increasing from 9.8 per cent of national output in 1952 to 21.7 per cent in 1987. Canadian trade grew from 36.2 to 51.1 per cent; the United Kingdom from 51.3 to 53.4; and Germany from 29.4 to 57.5. Japanese trade, however, declined from 23.2 to 21.6 per cent.[23]

Capital flows

The pattern of direct foreign investment is more complicated than that of trade. The importance of foreign investment compared with GNP increased for the major European countries throughout the nineteenth century reaching its apogee just before the First World War. The leading European States, especially Britain, were deeply involved in foreign loans and direct foreign investments. By 1900 about half of Britain's savings were being invested abroad. Just before the First World War, Britain's stock of overseas holdings was equal to about a quarter of its national wealth and approximately 10 per cent of Britain's national income was drawn from abroad. In 1914 about 6 per cent of French national income was derived from foreign loans and investments.[24] These levels fell markedly during the interwar period. Although the relative importance of direct foreign investment increased after the Second World War it has not returned to its pre-1914 levels.[25] In the 1980s direct foreign investment accounted for less than 3 per cent of gross fixed capital formation.[26]

Since 1960, however, there has been a dramatic increase in the level of international lending activity. Unlike the nineteenth century, when such flows were mainly in the form of bonds that were held by individuals, in the late twentieth century world bank credits are the most important form of international capital. The development of various Euro-currency markets has been spectacular: whereas net international bank credit amounted to about twelve billion dollars in 1964, by 1985 it had exploded to almost 1.5 trillion dollars. The role of foreign banks increased in all of the major industrialized countries during the same period, although the relative importance of non-national banks varied enormously accounting for 63 per cent of total bank assets (loans) in Britain in 1985, but for only 2.4 per cent in Germany, and 3.6 per cent in Japan. The international placement of bonds (in either foreign or Euro-currency markets) multiplied from three billion dollars in 1965 to 227 billion dollars in 1986.[27]

State response

Contemporary advocates of the notion that national States are withering away—in empirical if not in juridical theory—have emphasized pressures emanating from the international sphere but they have paid little attention to the capacity of States to respond. Yet, the fact is that national States have consolidated their governance in some domains while at the same time failing to do so in others. The extent to which *de facto* State control has been frayed by external pressures is a function of two variables: the level of pressure and the ability of States to respond. As indicated, States can respond to external threats and opportunities either unilaterally, or through co-operation with other States, by changing their policies or creating new institutional structures that re-establish or even enhance State control.

With regard to unilateral action, the critical issue is the extent to which policy-makers can secure resources—finance, money, military equipment—from internal as opposed to external sources. Over time this capacity has increased, especially for advanced industrialized countries. With regard to external action, the issue is whether States can engage in co-operative arrangements that enhance their interests either against non-state actors or other States. Since the Second World War such co-operative arrangements have become easier, at least for advanced democratic market economy countries.

SIZE AND STATE CAPACITY

The historical record is far more mixed than would be suggested by the conventional notion that interdependence is threatening effective State control. The basic long-term trend has been one in which States have become less dependent on the external environment. This has occurred primarily because political and economic development has made it generally easier for States to finance their activities, including those related to security, from internal sources rather than international borrowing. At the same time, however, growing disparities in power have increased the variation in the vulnerability of States to pressures emanating from the international environment. Smaller, less developed States are more dependent on the external environment and less able to adjust to it than are larger and more industrialized countries. The existence, however, of many small and weak States is itself mute testimony to the potency of juridical sovereignty which has swept away virtually all rival forms of political organization.[28]

Developing countries

While the relative importance of trade to aggregate economic activity has increased for almost all countries, the absolute importance of trade is considerably higher for smaller countries than for larger ones. There is an inverse statistical relationship between trade (as a proportion of GNP) and GNP. Smaller States have less diversified economies. They cannot achieve economies of scale in a wide range of industries. There are very high incentives for them to take advantage of the international division of labour. Hence, in the post-Second World War period, the average level of trade interdependence has increased because there are so many more small States in the international system.

The ability of poor countries to adjust to external pressures resulting from either changes in the pattern of international trade or in international capital markets is limited. Their bureaucratic capabilities are restricted. Labour mobility is lower than in advanced industrialized countries because levels of education are inferior; it is easier to move a skilled worker from one branch of industry to another than it is to convince a peasant to switch from one crop to another in the face of changing market conditions.

The manner in which independence came to many countries in the Third World, as a result more of the changing calculations of their colonial masters than of indigenous pressures for independence, left in place strong local actors within poorly integrated States that could only with difficulty be controlled by weak national political authorities. Often political leaders, wary of rivals at the centre, were anxious to empower peripheral actors whom they viewed as less threatening.[29] To guard against unrest in urban areas many political leaders in Africa exploited the agrarian sector by setting local agricultural prices far below world prices in order to make cheap food available in cities.[30] Such weaknesses and rigidities make adjustment to external pressures difficult because the stability of the regime, or at least the tenure of particular leaders, is hostage to an existing pattern of resource distribution that can only be changed at high political cost.

Most germane for an examination of the impact of economic interdependence on *de facto* sovereignty is the relationship between international economic activities and the government's ability to secure resources. In general, poorer countries are less able to extract material resources from their own societies than are richer ones. In 1987 government consumption accounted for 13 per cent of gross domestic product for low-income countries and 18 per cent for members of the OECD. Current government revenue accounted for 17 per cent of gross national product for low-income countries (excluding China and India), and 24 per cent for OECD members. Figures ranged from a low of 6.5 per cent for Sierra Leone to a high of 51 per cent for The Netherlands.[31]

Moreover a larger proportion of the revenues that governments in LDCs are able to extract comes from taxes on international trade. Given limited bureaucratic capacity, indirect taxation is problematic for many developing countries. Export levies and import duties are attractive because trading activities can be concentrated in a relatively small number of ports. Even with smuggling and corruption, it is easier to collect trade taxes than to secure other kinds of revenue. In

1987 poor countries secured 21 per cent of their revenue from taxes on international trade and transactions; members of the OECD secured 1.2 per cent of their revenue from the same source. The importance of taxes on international activity ranged from a high of 68 per cent for Lesotho to a low of zero for Italy, Belgium, The Netherlands, France, and Germany.

In sum, one of the striking characteristics of the contemporary international environment is an increase in the number of small, sometimes minuscule, States. They rely on taxes on international trade to a far greater extent than is the case for industrialized countries; they are often highly involved in international markets. The most painful manifestations of that involvement are the very high debt burdens confronting some LDCs, burdens that have led to austerity measures that have sharply reduced real standards of living.

Developed countries

Industrialized countries have hardly been able to extricate themselves from the constraints imposed by increasing trade and capital flows. Nevertheless, they are better able to adjust their domestic policies and even institutional structures to take advantage of opportunities and to mitigate threats presented by the external environment. This is not merely a question of size. The smaller European countries have developed effective corporatist structures which facilitate their ability to take advantage of opportunities presented by the world economy and to lessen the costs of adjustment. They have national value systems and corporatist structures that increase the participation of groups that might otherwise have little voice in policy-making. These structures facilitate ongoing relationships between the public and the private sector which make policy co-ordination and implementation easier.[32]

There is some evidence that even in the USA, a polity unusually devoid of corporatist-type practices, new institutional forms have been developed to cope with growing involvement in the world economy. The various industrial sector committees, first established during the Tokyo Round to increase co-operation between the office of the US Trade Representative and industrial groups, resembled corporatist structures in Europe more than the adversarial arms'-length relationship which sometimes characterizes interaction between the American executive branch and the private sector. This same arrangement was used during the Uruguay Round negotiations of the GATT.[33]

Communist countries and their successors

The satellites of the Soviet Union, as well as the newly independent States that were formerly part of the Union, with the exception of Russia, are more vulnerable than any of the polities of Western Europe. The economic systems of the former communist bloc countries are more rigid. Their level of development is lower. Their political institutions are fragile. The developed States of Western Europe, both large and small, can more readily adjust to external shocks, and are therefore less vulnerable and more economically secure. While the economic situation of Russia is problematic, its economy is both large and relatively isolated from the world economy. Russia is less vulnerable than any other members of the former communist system.

The components of the former Soviet bloc, with the exception of Russia, are the most likely targets of any specific efforts at economic coercion in which interdependence would be used to secure political or economic advantage. The most likely source of such coercion would be Germany which is the largest economy in Western Europe and is the most important source of direct investment and trade for the States of Central and Eastern Europe. During the 1930s Germany did use economic interdependence to secure political concessions from the smaller States of Central and Eastern Europe.

The replay of such a scenario is, however, unlikely. Germany would only be in a position to engage in economic coercion if the European Community disintegrated and the economy of Russia collapsed. Economic policy-making within the EC, especially in the area of trade, constrains the freedom of action of any one country. A substantial part of European assistance to Eastern Europe is being channelled through the European Development Bank, limiting the opportunities for Germany to act unilaterally. If the Russian economy does not completely collapse, it will remain an important economic partner for the other States of Central and Eastern Europe. The end of the Cold War will bring Eastern Europe closer to the norm that exists in other parts of the world: greater economic interdependence but, on balance, less vulnerability to explicit calculated threats from other States.

In sum, greater involvement in the world economy offers opportunities as well as imposing constraints on individual countries. Growing levels of world trade and capital flows have contributed to a historically unprecedented increase in the rate of economic growth, a boom that has been shared by both developing and industrialized countries. Expanding involvement in the world economy may limit the options open to policy-makers and present them with unexpected shocks over which they have little or no control. The erosion of *de facto* control, however, varies with size and level of development. Industrialized States—small and large—are far more able to respond to external pressures than developing ones because of their more sophisticated economies and more effective bureaucratic capabilities. Consequently, the extent to which economic interdependence has eroded *de facto* sovereignty is a function not only of the level of international involvement but also of the ability of States to adjust. The interdependence–independence relationship is dialectical and not one way.

CONCLUSIONS

The fundamental issue at stake in the literature is whether economic interdependence has constrained the *de facto* level of control exercised by national political leaders. There has been no challenge to juridical sovereignty; that is, no effort to replace sovereign statehood with some other authority structure.[34] The admittedly imperfect evidence presented in this chapter suggests that, if anything, State control has actually increased over the long term: *de facto* sovereignty has been strengthened rather than weakened. Contemporary developed States exercise greater and probably far greater *de facto* sovereignty than either their historical European ancestors or contemporary developing States. A major flaw in the interdependence argument is its tendency to ignore the available historical evidence on this point.

However, it cannot be doubted that greater economic openness and increased interdependence have placed some constraints on even the most powerful States of the West. These constraints are not the result of explicit policies adopted by other States. Rather, they are a consequence of the fact that national policies can be frustrated by global interactions that are beyond the control of any State. These constraints are most apparent in the area of international capital flows and macroeconomic policies. In the past large States could unilaterally control their own monetary policies. Nowadays the amount of international capital is so huge, and the ease of transfer so great, that even officials in the USA, the largest economy in the world, cannot conduct domestic monetary policy without considering the impact of international financial flows.[35] The 1992 European experience in which private capital markets were strong enough to shake the EC Exchange Rate Mechanism (ERM) to its foundations by forcing the Italians to devaluate the lira, obliging the British to let the pound float, and threatening the French franc are further examples. Of course, the situation is far more precarious for smaller developing countries. The economic fate of very small countries is critically determined by financial and other international conditions over which they have no control.

In conclusion, the particular activities associated with independent statehood have always been in flux which makes generalization difficult. Yet the survival of *de jure* sovereignty for more than 400 years in an environment of radically changing technologies, military capabilities, actors, and power distribution could only have occurred if the specific components of *de facto* sovereignty were malleable. States are actors and not things, and as such they can respond to new circumstances. Economic interdependence has constrained some policy options that have been traditionally associated with the exercise of sovereignty, especially for smaller less developed States. At the same time, some of the traditional anxieties of sovereign powers, especially the preservation of territorial integrity, have become less pressing. Interdependence inevitably poses challenges to sovereignty. Over time, however, economic interdependence has become less rather than more problematic for State control.

NOTES

1. On the question of whether the European Community should be conceived of as an international organization composed of sovereign States or as something else, see G. Garrett, 'The European Internal Market: The Political Economy of Regional Integration', *International Organization*, 46 (1992), and A. Moravcsik, 'Negotiating the Single European Act: National Interests and Conventional Statecraft in the European Community', *International Organization*, 45 (1991), 19–56.

2. F. Braudel, *The Perspective of the World: Civilization and Capitalism 15th–18th Century*, iii (New York, 1984), 97–8.

3. J. A. C. Conybeare, *Trade Wars: The Theory and Practice of International Commercial Rivalry* (New York, 1987), 19.

4. Ibid. 132–3, 136–9.

5. J. Brewer, *The Sinews of Power* (New York, 1989), 40.

6. D. S. Landes, *Bankers and Pashas: International Finance and Economic Imperialism in Egypt* (Cambridge, Mass., 1979), 10–11; see also D. C. North and B. R. Weingast, 'Constitutions and Commitments: The Evolution of Institutions Governing Public Choice in Seventeenth Century England', *Journal of Economic History*, 49 (1990).

7. J. Ferejohn, 'The Second Image Revised: Foreign Policy and Domestic Political Institutions in Early Stuart England', unpublished paper, Department of Political Science, Stanford University, Nov. 1991.

8. Brewer, *Sinews of Power*, 91–9.

9. Ibid. 114, 131–3.

10. C. Marichal, *A Century of Debt Crises in Latin America: From Independence to the Great Depression, 1820–1930* (Princeton, NJ, 1989), 4, 14, 17, 32–3.

11. H. Feis, *Europe: The World's Banker* (New York, 1965), 109, 148.

12. Ibid. 266–8.

13. Ibid. 120–2, 134.

14. Ibid. 84–92, 167–8, 172.

15. A. Hirschman, *National Power and the Structure of Foreign Trade* (Berkeley, Calif., 1945).

16. The American tendency to believe that all good things go together is elegantly demonstrated in R. Packenham, *Liberal America and the Third World* (Princeton, NJ, 1973).

17. These arguments are developed in D. Lumsdaine, 'Ideals and Interests: The Foreign Aid Regime, 1949–1986', unpublished Ph.D. Dissertation, Stanford University, 1987.

18. The relationship between economic leverage and international regimes is developed in R. M. Spaulding, Jr., 'German Trade Policy in Eastern Europe 1890–1990: Preconditions for Applying International Trade Leverage', *International Organization*, 45 (1991).

19. J. N. Rosenau, 'Global Changes and Theoretical Challenges: Toward a Postindustrial Politics for the 1990s', in E. O. Czempiel and J. N. Rosenau (eds.), *Global Changes and Theoretical Challenges: Approaches to World Politics for the 1990s* (Lexington, Mass., 1989), 5.

20. Quoted in J. Frieden, *Banking on the World* (New York, 1987), 114–15. See also W. Wriston, 'Technology and Sovereignty', *Foreign Affairs*, 67 (1988/89).

21. Figures derived from J. E. Thomson and S. D. Krasner, 'Global

Transactions and the Consolidation of Sovereignty', in Czempiel and Rosenau, *Global Changes and Theoretical Challenges*, Table 11-1.

22. Figures derived from GATT, *International Trade*, various issues.

23. Figures are reported in M. Webb and S. D. Krasner, 'Hegemonic Stability Theory: An Empirical Assessment', *Review of International Studies*, 15 (1989), Table 6.

24. Feis, *Europe*, 5, 14, 16, 48, 72.

25. Thomson and Krasner, 'Global Transactions', 201.

26. UN Center on Transnational Corporations, *Trends and Issues in Foreign Direct Investment and Related Flows* (New York, 1985), 19–20.

27. Webb and Krasner, 'Hegemonic Stability Theory', 191.

28. R. H. Jackson and C. G. Rosberg, 'Why Africa's Weak States Persist: The Empirical and the Juridical in Statehood', *World Politics*, 35 (1982).

29. J. Migdal, *Strong States and Weak Societies* (Princeton, NJ, 1988).

30. R. Bates, *Essays on the Political Economy of Rural Africa* (Cambridge, 1983).

31. Figures from World Bank, *World Development Report, 1989*, Tables 9 and 12.

32. P. Katzenstein, *Small States in the World Economy* (Ithaca, NY, 1985).

33. See J. Ikenberry, 'Manufacturing Consensus: The Institutionalization of American Private Interests in the Tokyo Trade Round', *Comparative Politics*, 21 (1989).

34. The European Community may be an exception to this generalization.

35. These relationships are lucidly developed in M. C. Webb, 'International Economic Structures, Government Interests, and International Coordination of Macroeconomic Adjustment Policies', *International Organization*, 45 (1991).

FURTHER READING

Clark, G., *The Seventeenth Century* (Oxford, 1960).

Cooper, R. N., *The Economics of Interdependence* (New York, 1980).

Gilpin, R., *The Political Economy of International Relations* (Princeton, NJ, 1987).

Keohane, R. O., and Nye, J. N., *Power and Interdependence* (Glenview, Ill., 1989).

Rosenau, J., *Turbulence in World Politics* (Princeton, NJ, 1990).

Waltz, K., 'The Myth of National Interdependence,' in C. P. Kindleberger (ed.), *The International Corporation* (Cambridge, 1970).

16

Ethnicity and Independent Statehood

FRED PARKINSON

Though it is having potentially far-reaching implications, ethnicity is a poorly understood part of the wider problem of independent statehood. Johann Gottfried Herder (1744–1803) was the first to realize that the behaviour of identity groups will not conform to the cosmopolitan image of human kind so expectantly projected by the intelligentsia of the eighteenth century.[1] On the contrary, time and time again it has been shown that the idea of the 'nation-state' has easily captured the imagination of political activists and gained the allegiance of wide sections of mankind. 'Both the theological and ideological doctrines have been so universalist in their assumptions that they have ignored, or worse, denied the cultural and political diversities of mankind.'[2]

Whilst problems connected with newly assertive identity groups have arisen regularly in Europe from the mid-eighteenth century, the most acute problems of that nature have occurred in the context of dissolving multinational States during the nineteenth and twentieth centuries and must therefore be analysed against that historical background.[3]

THE CONTEXT: NATIONALITY AND ETHNICITY

National States were largely achieved in Western Europe by the end of the eighteenth century.[4] In Central and Eastern Europe, however, the international order established after the First World War resulted not in the creation of nationally homogeneous States but, with very few exceptions, in the appearance of new multinational ones, in the image of the fallen Habsburg, Romanov, and Ottoman empires. The much coveted national statehood was achieved there only after the Second World War by the barbarous practice of unilateral mass expulsions.[5] However, even today unresolved and in some cases extremely troublesome nationality problems persist in Central and Eastern Europe. One of the most serious ones is now in the process of being lanced. Yugoslavia was originally an amalgam of territories carved out of the former Habsburg and Ottoman empires which faithfully reproduced both the socio-economic and cultural discrepancies of those two empires. It is now in the midst of chaotically violent disintegration. The prospects for its successor States are not good. Only Slovenia can be regarded as nationally compact. The remainder is to varying degrees of multinational composition posing thorny problems to all concerned.

Beyond Europe most of the successor States to the several overseas colonial empires wound up after the Second World War were multi-ethnic in composition. According to a recent count, out of 164 States in the then international system, only forty-five are national States.[6]

Frequently overlapping in time, three stages may be discerned in the socio-economic evolution of ethnic groups. Some of the latter find themselves still in a nomadic or semi-nomadic condition, roaming unselfconsciously across political frontiers along well-trodden, traditional routes close to their grazing grounds.[7] Whereas by definition nomads regard any territories accessible to them as their oyster, the abandonment of that way of life results in the development of a sense of territoriality which, in turn, breeds a sensitivity to the need for identifying, maintaining, and defending the frontiers of the territories claimed as theirs.[8] It is, however, during the incipient phases of the economically diversifying and industrializing stages that the impulse towards the formation of national sentiment is first registered. It is in this stage that ethnic groups become aware of their own cultural heritage and begin to claim the loyalties and support of their members.

THE POST-COLONIAL LEADERSHIP: A POLITICAL PSYCHOANALYSIS

With some exceptions, the governments of the colonial empires responsible for handing over their colonial estates took great care to ensure the passage of constitutions containing checks and balances to guarantee representative government. Yet, again with some exceptions, they failed to insist that the same be done in respect of ethnic self-determination. The reason was to ensure general stability, and to avoid horrendous ethnic upheaval of the kind that occurred in India and Pakistan in 1947.

The assumption that stability was all-important was shared by the post-colonial leaders of the successor States. Originally the very ones who had led their territories to independence—such as Nehru of India, Sukarno of Indonesia, Nkrumah of Ghana, the Bandanaraikes of Sri Lanka, Ben Bella of Algeria, Keita of Mali, and even San Martín in early nineteenth-century Latin America—were as a rule the product of a colonial education which had implanted in their mind a cosmopolitan outlook which to varying degrees tended to alienate them from their cultural roots.[9] The majority obtained their higher education at some centre of learning in the colonial metropolis or in its offshoot, the USA. Their choice of subject illuminates their cosmopolitan mentality, since most of them gave preference to courses reflecting faithfully the values of their colonial masters, rather than those of their original cultures. At a rough estimate, 40 per cent enrolled in law, and another 40 per cent in the humanities. Only exceptionally were preferences noted for subjects such as anthropology or ethnography, for although they had a direct bearing on the cultures of their own peoples, such studies were regarded as promoting tradition and obstructing independence.

The long-term effect of that education was twofold. On the one hand, those leaders were undergoing a process of partial but marked alienation, as already noted; but on the other hand they became increasingly and often painfully aware of their social isolation in their host countries, where they would suffer racial slights at the worst, and cheerful condescension at the best of times. Moreover, impressed by the technical achievements of the colonial administrations for creating admirably effective governmental structures in their dependent territories, those leaders tended to develop a resolve to take over those structures lock, stock, and barrel as going concerns. The last thing in their minds was an intention to dismantle those multi-ethnic colonial estates in order to replace them by ethnically based, pre-colonial ones. In theory, the post-colonial leaders had imbibed the notion of the ideal nation-state from Western thought, but in practice they were acting like Renaissance princes striving towards the status of *imperator esse in regno suo*, to emerge as Roman emperors in miniature within their own territorial estates.[10] That they were able to raise broad popular support for the struggle of independence from their colonial overlords is a proven historical fact. Yet, to note this is to say no more than that at an analogous juncture of history the rulers of the Habsburg Empire similarly were able to command general support for unity from groups of widely diverse national origins in their struggle against the perceived common enemy—the Ottoman Empire. Yet, going by European precedent it was to be expected that sooner or later identity groups would press for the granting of certain autonomies, or, in extreme cases, sovereign territorial independence where ethnogeographical conditions would permit.

POST-COLONIAL FRONTIERS: NEOCOLONIALISM OR ETHNIC SELF-DETERMINATION?

Uti possidetis

The nature of post-colonial frontiers of successor States provides further leads to the multi-ethnic problem.

The internal boundaries of imperial empires were drawn in a manner intended to serve the administrative convenience of the overseas powers. Ethnic considerations in their determination were of minor importance. In many instances, therefore, colonial boundaries would intersect entire ethnic groups. When on independence those boundaries were undergoing conversion into international frontiers, the question arose of redrawing them in accord with the ethnic principle or whether they were to be accepted in their colonial form as a parting gift from their former colonial masters. The problem first posed itself during the Latin American wars of independence at the beginning of the nineteenth century when it was decided to retain the colonial administrative boundaries as international frontiers for the time being, pending their revision once the danger of colonial reconquest had passed. This was the meaning of the doctrine of *uti possidetis*.[11] The Latin American example was followed by the newly independent successor States of the crumbling colonial empires of Asia and Africa upon emancipation. The colonial boundaries were preserved, the ethnic principle disregarded.

Unlike their Iberian predecessors of the nineteenth century, however, the ex-colonial powers of the mid-twentieth century cheerfully supported the post-colonial rulers in this respect, instead of wasting their efforts and energies in trying to achieve reconquest. A series of Resolutions passed by the General Assembly of the United Nations proclaiming the right of 'peoples' to their sovereign independence from colonial rule set the seal of legitimacy on the process of decolonization. The key Resolution on the *Declaration on Granting of Independence to Colonial Countries and Peoples* adopted by the General Assembly on 14 December 1960,[12] while upholding that right, added the important rider that 'every attempt to destroy partially or totally the national unity and territorial integrity of a country is incompatible with the aims and principles of the Charter of the United Nations'.

Two aspects of this Declaration deserve special comment. In the first place, the term 'peoples' is left undefined, but carries the implication that only legitimate independence movements recognized as such by sovereign States could qualify. In the second place, the false impression was conveyed that all post-colonial successor States' territorial confines had been established in conformity with the principle of national self-determination. The entire exercise was an attempt to perpetuate the colonial frontiers inherited by the successor States even where they were in blatant conflict with that principle. On the face of it this procedure had the merit of strengthening internal, as well as international stability. Only one attempt was made on the interstate plane to question the justice and wisdom, as distinct from the administrative and political convenience of the old colonial frontiers. At a conference held in Accra in 1958 called by President Kwame Nkrumah of newly independent Ghana, the post-colonial rulers (or those about to take over) divided over the issue. Those who wished to see a revision of the colonial frontiers—who included, besides Nkrumah himself, only Sékou Touré of Guinea and Léopold Senghor of Senegal—found themselves in a marked minority, while the remaining post-colonial rulers *in spe* were filing into the *status quo-uti possidetis* lobby. Typical of the sentiments expressed by members of the anti-revisionist lobby on that occasion was the observation made by President Tsirinana of the Malagasy Republic that 'if we were to take race, tribe or religion as criteria for determining our frontiers, there would be quite a few States wiped off the map of Africa'.[13]

Tsirinana had a good practical point. Once the principle of nationality is proclaimed as the criterion of legitimacy, neither the shape of any post-colonial frontier, nor the territorial integrity of any post-colonial State can be deemed safe any longer, and there might be no end in sight to the proliferation of new sovereign States. Consequently the conference of Addis Ababa, convened in 1963 to lay the foundations of the Organization of African Unity, declared the old colonial frontiers as the only internationally valid boundaries of independent

Africa, with only Somalia and Morocco—which had standing claims for frontier revision—dissenting.[14]

WILL STATE DEFEAT NATION?

With growing tension between the rival principles of *uti possidetis*, what was the attitude of the successor governments to be? To compete successfully in the existing system of international politics they have to promote the process of economic diversification and development as strongly as possible by associating their subjects with it, irrespective of their cultural loyalties. But they also need to discourage any thoughts of secession perhaps by emphasizing either the penalties for treason[15] or the political dangers of dissolution.[16] Other post-independence leaders tried to forge a supranational identity through a process of deliberate nation-building on the assumption that it is in the final analysis States that create nations, and not the other way round.[17]

However, what is clear from such empirical evidence as is available is that nation-building has done nothing to defuse ethnic tensions. On the contrary, such policies have brought about not the accommodation and refocusing of individual loyalties on to a supranational entity, let alone the merger of ethnic groups, as intended, but a deepening of the hegemony of already predominant ethnic groups, as happened in Myanmar (formerly Burma), Indonesia, Zambia, and Kenya.[18]

EXPLANATORY THEORIES

Explanatory theories are constructed on the basis of regularly observed empirical patterns. They are, in that sense, historicist in nature.

Unhistorical nations

The expression 'unhistorical nations' was first used in the present sense by the German philosopher Georg Friedrich Hegel (1770–1831) in describing groups of common identity which lacked a native literary class to articulate their values. While Hegel drew no conclusions from this, Friedrich Engels (1820–95)—who was not altogether untainted by the late nineteenth-century fashion of vulgar social Darwinism—considered those unhistorical nations as fit only for the proverbial dustbin of history, overrun as they would be, and should be, in the name of material progress by the culturally fitter and better-equipped, advanced historical nations.[19] Ernest Gellner, too, comments sceptically on aspiring ethnicities, noting that most of them 'go meekly to their doom, to see their culture slowly disappear, dissolving into the wider culture of some new national State'.[20]

However, far from suffering extinction, such European representatives of unhistorical nations as the Czechs, Slovaks, Ruthenes, Basques, Irish, Scots, and Welsh, have taken a prominent part in culture and politics. This vindicates Otto Bauer, who argued that under the impact of socio-economic diversification unhistorical nations were destined to play an important part in history.[21] Steeped in classical Marxism but mindful of its shortcomings in explaining the phenomenon of nationalism Bauer was attracted by the thoughtful ways in which Immanuel Kant (1724–1804) and Herder had elaborated their organic conception of nationhood in which the cultural element held pride of place.[22] He asserted that the need for industrialization required a work-force having reached minimum standards of formal education and that such education could only be provided by a much expanded corps of teachers at the grass-roots level of the village school who, by instilling national values and awakening folk memories, would engender a sense of national pride and, ultimately, a collective feeling of nationhood.[23]

Lenin's explanatory theory of nationality was diametrically opposed to Bauer's.[24] In 1913 Lenin postulated a correlation between budding capitalism and the awakening of national life on the one hand, and mature capitalism and the breaking down of national barriers on the other hand.[25] Because capitalism was developing unevenly on a world scale, Lenin maintained, the transition from budding to mature capitalism occurred in a different order in different areas of the world. This sequence he set out in 1916 as follows: (1) Western Europe and the USA; (2) Eastern Europe, especially Russia; (3) 'semi-colonial countries like China, Persia and Turkey, as well as all colonial territories.'[26]

While arguably grasping the essence of the connection between nationality and industrialization in its early stage, Lenin's theory suffered from a reductionism which obscured human allegiances, especially cultural ones, and led him to misread important parts of the ethnic problem.[27]

A test case of Bauer's and Lenin's explanatory theories of the dynamics of ethnicity under the impact of long-term socio-economic transformation is afforded by the reactions of the submerged and inchoate Amerindian nations in present-day Latin America.

Latin America's aboriginal population was estimated to be as high as 72 million in pre-Columbian times, shrunk to 5 million in the nineteenth century, and now amounting to a mere 8 per cent of the total population.[28] However, this latter figure requires some qualification in order to enable us to gauge the full potential impact of Amerindian identities on the vast socio-economic changes that have been taking place during the last seventy years. The proportion of survivors would swell to at least 30 per cent if partially assimilated Amerindians and mestizos were to be included in the count. Moreover, thirty million Latin American peasants, regardless of their biological origin or use of language, must be considered as of predominantly Amerindian culture. An Amerindian demographic recovery is now under way.

It was only after the Second World War, under the impact of industrialization (which affected Amerindian groups very adversely) that *criollo* groups (Latin American-born descendants of Iberian colonizers) started to show a serious inclination to pay heed to Amerindian sentiment. *Criollo*-initiated policies of enlightened integration amounted essentially to drawing Amerindians into the process of comprehensive economic development, cultural assimilation, and political participation. However, these were the policies that were being increasingly resented by Amerindian opinion as paternalistic and ultimately leading to their cultural extinction.

Enlightened *criollo* opinion—including its Marxist and Populist components—failed for a long time to realize that what they were facing was not a series of demands for one-off adjustments but a deep-rooted movement of protest and clamours for a wholesale reassessment of policies to match a rapidly altering mood of Amerindian opinion. The demands put forward by the Amerindians as part of their protest tended to escalate over time in clearly defined stages, assuming first a cultural and economic but finally a political nature. As they were gathering momentum, the protest movements tended to expand in scope and wax in emotional intensity.[29]

The spectacular exploits of the Peruvian guerrilla Shining Path (*sendero luminoso*) basically reflect general Amerindian opinion, differing from it only in the extreme nature of its cultural and political positions. *Sendero* is not simply opposed to development as a matter of principle, but only to foreign-imposed, post-conquista development, however sophisticated and prima-facie beneficial, which is seen as incompatible with and destructive of pre-Columbian values. What is wanted is a total return to pre-Columbian values as preliminary bases from which to trace out a path of culturally authentic socio-economic and technological progress.

In the terminology employed in Otto Bauer's explanatory theory, the Amerindian people of Latin America would seem to be in full process of converting themselves from an unhistorical ethnic group into a nationality, a process pregnant with disruptive effects on the *criollo*-initiated process of development in the region. The Amerindian experience in Latin America would also to a great extent bear out Gellner's assertion that socio-economic development requires a uniform culture, and that where such a condition does not apply, the process of development will stall.

NORMATIVE THEORIES

Normative theories are constructed on the basis of preconceived values, with the intention of bringing about essentially ideological solutions to practical problems.

The personalist prototype

In the mid-nineteenth century a point was reached in the socio-economic development of the Habsburg empire where its subject nationalities would no longer rest content to be mere recipients of German culture but demanded the right to pursue cultural activities of their own. At the Imperial Diet of Kremsier of 1848—held under the shadow of Eurowide revolutions—a constitution was drawn up, though never enacted, making generous provision for ethnic accommodation. The text of that constitution none the less served as a blueprint for a series of peaceful, though politically hard-fought constitutional *Ausgleiche* (literally compromises) in which the Empire made timely concessions which staved off the prospect of secession and— for a while—disintegration between: Austria and Hungary (1867), Hungary and Croatia (1867), Austria and Moravia (1905), Bukovina (1911), and the Polish and Ruthene constituent territories (1914).

Yet, what brought that fairly successful run of reforms to a halt was the intractability of the German–Czech antagonism in Bohemia, the last remaining hurdle. In retrospect that should not have caused much surprise, considering that the area was by far the most industrialized in the empire and exhibited the relatively most complex interpenetrated ethnic patterns—both standard recipes for political troubles, according to Bauer and Gellner alike.[30]

It was against a historical background of this kind and because of a desire to preserve the integrity of the Habsburg empire that Karl Renner devised his personalist solution of the ethnic problem in the multinational Habsburg empire. Renner started from the assumption that the cultural nation is an autonomous union of persons. The key to a problem-solving formula for areas of heterogeneous ethnic composition was identified by him in the separation of the cultural and political spheres of government in a manner reminiscent of the so-called 'millet' system in the Ottoman empire. The legal instrument by which to achieve that separation was to be the 'Kataster', a register of cultural allegiance made on a purely voluntary basis by individual members of cultural groups, however widely they might be dispersed within the area in question. Once neatly sorted out in this manner, individual members of a nationality of their choice would be placed under the authority of separate National Councils for the administration of a wide range of cultural activities including the arts and sciences, museums, galleries, theatres, and the like, leaving the residue of governmental functions in the hands of the political authorities of the area concerned. In this way each nationality would form a 'public legal corporation' fully recognized in constitutional law to guarantee its cultural autonomy.[31]

It would seem at first sight that Renner's personalist approach as exemplified in his normative theory of nationalities was eminently suited for application in regions of the developing world in which complex patterns of ethnic heterogeneity exist. Yet, Kedourie's comments are pertinent ones. For the preservation of multinational or multi-ethnic structures, he maintains, nationalism in the sense of the uncompromising quest for the much-coveted nationally homogeneous sovereign State is unsuited. As he puts it,

Cultural, linguistic and religious autonomy for the different groups of a heterogeneous empire is practicable only when it does not rest upon, or is justified by, nationalist doctrine. Such autonomy remained possible in the Ottoman empire for several centuries—the millet system—precisely because nationalism was unknown, and broke down when the doctrine spread among the different groups of the Empire.[32]

The territorialist prototype

At its foundation congress in 1898 the Russian Social Democratic Workers' Party proclaimed the rights of self-determination as the corner-stone of its policy on nationalities. In 1918 Lenin reaffirmed that right, in which he included secession 'for any nationality'.[33] However, unlike the Austro-Marxists, the Bolsheviks had next to no tsarist precedents to guide them in their quest for adequate solutions of the nationality question in Russia. Once in power they devised a system for the administration of autonomous republics and regions in the Russian Socialist Federated Soviet Republic to give constitutional form to the aspirations of non-Russian nationalities. After the creation of the USSR at the end of 1922 the same principle was applied on a smaller scale by other Union republics.[34]

NORMATIVE THEORIES TESTED

The Soviet Union

Soviet practice in matters of nationality after 1945 continued to be torn between the two rival principles of national self-determination along roughly territorialist lines and supranational socio-economic planning from the centre.

'The Russian empire has made a comeback,' Sir Charles Webster used to say in his famous lecture course at the London School of Economics after the Second World War. He was right; but even if Lenin's relatively enlightened territorialist nationality laws had not been perverted by Stalin, the latter's policies of enforced industrialization would have produced the classical Gellner effect of fostering heightened sentiments of national consciousness among non-Russian identity groups, rupturing the federal ties forged in 1922 among members of the Soviet federation and ultimately leading to the dissolution of the latter in 1991.[35]

Significantly, however, the successor States of the Soviet Union are based on crude territorialist principles leaving little or no room for accommodation of cohabiting identity groups of a national character—just as had happened after the First World War.[36] Sadly, therefore, the nationality problem on the territories of the former Soviet Union has been merely transformed. It has not been solved.[37]

The post-colonial successor States

If the Habsburg empire ultimately failed and the Soviet Union stumbled, are the multi-ethnic successor States to the various colonial empires likely to fare any better? Multi-ethnic problems, it is true, have been met head on by some of those successor States. But the results have been mixed.[38]

Consider, for instance, the cases of Myanmar (Burma) and Sri Lanka (Ceylon). Burma consists of a central valley inhabited by the majority Burmese population, and what used to be called Frontier Areas containing non-Burmese peoples taking up 47 per cent of the total area of the country and 16 per cent of its population.[39] A solution to the multi-ethnic problem was, partly under British pressure, attempted at the Panglong conference held in February 1947 at which Burmese independence leaders accepted the principle of ethnic equality. They also recognized the right of the ethnicities of the Frontier Areas to internal political autonomy, and reached an express understanding with the Kachin, Chin, and Shan leaders on their future relations with the projected Union of Burma. The traditionally pro-British Karens, on the other hand, were willing to be associated with those arrangements only if Burma remained within the Commonwealth—which it did not. The basic dilemma in implementing those agreements lay in the apparent incompatibility between economic planning and ethnic accommodation. In this event, the decision went in favour of ethnic Burma-ization. Thus, after 1949 the armed forces, originally organized along ethnic lines, fell under progressive military administration, Burmese was introduced as the lingua franca and Buddhism was brought to the fore. The Karens, Mons, and other disaffected ethnic groups revolted against this trend in efforts to secure territory of their own, as well as political self-determination. The full principle of centralized unity was enforced by the military regime of General Ne Win from 1962 onwards. Centralization and continued cultural subordination eventually provoked a violent backlash when in 1988 liberal elements in the cities spearheaded by students organized mass protests, in the course of which the students allied themselves loosely to long-standing ethnic rebels in a Democratic Front—a coalition of guerrillas made up in the bulk by Karens, Mons, and Kachins.[40] The military dictatorship which put down the revolt promulgated an electoral law that expressly excluded ethnic autonomy or independence.[41]

In Sri Lanka—unlike Burma—two territorially semi-compact major ethnic groups live side by side: a Sinhalese majority and a Tamil minority. In one or two areas there is ethnic interpenetration. The situation is further complicated by the fact that under colonial rule the Sinhalese majority became more commercially minded, while the Tamils, traditionally trade-orientated and constituting about 20 per cent of the population, became part of the administrative system. Since independence in 1950, however, the Sinhalese have dominated the government. Tamil migration into Sinhalese areas has taken place, whereas from time to time, and as part of ethnic-political jockeying, government-sponsored Sinhalese colonization has occurred in Tamil areas.[42]

Sinhalese–Tamil tensions reached a breaking-point in 1983 following government efforts to bring about an inter-ethnic accord being repeatedly obstructed by Sinhalese ground swells of opposition.[43] Tamil alienation eventually split into a moderate faction which would have been content with a decent measure of autonomy, and a radical faction—the fearsome Tigers—holding out for nothing less than sovereign statehood in a Tamil Eelam. Matters came to a head in 1987 when India, which contains a Tamil Nadu State of 50 million and therefore has a high political stake in seeing a satisfactory ethnic deal for Sri Lanka's Tamils, intervened. This created tensions with the Sinhalese-dominated government of Sri Lanka but an apparently satisfactory solution was found and set out in an important document— the Indo-Sri Lanka Accord—on 29 July 1987.

The Accord went to the heart of the problem by tackling the two crucial elements of territorial adjustment and local government autonomies. There was a basic commitment to Sri Lanka as 'a multi-ethnic and a multilingual plural society consisting, *inter alia*, of Sinhalese, Tamils, Muslims and Burghers', a formulation that effectively ruled out secession as a solution.[44] However, within that limitation the Accord contained an obligation to create a secure homeland for the Tamils, to be achieved by a merger of the mainly Tamil Northern and Eastern provinces,[45] subject to a referendum by the Easterners, in a single, territorially continuous province administered by a single Provincial Council. This on the face of it seemed an ingenious solution. However, to be perfect, it might have contained expressly personalist provisions for the ethnically mixed Eastern province which would have profited from a separation of cultural and political functions of local government, as originally canvassed by Renner. As things stand, it is to be feared that one day the Eastern province could be the scene of massive ethnic resettlement, or, infinitely worse, massacres of Indo-Pakistani proportions of 1947, all in the name of the hallowed principle of ethnic homogeneity.

The Sri Lanka government in the early 1980s had attempted to set up delegated administrative units.[46] This came as a disappointment to many Tamils who had expected to be given greater powers. All the Indo-Sri Lanka Accord could offer was delegated powers for the Provincial Council in respect of levying local taxes, the administration of the police—an important function—as well as the traditional running of local authority services. Tamil unhappiness, as always, sprang from the suspicion that a strongly self-willed and determined Sinhalese majority government could rescind those delegated powers.

As regards the issue of language, Sri Lanka's 1978 Constitution had introduced Tamil as a 'national language' alongside Sinhala but it was unclear whether the new status meant equality with the latter language, since Sinhala remained the only official language. It was only under the Indo-Sri Lanka Accord that matters were clarified when Tamil and Sinhala both became official languages, with English as the third official language.

Perhaps the Indo-Sri Lanka Accord bears comparison with the Kremsier Constitution of 1848 in the case of the Habsburg empire, since both contain numerous positive elements of compromise. However, it is as well to be realistic in appreciating the ever-present possibility of a unilateral declaration of independence proclaimed by either or both Tamil factions in the North. If the optimistic view is taken of a satisfactory agreement which has tightened up remaining loose ends, then it is likely to endure only if based on a hard, long drawn out and bitter *Ausgleich*.

IS *UTI POSSIDETIS* CRACKING?

It is becoming more and more apparent that the principle of *uti possidetis* is being placed in serious jeopardy by the ethnic fault-lines crossing the continents of which public international law, basically developed by *status quo*-minded statesmen in Western Europe and North America, refuses to take notice. In Africa that fault-line runs right across the continent from Djibouti to Senegal—a divide between Arabic and Black African peoples, rendering all frontiers based on *uti possidetis* extremely vulnerable. The ethnic fault-line in Asia extends all the way from Cyprus to Thailand, Indonesia, and beyond to the Philippines, while in Latin America the growing restlessness of Amerindian ethnicities is being felt throughout the Andean, Northern Brazilian, and Central American regions.

For how much longer can frontiers drawn without regard to ethnic realities withstand widespread pressures for national autonomies or statehood? As Gellner put it: 'The number of groups which in terms of the argument of "precedent" could try to become nations, which could define themselves by the kind of criterion which in some other place does in fact define some real and effective nation, is legion.'[47] In all parts of the developing world dissatisfied ethnic groups are stirring, creating unrest, and refuting the assertion that the stability of international frontiers springs eternal from *uti possidetis*. The call for the adjustment of frontiers is gathering strength and has already given rise to conflict between two of the poorest and half-starved West African countries of Mali and Burkina Faso.

Though, until recently, outright breaches of *uti possidetis* have been limited to the case of Bangladesh, there are signs that both in the former Yugoslavia and in the former Soviet Union, *uti possidetis* is being subjected to severe pressures as a result of the diabolical practice of 'ethnic cleansing'.[48]

Further afield, the prospects of a deal between the Amharic-dominated government of Ethiopia on the one hand, and the Eritrean and Tigrean secessionists, on the other, would no doubt have been greeted with relief by the successor States of Africa, terrified of seeing any African State breaking up for fear that disintegration will spread to other multi-ethnic structures left behind by the colonial empires of the past. But after their outright military victory, the Eritreans, if perhaps not the Tigreans, may be most reluctant to settle for anything less than independent statehood.

Yet another country that is experiencing the ethnic strain on its frontiers is Afghanistan. That multi-ethnic State was founded and has always been ruled by Pathans who made up about 40 per cent of the pre-1979 population. Numbering 15 million, the Pathans are the country's largest ethnic group. There are even more Pathans in Pakistan. When they ran the area, the British constantly fought and admired the Pathans who, in the mid-eighteenth century, had ruled a territory stretching across the mountains and down to the Indus river, in a loose confederation called Afghanistan. To frustrate alleged Russian designs, the British in 1893 incorporated into the Indian Empire the lands east of the Khyber Pass, thus dividing the Pathans along a line named after Sir Mortimer Durand, who had mapped it. The Pakistanis maintain this line was accepted by the tribesmen who joined their new State in 1947. The Afghans rebut this claim, insisting that those chiefs were bribed and never acknowledged the Durand line as an international frontier. Neither side pays much attention to the frontier, but sporadically the Pathans claim self-determination for an independent Pathoonistan.

The Soviet invasion of 1979 upset the ethnic balance within Afghanistan. As indicated, before 1979 40 per cent of all Afghans were Pathans, but since they live near Pakistan, a disproportionate number of them fled to that country. The Persian-speaking Tadhziks, once the second largest but increasingly the dominant ethnic group, tended to stay on to do most of the fighting. Both these groups are Sunni Muslims, but 15 per cent approximately of all Afghans are Shi'as who felt oppressed under the *ancien régime* of the Pathans. They are backed by Iran. Whatever happens to Afghanistan, now that the Soviet Union is no more and Russia and the USA have come to terms over that country, it will still have to contend with Pakistan and Iran pulling in opposite directions, suffering permanent pressures on its frontiers. If the principle of self-determination were to be applied rigorously in Afghanistan, it could spell the end to *uti possidetis* as regards the country's artificial frontiers.[49]

FINAL THOUGHTS

By imposing their political domination and cultural values on their dependent territories, the colonial powers distorted, and in many cases arrested, the free historical development of those areas. It should not therefore cause undue surprise, let alone consternation, that on acquiring formal sovereignty the genuine ethnic forces within them should wish to correct those distortions and recreate their own history. In this way ethnicities long in a state of hibernation, and therefore largely written off as politically marginal, such as the Kurds, could become and in many cases are now becoming vocal, and even violent in a single-minded pursuit for justice. Whether statesmen are dealing with ethnic disturbances in Afghanistan, Sri Lanka, India, Pakistan, or Lebanon, or facing ethnic pressures for the creation of an independent Kurdistan, Baluchistan, Pathoonistan, Khalistan, or Tamil Eelam, or grappling with a myriad of tangled claims emanating from aggrieved ethnic groups south of the Sahara, or coping with the increasing ferment among ethnic groups in Latin America, it must gradually dawn on them that these are not isolated cases but part of a global phenomenon exhibiting underlying similarities. Some evidence for this was presented in previous pages. What remains to be done is to draw the strands together as far as possible to bring underlying patterns out into the open.

Ethnicity and development

For a long time economic success, rather than ethnic welfare, has been the first preoccupation of multi-ethnic, as of other States. One of the explanations for this is the neo-mercantilist thinking which equates economic with the attainment of political power. In true eighteenth-century style, therefore, ethnicity has come to be looked upon as retrograde, and development as progressive. The history of the multinational empires of nineteenth-century continental Europe, as well as that of the overseas multi-ethnic colonial empires of the twentieth, has exposed this line of thinking as fallacious. An exclusive concern with economic development, especially in its most dynamic form—industrialization—has proved to exacerbate, not to solve ethnic problems. In retrospect it is pathetic to note the naïve expectations of Nigerian constitutional theorists that economic development would *ipso facto* do away with ethnic problems.[50] Where economic development is paired with intensive administrative measures of centralization, ethnicities will prefer detachment from multi-ethnic structures, rather than face the unpleasant prospect of cultural death by submersion. In some extreme cases, as in that of some Amerindian groups in Latin America, they will opt out of the development process altogether to seek alternative modes of livelihood which accord better with their culture, rather than risk total alienation. Attitudes like these are bound to encounter the baffled incomprehension on the part of benevolently inclined developer-governments who will consider them, in accordance with their single-minded rationalist-materialist philosophy, as wholly unreasonable.

Nation-building

Constructing nations out of separate ethnic groups is not only a difficult but also an unnatural process. It will not respond to simple government fiat but has to be brought about by coercion, through measures of intense administrative centralization. To persist in forcing ethnicities into a centralized strait-jacket for any length of time is to court State collapse, as happened in Lebanon and in Uganda.[51]

Nation-builders may avert collapse for a while by relying on general international solidarity, and more especially on the relative reluctance of States with ethnic affinities to intervene.[52] In the long run, however, they are bound to fail in solving their multi-ethnic problems. Even where nation-building governments succeed in forging a measure of inter-ethnic unity, this will commonly have been achieved through the domination of one particular ethnicity at the expense of the remainder. It is significant that even the most ideologically based political parties in developing countries—not excluding the communists—tend to be taken over by ethnic groups in pursuit of predominantly ethnic political objectives.[53] Thus, the disintegration of the Soviet and Yugoslav Communist Parties along ethnic lines heralded the crumbling of the Soviet and Yugoslav federations.

The United Nations' concept of self-determination

The present United Nations' concept of self-determination[54] based on ex-colonial boundaries was fashioned during the classical period of decolonization when it served a number of useful purposes. In the context of post-decolonization, when the multi-ethnic problem is at the fore in many of the successor States, that concept must be seen as anachronistic and counter-productive. It can be of no help in critical multi-ethnic situations, in which it will tend to encourage the inappropriate practice of 'nation-building'. Its out-of-date character should now be frankly recognized and attempts made to supplant the

1960 UN Declaration by a new one setting out the circumstances in which a right of ethnic self-determination is applicable, with due allowances to be made for the international duty not to intervene in the domestic affairs of sovereign States.

Ethnicity and independent statehood

The connection between ethnicity and independent statehood creates problems which have come to stay and cannot be ignored. On the basis of current trends, world ethnic forces for the rest of this century and in the coming one will prove as inherently potent and politically explosive as forces of nationalism proved to be during the nineteenth and twentieth centuries. The world at large, but in particular the vast arc of countries spanning Africa, Asia, and Latin America, represents a gigantic laboratory in which the connection between ethnicity and independent statehood is being tested every day. Academics in the social sciences should monitor the results very closely indeed.

NOTES

1. I. Berlin, *Vico and Herder: Two Studies in the History of Ideas* (London, 1976).
2. M. Howard, 'Ideology and International Relations', *Review of International Studies*, 15 (1989), 2.
3. A. D. Smith's contention that an *ethnie* is at the root of all nationhood is well taken, but applies in the main to late medieval and Renaissance Europe. It is of little help in analysing ethnicity in the context of decolonization and post-decolonization. See A. D. Smith, *The Ethnic Origins of Nations* (Oxford, 1988).
4. O. Dann and J. Dinwiddy (eds.), *Nationalism in the Age of the French Revolution* (London, 1988).
5. C. A. Macartney, *National States and National Minorities* (London, 1934); A. Cobban, *The Nation-State and National Self-Determination* (London, 1969) and B. F. Pauley, *The Habsburg Legacy, 1867–1939* (Malabar, Fla., 1972).
6. See S. Ryan, 'Explaining Ethnic Conflict: The Neglected International Dimension', *Review of International Studies*, 14 (1988), 161–77. Some scholars put the figure of nation-states as low as 12. The present writer prefers the higher figure. See also S. G. Seligman, *Races of Africa* (London, 1957).

7. A. I. Asiwaju (ed.), *Partitioned Africans. Ethnic Relations across International Boundaries, 1884–1984* (London, 1985); P. Bouvier, 'Un problème de sociologie politique. Les frontières des états africains', *Revue de l'Institut de Sociologie*, 4 (1972), 686–720.

8. E. A. Hoebel, *The Law of Primitive Man* (London, 1954); A. K. Mensah-Brown (ed.), *African International Legal History* (New York, 1975); R. Lemarchand, 'The Bases of Nationalism among the Bakongo', *Africa* (Winter 1961), 344–54; and H. H. Turney-High, *Primitive War* (London, 1949).

9. M. J. Akbar, *Nehru: The Making of India* (London, 1989); N. C. Chaudhuri, *The Autobiography of an Unknown Indian* (London, 1951); and I. Wallerstein, 'Élites in French-Speaking Africa', *Journal of Modern African Studies*, 3 (1965), 1–37.

10. On this point, see A. P. Sereni, *The Italian Origin of International Law* (New York, 1943) and F. A. von der Heydte, *Die Geburtstunde des souveränen Staates* (Ratisbon, 1952).

11. B. C. Drouet, *La Doctrina Americana de uti possidetis de 1810* (Buenos Aires, 1936); F. Barth, *Ethnic Groups and Boundaries* (London, 1969); I. Brownlie, *African Boundaries: A Legal and Diplomatic Encyclopaedia* (London, 1979); E. Hertslet, *Map of Africa by Treaty*, 3 vols. (London, 1909); E. Crowe, *The Berlin West Africa Conference, 1884–1885* (London, 1942); G. de Courcel, *L'Influence de la Conférence de Berlin de 1885 sur le droit colonial international* (Paris, 1935).

12. Resolution 1514 (XV) of the General Assembly, repr. in full in I. Brownlie (ed.), *Basic Documents on Human Rights* (Oxford, 1981), 28–30.

13. D. Bourjorl-Flecher, 'Heurs et malheurs de l'uti possidetis: l'intangibilité des frontières africaines', *Revue juridique et politique* (July–Sept. 1981), 811–35; Pheiphanh Ngaosyvathn, 'La Thailande conteste les frontières héritées de la colonisation', *Le Monde Diplomatique* (Nov. 1984), 14–15.

14. O. S. Kamanu, 'Secession and the Right of Self-Determination. An OAU Dilemma', *Journal of Modern African Studies*, 12 (1974), 355–76; N. L. Piame-Ololo, 'De l'état en Afrique a l'état africain. Problématique actuelle des chercheurs autochtones', *Revue juridique et politique* (Sept. 1984), 775–93; L. Ravi, 'On the Conflict Potential of Inherited Boundaries in Africa', *World Politics*, 4 (1966), 656–73.

15. Following an attempted coup in May 1989, Lt.-Gen. Mengistu, Head of State of Ethiopia, denounced the collusion of rebel generals with Eritrean separatists, accusing them of 'betraying the objective of the defence of the nation', *Le Monde*, 23 May 1989.

16. B. Neuberger, 'The African Concept of Balkanisation', *Journal of Modern African Studies*, 13 (1976), 523–9; 'State and Nation in African Thought', *Journal of African Studies*, 4 (1977), 198–205; A. Suhrke and I. G. Noble (eds.), *Ethnic Conflict and International Relations* (New York, 1977); A. D.

Smith, *State and Nation in the Third World: The Western State and African Nationalism* (Brighton, 1985); P. M. de la Groce, 'Risques accrus d'interventions étrangères au Tchad', *Monde Diplomatique* (Feb. 1987), 12–13.

17. President Sékou Touré, as cited by S. Ryan, 163. The notion of supra-nationality had some currency in the Soviet Union under Brezhnev but was quietly abandoned under Gorbachev. On the principal point, see G. W. Lapidus, 'Ethnonationalism and Political Stability: The Soviet Case', *World Politics*, 36 (1984), 555–80. See also I. M. Lewis (ed.), *Nationalism and Self-Determination in the Horn of Africa* (London, 1983); D. Lartin and S. S. Somatar, *Somalia. Nation in Search of a State* (Boulder, Colorado, 1987); D. Rothschild and V. Oluronosa (eds.), *State Versus Ethnic Claims: An African Policy Dilemma* (Boulder, Col., 1983); C. Thomas, 'Challenges of Nation-Building: Uganda—A Case Study', *India Quarterly* (July–Dec. 1985), 320–49.

18. Smith, *Ethnic Origins of Nations*, 148.

19. R. Rosdolsky, 'Friedrich Engels und das Problem der "geschichtslosen" Völker', *Archiv für Sozialgeschichte* 4 (1964), 187–282; I. Berlin, *Karl Marx* (London, 1939); D. Boersner, *The Bolsheviks and the National and Colonial Question* (Geneva, 1957); J. A. Petrus, 'Marx and Engels on the National Question', *Journal of Politics*, 33 (1971), 797–825.

20. E. Gellner, *Nations and Nationalism* (London, 1983), 470.

21. O. Bauer, *Die Nationalitätenfrage und die Socialdemokratie* (Vienna, 1907); C. Enloe, *Ethnic Conflict and Political Development* (Boston, 1973); and C. Geertz (ed.), *Old Societies and New States* (New York, 1973).

22. F. M. Barnard, *Herder's Social and Political Thought: From Enlightenment to Nationalism* (London, 1965); I. Kant, *Idea of a Universal History of a Cosmological Plan* (Hanover, NH, 1927).

23. It was no good, Bauer maintained, trying to iron out national peculiarities within multinational structures in vain attempts to create uniformity. On the contrary, unity could only be achieved through the frank recognition of national diversity. Bauer was among the first to realize that the multinational Habsburg Empire was doomed, not for its failure to satisfy the demands of the 'historical' nations but because of the awakening of the 'unhistorical' ones in its midst. The same general conclusion was reached many decades later by W. Connor, 'Nation-Building or Nation-Destroying?', *World Politics*, 24 (1972), 319–55.

24. Lenin, *Sochineniya*, xvii, 139–40.

25. Ibid. xix, 37–8.

26. E. V. Tadevosian, 'Leninskiye printsipy i formi resheniya natsionalnovo voprosa', *Voprosy filosofii*, 12 (1967), 15–25.

27. For E. Kedourie's perceptive comments on Lenin's theory of nationality, see his *Nationalism* (London, 1979), 90–1.

28. On these points, see a series of excellent papers on 'Le réveil des Indiens d'Amérique latine', *Le Monde Diplomatique* (Mar. 1982), 15–20. For a parallel case, see H. J. R. Roberts, 'The Economics of Berberism: The National Basis of the Kabyle Question in Contemporary Algeria', *Government and Opposition*, 18 (Spring 1983), 228–35.

29. The cultural demands put forward by the Amerindians were for the creation of certain autonomies, such as the opening of their own schools in which their children could be taught in their own languages, and for the right to express their views through their own media, such as broadcasting and newspapers. Economic demands would follow in the form of *recuperación*, the reclaiming of legal titles to land of which they felt they had been unlawfully dispossessed. The Amerindians would also object to plantation-farming and the alien agro-industrial technology associated with it, which was seen as destructive of their physical and social environment. Political demands would take the form of seeking backup for their claims in intensified forms of political organization. See *Le Monde Diplomatique*, n. 28.

30. A. Wandruszka, *Der österreichisch-ungarische Ausgleich von 1868: Seine Grundlagen und Auswirkungen* (Munich, 1968); M. Menger, *Der böhmische Ausgleich* (Stuttgart, 1891); A. Wandruszka and P. Urbanitsch (eds.), *Die Habsburgermonarchie 1848–1918*, iii: *Die Völker des Reiches* (Vienna, 1980); R. A. Kann, *The Habsburg Empire: A study in Integration and Disintegration* (London, 1957); B. F. Pauley, *The Habsburg Legacy: 1867–1918* (Malabar, Fla., 1972); Z. A. B. Zeman, *The Break-Up of the Habsburg Empire: 1914–1918* (London, 1961).

31. K. Renner (pseudonym Rudolf Springer), *Der Kampf der österreichischen Nationen um den Staat* (Vienna, 1902).

32. Kedourie, *Nationalism*, 117.

33. Lenin, *Sochineniya*, xix, 242–3.

34. E. H. Carr, *A History of Soviet Russia: Foundations of a Planned Economy, 1926–1929*, ii (London, 1971), 196, and R. Pipes, *The Formation of the Soviet Union: Communism and Nationalism, 1917–1923* (Cambridge, Mass., 1964).

35. According to the *Financial Times*, 25 Feb. 1989, Mr Gorbachev proposed that 'autonomous regions' be turned into 'national regions', an elevation of status by one rank. Such a solution in the Nagorno-Karabakh dispute would take the area out of the jurisdiction of Azerbaijan, while at the same time meeting the main demand of the majority Armenian population. On feelings in the Soviet Union itself on problems of nationality, see U. Halback, 'Sowjetische Nationalitätenproblematik—zu ihrer Rezeption in der sowjetischen Öffentlichkeit', *Osteuropa*, 38 (1988), 267–80.

36. *Izvestiya*, 1 July 1989. For a reasonably critical account of Soviet nationality practice, see T. V. Sathyamurthy, *Nationalism in the Contemporary*

World: Political and Social Perspectives (London, 1983), 51–3. Also P. Cockburn, 'Dateline USSR: Ethnic Tremors', *Foreign Policy* (Spring 1989), 168–84.

37. e.g. see 'Moldova's Poll Dominated by Ethnic Turmoil,' *The Times*, 7 Dec. 1991; and 'Welcome to Slugonia,' *The Economist*, 21 Dec. 1991.

38. R. B. Goldman and A. J. Wilson (eds.), *From Independence to Statehood. Managing Ethnic Conflict in Five African and Asian States* (New York, 1984); R. Sandbrook, 'Hobbled Leviathans: Constraints on State Formation in Africa', *International Journal* (Autumn 1986), 707–33.

39. Most of the information in this section of the chapter was obtained from J. Silverstein, *Burmese Politics: The Dilemma of National Unity* (New Brunswick, 1980).

40. *Guardian*, 29 Sept. 1988.

41. *Guardian*, 2 Mar. 1989.

42. L. Sabaratnam, 'The Boundaries of the State and the State of Ethnic Boundaries: Sinhala-Tamil Relations in Sri Lankan History', *Ethnic and Racial Studies*, 10 (1987), 291–316.

43. D. L. Horowitz, *Ethnic Groups in Conflict* (Berkeley, Calif., 1985), 132–4.

44. For an excellent analysis of that Accord, see M. L. Marasinghe, 'Ethnic Politics and Constitutional Reform: The Indo-Sri Lanka Accord', *International and Comparative Law Quarterly*, 37 (1988), 551–87. The relevant provisions of the 1978 Constitution, whereby (*a*) Sri Lanka was declared a unitary State, and (*b*) State sovereignty was made inalienable, were substantially unaffected by the Accord.

45. The Tamil shares are respectively: Northern Province: 95%, Eastern Province: 43%. Once the two Councils are linked the overall Tamil share will jump to nearly 69%. See Marasinghe, 'Ethnic Politics', 570.

46. B. Mathews, 'Devolution of Power in Sri Lanka: The Problems of Implementation', *The Round Table* (1987), 74–92. For a personal Tamil account of the negotiations between 1978 and 1983, see A. J. Wilson, *The Break-Up of Sri Lanka: The Sinhalese-Tamil Conflict* (London, 1988).

47. Gellner, *Nations and Nationalism*, 45–7.

48. For an able discussion, see M. N. Shaw, *Title to Territory in Africa* (Oxford, 1986), 113–14.

49. Data taken from *The Economist*, 18 Feb. 1989 and 14 May 1988.

50. Smith, *Ethnic Origins of Nations*, 221.

51. *The Economist*, 8 May 1989, and Sathyamurty on Uganda, *Nationalism in the Contemporary World*, 119–45.

52. Horowitz, *Ethnic Groups in Conflict*, 270–7.

53. Ibid. 197–8.

54. For a scholarly account of its genesis, see Shaw, *Title to Territory*, 59–80.

FURTHER READING

Asiwaja, A. I. (ed.), *Partitioned Africans* (Lagos, Nigeria, 1985).

Boucher, J., *Ethnic Conflicts: International Perspectives* (Beverly Hills, Calif., 1987).

Gellner, E., *Nations and Nationalism* (Oxford, 1983).

Horowitz, D. L., *Ethnic Groups in Conflict* (Berkeley, Calif., 1985).

Kedourie, E., *Nationalism* (London, 1960).

Smith, A. D., *The Ethnic Origins of Nations* (Oxford, 1986).

17

Continuity and Change in
the States System

ROBERT H. JACKSON

INTERNATIONAL DIVERSITY

The globe-encircling system of locally sovereign States that came into existence after 1945 encompasses variations between States and regions—in population, territory, topography, climate, customs, religion, social psychology, technology, economic development, political culture, and much else—which boggle the mind. Each region is unique, of course, just as individual States possess identities and personalities of which no two are exactly alike. Since much of this distinctiveness is reinforced by political independence which is a form of human freedom, it is likely to persist indefinitely. It is nevertheless the case, as the reader also will have noticed, that some regions have characteristics or face problems in common. There are also features which all States share and which make it possible to generalize meaningfully about the States system.

The purpose of this final chapter is to identify important points of difference and similarity in the regional States systems with a view to discerning some intimations of the overall dynamics and directions of our contemporary global society of States. Are the changes which are so evident in the contemporary world, particularly economic changes but also demographic, technological, ideological, and similar changes, fostering new varieties of international and transnational organization which undermine the foundations of sovereign statehood? Is the independent State becoming obsolete at least in some respects? Or is the existing States system based on the principle of sovereignty likely to adapt without fundamental alteration to all such changes? In short, what are the prospects for sovereign statehood?

Before considering these questions it is important to emphasize that the huge diversity which exists internationally is accompanied by, or—rather—is based upon, an identity and equality of status. All the territorial units (States) which collectively make up the international society enjoy the same formal condition: they are all equally sovereign. That means, given the way in which the term is used by States to refer to their international aspect, that their Constitutions are independent of any other Constitution. It is this international autonomy, and this alone, which makes them eligible to participate in international relations in their own right. When Namibia made her international debut on 21 March 1990, she did so in consequence of the fact that her independent Constitution came into effect on that day. Namibia thus now enjoys a status as a sovereign State which is the same as that of all other members of the international society. But, of course, in terms of her power she is in a weak position in relation to many of them, not least her neighbour and former overlord, South Africa.

It is the conjunction between equal status and unequal power which gives the relations of States so much of their intellectual and political interest, especially in this democratic age. The conjunction between equality of status and inequality of stature is not in itself at all an unusual political condition: citizenship, after all, is an equal legal status shared by individuals who may be very unequal in wealth, influence, intelligence, talent, and other respects. Status and stature rarely coincide. But the substantial inequalities and disparities between the formally equal States of the world are usually far greater than those between citizens within countries, and they take effect in a democratic context which now frowns on the projection of force across international boundaries to achieve national purposes—except in very restricted circumstances, such as responses to unambiguous acts of aggression as in the case of Iraq's invasion of Kuwait or desperate humanitarian crises as in the case of political anarchy and famine i' Somalia. The weakness or smallness of sovereign States was a gi eater international disability in the past than it is today. It was a concern to find out how States have got on in this historically unprecedented and still changing environment which led to the writing of this book.

STATE SURVIVAL

What general observations can be made concerning the relationship between equal statehood and unequal power in the post-1945 States system? A straightforward way of addressing this question is by reference to the analytical categories used in many of the foregoing chapters: birth, life, death, and future of sovereign States. The most important category is of course the life of States. This is because few States are expiring at the start of the final decade of the twentieth century, and those that are—East and West Germany, the Soviet Union, Yugoslavia, Czechoslovakia—have direct descendants which altogether are more numerous than their ancestors. In the twentieth century we have been witnessing a remarkable proliferation of independent States due to the breakup of empires, just as the nineteenth century witnessed a corresponding reduction owing primarily to political unification in Europe and colonization in Asia and Africa.

The global society of States has settled into a conservative middle-aged pattern in which death may be postponed indefinitely despite the continuing enormous variations of power between both regions and States. States do not expire naturally and existing States would either have to be killed off or willed out of existence. Almost everywhere today, however, it is unthinkable that State jurisdictions as represented on political maps could be changed by force without the consent of the sovereign governments involved—which was the historical practice well into the present century. As indicated in Chapter 4, Westphalian warfare and diplomacy created ten new States in Western Europe, but it extinguished forty-two. Because statesmen usually will not freely choose to go out of business, most contemporary States consequently seem destined to survive indefinitely. Even the momentous transformations which resulted in the demise of East and West Germany and the birth (or rebirth) of many territorial entities which previously were subordinate parts of the former Soviet Union ultimately depended on the consent of Moscow. The Berlin wall was knocked down only after Gorbachev signalled he would do nothing to stop it from happening.

The disintegration of Yugoslavia would appear to contradict this claim, but even in this tragic process it is worth noting the extreme reluctance of external powers and authorities, including the UN Security Council, to intervene by force to stop the conflict or even reduce the level of violence in what to outsiders looks more like a civil war and even a fratricide than anything else. The same aversion was evident in Somalia despite the extraordinary suffering brought about by clan warfare and drought. This post-1945 doctrine of non-intervention (and non-colonization) is making it possible for weak and disunified States to survive which in the not very distant past might have been conquered, partitioned, or in other ways eliminated by stronger internal or external powers. This poses a novel international problem which the States system has been wrestling with since the end of colonialism: accommodating and supporting independent States (which in other eras or circumstances might not have survived or even acquired independence in the first place) while at the same time responding to humanitarian crises (which are increasingly difficult for world opinion to ignore).

Since 1945 the world has witnessed the emergence of a large number of weak States of which many are extremely disorganized and divided internally. The fifty-one founding members of the United Nations—mostly historical European States—had expanded to 180 by early 1993—mostly former colonies of European powers or quasi-colonies of the Soviet Union and Yugoslavia. Apart from the immediate post-war rearrangement of frontiers between East and West which resulted in the birth of two sets of twins (East and West Germany, North and South Korea) this high birth-rate was until recently due entirely to Western decolonization in Asia, Africa, the Caribbean, and Oceania. Decolonization was one of the twentieth century's watershed changes which resulted in widespread and wholesale transfers of sovereignty from a few Western imperial States to a large number of ex-colonial Third World governments. Until recently this proliferation of new States seemed to be at an end. But the breakup of the Soviet and Yugoslav federations—which is strongly reminiscent of decolonization—has resulted in yet another wave of States which are either newly sovereign (e.g. Slovenia and Croatia) or have been born again (e.g. Estonia, Latvia, and Lithuania). Elsewhere the flotsam and jetsam of empire in the form of micro-States periodically bob to the surface in Oceania and could continue to do so both in this region and in the Caribbean where colonial jurisdictions still exist. But these developments involve tiny territories and populations which have no impact on the States system. Any significant births of new States in the future will have to entail changes in existing interstate boundaries—as happened in the former Soviet Union and Yugoslavia.

The possibility of it happening elsewhere is different from one region to the next and difficult to gauge, of course, but in general it is not great. This is owing in no small part to the fact that there are no more empires or quasi-empires to decolonize—unless one conceives as quasi-empires existing multi-ethnic States which are not democracies—of which there are many in Asia and Africa. Perhaps ironically, the egalitarian ethos which has spread from domestic to international politics underwrites the legitimacy of existing territorial jurisdictions whatever their internal conditions happen to be. Power differentials between States are today as great as at any time in the centuries-long history of the modern States system—probably they are greater—but they cannot have a lawful effect in the acquisition of territory by force against the will of an existing sovereign government. The doctrine of non-intervention enshrined in Article 2 of the UN Charter forbids it and a general inclination of major powers against intervention (except where a definite national interest is at stake) reinforces it. Otherwise there is a heavy reluctance to become involved in the problems of somebody else's sovereign jurisdiction—even where there are documented massive violations of human rights, as in Bosnia-Herzegovina and Somalia in 1992.

This egalitarian doctrine represents a fundamental change in international orthodoxy. It is underestimated by many students of contemporary international relations, who have perhaps not yet adjusted theories which are still based very considerably on historical power politics. The implications are profound: for if international boundaries can no longer be redrawn as a result of force they are (for reasons stated below) probably not going to change at all—unless some exceptional event occurs in which consent to such change is given, as happened in the former Soviet Union. The fate of Bosnia-Herzegovina and more generally of the formerly internal and now international boundaries of what was Yugoslavia may be a test case. If this State is carved up by Serbian and (to a lesser extent) Croatian armed militias with the tacit if not express backing of Belgrade and Zagreb it could be interpreted as a return to the classical method of drawing borders by force—particularly if those resultant borders are recognized by foreign powers and the UN. At the time of writing (summer 1992) Serbian militias were reported to have taken possession of more than 60 per cent of Bosnia-Herzegovina's territory from which non-Serbs had been evicted in an abhorrent process of 'ethnic cleansing'. The international community nevertheless was extremely reluctant to recognize any borders except the internal frontiers of former Yugoslavia which defined Bosnia-Herzegovina in the first place—unless all States' parties involved in the conflict could agree on new borders.

The long-term declining birth-rate of sovereign States is certainly not owing to any lack of candidates which aspire to self-determination.

Sub-Saharan Africa and Latin America contain numerous ethno-linguistic groups which might opt for independence if the opportunity presented itself. There are countries in South East Asia, South Asia, and the Middle East which frustrate the desire of certain segments of their populations to become independent countries themselves or to join independent neighbours. Even a few States in Western Europe (Spain and Britain) and in North America (Canada)—which are among the most integrated countries anywhere—also have their secessionists. The fact is that the political map could be very different if groups with a desire for independent statehood were accommodated by the States system.

The chapter on ethnicity gives an indication of the extent to which many States, particularly but by no means exclusively those in the Third World, are ambivalent in terms of political identity. The probably numerous 'ethnonations' today which do not possess sovereign statehood but harbour a desire for it are frustrated by the existing pattern of territorial jurisdiction which derives in most places from a process of colonial map-making that was often ignorant of indigenous boundaries or indifferent to them. It is interesting to speculate about the future of this sometimes violent friction between sovereign juris-diction and ethnic identity. Fred Parkinson argues that it is likely to be a cause of disruption and disorder in years to come as the doctrine of *uti possidetis* comes under extreme pressure from ethnic groups asserting a right of self-determination. It is most certainly a major source of the civil wars which have plagued ex-colonial regions in the post-1945 period: this is particularly evident in Africa where almost every major internal conflict including those in the Congo (Zaïre), Nigeria, Angola, Ethiopia, Sudan, and Uganda has involved ethnic divisions of one kind or another. It is also a marked feature of recent events in Eastern Europe and the former Soviet Union where ethno-nationalisms which for decades were suppressed by communist rule have reasserted themselves, sometimes with a vengeance—as in the conflicts between Croats and Serbs in the former Yugoslavia, or between Armenians and Azeris in the former USSR.

However, in a States system in which fundamental rules of the game are the recognition of existing international boundaries and the doctrine of non-intervention, a crucial (and sometimes overlooked) requirement in the formation of new States is (as indicated) the willingness of sovereigns to allow it to happen—as Gorbachev and Yeltsin allowed the birth or rebirth of (some of) the nationalities of the former USSR. It is noteworthy that the only acceptable and workable basis in this case was the former internal borders of the USSR which were simply internationalized. This fits conveniently with the doctrine of *uti possidetis*. Where sovereigns refuse it usually does not happen unless exceptional circumstances favour it—as in the case of Slovenian and Croatian independence against the will of (Serbian-dominated) Yugoslavia but with the blessing of Germany, Austria, and (more reluctantly and belatedly) other members of the EC as well as the USA. Again, the only legitimate basis was internationalization of the internal borders of former Yugoslavia. It will be interesting to see whether these borders can be repudiated and new ones established. If it happens a precedent may be set that goes against the predominant post-1945 practice.

Since Western decolonization there have been no generally recognized political births in the Third World resulting from the forced redrawing of borders. The impending emergence of Eritrea out of the Ethiopian civil war has involved consent from Addis Ababa, the capital of Ethiopia. The possible emergence of a Republic of Somaliland (the former British Protectorate of Somaliland) out of the anarchy in Somalia is a more puzzling case in so far as no recognizable government existed in Mogadishu, the capital of Somalia, when the republic declared itself independent in 1991. At the time of writing, however, neither the OAU nor the UN nor any important State had recognized the Republic of Somaliland. Self-determination of currently disenfranchised minorities has not even been contemplated in most cases—apart from the Palestinians.

Statesmen, as previous chapters indicate, are strongly disinclined to entertain any claims for self-determination which would involve loss of territory. Herein lies the tragedy of the Kurds, for example, who straddle the borders of Iraq, Iran, and Turkey, none of which is prepared to give up Kurdish-occupied territory and at least the first two of which are prepared to silence the Kurds—if necessary by State violence and terror. Even the 1990–1 Gulf War which resulted in the defeat of Iraq did not result in Kurdish independence—the UN and the coalition powers (especially Turkey) were at pains not to dismember Iraq. Most statesmen are prepared to collaborate to prevent the independence of ethnonationalities—as is evident from the chapters on South East Asia and Sub-Saharan Africa. In this respect, the doctrine of *uti possidetis* continues to have strong backing in a world of numerous multi-ethnic States.

The only significant post-colonial extinctions of juridical statehood was the emergence of independent Bangladesh from former East Pakistan as a result of military intervention by the Indian Army. One might be tempted to include Chinese conquest and integration of Tibet and the forcible incorporation of East Timor by Indonesia—except the latter was a Portuguese colony only in transition to self-government and the sovereignty of the former was ambiguous. The sociological potential and the political prospects for new sovereign States are consequently very different. Even if governmental force is not sufficient to put down rebellions, and separatists become in effect a State within a State, the international community can thwart the inner State's international emergence by refusing to recognize it or enter into overt relations with it. In short, international recognition and participation can 'trump' sociological determination or armed force in the game of sovereign statehood. At least this was the predominant tendency from 1945 until the time of writing.

The chances of jurisdictional death are also slight in every region surveyed in this book and for similar reasons. Indeed, death if anything is even less likely because births by separation are possible without a corresponding termination of sovereign statehood, as the cases of Bangladesh and Pakistan, Singapore and Malaysia, Slovenia and Yugoslavia, the Baltic States and the Soviet Union cum Russia have indicated. The death-rate of States fell almost to zero during the Cold War: before 1989 the last significant international jurisdictional disappearances in Europe—apart from Germany which was divided in 1945—were registered by Soviet absorption of the Baltic States of Estonia, Latvia, and Lithuania in 1940. It is interesting how memories of independence were kept alive and how rebirth of these sovereign jurisdictions was swift once it finally was clear that Moscow would no longer thwart it. A republic of Vietnam existed momentarily in 1954 before splitting into a communist north and a non-communist south and subsequently emerging as a single communist State twenty years later after extensive foreign intervention and a devastating civil war. The division of Germany after the Second World War into East and West and the reunification of that country following the end of the Cold War is another case of temporary disappearance. One might anticipate a similar development at some time in the future in the case of North and South Korea. The rebirth of Russia (but not in its pre-Soviet—tsarist—geographical shape, which was larger), of Armenia (which was briefly independent after the First World War), and of Serbia which existed as a sovereign State before the First World War are further examples. On the other hand, the emergence of the independent States of former Soviet Central Asia are all cases of new States (often based on old nationalities) resulting from the splintering of larger jurisdictions. Some of these 'Turkish' States look back to an earlier pre-tsarist colonial existence under the Ottoman Empire for their political identities.

Jurisdictional death (and birth) must of course be distinguished from the termination of a political regime and its replacement by another, such as was evident in the overthrow of the Shah and the establishment of a revolutionary Islamic State in Iran (1979) or in communist revolutions in Ethiopia (1974), Cuba (1958), China (1949), and Russia (1917)—or anti-communist revolutions in Ethiopia (1991) and Russia (1991). Between 1989 and 1991 we witnessed terminations of communist regimes and installations of non-communist regimes virtually throughout Eastern Europe and the former Soviet Union. Comparable regime changes in which autocracy was giving way to democracy also occurred in Latin America and in some Asian and African countries. In Western Europe and North America, of course, the displacement of democracy by something else is inconceivable. Indeed, these democratic and economically advanced States together with Japan are the reference group by which all States nowadays are judged.

Until as recently as the end of the First World War the birth and death of sovereign entities and the transfer of territorial jurisdictions from one State to another was a predictable and legitimate consequence of war and peace. Today, however, it is increasingly unimaginable owing not least to the norm of territorial legitimacy which has spread around the world and has preserved thoroughly disintegrated States, such as Chad, Sudan, Uganda, Ethiopia, and even totally anarchic Lebanon and Somalia. Most deaths in the future may have to depend on voluntary acts of political euthanasia. This could occur, for example, if the Caribbean States submerged their separate sovereignties to form a single federation. Marginal African States may come under pressure from the IMF and the World Bank to unite into more economically promising jurisdictions. But the chances of such political happenings are poor if the regional chapters in this book are anything to go by. As indicated, most sovereign governments are extremely reluctant either to give up territory or to combine their jurisdictions voluntarily. On the contrary, the existing territorial pattern of sovereign statehood in all of the major regions of the world seems to have acquired a sanctity which few if any powers are prepared to violate or even dispute, presumably because they desire to avoid not only the universal condemnation but also the threat to international order which such an action would provoke. Since 1945 there have been very few significant territory grabs anywhere in the world. Israel is one State that has attempted territorial conquest but this can be explained by her national insecurity and her siege mentality. The Israeli military occupations of the West Bank, the Golan Heights, and the Gaza strip have never been internationally recognized.

WAR AND CIVIL WAR

One of the more promising developments of international relations since 1945 has been the declining incidence of war—that is, international warfare. Although Europe and America experienced the Cold War they have not faced unambiguous international war since 1945: the superpowers were poised for war for four decades but managed to avoid going to war. The Cold War of course involved several hot wars outside the West, most notably the Korean and Vietnam Wars and also various wars between Israel and some of its Arab enemies in the Middle East. The most devastating and long-lasting was the Vietnam War which involved major intervention by outside powers—but this was in many respects a civil war and not an international war.

Perhaps the most serious regional conflict (measured by death and injury, destruction and damage) was the first Gulf War between Iraq and Iran (1980–8) which inflicted heavy casualties on both sides but primarily on very young, poorly trained, and ill-equipped Iranian conscripts mobilized by the Mullah disciples of Khomeni to carry out fanatical and what proved to be useless bloodletting assaults against well-dug-in Iraqi soldiers. The second Gulf War between Iraq and a coalition of Western and Arab powers led by the USA (1990–1) was internationalized and also far sharper and shorter. It involved significant casualties—but only to the Iraqi soldiers who occupied Kuwait and to Iraqi civilians who were victims of Coalition bombing. It is noteworthy for being not only the first international conflict following the end of the Cold War but the first UN-authorized war since the Korean War (1950–3). There have also been conflicts involving

India and Pakistan and India and China in South Asia. Several wars have occurred in Sub-Saharan Africa—between Libya and Chad, Somalia and Ethiopia, Tanzania and Uganda, Morocco and Western Sahara. And there was of course a brief war between Argentina and Britain in the Falkland (Malvinas) Islands of the South Atlantic in 1982. As indicated, it is difficult to judge whether the wars in the former Yugoslavia and Soviet Union—for example between Croats and Serbs or between Armenians and Azeris—are international or civil conflicts.

But if the following points are considered it seems surprising that there have not been more international wars in recent decades: the number of sovereign States has multiplied more than threefold since 1945; local sovereigns are now located in every quarter of the globe; Third World governments are far more heavily armed than their colonial predecessors ever were; and very few are democratic or even constitutional governments and many are controlled by military regimes. Consequently there are many more national interests and military powers than there used to be with a corresponding potential for international armed conflict. But wars have not increased in proportion to the number of States and their potentially conflicting national interests.

On the other hand, however, violent discord within States between governments and armed opposition groups is almost a common occurrence—particularly in the former colonial regions of Asia and Africa and also in Latin America. In the late 1980s serious civil wars were being waged in Angola, Ethiopia, Sri Lanka, Sudan, Mozambique, Cambodia, Burma, Afghanistan, Nicaragua, and El Salvador. Foreign intervention by one or both superpowers in some of these wars profoundly increased their production of casualties and refugees: for example the Afghanistan War. When the Cold War came to an end in 1989–91 and the superpowers withdrew many of these wars began to be wound down: Angola, Ethiopia, Cambodia, Nicaragua, El Salvador, and (perhaps) Mozambique. But civil wars occurred without major foreign intervention (Sudan) and continued in spite of foreign withdrawal (Afghanistan). The various internal factions at war in Afghanistan were well able to wage war after Soviet withdrawal and declining American interest and support. Some civil wars may even be caused by foreign withdrawal: the conflict in Somalia broke out in 1991 following the end of the Cold War and the withdrawal of the superpowers from the Horn of Africa. The quasi-civil wars in parts of the former Yugoslavia and USSR were provoked by the breakdown of communist States at the end of the Cold War.

Some anti-government rebels persist in their warfare against State authorities for extended periods: a civil war in Ethiopia began in 1962 and lasted almost thirty years. The on-again, off-again civil war in Sudan has lasted for almost as long. This is surprising in light of the fact that very few post-1945 civil wars have resulted in the dismemberment of existing States or formation of new States: the partition of Pakistan which led to the independence of Bangladesh is one exception; perhaps a dismemberment of Bosnia-Herzegovina will prove to be another exception. Secessionists seem not to realize that their chances of gaining sovereign statehood in the contemporary international society are slim without consent of the sovereign government they are fighting against and recognition by the international community. Perhaps they believe they can use force to coerce such consent, but this has rarely happened and usually requires the total defeat of a sovereign government—as in Ethiopia in 1991. Consequently, civil wars—with or without foreign intervention—drag on endlessly with neither winners nor losers—just prolonged and seemingly useless bloodletting—as in Sudan. Only when there has been exceptional external pressure have such wars been terminated or markedly reduced in their level of violence. This happened following involvement by the EC and the UN in the brief bloody 1991 conflict between Croatians and Serbians in Yugoslavia. But by the summer of 1992 it had not happened in the war in Bosnia-Herzegovina. But many civil wars seem to fester indefinitely without any clear winners or losers. This, too, may be owing—at least in part—to the conservative inclination and practice of contemporary States and the States system to recognize the international legitimacy and territorial integrity of all existing States, including even countries which lack internally legitimate governments and contain profoundly alienated ethnonational regions.

SOVEREIGNTY, INEQUALITY, AND DEPENDENCY

'Sovereignty' has been aptly characterized by Anthony Payne as 'the ideology which legitimizes the post-war international system.' As J. D. B. Miller puts it: 'a sovereign State, however small, is a formidable adversary in terms of publicity.' These remarks point to the normative means by which the survival of even the tiniest countries is internationally guaranteed today. State survival nowadays is seen as a matter of right rather than power.

The smallness or weakness of many States draws them into external relationships of quasi-trusteeship with international organizations and important States. The Caribbean and Pacific countries and also many Sub-Saharan States are for all intents and purposes wards of the United Nations system, the European Economic Community, the Commonwealth, Francophonie, and other international organizations. Many Third World States are heavily dependent on the IMF and the World Bank. They rely on the international community not only for their liberty but also for their welfare. This dependency system is in many important respects the successor to Western colonialism. It is difficult to imagine how such countries would manage to get on without some such supporting and sustaining external framework.

Of course, many weaker States have also entered into bilateral relations with more significant powers located either within their region or outside. Such relations often have earmarks not of classical suzerainty in which sovereignty becomes 'an empty shell'[1] but rather of international clientelism and dependency. The historical role of the former Soviet Union in Eastern Europe and that of the USA in Central America is illustrative. The superpowers during the Cold War supported faithful clients across great distances, as in the case of the USA and Israel and the Soviet Union and Cuba. China provided patronage, often in rivalry with the Soviet Union, to certain clients in South East Asia and Sub-Saharan Africa. Cuba under Fidel Castro endeavoured to play the role of military patron to various Marxist African States presumably in order to enhance Cuba's standing among Third World States in rivalry with America. There have also been noteworthy regional powers upon whom lesser States in the region are somewhat dependent. Obvious examples are Brazil, Mexico, and Venezuela in Latin America, India in South Asia, Indonesia and Vietnam in South East Asia, Australia in Oceania, Egypt and Saudi Arabia in the Arab Middle East, and Nigeria in West Africa. South Africa could play a similar role in Sub-Saharan Africa if apartheid is successfully brought to an end.

In addition to these more conventional patron–client relations there have also been instances of what could be termed 'reverse suzerainty' in which richer powers actively solicit requests for support, for example in votes at the UN, from countries which in most respects are poor and insignificant. The USA, France, and various other wealthy States have cultivated clienteles from among Third World States mainly through the allocation of foreign aid. Japan has been moving in this direction in North East and South East Asia. Canada has sought to play the role of benefactor to numerous minor States of the Commonwealth and Francophonie presumably for the purpose of increasing her stature in these organizations as a rival to Britain and France. Australia plays a similar role in the Commonwealth particularly in relation to Oceanic members.

These relations are bound to continue indefinitely because they are driven by the sharp and indeed profound material inequalities between States both within regions and in the world at large. Following the end of the Cold War the impoverished States of Sub-Saharan Africa became noticeably worried that Western-funded international aid would be redirected from the Third World to Eastern Europe and the former Soviet Union. Their fears have not been groundless: the West's interest in Africa has declined and its corresponding interest in Russia and other East European or ex-Soviet States has undoubtedly increased since the remarkable international changes of 1989–91. The finances and other economic resources available for international aid are definitely limited and will no doubt be distributed where the political and economic returns are greatest. Sub-Saharan Africa is not likely to be a very high priority. On the other hand, the existing international framework for distributing aid is well entrenched and the many aid agencies, public and private, can be expected to demand that there be no substantial reductions of financial and technical assistance to Sub-Saharan Africa and other poorest parts of the Third World. This framework prevents international aid from being directed wholly by the individual and collective interests of the developed donor countries, somewhat in the same way that institutions of the Welfare State constrain the allocation of resources by markets within States.

However, there is little sign that gross existing inequalities between States and regions (such as are recorded in annual reports of the World Bank) will begin to be substantially reduced in the foreseeable future.[2] It would require very substantial foreign investment to begin to roll back the vast ocean of poverty and underdevelopment. The poorest countries are often far from the most attractive investment opportunities in a world in which private capital is highly mobile and can be invested where the returns are greatest and safest. It would

require determined international collaboration between States deliberately to transfer wealth from rich countries to poor ones to counter
market dictates. The public funds required would also be very great
and could only be mobilized either from taxation or borrowing in the
developed countries—both of which were unpopular in most of these
countries in the early 1990s.

Furthermore, any such international transfer of wealth might involve
some limits on sovereign rights, just as transfer payments within
States ordinarily require taxation and expenditure policies which
interfere with the freedom of citizens and the domestic market-place.
Would independent governments accept such limitations even if they
stood to benefit from the transfers? Would for example the new (or
renewed) States of Eastern Europe give up some of their recently
acquired (or reacquired) independence if that is necessary to receive
aid from Western Europe? Would Russia or Ukraine permit significant
involvement in their domestic economies by the IMF, the World
Bank, and the European Bank for Reconstruction and Development
as a condition of receiving loans from Western governments and
banks? If there are to be such transfers they will have somehow to
accommodate both the demands of lenders that the loans be invested
properly and paid back on time, and the demands of borrowers that
their independence not be trespassed upon. This may prove to be a
difficult dance for both parties to master.

What is perhaps easiest to foresee is the perpetuation of certain
underdeveloped or underpopulated regions in their current marginal
conditions. Sub-Saharan Africa apart from South Africa has been in
a situation of stagnation for two decades and in some places even
longer and there is little reason to expect this region to be other than
a global backwater in the foreseeable future. South Asia, the other
centre of global poverty, could also remain largely unchanged indefinitely although parts of India could with luck and political stability
become a regional engine of economic growth. The demographic
insignificance and territorial remoteness of Oceania strongly suggests
that its future will be more or less a continuation of its past—perhaps
it together with Sub-Saharan Africa will indefinitely remain as regions
defined by a nearly total dependence on international hand-outs. The
same might be expected of the Caribbean except that it is located
near by one of the great centres of the global economy and could
experience significant improvements to its economic fortunes as a
result. But it is still difficult to imagine the Caribbean as anything

much more than a tropical haven for Western tourists. Regions such as the Caribbean and Oceania are almost bound by geographic and demographic circumstances to remain peripheral places indefinitely.

CHANGE OR CONTINUITY?

If most chapters of this book are any indication the majority of existing States and regions and the global States system as a whole seem destined to persist indefinitely more or less in their existing shape. Most contributors foresee no withering away of the States system: there is no definite intimation of any alternative arrangement and certainly not a world government of some kind. The current pattern of sovereign-state jurisdiction is not expected to change either. International boundaries are of course changing in what formerly was the Soviet Union and Yugoslavia as these areas experience a postponed process of national self-determination reminiscent of decolonization. These changes could create demonstration effects elsewhere especially where mobilized and politicized ethnicity runs counter to the doctrine of *uti possidetis*. But it seems more likely that the existing pattern of sovereign-State jurisdiction will hold if only because it is almost impossible to contemplate change without a corresponding threat of instability. The customs and habits and inclinations of States are mostly conservative and *laissez-faire*—even during periods of remarkable international change such as the transformation of 1989–91. Existing regions also appear destined to persist without substantial alteration in their shapes or identities—although obviously not their material conditions which in some cases could change significantly. The one major exception at the time of writing was of course Eastern Europe whose future shape was still unclear. However, such monumental changes happen rarely in international relations.

What should probably be expected, therefore, is continuing shifts in the broadly defined balance of power, as States, and increasingly also regions, compete in the great race for economic, technological, and scientific supremacy. Some will gain while others will lose ground and still others will stay more or less in the same position. Perhaps Mexico (and even some other countries of Latin America) will develop more rapidly with new opportunities for investment and markets provided under the terms of the 1992 North American Free Trade Agreement (NAFTA) with the USA and Canada. Perhaps North

East and possibly even South East Asia will advance significantly under Japanese commercial leadership. Perhaps parts of Eastern Europe (the Czech Republic successor to Czechoslovakia, Hungary, Poland, possibly Slovenia, and perhaps Croatia and the Baltic States) will progress more speedily as a result of their geographical proximity to the new Germany—the dynamic heartland of the European economy. Location alone can be opportunity. What will happen in that huge area once occupied by the USSR it is still too early to say. Will it (or parts of it) develop into a dynamic Western-style market economy, will it stagnate, or will it decline? Will Russia, Ukraine, and Belorussia find their feet in the world economy or will they stumble along unable either to return to communism or to accept the disciplines of capitalism? Will the weaker and peripheral States (Albania, Bulgaria, Romania, Moldava, Georgia, Armenia, Azerbaijan, and the States of former Soviet Central Asia) remain outside the race altogether, in effect becoming part of an expanded Third World?

In the regional chapters of this book the long shadow of the superpowers can be discerned. But what seems even more noteworthy following the end of the Cold War is the definitely limited influence of such powers. Russia has abandoned even the pretence of exercising global influence and the shadow of America is not as long as it once was. If Russia and America are not yet merely the equals of other major powers owing to their still awesome military might, they are no longer the paramount powers they once were. The USSR was never an economic power and Russia will remain in the position of its predecessor until economic reforms have an effect which could be years if not decades away. The US share of world economic production has declined significantly from its artificially high levels at the end of the Second World War. At the same time Japan (the hub of North East Asia) and Germany (the engine of the EC) are economic powers which together with associated countries are beginning to rival the USA. But Japan is extremely cautious and even inhibited in its outward projection of non-commercial and particularly military influence, and the EC has proven more often than not to be seriously deficient in any capacity to articulate and project a co-ordinated foreign and military policy—as the (second) Gulf War and the wars in the Balkans clearly indicate. This may leave the USA as the solitary superpower possessing both unrivalled military clout and still consequential economic strength.

However, neither the USA nor the EC nor Japan is a hegemonic power in the classical imperial sense. There is today less economic reason to expand one's national territory than there was in the past. Economic interests of States can be pursued through international trade and other transactions and agreements without going to the enormous trouble of acquiring and governing foreign territory. There is more to be gained economically from respecting than from denying the sovereign rights of others. Economic powers—such as the USA—almost automatically dominate neighbouring States economically—such as Canada or certain Caribbean or Latin American countries—without resorting to colonization. Territory is still important but it evidently is not sufficiently important to induce powerful States to acquire it at the expense of the powerless—as was the case in the not very distant past. The economic value of land and even natural resources as factors of production have declined, as compared to that of a skilled and flexible work-force able to produce or employ high technology or to operate a modern service economy. Human capital and the institutional arrangements that can best generate it and take advantage of it are the *sine qua non* of State prosperity and status in the contemporary world.

And to the extent that States today are eager to enter into international economic relations in order to develop, they also must be willing not only to trade with other States but do whatever else may be necessary to compete internationally—including making themselves available to foreign investment. Such an 'open' international economy makes territory (and the economic resources contained within it) accessible and exploitable without resort to sovereign control. Indeed, States nowadays are far more likely to clamour for investment from abroad than erect barriers to it in the recognition that otherwise they will not be able to deliver the goods their populations increasingly demand and even expect. If the experience of recent decades is any guide, communism, State capitalism, economic nationalism, mercantilism, or any other autarkic system is detrimental to the wealth of nations in an increasingly competitive global trading economy. The sorry economic performance (outside the military-industrial complex) of the Soviet Union and its successor Russia—which arguably is one of the few countries of sufficient size for autarky to be a reasonable economic option—is testimony.

However, an open international economy does not require the abandonment or even any substantial loss of State sovereignty properly understood as constitutional independence. Canada and Mexico may be willing to trade more freely with the USA but they certainly are not about to surrender to America's manifest destiny to enclose the entire North American continent within its domestic jurisdiction. The Japanese may invigorate the economies of North East and South East Asia but it is inconceivable that their regional investment and trading partners will accept any significant loss of political independence as a price for such economic opportunity.

When a future different from the present is foreseen it usually involves the expectation of increased regionalism in the form of trading blocs. The most elaborate example is of course the EC which other regions cannot ignore and must to some extent imitate. But far from reducing the significance of member States, the European community has in fact strengthened them. What has evidently changed is not the location of sovereignty or the legal standing of member States *vis-à-vis* the community: Brussels is still the servant and not the master of the EC States. Europe is still far from being a federal State under a government responsible to an elected European parliament: it remains a conventional international organization under a Council of Ministers representing the member States of the Community.[3] What Western European governments have evidently been constructing for the last thirty years according to Donald Puchala is a system of institutionalized co-operation in many areas of mutual interest or concern. It is the character and *modus operandi* of European international relations which are different today: they express coalitional rather than confrontational politics and are conducted through regional organizations more than in the past. Furthermore, if (unanticipated) disintegrative consequences of the 1991 Maastricht Treaty are anything to go by—particularly the referendums in Denmark and France and the disruptions in the Exchange Rate Mechanism—there is very little indication that the EC is becoming a focus of political identity and loyalty. On the contrary, Maastricht (unwittingly) seems to have aroused existing national identities in Western Europe.

However, even if the EC is becoming a kind of sovereign entity and political identity above its member States—which is still far from clear—all this would mean is that Europe is emerging as a superpower (at least in population and wealth if not in arms). In which case sovereign statehood (and the power annexed to it) in Western Europe is merely expanding and unifying, just as in the former USSR it has been contracting and fracturing. This process of State-building and State-dismantling is entirely consistent with the history and *modus operandi* of the States system and need not be interpreted as contrary to it.

If the European experiment in regionalism proves successful, States in other regions might well imitate it by developing comparable and to a certain extent rival economic blocs. However, even if that were to happen the future would not be one of transcending existing States so much as reordering their relations in accordance with regional requirements. There has been much talk recently of organizing a Pacific Rim bloc of trading States stretching in an ocean-wide arc from New Zealand to Chile and including Japan and the USA. Perhaps the Japanese might promote the idea of transforming North East and South East Asia into a more formally organized economic area. They may feel obliged to do this if exclusive trading blocs coalesce among their Western trading partners and they are forced to confront a prospect of transferring their investment and production to countries in these blocs rather than exporting to them—which is already occurring in North America and Western Europe. Under the leadership of rich and dynamic Japan and with the co-operation of populous China and the participation of the rapidly developing NICs, East Asia could become a rival centre of global economic activity. Indeed, according to Gerald Segal it already is. The 1992 free-trade agreement between the USA, Canada, and Mexico could in the future include other Latin American countries: another conceivable bloc of formidable population, technology, and natural resources. At the time of writing one could already foresee more than the outlines of these three primary regions which if present trends continue will serve as the principal political and economic (if not military) counter-weights of a triangular (rather than bipolar or multipolar) States system in which other regions of the world are increasingly peripheral.

But the most significant prospects for regional ascendancy in the longer term lie, perhaps paradoxically, in the old heartland of the international system: Europe. The division in this book between Eastern and Western Europe which is entirely faithful to a reality that lasted for more than forty years has been undermined by dramatic and almost entirely unforeseen political changes in the East. For consider what could be in the offing if Gorbachev's rhetoric about a 'European home' were to turn eventually into some kind of reality. What would happen if Eastern Europe and European parts of the former Soviet Union became reintegrated with Western Europe after a fifty- and in some cases a seventy-five-year absence? In other words, what would be the result of an expansion and intensification of trade, commerce, investment, communications, travel, and migration in a land mass stretching from the Atlantic to the Urals (not to mention the Pacific in the case of Russia) with a highly educated population of half a billion and a concentration of wealth that is unrivalled anywhere? The potential for economic development of the whole of Europe assisted by the EC is greater than in any other major region, including the Americas and North East Asia—not to mention the Pacific Rim as a whole—where intra-regional differences of geography, culture, ideology, education, living standards, and the rest are far greater. The European continent could once again become the global centre: a 'super-Europe'. Of course this scenario assumes that European armed conflicts which have also broken out with the end of the Cold War will not expand beyond their present confines in the Balkan peninsula and isolated pockets of the former USSR—an assumption that many sceptics with knowledge of European history may find it difficult to accept.

But even this grandiose scenario need not entail any decline of sovereign statehood. Whereas Western Europe already discloses a process of regional integration based on economics which is remarkable in the annals of the States system, at the same time there is to date no firm indication that constitutional independence is clearly on the wane for its component States. The EC still has a long way to go before it resembles the USA. In short, the emergence of organized regional blocs is entirely consistent with a States system and only discloses a change in the ways in which sovereign governments choose to relate to each other: regionalism only means that they relate far more intimately and intensively to their geographical neighbours than to other States or regions. This is in sharp contrast to the age of imperialism, when Britain, France, and other colonial powers had intensive commercial as well as political relations with geographically distant dependencies.

If these speculations are consistent with present realities and possibilities it suggests that sovereign States and the States system formed by them will be around at least for the time being and probably for much longer than that. The development of regionalism is not undermining the sovereign State as the foundation upon which the political organization of the world is erected; it is not an alternative framework of political life. Instead, it is a new adaptation of a long-standing method of organizing and conducting relations among peoples. Regionalism as manifested in the NAFTA or even the EC is more like a rearrangement of the deck-chairs or rather an alteration in the arrangement of cabins and other quarters on a *Titanic* which has not hit any iceberg or even sprung any minor leaks and is not likely to do so owing to the fact that unlike the real *Titanic* the States system is still remarkably seaworthy despite being more than four centuries old.

Granted the States system can be exploited by abusive or corrupt élites, often encourages national parochialism and prejudice, and has periodically—some would say regularly—led to devastating wars and other kinds of human suffering. But no human institution is fail-safe or foolproof. The States system still remains a remarkably flexible political arrangement that has accommodated if it has not actually facilitated arguably the greatest freedom and certainly the highest living standards ever recorded in human history. The affluent and democratic countries of the West are proof of what can be achieved within the framework of independent statehood. Why should anyone expect such a system to be abandoned at the very moment of its greatest success?

NOTES

1. See G. Schwarzenberger and E. D. Brown, *A Manual of International Law* (London, 1976), 48.
2. See *World Development Report 1991* (Washington, DC, 1991).
3. For a different interpretation see J. Pinder, *European Community: The Building of a Union* (Oxford, 1991).

INDEX